Alger Hiss,
Whittaker Chambers
and the Case That
Ignited McCarthyism

Alger Hiss, Whittaker Chambers and the Case That Ignited McCarthyism

Lewis Hartshorn

McFarland & Company, Inc., Publishers
Jefferson, North Carolina, and London

LIBRARY OF CONGRESS CATALOGUING-IN-PUBLICATION DATA

Hartshorn, Lewis, 1948–
Alger Hiss, Whittaker Chambers and the case
that ignited McCarthyism / Lewis Hartshorn.
p.   cm.
Includes bibliographical references and index.

ISBN 978-0-7864-7442-4
softcover : acid free paper ∞

1. Hiss, Alger.   2. Chambers, Whittaker.   3. Communism—United States—
History—20th century.   4. Trials (Political crimes and offenses)—United States.
5. Political culture—United States—History—20th century.
6. United States—Politics and government—1945–1953.   I. Title.
E748.H59H38 2013   364.1'31—dc23   2013021931

BRITISH LIBRARY CATALOGUING DATA ARE AVAILABLE

On the cover: *left to right* Whittaker Chambers (Library of Congress),
Alger Hiss testifying before the HUAC (Library of Congress),
Hiss in Lewisburg Federal Penitentiary (Federal Bureau of Prisons);
background image (iStockphoto/Thinkstock)

Manufactured in the United States of America

McFarland & Company, Inc., Publishers
Box 611, Jefferson, North Carolina 28640
www.mcfarlandpub.com

To the memory of
Albert Goldman and Bess Marie

Table of Contents

Acknowledgments

Since the Hiss-Chambers controversy broke publicly in the summer of 1948, a number of books have been written to which I'm indebted. Many are noted in the text but I especially acknowledge Meyer Zeligs' *Friendship and Fratricide* (1967) and Allen Weinstein's *Perjury, The Hiss-Chambers Case* (1997). Both books were meticulously researched, though I find fault with their interpretations. Zeligs' Freudian slant added little to the essential common sense truths he discovered, yet provided a weapon for his detractors to critically flail him, and Weinstein's major interpretations simply fly in the face of his research and investigations, largely because he relied heavily on Chambers as a credible source or he suppressed evidence favorable to Hiss.

The writings and papers of the late William A. Reuben, a veritable encyclopedia on the "case" for over fifty years, were indispensable.

Thanks to Robert (Bob) Clark, FDR Library archivist, who found Adolf Berle's 1939 handwritten notes of his meeting with Chambers, believed lost for decades. Those original notes prove that Berle's designations "underground espionage agent" did not apply to Chambers himself (as suggested by the FBI's copy of the notes) but to Philip Rosenbliett, accused by Chambers. The whole truth of the Berle-Chambers meeting, distorted and misrepresented by Chambers, Weinstein, and others, is presented here for the first time.

Thanks also to Jeff Kisseloff, especially for helping me obtain the Hiss grand jury transcripts, and to Svetlana Chervonnaya for information on Col. Boris Bykov (actually Bukov) and on Chambers's expulsion from and readmission to the Communist Party.

Roger Sandilands, professor of economics at the University of Strathclyde, Glasgow, and biographer of Lauchlin Currie, read the transcript as it developed and provided valuable criticism and enthusiastic encouragement, for which I'll always be grateful.

The H-Net web site H-HOAC (History of American Communism), http://www.h-net.org/~hoac/, supported a spirited debate on the Hiss-Chambers affair for several years, particularly from 2003 to 2007. Most interesting were the posts by Julius N. Kobyakov, a former Soviet intelligence officer who had personally conducted an official search of KGB archives to see if Alger Hiss had ever been a paid or unpaid Soviet agent or source. Kobyakov discovered nothing to implicate Hiss, and he was further assured by his colleagues with access to the classified GRU archives that Hiss had never been a source for military intelligence.

Preface

This book does not pretend to present an exhaustive chronicle of the Alger Hiss–Whittaker Chambers controversy — one which encompassed months of congressional and grand jury hearings in 1948–49, two of the longest federal criminal trials in U.S. history, legal appeals spanning thirty years, dozens of books and innumerable articles, a three-hour documentary, a television dramatization, and Internet web sites (AlgerHiss.com, WhittakerChambers.org) obligatory for the twenty-first century — but this book does purport to be definitive of Alger Hiss's innocence, for it reveals without question that the story Whittaker Chambers told about himself to the authorities and in his bestselling autobiography, *Witness* (1952), is largely untrue and that the story he told about himself and Alger Hiss as confederates in the U.S. Communist underground of the 1930s is completely fraudulent.

My narrative focuses on the early months of the affair, from August 1948, when Chambers publicly denounced Hiss and several others as dues-paying Communists in testimony before the House Committee on Un-American Activities, to the following December, when Alger Hiss was indicted for perjury. The truth emerges during these months, so I leave it to others to examine and elaborate on the subsequent trials and appeals, or to futilely debate whether Alger Hiss was a Soviet agent codenamed ALES as suggested (though only in a qualified footnote, added to the document years later by the FBI) by Venona decrypt number 1822.

My goal is to illustrate that in a case long considered closed and picked clean, history may not always be what we so confidently believe.

CHAPTER I

Enemies Within

"There could be no greater error than to suppose that historical myths cannot be actually created by design."[1]— George F. Kennan

In the late 1990s historian Theodore H. Draper remarked that anyone under the age of fifty — and certainly forty — knows hardly anything about the Alger Hiss-Whittaker Chambers affair.

> Yet not so long ago the case stirred up the most agonizing conflict; it separated friends and divided families. The reason for the difference today is the change in the country and the world. The Hiss-Chambers case turned on the threat of communism and was exacerbated by the element of espionage. That threat has evaporated; the espionage is antiquated; and it is necessary to use some historical imagination to see into the innards of the case.

Draper wrote those words in a favorable 1997 review of two books which are still largely accepted as the affair's defining texts: *Perjury: The Hiss-Chambers Case* by Allen Weinstein, and *Whittaker Chambers: A Biography* by Sam Tanenhaus.[2] Weinstein concluded that the jury made no mistake in convicting Alger Hiss of perjury in 1950, and much of Weinstein's research was made available to Tanenhaus, who concurred. But after two decades of my own investigation of the Hiss-Chambers case I am convinced that those two books, along with much else written about Hiss and Chambers, are deliberately constructed myths (i.e., stories or narratives, as myths were defined by the Greeks) contrived, for political and professional reasons, to feed the self-satisfied chauvinism of the Right and to validate the prejudices of the generations who accepted and still accept the Cold War clichés symbolized by the Hiss-Chambers case: that the liberal, the New Deal Democrat, the socialist, and the Communist were all of the same type; that a Communist equals a spy equals a traitor.

Ignorance is the first requisite of the historian, but his only sacred imperative is to seek the truth about what he has been told and read, and to disseminate that truth to others.[3] By that standard, Weinstein and Tanenhaus, foremost among many, have violated that revered trust. Instead of exposing the myths surrounding Alger Hiss and Whittaker Chambers, and revealing the men behind the masks, they have remodeled the facts to fit the fantasies that shaped the myths and glossed the masks with pseudo-historical cosmetics. "Myth, after all," biographer Albert Goldman wrote, "is what we believe naturally. History is what we must painfully learn and struggle to remember." The conflict of myth and history is the quintessence of the Hiss-Chambers story.[4]

Nevertheless, Allen Weinstein deserves credit where it is due. He begins the 1997 edition of *Perjury* by conveying a sense of fairness:

> [S]ince the jury at Alger Hiss's second trial [the first jury had deadlocked, eight to four for conviction] pronounced him guilty of perjury, the case remains controversial and the verdict leaves questions unanswered. Did Hiss become an underground Communist while serving as a New Deal official? Did he turn over classified State Department files to Whittaker Chambers, a self-confessed former underground agent for the Communist Party? Or did Chambers, for obscure and malevolent reasons, deliberately set out to frame and destroy a respected public official?
>
> No critical reception of any book on the controversy, whether favorable or hostile, will resolve the debate. For any historian to assume that his research has conclusively resolved the case in all its varied dimensions would constitute self-deception at a level even higher than that achieved by the two protagonists.

And then Weinstein sets out to show how deceptive he can be. He also tells us that he once believed Alger Hiss was innocent. His interest in the case began in 1969, and he subsequently published an article on Hiss-Chambers that concluded "both men had probably lied; that Hiss hid facts concerning his personal relationship with Chambers, while the latter had falsely accused Hiss of Communist ties and espionage."

Perhaps Weinstein actually changed his mind. Or perhaps, like an ancient Greek logographer, he elected to legitimize a myth.

The Hiss case was the trial of the century of its day, yet it was much more than two divisive trials, and anyone interested in post–World War II domestic politics who attempts to understand the battles over the New Deal, Communism, and the Cold War can scarcely ignore it. The case emboldened Senator Joseph McCarthy to make his first pugnacious assault on the State Department in 1950, less than a month after Hiss's perjury conviction. It launched future president Richard Nixon, a first-term congressman who stage-managed most of the Communist espionage hearings of the House Committee on Un-American Activities (HUAC) in 1948, to a Senate seat in 1950 and the vice-presidency in 1952. Moreover, Hiss's guilty verdict marked the reemergence of the conservative movement and elevated Whittaker Chambers from renegade Communist informer to hero of the Right. Though the case had little, if any, bearing on United States foreign policy, Victor Navasky, *The Nation*'s editor, said in 1980 that if any "single individual can claim credit for establishing the link between the international cold war and the domestic one, between Soviet aggression abroad and the red menace at home, it is Whittaker Chambers ... [who] established the fundamental cold war assumption that to be a Communist was to be an agent of a foreign power."[5]

Conservatives seized on the guilty verdict to further rebuke the policies of the Roosevelt and Truman Administrations. Hiss had joined FDR's New Deal in 1933, advised Roosevelt at the infamous Yalta Conference in February 1945, presided over the founding of the United Nations and personally delivered the UN Charter to President Truman. The Right had maintained since the 1930s that Roosevelt was a "useful idiot" of the Soviets. Truman defended Roosevelt's policies; they were sound, but we had been betrayed by Russia, our wartime ally. By early 1947 Truman was proclaiming Communism a grave threat to the nation. So why, conservatives asked, had we once allied ourselves with that threat? Whittaker Chambers provided the answer they wanted to hear:

The simple fact is that when I took up my little sling and aimed at Communism, I also hit something else. What I hit was the forces of that great socialist revolution, which, in the name of liberalism, spasmodically, incompletely, somewhat formlessly, but always in the same direction, has been inching its ice cap over the nation for two decades.... And with that we come to the heart of the Hiss Case.... Alger Hiss is only one name that stands for the whole Communist penetration of Government. He could not be exposed without raising the question of the real political temper and purposes of those who had protected and advanced him, and with whom he was so closely identified that they could not tell his breed from their own.[6]

For Alger Hiss and his supporters the case stood for something quite the opposite. Hiss wrote in 1988:

I have had forty years to reflect on the origins of my case, as it was fabricated by an unholy trinity bound together by the theology of anti-communism. They joined forces against me — each at an important time in his career — in their zeal to make their theology the dominant religion of the land. They were Richard Nixon, the power-hungry politician; J. Edgar Hoover, the ultimate bureaucrat; and Whittaker Chambers, the perfect pawn.[7]

But for Democrats and liberals who sided with Whittaker Chambers at the time (and from blue-collar workers to cosmopolitan intellectuals there were many), the choice must have been excruciating. Not only were they helping to promote an era of political reaction and ideological mythmaking, they were also condoning an informer who turned on his erstwhile friend.

Even the mythmakers agree on the salient facts of the case. Whittaker Chambers, an editor of *Time* magazine, appeared publicly on August 3, 1948, as an expert witness on Communist infiltration of government before HUAC's hearing on Communist espionage. He testified that he was one of the few people in the Western world who knew the truth about the insidious nature of Communism. On his oath he said he had been a paid functionary of the Communist Party from 1924 to 1937, when he broke from the Party and commenced to live a God-fearing life as a free man. Chambers testified:

In 1937 I repudiated Marx's doctrines and Lenin's tactics. Experience and the record had convinced me that Communism is a form of totalitarianism, that its triumph means slavery to men whenever they fall under its sway, and spiritual night to the human mind and soul. I resolved to break with the Communist Party at whatever risk to my life or other tragedy to myself or my family.... For a year I lived in hiding, sleeping by day and watching through the night with a gun or revolver within easy reach. That was what underground Communism could do to one man in the peaceful United States in the year 1938.

Chambers said he had had good reason for believing the Communists might try to murder him because for several years he had served in a secret apparatus in Washington, D.C.:

The head of the underground group at the time I knew it was Nathan Witt, an attorney for the National Labor Relations Board.... Lee Pressman was also a member of this group, as was Alger Hiss, who, as a member of the State Department, later organized the conferences at Dumbarton Oaks, San Francisco, and the United States side of the Yalta Conference. The purpose of this group at that time was not primarily espionage. Its original purpose was the Communist infiltration of the American Government. But espionage was certainly one of its eventual objectives. I should perhaps make the point [Chambers later clarified] that these people were specifically not wanted to act as sources of information. These people were an elite group, an outstanding group ... and their position in the Government would be of very much more service to the Communist Party.

Donald Hiss, Alger's brother who was a government official in the 1930s, was also accused by Chambers of membership in the underground apparatus. Chambers claimed that Priscilla Hiss, Alger's wife, was a dues-paying Communist but Donald's wife was not. After his break with the Party, Chambers told the committee, he pleaded with Alger Hiss to join him:

> I went to the Hiss home one evening at what I considered considerable risk to myself, and found Mrs. Hiss at home. [She] attempted while I was there to make a call, which I can only presume was to other Communists, but I quickly went to the telephone and she hung up, and Mr. Hiss came in shortly afterward, and we talked, and I tried to break him away from the party.
>   As a matter of fact, he cried when we separated; when I left him, but he absolutely refused to break.

"He cried?" Representative John McDowell of Pennsylvania asked in astonishment. "Yes, he did," Chambers replied. "I was very fond of Mr. Hiss."[8]

The *New York Herald Tribune* published photographs of Alger Hiss, Lee Pressman, and Nathan Witt under the caption "Implicated in Yesterday's Testimony on Espionage Ring." Later that day, August 4, HUAC read into the record a telegram from Alger Hiss which stated: "I do not know Mr. Chambers and, so far as I am aware, have never laid eyes on him. There is no basis for the statements about me made to your committee. I would ... appreciate the opportunity of appearing before your committee to make these statements formally and under oath." Appearing before HUAC the next morning, Hiss, who had left the State Department in 1947 and was now president of the Carnegie Endowment for International Peace, read a statement in which he denied being a Communist or ever having been one; that he had never adhered to the tenets of the Communist Party or followed its Party line; that he had never been a member of any Communist front organization; that to the best of his knowledge none of his friends were Communist; and that his government contacts with any foreign official who was a Communist were strictly official. Hiss read:

> I never heard of Whittaker Chambers until in 1947 when two representatives of the Federal Bureau of Investigation asked me if I knew him and various other people, some of whom I knew and some of whom I did not know. I said I did not know Chambers. So far as I am aware I have never laid eyes on him and I should like to have the opportunity to do so.... Except as I have indicated, the statements about me made by Mr. Chambers are complete fabrications.

Robert Stripling, HUAC's chief investigator, asked Hiss to give the committee a resume of his education and Federal employment. Hiss replied that he was educated in Baltimore public schools, graduated in 1926 from Johns Hopkins University and then entered Harvard Law School, from which he graduated in 1929. He was then immediately employed with the Federal government for a year as a secretary to Oliver Wendell Holmes, Jr., an associate justice of the Supreme Court. Hiss then entered private law practice with firms in Boston and New York for about three years, after which, at the request of government officials in May 1933, he came to Washington to serve as an assistant general counsel to the Agricultural Adjustment Administration.

At this point Representative Richard Nixon of California interrupted to ask if Hiss would "give the names of the Government officials who requested you to come to Washington with the AAA?"

"Yes," Hiss responded. "Judge Jerome Frank was general counsel. He requested me to come to Washington to be an assistant on his staff."

"You said it in the plural," Nixon stated. "Was he the only one then?"

"There were some others. Is it necessary?" Hiss said. "There are so many witnesses who use names rather loosely before your committee, and I would rather limit myself."

"[B]ut you indicated," Nixon insisted, "that several Government officials requested you to come here and you have issued a categorical denial to certain statements that were made by Mr. Chambers concerning people that you were associated with in Government. I think it would make your case much stronger if you would indicate what Government officials."

Hiss said it did not matter whether it strengthened his case or not, he did not want to mention names he felt were not necessary. "If you insist on a direct answer to your question, I will comply."

Nixon wanted names, so Hiss told him that Supreme Court justice Felix Frankfurter (Hiss's professor at Harvard who had recommended him for the Holmes clerkship), who was in 1933 an adviser to President Franklin Roosevelt, strongly urged him to come to Washington.

Hiss continued with the account of his government service. From AAA he was loaned to a senate committee as a legal assistant. He then joined the Solicitor General's office, and in 1936 Assistant Secretary of State Francis Sayre asked Hiss to work for him in the Trade Agreements division. In various capacities he served in the State Department until January 1947. He said he was asked to take his present position with the Carnegie Endowment by John Foster Dulles, foreign policy advisor for New York governor Thomas Dewey who was the Republican presidential candidate in the upcoming election.

Stripling asked Hiss when he had first heard of "these allegations on the part of Mr. Chambers?" Hiss answered that the night before Chambers testified he received a call from a reporter who told him that Chambers would testify before HUAC the next morning and name him as a Communist.

"You say you have never seen Mr. Chambers?" Stripling asked.

"The name means absolutely nothing to me, Mr. Stripling."

Stripling showed Hiss a recent photograph of Chambers and remarked that Chambers was now much heavier than he was in the 1930s. Said Hiss:

> I would much rather see the individual. I have looked at all the pictures I was able to get hold of in ... yesterday's paper.... If this is a picture of Mr. Chambers, he is not particularly unusual looking. He looks like a lot of people. I might even mistake him for the chairman of this committee. [The acting chairman on August 5 was Karl Mundt of South Dakota.] I would not want to take oath that I have never seen that man. I would like to see him and then I think I would be better able to tell whether I have ever seen him. Is he here today?

"Not to my knowledge," Mundt replied.

"I hoped he would be," Hiss said.

"You realize that this man whose picture you have just looked at," Mundt said, "under sworn testimony before this committee, where all the laws of perjury apply, testified that he called at your home, conferred at great length, saw your wife pick up the telephone and call somebody whom he said must have been a Communist, plead with you to divert yourself from Communist activities, and left you with tears in your eyes...."

"I do know that he said that." Hiss responded. "I also know that I am testifying under those same laws to the direct contrary."

Stripling wanted to know if Hiss had been investigated under the loyalty program. Hiss said he did not know. "You went to the FBI and made a statement?" Stripling asked.

> In 1946, [Hiss recalled,] Mr. Justice Byrnes, then Secretary of State and my chief, called me into his office. He said that several Members of Congress were preparing to make statements on the floor of Congress that I was a Communist. He asked me if I were, and I said I was not. He said, "This is a very serious matter. I think all the stories center from the FBI. I think they are the people who have obtained whatever information has been obtained. I think you would be well advised to go directly to the FBI and offer yourself for a very full inquiry and investigation."
>
> He also said he thought it would be sensible for me to go to the top man, and I agreed.
>
> I immediately ... put in a call for Mr. J. Edgar Hoover, who was not in town. I was courteously received by his second in command....
>
> I told him my conversation with the Secretary of State and said I offered myself for any inquiry. They said did I have any statement to make? I said I was glad to make any statement upon any subject they suggested, and they had no specific one initially. So I simply recited every organization I had been connected with to see if that could possibly be of any significance to them. They asked me if I knew certain individuals. Among the names I remember was that of Lee Pressman. I told them how I had known him and the extent to which I had known him.... They did not mention the name Chambers, I am quite sure.

Representative Mundt asked Hiss if he could "think of anything which might throw any light on the reason why these charges have been made, either by Chambers or by some Members of Congress?" Hiss replied that as to the congressmen he had the same impression as Secretary of State Byrnes: that the information came from the same source. "As to the FBI information," Hiss added, "it seems in the light of Chambers' testimony that they, too, had only that source of information. I have no basis ... for imagining why he should have used my name."[9]

As the hearing concluded, Stripling, underscoring the obvious, remarked: "There is very sharp contradiction here in the testimony. I certainly suggest Mr. Chambers be brought back before the committee and clear this up."

"It would seem that the testimony is diametrically opposed," Mundt reiterated, "and it comes from two witnesses whom normally one would assume to be perfectly reliable. They have high positions in American business or organizational work. They both appear to be honest. They both testify under oath. Certainly the committee and the country must be badly confused about why these stories fail to jibe so completely."

In the initial phase of the Hiss-Chambers affair, after both men had publicly testified before HUAC, the myths implore us to believe — for if we do not rise to the bait the myths die aborning — that Alger Hiss's reaction to Whittaker Chambers's attack was *not* the spontaneous response of an innocent man but rather Hiss was posing to save his reputation. This is the recurring theme of the most bizarre, egregious myth-making book to date: *Alger Hiss's Looking-Glass Wars* (2004) by G. Edward White. Sloppily researched, replete with howlers and infantile psychological analyses, the book purports — and utterly fails — to reveal the "secret life of a covert Soviet spy."

"So when Chambers surfaced in 1948," White wrote, "with claims that Hiss had been a Communist in the 1930s, Hiss's first impulse was to launch a reputational defense. He simply denied any such affiliations, and asked the House Un-American Activities Committee who they were inclined to believe."[10]

In actuality, HUAC was eagerly inclined to bring a perjury indictment against anyone who lied under oath. Alger Hiss was a meticulous lawyer who knew all about security matters and the dangers of lying to congressional committees. Hiss's reputation was secure with those who mattered; his colleagues had advised him to ignore the charges. If Hiss had been a Communist and a confederate of Chambers there never would have been a Hiss case because he never would have testified.

But let's assume Chambers was telling the truth. He used aliases in the 1930s; Hiss did not know his name was really Chambers, and Hiss could no longer recognize his former comrade because he had put on so much weight. Perhaps Hiss thought he could brazen out a denial and get away with it. However, our assumption is somewhat deflated when we reflect that Hiss must have known who Chambers really was even if he could not recognize him. After all, tearful departures are hard to forget.

And if we believe Chambers, our assumption that Hiss did not know him in the 1930s as Chambers falls completely flat because in his autobiography *Witness* (1952) Chambers recalls the final weeping meeting of December 1938 in which the Hisses told him: "You don't have to put on any longer. We have been told who you are."[11]

Also in *Witness*, Chambers maintained that Hiss knew he worked at *Time* and had been keeping a close watch on Chambers (his old friend Carl) for years. Chambers stated that Hiss knew much about him at a time when Chambers knew almost nothing about Hiss.[12]

Alger Hiss lived a long life. He died in 1996 at age 92, and no one ever thought he was insane (though Chambers's sanity has been called into question); but if Chambers was telling the truth on August 3, 1948, then Hiss's appearance before HUAC two days later was the audacious performance of a lunatic.

One of the defining elements of myths is the recounting of events that never happened, and the Hiss-Chambers myths are full of them. So I am obliged to present here a piece of hard evidence that *never* appears in any of the Hiss-Chambers myths.

During his August 3 HUAC testimony, Chambers was asked the identity of the actual head of his Communist underground apparatus. Chambers answered that "the organizer of the group had been Harold Ware. The head of the whole business was J. Peters."

Harold Ware is a very important character because, according to Chambers in *Witness*, it was Ware who introduced him to Alger Hiss. Chambers's sympathetic biographer, Sam Tanenhaus, faithfully echoes his hero's account of his introduction to Harold Ware: "In the summer of 1934, after the Ware Group had been in existence a year, Peters introduced Chambers to Ware at a Manhattan Automat. Chambers sensed right away that he and Ware would make a good team."[13]

Tanenhaus has been commended for his empathy, but he should be reproached for not investigating a lie. The August 3 testimony continues:

HUAC: Do you recall what happened to Harold Ware?
CHAMBERS: He was killed in an automobile accident.
HUAC: What was his real name?
CHAMBERS: As far as I know, Harold Ware. I never knew him.

CHAPTER II

Richard Nixon Ascending

"He's going to be a good man for us."[1] — J. Edgar Hoover on Richard Nixon, 1947

Richard Milhous Nixon was a lieutenant commander in the U.S. Navy serving out his final months settling civilian contracts along the east coast in September 1945 when he received a letter from a family friend asking if he wanted to run as a Republican candidate for the 12th Congressional District of California in the 1946 midterm elections. The thirty-three-year-old Nixon would be running against Jerry Voorhis, a Yale-educated, five-term Democrat. "The idea that I might play even a minor part in practical politics," Nixon later insisted, "never previously occurred to me." Like much else he claimed about his start in politics, Nixon biographer Anthony Summers wrote, "The assertion was not true."[2]

After his discharge from the Navy, Nixon went home to Whittier and devoted all his energy to the campaign, researching Voorhis's record in detail and furtively watching his opponent speak. To California Republicans, Voorhis seemed unbeatable; the Washington press corps named him the representative with the most integrity, and his peers voted him the hardest-working man in the House.

Nixon executed accomplished speeches, but his campaign was going nowhere until his backers hired Murray Chotiner, a diabolical public relations consultant renowned for his ruthlessness. Though Voorhis was a member of HUAC and had a 1940 anti-communism act named after him, he was a New Deal Democrat who had once registered as a Socialist during the Depression. Chotiner, by way of an onslaught of contemptuous advertisements and press reports, portrayed Voorhis as a dupe of the Communists.

There was a growing anxiety, if not frenzy, throughout the country over Communist infiltration. In a speech before an American Legion convention in California a month before the election, FBI director J. Edgar Hoover said that at least 100,000 Communists were running loose in America. The actual number of Communists didn't worry Hoover; his fear was that ten sympathizers stood behind every dues-paying Party member "ready to do the party's work. These include their satellites, their fellow travelers and their so-called progressive and liberal allies. They have maneuvered themselves into positions where a few Communists control the destinies of hundreds who are either willing to be led or have been duped into obeying the dictates of others."[3]

At the same time, Nixon was on the offensive, publicly contending that Voorhis had been endorsed by the Political Action Committee (PAC) of the CIO, the Congress of Industrial Organizations, which undeniably included Communists and fellow travelers. However, the charge was false; Democratic leftists had prevented a PAC endorsement of Voorhis. But the allegations of Communist sympathy killed Voorhis's career; he left politics forever after Nixon's easy victory.

The midterm election of 1946 was a disaster for Democrats all across the land. Only three-eighths of the electorate went to the polls, and the Democratic vote fell by ten million from 1944. Candidates supported by the PAC-CIO won less than a quarter of the races they entered. Republicans now controlled both the House and Senate for the first time since 1932. Democratic seats in the House fell to 188, from 242 in 1944, a freefall from the 331 seats they won in 1936. A Gallop poll gauging campaign issues a month before the election found "foreign policy and relations with Russia" ranking the most important, followed by reducing inflation, curbing labor strikes, making the UN succeed, and ending shortages of housing, food, and clothing.[4] Republicans had campaigned on the themes that Democratic government was riddled by "communism, confusion, and corruption," and many political commentators believed that the communism charge was the most potent force in the shift of power.[5] The day after the election the *Chicago Tribune* editorialized that the voters were "aroused by the manifest dangers to their country's future and to their own welfare. They won the greatest victory for the Republic since Appomattox.... They have broken the evil combination that so long has held the government of this country captive — the combination of corrupt metropolitan machines with disloyal Communists."[6]

American politics for more than a decade prior to 1946 represented an ideological battle between the coalitions comprising the "Roosevelt Revolution"— of business regulation, redistribution of wealth, and internationalism — and their enemies who desired tax cuts, anti-labor legislation, a balanced budget, and for the world beyond American shores to fade away. But Roosevelt died a month before the Allied defeat of Germany, and FDR's liberal vice president of 1940, Henry Wallace, was replaced in 1944 with the more centrist Harry Truman. From the moment Truman ascended to the executive office until the present, the center in U.S. politics has increasingly adopted the notions and policies of the Right. As Christopher Lasch wrote in 1968: "The dynamics of Cold War politics demanded of centrist liberals a continual effort to outmaneuver the Right by preempting it. This strategy, however, far from putting down the Right, merely contributed to its amazing growth."[7]

The Allied war against Hitler and the Axis was born of necessity to defeat a common enemy, but other than that paramount need, the United States, Great Britain, and the Soviet Union shared no unifying political or economic peace objectives — except, in the case of the U.S. and Britain, the negative aim of containing Russia and the Left. According to historian Gabriel Kolko, when the war ended, the U.S.

> refused to negotiate in any serious way, simply because as self-confident master of economic and military power the United States felt it could ultimately define the world order. It had the greatest amount of force in the world as well as the readiness to employ it. Containing the USSR within its bloc, and then integrating the vast remainder of the world, was not so much a new policy but rather a continuation of the quarantine strategy of the United States and its allies after 1918.[8]

To encourage Truman's foreign policy of "ritualized deceit,"[9] the State Department presented him with a top-secret study in 1945 offering this advice: "Decisive action against the American Communists would be a convincing demonstration to Stalin of the inherent strength of this country and would strengthen relations between the two countries."[10]

Yet the Cold War was not an illusion, and Americans were justifiably alarmed about the intentions of the USSR. By early 1946 almost sixty percent of Americans polled believed Russia's actions in Eastern Europe and elsewhere portended a desire to rule the world. Twenty-five percent of those sampled were ready to go to war immediately to stop Soviet aggression. In the first three Cold War months alone of 1946 ominous events transpired.

In a speech to the Russian people on February 9, Stalin denounced the evil "monopoly capitalists"[11] and the inherent contradictions of capitalism that produced fascism and World War II — which the Soviets won in Germany — and now threatened to engulf Russia herself. Those evils would continue, the Soviet leader proclaimed, until capitalism was supplanted by Communism. American liberal William O. Douglas said the speech was the "declaration of World War III."[12]

On February 11, Undersecretary of State Dean Acheson was forced to admit the existence of a secret Yalta protocol on the Far East, only two weeks after he publicly denied it, when the Soviet Union published them.

On February 15, the Canadian government announced the arrest of twenty-two people charged with spying for the Soviet Union. This followed the defection of Igor Gouzenko, a cipher clerk in Ottawa's Soviet Embassy. Gouzenko took with him incriminating documents which proved the existence of an espionage network in the United States and Canada. When questioned by the FBI and Canadian security officials, Gouzenko said he had been told by a lieutenant "in the office of the Soviet military attaché that the Soviets had an agent in the United States in May 1945 who was an assistant to the then Secretary of State, Edward R. Stettinius."[13] Because of other sources, particularly statements made by Whittaker Chambers to the FBI earlier in the 1940s, the Bureau concluded that Gouzenko's hearsay information could only apply to Alger Hiss, who had worked for Stettinius.

On February 22, George Kennan, charge d'affaires of the U.S. Embassy in Moscow, dispatched his "Long Telegram" to Washington. It must have relieved Truman to be assured that conflict with the Russians was inevitable because of the very nature of the Soviet regime. The Soviet myth of capitalist encirclement was a continuation of the fear of foreign penetration the weak regimes of the Czars employed to shore up their archaic political system. "At bottom of Kremlin's neurotic view of world affairs," Kennan wrote, "is traditional and instinctive Russian sense of insecurity.... And they have learned to seek security only in patient but deadly struggle for total destruction of rival power, never in compacts and compromises with it." Kennan remarked it was no coincidence that Marxism, which viewed economic conflicts of society as insoluble by peaceful means, caught hold for the first time in Russia who had never known a peaceful neighbor or tolerated separate internal powers. Lenin's truculent interpretation of the dogma heightened the sense of insecurity even more than the former Russian rulers. In the name of Marxism the Bolsheviks "sacrificed every single ethical value in their methods and tactics. Today they cannot dispense with it."

"In summary," Kennan continued, "we have here a political force committed fanatically to the belief that with U.S. there can be no permanent *modus vivendi*, that it is desirable and necessary that the internal harmony of our society be disrupted, our traditional way of life be destroyed, the international authority of our state be broken, if Soviet power is to be secure." The Soviets had "an elaborate and far flung apparatus for exertion of its influence in other countries, an apparatus of amazing flexibility and versatility, managed by people whose experience and skill in underground methods are presumably without parallel in history." However, Kennan reminded Washington that the USSR did not take unnecessary risks, was impervious to logic of reason but highly sensitive to logic of force, and would usually withdraw when it encountered strong resistance. "Thus, if the adversary has sufficient force and makes clear his readiness to use it, he rarely has to do so." And if situations were properly handled there need be no showdowns.

On March 5, Winston Churchill delivered the famous "Iron Curtain" speech at Fulton, Missouri: "Nobody knows what Soviet Russia and its Communist International organization intends to do in the immediate future, or what are the limits if any to their expansive and proselytizing tendencies.... From Stettin in the Baltic to Trieste in the Adriatic, an Iron Curtain has descended across the continent."

Since assuming the presidency in April 1945 Truman's approval rating plummeted over fifty points to nearly thirty percent after the Republicans' congressional victory in 1946. Truman's leadership was so little regarded that a prominent Democrat, Senator William Fulbright of Arkansas, suggested he resign and hand the presidency over to the Republican leader of the House.

Truman's appeasement of the Right commenced in earnest when he established the Temporary Commission on Employee Loyalty in November 1946. Designed to preempt legislative action, the temporary measure became law by Executive Order 9835 on March 25, 1947. The Federal Employees Loyalty Program, including the Attorney General's list of subversive organizations, ordered the immediate fingerprinting and processing of loyalty questionnaires of more than two million federal officials and workers. The information gathered would be crosschecked against the files of the FBI, the Civil Service Commission, military intelligence, and HUAC in a search for "derogatory information" and "reasonable doubt" of an employee's loyalty. Those accused of disloyalty were virtually presumed to be guilty and would not have the right, among other basic legal niceties, to confront the accuser.

The "Truman Doctrine" was unveiled in a speech by the president before a joint session of Congress on March 12, 1947. With devastated Western Europe on the verge of economic collapse, and Great Britain broke and withdrawing its commitments from the Balkans, Truman evoked the looming specter of Soviet expansion to persuade the American people to bail out Europe. The president wanted economic and military aid for Greece and Turkey (though the Red Army was not threatening either country), and he committed the U.S. to a global policy of containing Russia. The doctrine was couched in ideological rhetoric and entailed a massive increase in military spending, the intimidating twin arms of Washington's foreign policy straightjacket for decades to come.

Appearing that March for the first time before HUAC at the behest of its Republican chairman, J. Parnell Thomas, J. Edgar Hoover spoke of how Communism was being spread by "the diabolic machinations of sinister figures engaged in un–American activities," and that American liberals had been "hoodwinked and duped into joining hands with the Communists."[14] Truman despised the Red-baiting committee, and though ostensibly Hoover served the Administration, his presence before HUAC revealed the measure of his power to confront superiors. No Attorney General (Hoover's boss in the Justice Department) dared risk confrontation with the Bureau's mighty publicity machine — or with Hoover's secret files and army of fawning Special Agents. He was cherished as a national symbol of integrity and strength by an adoring public.

It was the liberals' beloved FDR who encouraged J. Edgar Hoover to put American Communists under surveillance, and it was while working in the Democratic Administration of Woodrow Wilson that Hoover acquired the skills needed to create his legendary filing system of leftwingers. During the "Red Scare" of 1919-20, when Wilson's Attorney General, A. Mitchell Palmer, was arresting without warrants thousands of Communists who were illegally searched and denied legal counsel, Hoover, who was leading the General Intelligence Division, had prepared a catalog of "subversives" comprising 500,000 names, along with biographical notes on 60,000 people, so efficiently organized that names and cross-references could be located in minutes.

Hoover refused to accept solid research showing the Civil Rights movement was not Communist-inspired (or that the Mafia really existed), and he laid responsibility for almost all of America's social problems, including juvenile delinquency, sexual promiscuity, and homosexuality, on Communism. Hoover's former assistant, Charles Brennan, recalled that FBI insiders never really knew the enemy they were fighting: "There was never any substantive understanding of what Communism meant. The word was just used as a general category for that which was foreign, unfamiliar, and undesirable."[15]

Communism in the U.S. in the late 1940s, by Hoover's estimate, was such a dangerous threat that if America did not successfully cope with it then she need not worry about any other threat to internal security because it was possible that there would be no nation. Communist Party membership, about 50,000 in 1946, had climbed to 75,000 by 1947. The Party was capable of raising $300,000 in a month, and their rallies could draw 20,000 people to Madison Square Garden. McCarthyism historian Ellen Schrecker wrote that in 1947 Communists still controlled dozens of "vibrant front groups and retained considerable power within the labor movement."[16] Communist Party membership had fallen to 60,000 by the summer of 1948 when HUAC held its Communist espionage hearings. Communism never took lasting root in the United States, certainly not after the disclosures in the mid–1930s of Stalin's monstrous crimes and the Nazi-Soviet non-aggression pact of 1939. In 1944, during the wartime alliance, CP membership reached its peak of 100,000 in the U.S., but its ideology had been long since discredited and was bankrupt to all but a few lumpen intellectuals and their alienated followers. Yet the FBI pursued them almost to the last man. By the mid–1950s, with CP membership less than 5,000, a third of the members were FBI informants who often informed on each other or recruited acquaintances into the Party, only to turn them in to the FBI.

Hoover took several questions after his March 1947 HUAC speech from newly-elected Representative Richard Nixon. As a law student a decade earlier, Nixon, inspired by a recruiting speech given by one of Hoover's aides, had applied to become an agent, but the Bureau deemed him to be "lacking in aggressiveness."[17] But now, after hearing of Nixon's Red-smear campaign against Jerry Voorhis, Hoover had no doubts about the Congressman and told an aide that day: "He looks to me as if he's going to be a good man for us."

One of Nixon's contributions to the myths of the Hiss-Chambers case, a myth he insisted was true until he died in 1994 (though refuted decades ago), was that he had never heard of Alger Hiss before Whittaker Chambers's HUAC testimony of August 3, 1948. Garry Wills exposed the lie in *Nixon Agonistes* (1970). A year and a half before Chambers testified, Nixon had heard that Hiss was "the most influential Communist in the State Department" from Father John Cronin, a priest active in Baltimore dockside union affairs in the early 1940s who was interviewed by Wills. Cronin discovered Communist cadres were rigging union elections, and the FBI approached him about what he knew. Soon the FBI was using Cronin as a conduit for deliberate leaks, providing him with classified material for a secret 1945 report on Communism for the American bishops. Nixon biographer Summers and Allen Weinstein wrote that Cronin had shown the report to Nixon and discussed Hiss with him.

Cronin's revelation killed another Nixon myth: that the FBI "played no role whatever in the Hiss case,"[18] a remark made *after* HUAC's Chairman Thomas boasted in 1948, "The closest relationship exists between this committee and the FBI. I think there is a very good understanding between us. It is something, however, that we cannot talk too much about."[19] Once the HUAC investigation of Hiss was in full swing, Cronin said, "the really hard-core material was given to me ... informally ... by my friends of the FBI." They would "tell me what they had turned up.... I told Dick, who then knew just where to look for things and what he would find." By the time the HUAC probe became serious, Summers wrote, "Nixon was on the phone late at night with one of Hoover's top aides, Louis Nichols, and meeting in his hotel room with former FBI agents." The FBI leaked information to HUAC and other congressional committees expressly to publicize cases it couldn't prosecute. It was the FBI that provided conservative congressmen in 1946 with allegations that Hiss was a Communist, allegations which were going to be used to denounce Hiss until he met with the FBI by order of his superior, Secretary of State James Byrnes. "One of Hoover's top lieutenants," Ellen Schrecker wrote, "apparently hand-delivered a Bureau report on Hiss to Mississippi Senator James Eastland."[20] Ironically, Hoover and his agents were contemptuous of HUAC's headline-hungry members for habitually leaking information that might embarrass the Bureau.

There is no doubt HUAC would have subpoenaed Alger Hiss to appear had he not volunteered to testify on August 5, 1948. But if Whittaker Chambers's sworn testimony two days prior, and his later recollections in *Witness* about Hiss knowing who he was were true, there would have been no conceivable motive for Hiss to lie. Like the other "Communist underground members" Chambers named, except for Donald Hiss and former assistant secretary of the treasury Harry Dexter White, both of whom also immediately denied the charges and answered all HUAC's questions, Hiss would have asserted his right not to incriminate himself. Thirty-five years after the event Hiss said he "never had any choice but to testify. At the time of the HUAC hearings, I thought my testimony would clear the whole thing up. I soon learned it wasn't that kind of committee." When interviewer David Remnick asked if he was sorry he didn't take the Fifth, Hiss replied: "With the hindsight I have now, well, who would want to undergo the deprivation that I have? I only hope that I would do the same."[21]

After HUAC staffer Robert Stripling announced on August 5 that "there is very sharp contradiction here in the testimony. I certainly suggest Mr. Chambers be brought back before the committee and clear this up," the committee assured Hiss that a prompt confrontation between the two men would be arranged. However, twelve days elapsed before the committee brought the two men face to face. Why didn't Alger Hiss confront Whittaker Chambers on his own by simply walking the few New York City blocks from his office at the Carnegie Endowment to Rockefeller Center where Chambers worked at *Time*? Hiss told an interviewer in the 1960s:

> It did *indeed* occur to me. I discussed it by telephone with my lawyer, William Marbury, who was in Baltimore and saw no particular disadvantage, and with Foster Dulles [then chairman of the Board of the Carnegie Endowment]. But Dulles was strongly opposed to it as improper, in view of the fact that the House Committee had assumed jurisdiction of the topic of my knowing Chambers as a subject of inquiry, and on the first day Nixon had said a confrontation would be arranged by the Committee.[22]

"He was rather insolent toward me," Nixon later wrote of his first encounter with Hiss. "His manner and tone were insulting in the extreme."[23] Though hostility is not communicated in the cold print of the transcript, Hiss had a low opinion of the committee and probably showed it but said he had "no reason for selective contempt for Nixon, a pale nonentity placed inconspicuously on the hearing room dais among the well-known bullies of the committee who played major roles."[24]

Robert Stripling told an interviewer years later:

> Nixon had his hat set for Hiss, it was a personal thing. He was no more concerned about whether Hiss was [a Communist] than a billy goat.... I was surprised one day, sitting in [Nixon's] office.... He said to me "Hiss, that son of a bitch is lying ... lying, lying, lying!" He was just *outraged*. Of course, I knew nothing about him being briefed.[25]

But Nixon genuinely admired Whittaker Chambers. At first, Chambers made scant impression on Nixon or the other HUAC members because his accusations did not involve espionage — they were impatiently waiting for the "spy stories" which never came. Chambers was halfway through his opening statement when Nixon realized "he had some extraordinary quality" which raised him far above HUAC's usual suspects. "It was not how he spoke; it was, rather, the sheer, almost stark eloquence of phrases that needed no histrionic embellishment." Despite Chambers's unsightly appearance ("he was short and pudgy; his clothes were unpressed; his shirt collar was curled up over his jacket"), Nixon realized that here was a man of "extraordinary intellectual gifts and one who had inner strength and depth ... careful with his words, speaking with what sounded like the ring of truth."[26]

Hiss's initial HUAC "performance," Nixon recalled, was brilliant compared to the lackluster testimony of Chambers, and had he concluded his testimony after denying Communist affiliations or sympathy "he would have been home free." But Hiss made an "irreversible mistake" when he went a step further and "denied ever having heard the name Whittaker Chambers."[27] (Actually, Hiss testified that he *had* heard the name but it meant nothing to him.) Hiss never once said outright "I don't know Whittaker Chambers" but "qualified it carefully" by saying, "I have never known a man by the name of Whittaker Chambers." So fraught with significance was this distinction to Nixon that in the midst of Hiss's testimony he asked a staffer to call Chambers in New York to find out if he used an alias when he was a Communist functionary. The hearing was over before Chambers responded that Hiss and the other members of the underground apparatus with whom he had worked in the 1930s had known him only as "Carl." Why Chambers later embellished his story, insisting that Hiss knew his real name since at least 1938 and had been keeping tabs on him at *Time* prior to his testimony, is one of the enigmas of pathological lying.

In the timeline of Richard Nixon's astonishing political career, his actions the afternoon following Hiss's testimony highlight a preeminent benchmark. Hiss had so superbly deflected Chambers's accusations that the committee was in a virtual panic as the hearing ended. Most HUAC members, and probably ninety percent of the reporters present, were certain a horrible mistake had been made and that the committee owed Hiss an apology for having allowed Chambers to testify without first checking his story. Editorials and news stories the next day blasted HUAC for its careless procedures and, in Nixon's view, "completely overlook[ed] the possibility that Chambers rather than Hiss might have been telling the truth."[28] A *Washington Post* correspondent told Nixon: "This case is going to kill the Committee unless you can prove Chambers' story." HUAC's existence depended on demonstrating that the Communist threat in government was authentic, but now there was a growing awareness that Chambers — false rumors were flying that he was an alcoholic who had been in a mental institution — had conned them.

When the committee privately reconvened after Hiss's departure, "you could have cut the gloom with a knife," Stripling recalled. One Republican member lamented, "We've been had. We're ruined." Louisiana Democrat Edward Hébert proposed turning the files over to the Justice Department and holding no more "spy" hearings: "Let's wash our hands of the whole mess." According to Nixon, if Hébert had put his suggestion up for a motion, it would have carried overwhelmingly. Armed with Father Cronin's secret report innuendos on Hiss (which he kept to himself) and his gut feeling that Hiss had known Chambers, Nixon pressed to carry on with an investigation. Also, unlike the other congressmen, Nixon was unopposed for reelection in November and thus in no hurry to go home and campaign. Nixon argued that turning the case over to the Justice Department would probably destroy HUAC; "It would be a public confession that we were incompetent and even reckless in our practices." Moreover, Nixon stressed the committee's responsibility not to drop the matter now that they had opened it up but to see it through. He reminded the others that Chambers had told his story privately many times to "representatives of government agencies and that no action had ever been taken to check the credibility of his charges." Apparently the likelihood that Chambers's serial accusations could not be corroborated and had no merit never dawned on Nixon. His lone suspicion that "while Hiss had seemed a completely forthright and truthful witness, he had been careful never to state categorically that he did not know Whittaker Chambers" was a rather lame criterion for pushing ahead with the case. As Stripling was quoted above, Nixon was not concerned about whether Hiss was a Communist or not. When Nixon closely read the transcript of Chambers's testimony he disregarded "those sections which bore on Chambers' charge that Hiss had been a Communist. I concentrated my sole attention on one question — had Hiss known Chambers? — because it was obvious from reading Chambers' testimony that not only did he claim to know Hiss, but that he knew him very well." Ergo, if Hiss were lying about not knowing Chambers, "then he might also be lying about whether or not he was a Communist" — though Nixon knew he would never be able to prove that Hiss was or had ever been a Communist. From the outset Nixon wanted only to establish Hiss's guilt by association with Chambers at a time when Chambers was admittedly a nefarious Communist bent on infiltrating the government with Communists and sympathizers. Even if Hiss had known Chambers under completely innocuous circumstances that were the opposite of what Chambers claimed, it would be incumbent on Hiss to prove his innocence. If he couldn't, then Chambers must be telling the truth, and "this meant," Nixon wrote in *Six Crises* (1962), "that the Communists had been able to enlist the active support of men like Alger Hiss — in education, background, and intelligence, among the very best the nation could produce." In fairness to Nixon, he could not have known on August 5, 1948, which man was lying, and his feeling that HUAC had an obligation to see the case through is commendable: "If Chambers is lying, he should be exposed. If Hiss is lying, he should be exposed." At the end of the day Nixon's arguments won out and the freshman congressman was appointed to head a subcommittee to interview Chambers again, this time privately. Stripling was directed to subpoena Chambers to a hearing in New York two days later.

More bad news hit HUAC the day of Hiss's testimony. President Truman held a press conference and fumed: "They are using these hearings simply as a red herring to keep from doing what they ought to do. No information has been revealed that has not long since been presented to a federal grand jury and that has not long since been known to the FBI."

After a three-year investigation costing half a million dollars, the Department of Justice announced it had "failed to turn up evidence that would justify prosecution of the Communist espionage now unfolding before congressional committees."[29]

"There was little optimism," Robert Stripling recalled, "in our little subcommittee as we rode to New York on the night of August 6, 1948, to confront Chambers with the brunt of Hiss's denial."[30]

CHAPTER III

Close Friends

"No one could invent all the little items that Chambers has told. I don't believe, either, anyone could learn them merely by studying a man's life. It just doesn't make sense."— Reporter Bert Andrews to Nixon after interviewing Chambers about Alger Hiss

On the same day the subcommittee interviewed Chambers the *New York Times* reported that a HUAC spokesman promised "the whole spy case" was about to be "broken wide open." "A special subcommittee," the report said, "its members unidentified, left Washington tonight for an undisclosed destination." The *New York Herald Tribune* wrote that the sub-committee "left Washington today for a clandestine rendezvous with a mysterious witness billed as able to 'crack wide open' current espionage investigations."

Within the span of four days, from Chambers's testimony of August 3 to the day after Hiss testified, the "case" became a *cause célèbre*; the public, as well as HUAC, fixated on personalities. Though Chambers accused others of Communist ties and government infiltration — but never espionage — he singled out Hiss for special attention, with the obvious expectation that the committee would devote most of its investigation to his charges against Hiss.

Also notable was HUAC's unusual handling of those accused by Chambers compared with those accused by "spy queen" Elizabeth Bentley, star witness of the first day of the hearings on Saturday, July 31. For example, when former government employee Nathan Gregory Silvermaster, accused by Bentley of heading an espionage ring, appeared before HUAC on August 4, Bentley was in the hearing room prepared to confront him. This was the appropriate procedure, and it should have been followed the next day when Alger Hiss testified. If Whittaker Chambers had been present, Hiss's equivocations about not being able to identify Chambers from photographs could not have happened, and without question the Hiss-Chambers "Case" would have ended that day.

Another mystery is why Richard Nixon and his subcommittee went to New York to "confront Chambers with the brunt of Hiss's denial" instead of demanding that Chambers return to Washington. And why, having made the trip, did they not confront Chambers with Hiss himself instead of Hiss's mere denials? After all, Hiss lived in New York. The courtesy was not extended the following week to Hiss. He was subpoenaed to appear in Washington on August 16.

The private meeting, or executive session, with Chambers was held in a vacant courtroom in the Foley Square Federal Courthouse. The subcommittee was comprised of Representatives Nixon, McDowell, and Hébert. Chief investigator Stripling was accompanied by three underlings, the research director, and a stenographer. The questioning began at 10:30 A.M. and continued for almost three hours, mostly off the record at Chambers's request. The on-the-record transcript, not published until two months later but ostensibly made public on August 25, is one of the most important documents of the Hiss-Chambers case, not only for the details of Chambers's demonstrable bald lies and embroideries of fact, but also for what Chambers purposely left unsaid but admitted to not long afterwards — admissions that even HUAC would have found troubling on August 7 and at two later August hearings with Chambers.

By not confronting Chambers and Hiss early on, HUAC — or, rather, Nixon and Stripling, who now controlled the investigation — discounted the possibility that Hiss had known Chambers not only under a different name but also in another context from the one Chambers alleged. However, nine days later, on August 16, this was exactly what Hiss claimed. Though Hiss was then still unable to identify photographs of his accuser, the only person he could think of whom the newspapers said (by way of Nixon's leaks) had spent time at his home in the mid–1930s was a man named George Crosley, a needy freelance journalist Hiss befriended and to whom he had sublet an apartment.

Those facts that Chambers later confirmed — that Hiss knew him as George Crosley, that he often passed himself off as a journalist in the mid–1930s, and that he and his wife and baby occupied (*sublet,* according to Chambers's wife, Esther) for two months an apartment formerly occupied by the Hisses — were not even hinted at during the August 7 private session.

Calling someone a Communist, even knowing it was a lie, was not remarkable for Chambers and did not weigh on his conscience. He frequently accused colleagues at *Time* magazine of being Communists, and during his tenure as foreign news editor in 1944 and 1945 he manufactured wartime reports from abroad to fit his anti–Communist bias, an outlook shared and promoted by *Time* publisher Henry Luce.

Chambers had nothing to lose by testifying — falsely or otherwise — before HUAC, and Luce believed it was Chambers's patriotic duty to appear. Accusing and lying — and posing — were as natural as breathing to Chambers. He was confident HUAC would not expose his lies or hold him to account — so confident that near the end of his August 7 testimony he agreed to take a lie-detector test, an exercise that requires a subject who feels guilty or anxious about lying. HUAC dropped the idea anyway.

"At the start," Stripling later wrote of the meeting with Chambers on the 7th, "we were frankly skeptical of him, but he blandly ignored this and began adding a great store of detail to the astonishing story he had told earlier."[1]

Nixon began the interview and ascertained from Chambers that there was no question of mistaken identity. He knew Hiss from about 1935 to 1937 by his real name, but Hiss and the others in the Washington group knew him only as "Carl," his Communist Party name. How did Chambers know that Alger Hiss was a member of the Communist Party? J. Peters told him so. What facts did J. Peters provide? No facts, but Peters was the head of the American Communist Party underground. Was there any other evidence? Nothing, Chambers said, beyond the fact that Hiss "submitted" himself as a "dedicated and disciplined Communist."

Chambers testified that he obtained Communist Party dues once a month from Hiss over a two or three year period. Hiss "would simply give me an envelope containing Party dues which I transferred to Peters," and Hiss "was rather pious about paying his dues promptly." But Nixon didn't question how he squared that with his public testimony four days earlier when Chambers swore that Henry Collins, treasurer of the Washington group, collected the dues from everyone and then turned the money over to him. Nixon instead asked, "Is there any other circumstance which would substantiate your allegation that [Hiss] was a member of the Party?" Only, Chambers replied, "that all Communists in the group in which I originally knew him accepted him as a member of the Communist Party."

Turning to more personal matters, Nixon asked Chambers if he had ever spent time in Hiss's home. Chambers said he had.

NIXON: Did you stay overnight?
CHAMBERS: Yes; I stayed overnight for a number of days.
NIXON: You mean from time to time?
CHAMBERS: From time to time.
NIXON : Did you ever stay longer than one day?
CHAMBERS: I have stayed there as long as a week.
NIXON: What would you be doing during that time?
CHAMBERS: Most of the time reading. I made that a kind of informal headquarters.
MANDEL (the research director): What was Mr. Hiss's library devoted to?
CHAMBERS: Very nondescript, as I recall.

Nixon inquired if Chambers could describe any of the several different houses the Hisses had lived in when he knew them.

CHAMBERS: It seems to me when I first knew him he was living on 28th Street in an apartment house. It also seems to me that apartment was on the top floor. Now, what was it like inside, the furniture? I can't remember.

Chambers recalled the approximate locations of the other Hiss residences during the period he claimed to have known Hiss. The Hisses moved from 28th Street to P Street in April 1935. They moved from P Street to 30th Street in the summer of 1936, and then moved to Volta Place in December 1937 where they lived when Chambers said he last saw them in December 1938. (The Hisses' lease on the 28th Street apartment expired at the end of June 1935, though they had moved out two months earlier. Hiss testified at his next HUAC hearing that because of the overlapping leases he sublet the apartment at cost to George Crosley [Whittaker Chambers] and his family. Chambers later admitted living there for two months but insisted that Hiss provided the place for free, as a friendly gesture from one Communist to another. In any event, Chambers suppressed this significant fact at the August 7 hearing.)

Chambers could not remember anything about the interiors of the four Hiss residences he claimed to have visited or stayed in overnight. He drew a blank when Nixon asked if he could describe any pictures on the wall or furnishings or china or silver or cocktail glasses. The only item Chambers could recall was a cigarette box, "small red leather-covered ... with gold tooling on it." Nixon asked if the Hisses had a piano. "I don't believe so," Chambers replied, "I am reasonably sure they did not." But at their 30th Street house, an "informal headquarters" for Chambers, a spinet piano was the biggest object in their small living room, and Priscilla Hiss was an inveterate pianist who often played it.

Despite Chambers's uninformative, question-begging answers, Nixon later wrote that "his mind's retentive capacities were developed to an astonishing degree." And Allen Weinstein, master manipulator of Chambers's lies, wrote in *Perjury* that Chambers displayed during the August 7 hearing "remarkable familiarity with the domestic arrangements of the Hisses," including "numerous homey details" and "descriptions of their furniture."

Some of the subcommittee's questions evoked spontaneous, seemingly involuntary and outlandish inventions from Chambers.

> STRIPLING: Did [Hiss] go to church?
> CHAMBERS: He was forbidden to go to church.

Though HUAC investigators made no attempt to find out, Hiss was a lifelong Episcopalian, and during the period Chambers was supposed to have known them so well, the Hisses attended Christ Church in Georgetown. The rector was a college friend of Hiss, and Hiss's stepson, Timothy Hobson, sang in the choir.

> MANDEL: A picture of Hiss shows his hand cupped to his ear.
> CHAMBERS: He is deaf in one ear.
> HÉBERT: Which ear?
> CHAMBERS: I don't know.
> NIXON: Did he tell you how he became deaf in one ear?
> CHAMBERS: I don't recall that he did.

Hiss had never been deaf in either ear. In 1948 an audiologist at Columbia Medical Center certified that his hearing was excellent in both ears.

> NIXON: Did they drink?
> CHAMBERS: They did not drink. They didn't drink with me. For one thing, I was strictly forbidden by the Communist Party to taste liquor at any time.

However, Hiss drank frequently and collected vintage wines.

> NIXON: Was there any special dish they served?
> CHAMBERS: No. I think you get here something else. Hiss is a man of great simplicity and a great gentleness and sweetness of character, and they lived with extreme simplicity. I had the impression that the furniture in that house was kind of pulled together from here or there ... nothing lavish about it whatsoever, quite simple. Their food was much the same pattern, and they cared nothing about food. It was not a primary interest in their lives.

Chambers's most outrageous and gratuitous fabrications concerned Timothy Hobson, Priscilla's son by a previous marriage, who was ten years old in 1936 and lived with the Hisses at the time they were acquainted with Crosley/Chambers. Chambers told Nixon he called the boy Timmie. He was the son of Thayer Hobson, who, Chambers thought, worked for publisher William Morrow in New York. Chambers described Timothy as "a puny little boy, also rather nervous" and "slightly effeminate." "Do you recall where he went to school?" Nixon asked. Chambers couldn't recall the names of the schools Timothy attended in 1936 or 1937, but he said the Hisses told him that Thayer Hobson was paying for Timothy's schooling, and they were "diverting a large part of that money to the Communist Party."

> NIXON: Hiss told you that?
> CHAMBERS: Yes, sir.
> NIXON: Did he say how much he was paying?
> CHAMBERS: No; I don't know how much he was paying.
> NIXON: Did he name the Communist Party as the recipient?
> CHAMBERS: Certainly.
> HÉBERT: Hobson was paying for the boy's education?
> CHAMBERS: Yes; and they took him out of a more expensive school and put him in a less expensive school expressly for that purpose.

Again, Robert Stripling and his team of investigators made no attempt to find out if this appalling accusation was true or false. Had they asked Thayer Hobson, he would have informed them that Hiss could not have diverted any of Timothy's tuition to the Communist Party or anyone else because Hobson paid the schools directly. It was true that Timothy did change schools. But the latter school was *more* expensive, not less. Moreover, Hobson couldn't afford the increase, so Hiss made up the difference. "I knew the son of a bitch was a liar," Hobson said of Chambers, "when I heard that." Stripling later published the story as the truth ("facts which only an extremely intimate friend of Hiss ... could have provided") in his 1949 book *The Red Plot Against America*.

Timothy Hobson was a grown man in August 1948, but he was never approached by HUAC for his recollections of the years in question. Now a retired physician living in California, Timothy told an interviewer in 2001 that he could not remember ever seeing Chambers, though he did recall seeing Chambers's wife on one occasion. In February 1937, when Chambers asserted he was a frequent visitor at the Hisses home on 30th Street, Timothy (who was large for his age, not puny) was struck by a car while riding his bicycle. "I was in a cast in the front bedroom," he said. "I was immobilized for well over a month. If he was in the house, he would have known about it, and I would have known he was there."

It is disconcerting to be in the presence, even a literary one, of a liar as composed as Chambers and not believe him. And because Chambers actually had known the Hisses — it was the duration and nature of the acquaintance that would be disputed — a few of his answers were on the mark; others, if not sweeping inventions, were only partly true, yet, as Nixon believed, "had a personal ring of truth about them beyond the bare facts themselves." Two half-truths Chambers told were later exploited, as we shall see, by the committee to devastating effect against Hiss. One concerned Hiss's interest in birds.

> MANDEL: Did Mr. Hiss have any hobbies?
> CHAMBERS: Yes; he did. They both had the same hobby — amateur ornithologists, bird observers. They use to get up early in the morning and go to Glen Echo, out the canal, to observe birds. I recall once they saw, to their great excitement, a prothonotary warbler.
> McDOWELL: A very rare specimen?
> CHAMBERS: I never saw one. I am also fond of birds.

The other partial truth was about an old car Hiss had given away in the mid–1930s. Chambers recalled that when he first knew them the Hisses drove a dilapidated Ford, a black roadster. But they got rid of it in 1936 and bought a new Plymouth sedan.

> MANDEL: What did he do with the old car?
> CHAMBERS: The Communist Party had in Washington a service station — that is, the man in charge or owner of this station was a Communist — or it may have been a car lot.... I never knew who this was or where it was. It was against all the rules of underground organization for Hiss to do anything with his old car but trade it in ... but Hiss insisted that he wanted that car turned over to the open party so it could be of use to some poor organizer in the West or somewhere. Much against my better judgment and much against Peters' better judgment, he finally got us to permit him to do this thing.... I should think the records of that transfer would be traceable.

In summary, Chambers contended a *close association* with the Hisses from about 1935 to the end of 1937. Yet he was ignorant of all the major events in the Hisses lives after the first half of 1936, such as Timothy's accident in early 1937 or Hiss's pneumonia in 1936 or the fact that the Hisses lived in a hotel for two weeks before moving to 30th Street in 1936. Moreover, Chambers was consistently inaccurate or unaware of precisely the sort of details that a close friendship would have divulged, ignorance he attempted to camouflage with inane digressions, such as his bit about Hiss's "great gentleness and sweetness of character."

The facts Chambers did know were of a type easily learned in casual conversation with Hiss or perhaps lifted from standard reference books. The listing for Alger Hiss in the 1947 *Who's Who in America* provides his wife's maiden name, her former married name, and her son's name. There is also an entry for Thayer Hobson which indicates his profession and employer. The 1947 *Current Biography* added that Hiss was an "amateur ornithologist" (the same words Chambers used) and liked to play tennis — also noted by Chambers during testimony.[2]

Robert Stripling later wrote that when the subcommittee returned to Washington he prepared a "list of every statement Chambers had made" and detailed a researcher to check each item. "She worked diligently, combing the records of Timmie's schools, employment agencies, the veterinarian concerned, car registrations, real estate offices and the like." Not to be outdone, Nixon wrote in *Six Crises* (1962): "In the next nine days, from August 8 to August 16, the Committee staff under Stripling's direction worked round the clock in a search for documentary or other proof ... of Chambers' story.... And in detail after detail, where the Chambers story could be checked with third parties, it proved to be true."

But according to Bert Andrews, Washington bureau chief of the *New York Herald Tribune*, Nixon's account to him of the investigation the week following Chambers's testimony was somewhat more indecisive and faltering. "We have established two facts," Nixon said. "Hiss did live in the Twenty-eighth Street apartment. He did have a dog."[3] Nixon asked Andrews to read Chambers's testimony on a confidential basis. Nixon still didn't know which man to believe, and he wanted an outside judgment. Andrews concluded that Chambers must have known Hiss well.

Nixon also solicited the opinions of William P. Rogers, chief counsel for the Senate Internal Security subcommittee investigating the espionage charges of Elizabeth Bentley; and Charles J. Kersten, Republican congressman of Wisconsin and a Nixon mentor. Both reached the same presumption as Andrews. Kersten suggested that Nixon ask John Foster Dulles to read the August 7 transcript because he had heard that Hiss was attempting to get Dulles and other Carnegie board members to make reassuring statements to the press on Hiss's behalf. Nixon phoned Dulles the next day, and they agreed to meet that afternoon in New York, where Dulles was working on Thomas Dewey's presidential campaign. Allen Dulles, John Foster's brother (who later became director of the Central Intelligence Agency), was also there when Nixon arrived. Both men read Chambers's testimony and both were disturbed by it. John Foster Dulles worriedly paced the floor, then halted and said to Nixon: "There's no question about it. It's almost impossible to believe, but Chambers knows Hiss."[4]

Nixon was still not satisfied. On August 12 he drove alone from Washington to Chambers's Westminster farm, a two-hour trip. He wanted to talk to Chambers in private "to gain a more intimate impression of what kind of man he really was ... to sense whether or not he was telling the truth." "It was the first of many long and rewarding conversations," Nixon wrote fourteen years later, "I was to have with him during the period of the Hiss case, and through the years until his death in 1961." Though Nixon's visit was "not too productive in obtaining any additional information" about the putative Hiss-Chambers relationship, he gathered from Chambers that there was much more at stake — such as the fate of the nation — than what happened to either of them as individuals. With "great feeling," Nixon recounted, Chambers implored: "*This is what you must get the country to realize.*"

A week after the private meeting with Chambers, HUAC's "investigation" of his charges still had not produced much. They had not even located the records of the title transfer of Hiss's car, the one he supposedly gave to the Communists, the one whose title Chambers believed was traceable. Stripling had managed to obtain photographs of the exteriors of the four residences the Hisses had lived in from 1935 to 1938, and Nixon took the photographs with him on yet another visit to Chambers's farm, this time accompanied by newsman Bert Andrews. For lack of evidence that would corroborate Chambers's story, Nixon was forced to rely on his gut feelings and the hunches of others who had read Chambers's testimony. Andrews, an ace reporter who had won a Pulitzer Prize for his investigations of the egregious practices of the State Department's loyalty program, was along to put some tough questions to Chambers.

At first Chambers was reluctant to talk to Andrews because of his reputation as a somewhat liberal journalist who had been critical of HUAC. "I thought you were unfriendly to the Committee," Chambers said in HUAC's defense. "Ask Congressman Nixon here," Andrews replied, continuing:

> He'll tell you that the Committee is very close to dropping this whole case because it is loaded with dynamite and because they don't have enough evidence. If they drop it, what happens then? It's still a case of your word against Hiss's. And Hiss's record is so much better than yours the chances are you will still be indicted for perjury just because his story will be believed over yours. After all, nobody has really believed your story for the last nine years, have they?

But if Andrews "interrogated" Chambers there is no indication of it in his 1962 book *A Tragedy of History, A Journalist's Confidential Role in the Hiss-Chambers Case.* He posed a couple of embarrassing questions he knew Chambers would deny: Was he an alcoholic? Had he been in an insane asylum?

Nixon had noted Hiss's former address on the back of each house or apartment photograph he brought. He showed them to Chambers without letting him see the backs, and Andrews confirmed that Chambers's identifications were all correct. Then Andrews asked Chambers about his shared interest with Hiss of bird watching. "Certainly," Andrews remarked, "if that is true you *must* remember more about that hobby in connection with him." Chambers went into an adjoining room and returned with two books of Audubon prints. "Alger Hiss gave me these books," Chambers said. He flipped through the pages and stopped at the picture of a hooded warbler. "Hiss had a picture," Chambers said to Andrews and Nixon (both recounted this episode), "of the same species on the dining room wall in one of his homes." This is a perfect illustration of how Chambers launched ever-expanding charges against his luckless victim Alger Hiss. Only one week before this statement Chambers recalled to HUAC how excited the Hisses were when they told him they had once seen a prothonotary warbler — and just a few questions later in the August 7 transcript there is this exchange:

NIXON: [D]o you recall any pictures on the wall that [the Hisses] might have owned at the time?
CHAMBERS: No; I am afraid I don't.

"Later," Andrews wrote, "the committee tried to trace the books to Hiss. It was never able to do so."

"I've made up my mind on one thing," Andrews remarked to Nixon. "No one could invent all the little items that Chambers has told. I don't believe, either, anyone could learn them merely by studying a man's life. It just doesn't make sense."

Richard Nixon and Robert Stripling created the myth of guilt by close association between Hiss and Chambers. Even more damaging was the impression built up over two weeks that Hiss had denied knowing Chambers *by any name or under any circumstance*. By interviewing Chambers secretly, where Hiss could not promptly respond, and then leaking selected testimony to the public, they fashioned the general perception that Hiss was a sinister liar — all in keeping with HUAC's and Chambers's mantra that the public should identify Hiss with what they believed was nefariously characteristic of the New Deal, Yalta, and the UN.

During this week of rumors and press leaks Alger Hiss indeed called on his Carnegie superior John Foster Dulles. Hiss was concerned and annoyed about the rumors and decided he should pay a visit to Whittaker Chambers at his *Time* office and find out who he really was. But Dulles, who had already been primed by Nixon, told Hiss not to and that the Committee would arrange for him to see Chambers; they were now officially in charge of the investigation, and Hiss should leave matters to them. And on Friday the 13th a telegram from HUAC summoned Hiss to Washington the following Monday.

CHAPTER **IV**

Star Chamber

"Dr. Silverman, you are now before the greatest open court in this country."[1]—
Representative F. Edward Hébert of Louisiana (HUAC 80th Congress) to Abraham
George Silverman, witness

J. Parnell Thomas, Republican of New Jersey and chairman of the House Committee
on Un-American Activities of the 80th Congress (1947-1948), told a *New York Times* interviewer in 1954 that the Republican National Committee chairman "was urging me in the
Dewey campaign to set up the spy hearings. At the time he was urging me to stay in Washington to keep the heat on Harry Truman."[2] The heat was also rising on Chairman Thomas
in the first two weeks of August 1948. *Washington Post* columnist Drew Pearson learned that
Thomas was padding his congressional office payroll and taking kickbacks from nonworking
"employees." In one of the most poetically brutal ironies of American politics, Thomas—
after months of reproaching a parade of witnesses, accused by Bentley and Chambers, for
"taking the Fifth"—on advice of counsel refused to testify before a federal grand jury investigating the charges against him on the ground of self-incrimination. Finished politically,
he was indicted in November 1948, convicted a year later, and ultimately served almost a
year in prison.

Thomas had been with HUAC from its inception, when it was renowned as the Dies
Committee. The creation of the Special House Committee on Un-American Activities in
May 1938 as a temporary investigating committee was largely the result of the outrage of
east Texas Democrat Martin Dies over the legendary sit-down work stoppage of auto workers
in Flint, Michigan, the year before. Dies denounced the strike as a communist tactic
imported from France. The House of Representatives authorized Dies to embark on an
investigation of un–American propaganda, and his committee became one of the first insti-
tutional weapons against the New Deal. Dies protested that the federal bureaucracy was
swollen with "hundreds of left-wingers and radicals who do not believe in our system of
private enterprise,"[3] and his demand for removing "communists" from the federal payroll
had vast public and congressional backing. Opinion polls recorded consistently high approval
ratings for the committee's investigations, and neither the Roosevelt administration nor
many congressmen dared oppose Dies. Spectacular inquests were conducted to attract max-
imum attention. "The room where it held its hearings," British journalist Alistair Cooke

noted, "was a Roman circus panting for the entrance of dazed Christians."[4] The specter of communist subversion, HUAC asserted repeatedly, was a great peril to American society. "The anticommunist scenario that Dies and his colleagues purveyed," historian Ellen Schrecker wrote, "was a remarkably effective weapon for attacking the Roosevelt administration. Anticommunism, it turned out, made headlines, and the committee's investigations invariably received enormous publicity." And in the temper of J. Edgar Hoover's index of leftists and subversives was "Dies's list," comprising the New Deal's most astute and effective lawyers, economists, and bureaucrats — such as Harry Dexter White and Alger Hiss. The list read like a "Who's Who of Popular Front Washington," Schrecker wrote, and "was to become a lethal time bomb."[5]

By 1942, after the United States had entered the war and allied with the Soviet Union, the Dies committee had become increasingly inactive, and in 1944 it held only a few brief hearings. Dies declined to run for reelection, and three other committee members were defeated in November 1944. In the hopeful months before the end of the European war, many Americans believed they were entering a new era of international cooperation and peace which would be reflected in a less frenetic atmosphere of domestic politics. Despite its crass mischief and grasping for the limelight, it was assumed that Dies's HUAC would be gently retired.

But at the opening of the 79th Congress in January 1945, a coalition of Republicans and Southern Democrats led by John Rankin of Mississippi resolved to make HUAC a permanent committee. Rankin took the initiative, and it was solely his idea, for in addition to wanting to keep the committee alive (though he had never been a member), he was convinced there was a plot to destroy the files and records of the Dies years.

Rankin had served in the House since 1921. He was a World War I veteran and a former prosecuting attorney in Mississippi. His legislative obsessions were veterans' benefits, the promotion of white supremacy and the maintenance of Jim Crow laws in the South, and the suppression of communism. He hated Jews and believed "slavery was the greatest blessing the Negro people ever had." In 1945 he asked William C. Bullitt, former ambassador to the Soviet Union: "You said before that sixty percent of the Communist Party here are aliens. Now what percentage of these aliens are Jews?"[6]

How Rankin engineered the creation of a standing Committee on Un-American Activities was, according to HUAC historian Robert Carr, "one of the most remarkable procedural coups in modern Congressional history."[7] On the first day of the 79th Congress the Rules Committee chairman offered the resolution that the rules of the previous Congress remain in effect for the new one. Immediately Rankin recommended an amendment to the resolution that the Un-American Activities Committee be added as a standing committee. Technically, *no* committees existed until the chairman's resolution itself was adopted, and it had to be voted upon at once. It was a railroading maneuver, but Rankin cleverly deduced that House members would continue to find no political wisdom in voting against un–American activities investigations. In the debate over his amendment Rankin asserted that the destruction of the Dies archive was prevented only because of the presence of a police guard. However, Speaker Sam Rayburn pointed out that under House rules the records of a defunct committee went to the House clerk for safekeeping and then to the Library of Congress. When the roll was called, Rankin's amendment was carried by 207 to 186, with 40 members not voting. His proposal was supported by 137 Republicans and 70 Democrats, 63 of whom were Southerners. 150 Democrats and 34 Republicans voted against the amendment.

The House voted 315 to 54 to give the now permanent committee an appropriation of $50,000 and all of the files and records of the former Dies committee. Under Public Law 601, 79th Congress, the House Committee on Un-American Activities was authorized to investigate

> the extent, character and objects of un–American propaganda activities in the United States; the diffusion within the United States of subversive and un–American propaganda that is instigated from foreign countries or of a domestic origin and attacks the principle of the form of government as guaranteed by our Constitution; and all other questions in relation thereto that would aid Congress in any remedial legislation.

The 79th Congress was in its fourth month when President Roosevelt died on April 12. Almost immediately diplomatic relations between the U.S. and the U.S.S.R. soured — as Truman from the outset of his presidency took a tough stand — and the national mood of friendliness toward Russia also darkened. And then the fear conditioning began. Fear was no longer the "only thing we have to fear," as FDR said in 1933. Fear, as John Foster Dulles now put it, is "a feeling of need in the face of danger."[8] The danger was a worldwide communist movement, arising from the imminent defeat of the fascist powers, led by the Soviets who were breaking allied agreements on the fate of Eastern Europe. The *need* of an evil enemy was becoming embedded in America's psyche. Playwright Arthur Miller believed it was "an ignoble thing … this wrenching shift, this ripping off of Good and Evil labels from one nation and pasting them onto another…. If last month's friend could so quickly become this month's enemy, what depth of reality could good and evil have?"[9]

After the atomic bombs were dropped on Japan in August, the illusion that by keeping the technology "secret" the U.S. could prevent the Soviets from developing their own bomb was almost universally prized by the public. Thus, tracking down domestic Communists — all considered potential spies — was simply an obligation of preserving the secret weapon, never mind the abuses of power. The already edgy and wary nation was stunned on February 3, 1946, when Drew Pearson announced on his popular radio program that a Soviet spy was in the custody of the Canadian government, having confessed to a "gigantic Russian espionage network inside the United States and Canada." Pearson's source was almost certainly FBI director J. Edgar Hoover, who wanted to force the issue and exploit the people's fear.

The paramount interest of HUAC after 1945 was the alleged subversive exploits of communist provocateurs and fellow travelers. The loyalty and patriotism of anyone to the left of a centrist Democrat was questionable. The committee assumed the nation's citizens were weak and corrupt and did not trust each other. HUAC made Americans suspicious of democratic organizations and institutions, those which contributed immensely to the stability and vitality of the nation, by insinuating that the social structure was layered with disloyal individuals; they asserted public officials were spies for the Soviets, teachers were Communists, scientists were ceding atomic secrets to the enemy, the film industry was a Red propaganda machine, organized labor was treacherous. The fear-mongering and denigration of Americans were astonishing in light of the dismal achievement of communism to win converts in the United States. A country sustained for centuries by self-reliance and religious faith was scarcely going to fall prey to the doctrines of Marx and Lenin. The domestic anti-communism of the decade following World War II transcended political adventure and opportunism. It was essentially irrational — ideology trumping reality. Ellen Schrecker remarked that it was tapping into something "dark and nasty in the human soul."

Though HUAC was primarily an investigating committee, it employed no logical procedures or systematic methods for carrying out investigations. Because most of their inquiries were either groundless or foolish they shifted expediently with the political winds of the hour or the willy-nilly prejudices of committee members or staff. Just as inconsistent and whimsical as its investigations was the conduct of hearings. If the hearing was public, quite often it was not preceded by even the most rudimentary investigation, thus permitting irresponsible and emotionally unbalanced witnesses, especially HUAC's darlings, Elizabeth Bentley and Whittaker Chambers, to slander innocent people under privileged circumstances. If the hearing was private, unfriendly witnesses were often grilled and browbeaten and denied their rights, and the next day the most damaging parts of their testimony, leaked to the press against all the rules of the House, were printed in the major newspapers. But friendly witnesses were allowed to tell their stories at great length without embarrassing questions. The ex–Communist witnesses, particularly Bentley, Chambers, and Louis Budenz, were allowed to indulge in monologues. When Budenz testified before the committee in 1946, for example, he spoke at immense length without committee guidance about his conviction that a "conspiratorial apparatus" existed within the formal Communist Party organization. Chambers became the favorite "committee witness," and they depended upon him almost totally for the development and continuation of the August 1948 spy inquiries — though he continued to deny any knowledge of espionage.

HUAC's public hearings nevertheless were fascinating and compelling. They mirrored, without doubt, the nation's obsession in the late 1940s with all things subversive and communist. And as Herbert L. Packer persuasively noted in *Ex-Communist Witnesses* (1962), the "facility of narration" and what "appears to be a coherent account" of witnesses unencumbered by rules of evidence and "unscathed by cross-examination" are the advantages of congressional inquiries as opposed to court trials where the meager narrative, confined to points on the indictment, must then be punctuated by cross-examination, an often slow and unrevealing process though its cumulative effect may be great, to test the credibility of the witness. The nonadversary aspects of HUAC's hearings, "often deplored on grounds of personal fairness," Packer wrote, "is at once a boon to the facile narration of complicated facts and a bane to the careful verification of those facts."

Returning to HUAC's members of the 80th Congress, Walter Lippmann reflected in his opinion column shortly after the 1946 midterm elections that he hoped the new Republican majority would "strip Representative Rankin of the tyrannical power which he has usurped, and put an end to this man's lawless, subversive, and outrageous attacks on the constitutional liberties of the American people."[10] But under incoming chairman J. Parnell Thomas, HUAC sunk even lower in the quagmire of capricious invective.

A less qualified candidate for a congressional committee chairmanship can barely be imagined, but because Thomas had been with the committee since 1938, seniority prevailed. Also, Republican leaders were confident that Thomas, who despised the New Deal and all its work, would not pass up an opportunity to attempt to discredit supporters of Roosevelt's or Truman's programs. HUAC historian Robert Carr characterized Thomas as completely undignified, vulgar, raucous, course, small, vain, stupid, arrogant, opinionated, flamboyant, prejudiced, emotional, vindictive, blindly partisan, and utterly irresponsible. His two-year term as HUAC's presiding officer was fittingly capped with a criminal conviction.

Mississippi Democrat John Rankin, the most scandalous member, faded into the background of the committee during the 80th Congress, and in 1949 he was forced by House rules to forgo HUAC membership when he became chairman of the Veterans' Affairs committee.

Karl Mundt of South Dakota, the most senior Republican after Thomas, was elected to the House in 1938, appointed to the Dies committee in 1943, and remained with HUAC until he became a Senator in November 1948. Before joining the House he was employed with various business interests and had worked as a magazine editor and writer. Throughout much of 1948 he served as HUAC's acting chairman. Like Thomas, he hated the New Deal and attacked the Democratic administration at every opportunity. He adamantly disapproved of the United Nations, the State Department, and U.S. postwar foreign policy as being too soft on the Soviet menace. Mundt was one of the most intelligent members of the committee and was a competent acting chairman and subcommittee chairman who regularly attended sessions and carefully followed the development of hearings.

Richard Nixon, though a freshman congressman propelled into office by California businessmen and a campaign remarkable for smearing Jerry Voorhis as a Communist sympathizer, became the star of the committee by the close of the 80th Congress. He was the brightest, most able, and hardest working member, particularly during the Hiss-Chambers sessions, which he dominated. Nixon's first year was rather quiet, and he was not much involved even in the Hollywood hearings, and was understandably somewhat inclined to defend his state's movie industry against the charges and attacks of chairman Thomas and others. But despite his initial display of fairness and detachment, as time went on he became stridently partisan and deviously opportunistic. In early 1948 he chaired a subcommittee which proposed legislation to curb the Communist Party by requiring members to register and barring them from public office, resulting in the Mundt-Nixon bill.

John McDowell, Republican of Pennsylvania, was a one-term mediocrity who swept into office with the 1946 GOP landslide. A former newspaperman of limited ability and strong reactionary political prejudices, he took part in several of the Hiss-Chambers hearings, most prominently in the executive session with Hiss on August 16 (which shall soon be examined) when he set up Hiss with the question, "Have you ever seen a prothonotary warbler?"

Democratic Representative F. Edward Hébert of Louisiana was appointed to HUAC to fill a vacancy in January 1948, only to be expelled a year later because other Democrats on the committee insisted that only lawyers serve. Hébert was a prominent New Orleans newspaperman before his election to the House in 1940. He questioned many witnesses during the espionage hearings the summer of 1948, and was a steadfast and enthusiastic worker who believed the hearings should be fairly conducted and witnesses not badgered or bullied. But like the other committee members, Republicans and Democrats, he shared a distorted, surreal view of the insidious reach of communism into American society. He was convinced, for instance, that American college campuses were overrun with Communists.

Next to Richard Nixon and perhaps Martin Dies, the person most closely associated in the public's mind with the Un-American Activities committee was Robert Stripling, the committee's longest-serving staff member and, from 1939 until he retired in 1948, its chief investigator. Because of his fanatical devotion to the committee's work and his great ability as an inquisitor, if not an investigator, one of his otherwise leading critics, muckraker Drew Pearson, called Stripling "the real brains" of HUAC. "He functions as a unique combination of master of ceremonies," said the usually unfriendly *Washington Post*, "chief counsel, main interrogator, and front-running guide through the labyrinths of subversive organizations."[11]

He was born in 1912 and retired from HUAC at the tender age of 36, when most professionals are just getting started. Martin Dies brought Stripling from Texas to Washington in 1932 after Stripling had attended for a time, without graduating, both Texas A&M and the University of Texas. Dies provided him with a low-paying patronage job as a door-keeper at the House of Representatives, and Stripling attended law school at night but never finished. When Dies was appointed to chair the Special Committee on Un-American Activities in 1938, Stripling volunteered to work without salary as the committee's clerk. A month later they put him on the payroll, and a year after that he carried the title Chief Investigator.

Stripling was the first to admit he had no qualifications as an investigator except what he learned in the process of his own investigations. In fact, he was totally unprepared, with no training or experience, for such an important position. Yet, typically, the committee never aimed above the second-rate in recruiting staff. A random ex–FBI hand without much of a track record, or a former Communist Party member who could do a little research, was the best HUAC obtained for investigative work.

Upon retirement in December 1948, Stripling was showered with praise for his knowledge of subversives and un–American types. "It is our studied opinion," according to a HUAC statement, "that Bob Stripling has become one of the best informed men in the United States on the identities, the tactics, and the end objectives of the Communist conspiracy. He has few equals and no superiors in his knowledge of the treacherous methods of disloyal … elements in this country."[12]

Throughout the era of fear conditioning, particularly the first postwar decade, the very definition of a Soviet-inspired Communist in America underwent curious and enlightening vicissitudes. If, as Richard Nixon pointed out, Alger Hiss — "in education, background, and intelligence, among the very best the nation could produce" — had been enlisted by the Communists, "then surely the country should be informed" and Congress should take action to deal with the problem.[13] Stripling adds that "Red agents are brilliantly trained, fanatically dedicated, physically brave, and industrious beyond the comprehension of Americans."[14] But by the early 1950s Senator Joe McCarthy was saying that "practically every active Communist is twisted mentally or physically in some way." And that is not a quote taken out of context, for it was commonly assumed — and there were psychological studies to back it up — that the Communist Party embraced "a large proportion of emotionally maladjusted individuals who were seeking to solve their emotional problems by attacking society, rather than face up to their personal inadequacies and conflicts." Or, as Arthur Schlesinger, Jr. wrote, it gave those who joined the "social, intellectual and even sexual fulfillment they cannot obtain in existing society."[15]

In the first month of the 80th Congress, HUAC authorized Chairman Thomas to announce their forthcoming inquiries into Communist subversion of the motion picture industry and of the Federal Government. In advance of the October 1947 Hollywood hearings, HUAC circulated the rumor that the Roosevelt administration had brought pressure upon the movie industry to produce pro–Soviet films. Robert Stripling declared that if the CP could "seize the motion picture industry … it could hasten by many years its … plan to communize the country. About 75,000,000 Americans attend movies each week. Most of the patrons believe what they see."[16]

HUAC's first Hollywood witnesses — by way of the Motion Picture Alliance for the Preservation of American Ideals — laid the foundation for charges of a vast systematic "communization" of the film industry. Producer-director Sam Wood (*For Whom the Bell Tolls*) named many writers and other creative people as Communists. "If I have any doubt," Wood said, "then I haven't any mind. These Communists thump their chests and call themselves liberals. But if you drop their rompers you'll find a hammer and sickle on their rear ends."[17]

The ensuing "degradation ceremonies" (so labeled by leftist Victor Navasky) of the Unfriendly Ten or Hollywood Ten, as the screenwriters came to be called, ended in contempt of Congress citations and prison sentences — and subsequent blacklisting until the 1960s — when they refused to answer that era's most fearsome question: "Are you now or have you ever been a member of the Communist Party?"

The committee's Hearings Regarding Communist Espionage in the United States Government commenced July 31, 1948. Two weeks before, President Truman had called a special session of Congress while delivering his acceptance speech at the Democratic National Convention in Philadelphia. He demanded that the "do nothing" 80th Congress go back to work and pass legislation stalled earlier in the term. The House and Senate retaliated with inquiries into subversive activities.

The timing was perfect because only a few days earlier, on July 20, a federal grand jury in New York, impaneled for over a year, had returned indictments against twelve members of the National Board of the Communist Party. They were charged with conspiring to overthrow the U.S. government in violation of the Alien Registration Act (or Smith Act) of 1940. But the grand jury had not acted on the testimony of an anonymous witness, and, according to the *World-Telegram*, that testimony was the most important heard. The putatively secret proceedings of the grand jury had been leaking to the press for months. Edward Nellor of the *New York Sun* had already revealed the nature of the grand jury's investigation, broke the news that the Communist officials would be indicted, and disclosed that a "well-educated woman," who had been a courier for the Communists, "had told her story to the Federal authorities."[18]

The mystery woman was Elizabeth Bentley, and she testified for five hours at HUAC's first spy hearing. But she had been talking to the FBI and the grand jury for three years. Their investigations cost hundreds of thousands of dollars and resulted in no indictments. The day after her first interview with the FBI in 1945, Director Hoover relayed to President Truman that "a number of persons employed by the Government" were passing information to "persons outside the Federal Government" who in turn were giving it "to espionage agents of the Soviet Government."[19] Hoover avowed there would be "no limit" to the number of Special Agents assigned to Bentley's story, the FBI's biggest spy case to date and, as it turned out (according to historian Gary May), "one of the longest, most expensive, and ultimately fruitless investigations in the Bureau's history."[20] They were utterly unable to corroborate her story with other witnesses, documentation, wiretaps, or surveillance.

Elizabeth Bentley, like Whittaker Chambers, was an informant for the FBI well into the 1950s. And the traits she shared with Chambers are notable. Like Chambers, she was not a reliable witness: she embellished her stories habitually or outright fabricated some accounts; she was a serial accuser who couldn't substantiate her charges; she made friendships under false pretenses only to alienate them and then turn against her erstwhile friends; she claimed a religious awakening helped her break from the Communist Party. One of Bentley's biographers, Kathryn Olmsted — in a passage that could apply to Chambers by changing the gender — wrote: "At times, she did tell the truth; at other times, she was a lying, manipulative opportunist. Throughout her life she was a bundle of contradictions ... a fan, at different times, of Mussolini, Stalin, the pope, and J. Edgar Hoover; a shrewd woman who outsmarted the NKGB and the FBI."[21]

Elizabeth Bentley's story, as told with some "improvements" to HUAC, began with the usual background. She was born in 1908, graduated from Vassar College in 1930, taught for two years in Virginia at the Foxcroft School, received a master's in Italian (by submitting a completely plagiarized thesis) from Columbia University in 1935, worked as a secretary, and was vice president of United States Service and Shipping, a Soviet front company, for six years.

She joined the Communist Party in 1935 while attending Columbia, where radicalism was in vogue. "I suppose," Bentley testified, "I was a very confused liberal, and, unfortunately, we confused liberals have a tendency to look for guidance some place and a tendency to admire efficient people who know where they are going and seem to be doing a good job in the right direction."

In October 1938 Bentley met Jacob Golos and became his lover. Golos, a high-level American Communist, operated the Soviet Union's official tourist bureau in New York, and he had set up an espionage organization to obtain information from government employees and officials for transmission to the U.S.S.R. Bentley said Golos asked her to become involved in this operation about the time of Germany's invasion of Russia, around June or July 1941. By a "gradual process" she "took charge of individuals and groups" who were employed in the U.S. government and in positions to furnish information.

Bentley learned from Golos that a man named Nathan Gregory Silvermaster, a government official in the Farm Security Administration in Washington D.C., was interested in organizing a group of government employees who could provide information for the Soviets. It was arranged that Bentley, using an alias, would go to the Silvermaster home every two weeks — "and I knew them until the end of September 1944" — "very often have dinner with them," Bentley testified, "spend the evening and collect ... information which they had previously collected from the members of the group." What type of information? "Military information, particularly from the Air Corps," Bentley continued, "on production of airplanes, their destinations to the various theaters of war and to various countries, new types of planes being put out, information as to when D-day would be, all sorts of inside military information." But nothing, she made clear, about the atomic bomb. These documents were photographed, she claimed, in the Silvermasters' basement. Bentley admitted that she had never seen anyone deliver documents to the Silvermaster house, but that she nevertheless dispatched the films to Jacob Golos in New York. She did not know how Golos then transferred the materials to the Soviets — "he was very close-mouthed." Bentley said she only received travel expenses from Golos for her work, and that she was employed during this period with the United States Service and Shipping Co., a corporation which contracted with Intourist Moscow to forward packages to Russia.

Bentley told the committee she had been "thoroughly sold on the conviction that no matter what happened in my lifetime I was building a decent world in the future."

"Even if it was betraying your own government," Rep. Hébert interjected, "in time of war?" Bentley replied that she hadn't thought of it as betrayal.

Jacob Golos was the only high-ranking Communist Bentley knew, and she thought he was a "great idealist ... who was working for ... the betterment of the world." But Golos had shielded Bentley "from the realities behind this thing," and when Golos died in November 1943 she was "thrown in direct contact with Russians" who "thought that I was much more sophisticated than I was. They thought that I knew what was going on, and unfortunately they landed on me with both feet, made no bones of the fact that they had contempt for American Communists with their vague idealism, no bones of the fact that they were using the American Communist Party as a recruitment for espionage, and, in general, they were about the cheapest type of person I have ever seen — the gangster type."

Rep. McDowell remarked, conveying the sentiments of the entire committee: "I hope all the foggy-minded liberals in America who are playing with this thing read this evidence."

Adrift, lonely, and frightened, Bentley headed to the FBI in August 1945. Within days of her confession Hoover charged his counterespionage chief, Tom Donegan, to lead the massive effort to verify her accusations. Phones were tapped and suspects followed. Several government employees fingered by Bentley were friends and professional colleagues, and the FBI ascertained that they saw each other often. Agents surreptitiously entered the Silvermaster home and discovered a darkroom in the basement. But no corroborating evidence was uncovered that would stand up in court, and Hoover was particularly agitated because Bentley divulged that many of her sources did not have "actual knowledge of the disposition of the information they were transmitting."[22]

Nathan Gregory Silvermaster was a 49-year-old self-employed house builder living in New Jersey when HUAC called him to testify on August 4, 1948. He was Jewish and had been born in Russia, but had been a naturalized American citizen for over twenty years. He refused to answer questions about Communist affiliations and about people he may or may not have known, asserting his Fifth Amendment privilege. Silvermaster had been employed by the federal government from 1935 until 1947 when he resigned in the wake of, in his words, "groundless accusations of disloyalty," having been almost constantly under investigation for twelve years "because I have never attempted to conceal my strong advocacy of the rights of the underprivileged and of all New Deal principles." Yet he was always cleared by various agencies, including the Secret Service. An economist, Silvermaster directed studies for the Board of Economic Warfare in 1942 of the enemy's economic potential in order to cut the flow of strategic materials to Axis countries. But for most of his government service he developed transportation programs for migratory farm workers in the Farm Security Administration. In a statement HUAC permitted him to read, Silvermaster said Bentley's charges were "false and fantastic. I can only conclude that she is a neurotic liar. I am and have been a loyal American citizen and a faithful Government employee. I am not and never have been a spy or agent of any foreign government.... If I committed a crime, I should be indicted and prosecuted in the courts. Without such indictment and prosecution, my reputation should not be smeared."

No legal action was ever taken against Silvermaster, and more than forty years after his death his family continues their efforts to clear his name.

The most important former government officials Elizabeth Bentley publicly accused of complicity in her espionage ring were Lauchlin Currie, an economist and White House aide to President Roosevelt from 1939 to 1945; Harry Dexter White, Assistant Secretary of the Treasury, an FDR appointment in 1944; and Duncan Lee, Chief of the Secretariat in the wartime Office of Strategic Services (OSS). Each man would testify publicly before HUAC, openly answer all questions, and unequivocally deny Bentley's accusations. Bentley allowed that she had never even met or communicated in any way with Lauchlin Currie or Harry Dexter White, thus her attacks on them were founded merely on hearsay; but Duncan Lee acknowledged that he had known Bentley, though not by her real name, for about two years, from 1943 through 1944.

At a Washington D.C. cocktail party in the spring of 1943, Lee's story goes, he was introduced to Helen Grant (Bentley) by a mutual friend, Mary Price, a secretary of political columnist Walter Lippmann, and the sister of Mildred Price, a good friend of Lee and his wife, Ishbel. "Helen" spent much of the party in the Lees' company. She was a few years older than the couple, and they were flattered by her attention and found her seemingly upper class old American background, reflected in her appearance and manner, attractive and congenial. She told them she was an executive for a firm in New York that imported and exported leather products, and often traveled to Washington on business. The Lees invited her for drinks on her next trip.

Within a few weeks Helen returned, and she joined the Lees at their apartment for an after dinner drink. Lee believed that on the following visit Helen brought along a friend, a man named John whose foreign-sounding last name Lee could not recall, and the couples met for dinner at a local restaurant. Years later Lee would discover that John was Jacob Golos, but at the time he was introduced as Helen's dear friend, a refugee writer who had never been to Washington. Lee remarked that the man was quiet and obviously very ill, and that he only saw him once more some months later, in Helen's company, and that shortly thereafter John died.

Golos's death marked the beginning of a disquieting strain in the relationship between the Lees and Helen. In her bereavement and loneliness she turned increasingly to them for emotional support. She would protest how much they meant to her and how dependent she was on their friendship. "We were truly sorry for her," Lee recalled, "and offered as much sympathy and affection as we could. At the same time we began to feel that we were being asked to assume more of an emotional burden than we could carry and that her dependence upon us was exaggerated and unhealthy."

During his August 10, 1948, HUAC testimony, Duncan Lee was asked by Robert Stripling: "Why did you meet Miss Bentley at the drug stores on Wisconsin Avenue?"

"I will be glad to tell you," Lee responded, "but ... I would like to give this background."

Lee said it was about October 1944 that he and his wife decided the acquaintance with Bentley had to be ended because she "had become a personal nuisance to us.... One evening when she called on us I put it to her quite bluntly that we thought we should not see her anymore." Bentley cried, Lee said, and protested how fond she was of Lee and his wife and what a great deal they meant to her. After half an hour of weeping, Bentley pleaded with them to at least occasionally meet her outside of their home, at a restaurant or some other public place. "In order to get her out of the house," Lee told Stripling, "we agreed to do it." After that scene, Lee continued, he saw Bentley perhaps three more times, once at Martin's Restaurant, and "I believe on two occasions after that when Miss Bentley called, she called from a neighboring drug store, and on both those occasions either we couldn't get a sitter or my wife didn't want to go out and simply told me to go out and see her and get rid of her as quickly as possible, which I tried to do."

And there was another distressing factor, Lee claimed, that contributed to their decision to quit the friendship with Bentley — her increasingly left wing, intemperate, and extreme political views might prove embarrassing to his position in the OSS. Lee said he told Bentley at the time of the rupture that her "expressed views were apparently a good deal more extreme than we had originally thought," because one of her traits that initially attracted Lee and his wife was her moderate liberal outlook.

"Did you ever tell Miss Bentley anything that you learned in a confidential capacity while you were in the OSS?" Stripling asked.

Lee replied he had not, and that he had made it a rule during his OSS service never to discuss anything that had not previously appeared in the newspapers, and then only to the extent made public. In recalling his acquaintance with Bentley, Lee remarked, "I have been puzzled that I do not remember that she ever tried to get any information out of me. In view of that fact I am tempted to believe that Miss Bentley used her social relationship with me merely to help her misrepresent to her employers for her own personal build-up that she had access through me to someone of the importance of General Donovan."

However, Duncan Lee's political ideology and opinions were not conservative by any stretch, and as late as 1942 he still considered himself a socialist. A distant relative of the Confederate General Robert E. Lee, and the son of a missionary, Lee was born in China in 1913 but arrived in the United States before he was a year old. He attended Yale for four years, graduating with a B.A. degree in 1935, and won a Rhodes scholarship to study at Oxford for three years, taking both a B.A. in jurisprudence and a bachelor of civil law degree there. He married Ishbel in 1938 while they were attending Oxford. They shared the attitudes of most of their college friends. They were left wing socialists sympathetic towards the Soviet Union who supported the British Labour Party and the Loyalists in Spain, but the Lees were not doctrinaire Marxists or members of the Communist Party then or later. Following Oxford was a year at Yale Law School before joining the law firm of Donovan & Leisure whose senior partner was the World War I hero Colonel William "Wild Bill" Donovan, who became Director of the OSS during World War II. Lee stayed at the firm three years and then served in the army throughout the Second World War in the OSS, working closely with Donovan. As Lee's responsibilities increased at the OSS, his "Oxford-born radicalism" became largely a matter of "unconscious posturing," realizing that leftist activism wasn't in his nature. Lee entered the army as a first lieutenant and was discharged lieutenant colonel. He went to the OSS as legal adviser, drawing contracts, negotiating leases, and ensuring the budget was spent in accord with the General Accounting Office. After military service Lee practiced law independently in Washington.

Thirty-five years after his HUAC testimony, Duncan Lee surmised, in an unpublished letter to his family in 1983, that J. Edgar Hoover was the Wizard of Oz behind Elizabeth Bentley's charges against him. Hoover bitterly opposed what he considered encroachments by the OSS on FBI jurisdictions outside the United States. He feared General Donovan, regarding him as a rival and a threat, and Lee believed Hoover was striking at Donovan through him. "Getting me," Lee wrote, "would serve a double purpose and the FBI certainly did its best to do me in. When it found it could not it vented its frustration in a campaign of extra-legal punishment and harassment" by cajoling the State Department to lift his passport and persuading the Bermuda government, where Lee was practicing law in the early 1950s, to deport him.

After Lee's HUAC testimony, Elizabeth Bentley was called to the stand to rebut him. Bentley agreed with Duncan Lee that she had used the name "Helen" and they met in early 1943 by way of Mary Price, but that was all they agreed on. Mary Price, Bentley maintained, was a member of Jacob Golos's spy ring. Price was also employed by Walter Lippmann as a secretary, and, Bentley claimed, "she was giving us information which she had taken from Mr. Lippmann's files. We told Miss Price that if she ever found any likely prospect for giving information she should let us know."

When Duncan Lee went to Washington to join the OSS, "Mary came to us," Bentley swore, "told us about him, and we were to take him on. Mary took care of him for awhile, and then Mary left Washington, and I took him over at that point." "He knew Mary personally, you see, through her sister, and Mary had told him about me, and the name I had gone by, which was Helen, and I just walked into his apartment and said, 'I am Helen,' and spoke about things that only the two of us would know, and that is how we made our contact. It started with his apartment, and then he got very nervous and wished to meet me in the street, so we would meet in drug stores, and so on."

"What business did you discuss?" HUAC's chief investigator asked.

"I discussed the fact that he had been giving information from the OSS to Mary Price and I said that I would continue with that," Bentley replied.

She added that Lee was a Communist Party member, and, though "I have never seen his party card," she collected his dues and brought him CP literature.

"What type of information," Stripling asked, did Lee give Bentley "which you in turn furnished to the Russian agents?"

"I would say it was various types of information that was valuable to us," Bentley said, begging the question. "One type was checking on whether the OSS had spotted any of our people who were then working for the OSS."

When asked if Lee had met Jacob Golos, Bentley replied, "Yes. I remember distinctly because it was about a month or so before Mr. Golos died"; thus the meeting would have occurred in October 1943. "I had told Mr. Golos about Mr. Lee," Bentley allowed (though Golos obviously already knew about Lee according to her earlier testimony), "and he thought that the prospect was very interesting. He wanted to meet him personally." Yet Bentley already insisted she had been seeing Lee for months, so he was long past the prospect stage. "At this meeting we sat and I think we drank beer," Bentley continued, "and Mr. Golos introduced himself as a high functionary of the Communist Party, explained that they were very much interested in the material Mr. Lee was furnishing, and had a long chat with him on the type of information that was available and what he should look for."

"Did [Lee] ever tell you anything about Oak Ridge, Tenn.?" Stripling inquired.

"Yes. Toward the end of the time I knew him … he told me that he had word that something very secret was going on at that location. He did not know what, but he said it must be something supersecret because it was shrouded in such mystery and so heavily guarded."

"Well, now, Mr. Chairman," the irrepressible Representative McDowell chimed in, "here, for, I believe, the first time since the conspiracy of Aaron Burr, a high officer of the Army has been accused publicly of the violation of the Articles of War, which he must certainly realize the penalties of and the punishment. The questions which are flooding my mind at this moment, I feel, should not be given here."

But questions remain unexamined, much less unanswered. If Duncan Lee only "briefed" Elizabeth Bentley and never gave her any actual documents — for such is what she told the FBI consistently in her many confessions — why, after their initial introduction, did Bentley visit the Lees so many times when it would have been much safer and easier to transfer the oral information using pay telephones? And Bentley always maintained that Lee was "petrified" of FBI surveillance. So why would he allow a Soviet agent to possibly lead the authorities to his home? Or why would he take the chance of meeting Bentley in a public place, such as a drugstore, only to breathlessly relay the latest secrets while insisting that she not write them down?

Elizabeth Bentley's victims were to her scheme of magical thinking former collaborators who, as she wrote in her 1951 memoir *Out of Bondage*, "had become in the hands of the Communist movement, no longer individuals but robots; they were chained in an intellectual and moral slavery." And in her putatively cogent words and testimony her fantasy confederates indeed evoke images of automatons and evil androids whom she "disconnects" from an "apparatus" in New York and plugs in like an appliance to a "cell" in Washington.

Mary Price always denied involvement in Bentley's implausible espionage tales. When interviewed by the FBI in 1947, Price told the agents she had known Bentley and Duncan Lee only socially. In 1976 she recalled in an interview that Bentley was a casual acquaintance she had met in New York, and when she moved to Washington Bentley "would call up and say she was on an expense account and how would I like to have dinner?" Price was working for the Progressive Party on Henry Wallace's historic 1948 summer campaign in the South when reporters confronted her in North Carolina about Bentley's HUAC appearance. "It was a surprise," Price said, "that Bentley had gotten to the point of getting people taken in by it." But a year before the press avalanche Price knew trouble was up when the FBI questioned her about Bentley. She then sought legal counsel and was advised "just not to talk about it." After the 1947 FBI interview Price took the Fifth before a New York grand jury when asked if she knew Bentley and others. HUAC never subpoenaed her for the spy hearings, but the FBI continued to harass Mary Price and her employers for years.[23]

On Friday the thirteenth of August 1948, the day Lauchlin Currie and Harry Dexter White, the former leading economists in the Roosevelt Administration, testified before the House Committee on Un-American Activities to answer Elizabeth Bentley's charges of espionage against them, William H. Taylor, an economist at the International Monetary Fund (IMF) of the World Bank, wrote a letter to HUAC Chairman Thomas.

Early in her testimony of July 31, Bentley accused Taylor of being a Communist and a source for the Silvermaster spy ring who "was sent abroad at various times" by the Treasury Department ("I believe he went to China"). Like many others Bentley attacked, she never made the direct statement that she actually knew Taylor, but it was implicit.

Taylor informed the committee that he had recently returned from a trip and learned of Bentley's charges through the newspapers. His letter included a statement given to the press the day before in which he denied her accusations. Taylor asked to appear before HUAC to deny Bentley's "allegations or implications arising therefrom concerning myself." But the committee did not reply, so Taylor wrote again on September 3. He enclosed an affidavit and requested it be included in the public record. In the affidavit Taylor noted he was born in Canada in 1906 and became a naturalized American citizen in 1940. He had held several academic positions in the U.S. and Canada. He worked in the Division of Monetary Research of the Treasury Department from 1941 to 1946, and then accepted a position with the IMF. He swore he had never been a member of the Communist Party or any group affiliated with or sponsored by the CP; never participated in any espionage group or plot; never transmitted confidential information except as authorized in the line of duty; never met, seen, or communicated in any way with Elizabeth Bentley — "So far as I know she does not contend that she ever knew or met me." Taylor admitted he knew most of the people Bentley accused of supplying unauthorized information, but only in a proper way in keeping with his position as a government employee. He also confirmed he had been sent to China, where for nine months he was held prisoner by the Japanese.

William H. Taylor's letters and affidavit were published in HUAC's 1948 report — in fine print in the appendix and following a list of Bentley's alleged sources, in which Taylor's name was still prominent.

And yet, as Taylor feared from the outset, there were "implications arising." *Seven years later*, in 1955, the International Organization Employees Loyalty Board of the IMF found William H. Taylor "disloyal" because the *Washington Daily News* had printed rehashed allegations by Bentley. But Taylor defended himself brilliantly — with the truth — and the Loyalty Board reversed its decision. He then sued Bentley and the *Daily News* and won an out-of-court settlement.

Lauchlin Currie and Harry Dexter White were the most influential economists in the nation in the later years of the Roosevelt Administration. Currie, a senior aide to FDR, advised the White House on taxation, social security, and production plans for the war and postwar. He had been in charge of Lend-Lease to China, closely involved in loan negotiations with England and Russia, and a participant in the 1944 Bretton Woods conference. White, along with the legendary British economist John Maynard Keynes, founded the World Bank and the International Monetary Fund at Bretton Woods, and drafted the American plan of the compromise with Keynes. When World War II began, Treasury Secretary Henry Morgenthau, Jr. appointed White to head all international matters for the department. He was named Assistant Secretary the year before Roosevelt died, and in 1946 President Truman selected White as the first executive director of the IMF.

Both Currie and White had taught at universities and were considered relatively conservative mainstream economics professors. White, in fact, was among the more anti–Russian officials in Washington. In 1940 the Treasury Department froze funds of the Baltic nations in the U.S. in a manner the Soviets thought highly unfriendly; the same year White suspected that the U.S.S.R. would harm United States interests in the Far East by agreeing to a nonaggression pact with Japan; and several days after the Nazi invasion of Russia the Treasury Department refused to initiate any aid to the Soviets. "The real reason in support of a strong Germany," White wrote near the end of the war, "is a desire to maintain a strong enemy of the Soviet Union in Europe." White's plan for the postwar world proposed the creation of global markets for U.S. exports and the hegemony of the United States over the world financial system.[24]

Currie was the first to testify the morning of August 13, and he welcomed the opportunity to "state again under oath," as he had previously before a grand jury investigating the same charges, that he had never been a member of the Communist Party or any of its front organizations, nor was he sympathetic to the tenets or doctrines of communism. He added he never had the slightest reason to believe that any of his associates, friends, or even acquaintances were Communists.

One of the lies Elizabeth Bentley told on Currie — "hearsay three times removed," Representative Rankin noted — insinuated he had learned and gossiped to others that the U.S. was about to break a Russian code. "Well," Bentley testified two weeks earlier, "Mr. Silvermaster told me that one day Mr. Currie came dashing into Mr. Silverman's house, sort of out of breath, and told him that the Americans were on the verge of breaking the Soviet code. Mr. Silverman, of course, got immediately — in due course, got in touch with Mr. Silvermaster." Bentley added that she passed this on to Russian agents. She also accused Currie of harboring Soviet spies in government agencies and disclosing "inside information" about China to unauthorized individuals.

Currie absolutely denied providing anyone with information who was not officially entitled to receive it. "I did not know during the war," Currie swore, "nor do I know now, that any branch of the Government or of its military forces attempted to or was about to break the Russian code. I knew nothing and I know nothing about whatever work was done in connection with our own or foreign codes."

Currie admitted that he had known both Nathan Gregory Silvermaster and Abraham George Silverman for years. He met Silvermaster, who had briefly worked for Currie, in 1940. His impression was that Silvermaster was entirely competent, and "no question of [his] loyalty arose or entered my mind." They saw each other many times at social gatherings until Currie left government service in 1945. Currie was a graduate student at Harvard when he met Abraham George Silverman, who was teaching economics at the Massachusetts Institute of Technology. Both later joined the government as economists but had little official contact. Currie respected Silverman's high technical ability, and never had any reason to question his loyalty or suspect him of Communist affiliations. "I had no occasion to discuss with him," Currie testified, "any matters of public importance and certainly none of a confidential nature."

Abraham George Silverman had been summoned by HUAC to testify the day before. Though he had answered all questions asked of him by grand juries *before and after* his appearance before the House committee, he refused to answer many of the committee's questions in the presence of his lawyer. Silverman considered the charges to be politically motivated to discredit the New Deal by accusing those who supported its programs and devoted years to its realization. He remarked that he had testified before a grand jury investigating the same charges a year before. "I did so conscious of my own innocence," Silverman said, and he was deeply thankful "for a legal system designed to prevent the publication of malicious slanders against innocent individuals, to prevent the vilification of their characters without indictment and trial in open court where they would be afforded full opportunity to confront and cross-examine their accusers.... Yet, now, incredible slanders have been given wide publicity in the absence of indictment."

Silverman was born in Poland in 1900, received a Ph.D. in economics from Harvard, and taught at MIT until 1933 when he became a statistician and then negotiator for the U.S. Tariff Commission. In 1936 he was appointed director of Bureau of Research, U.S. Railroad Retirement Board, where he worked until 1942. From then until the war ended he was an economic adviser in the Air Force.

Elizabeth Bentley swore on July 31 that at the time in question Silverman was a member of the Communist Party, and that she collected his dues on occasion. She alleged he furnished "prolific information" and "military information" to her spy group. But further questioning had revealed she did not know Silverman and had never seen anyone deliver documents to the Silvermaster residence — her reputed collection point — where she was in actuality an occasional dinner guest. Silverman, on his oath before grand juries, swore he had never seen Bentley prior to her public accusations and had never communicated with her in any way.

But HUAC was solidly with Bentley, and Representative Hébert declared: "Dr. Silverman, you are now before the greatest open court in this country ... beyond the confines of any limited courtroom in this country.... I tell you, Dr. Silverman, that this lady standing here ... accuses you in open court before the American people of being an espionage agent...."

"In my opinion, she is telling a huge web of lies," Silverman responded.

"Miss Bentley has made these charges and you are familiar with them," Hébert continued. "Now, you have your opportunity in open court to tell this lady that you have never seen her before, that you have never received anything from her...."

All Silverman would say was, "I do not consider this to be an open court."

Harry Dexter White was next after Currie to be sworn in, and he carried the additional burden of having to answer not only the charges of Bentley but also those of Whittaker Chambers, who, unlike Bentley, claimed he had actually known and conspired with White. Both Bentley and Chambers accused White of having placed Communists in government posts to influence policy. Bentley, but not Chambers, further accused White of providing information to the Silvermaster ring.

When Whittaker Chambers made his first public HUAC appearance on August 3, he was clear to differentiate that he had been a courier in an underground apparatus of the American Communist Party in the mid–1930s that had no connection with the Soviet Union or with espionage. About Harry Dexter White, Chambers said he tried to "break [him] away from the Communist movement" but couldn't positively swear that White had been a "registered member" of the CP, though he "certainly was a fellow traveler so far within the fold that his not being a Communist would be a mistake on both sides."

"Was he considered a source of information to the Communist cell?" Representative Hébert asked.

"No," Chambers replied, "I should perhaps make the point that these people were specifically not wanted to act as sources of information. These people were an elite group, an outstanding group ... and their position in the Government would be of very much more service to the Communist Party."

"In other words," Hébert said, "White was being used as an unwitting dupe?"

"He was ... perfectly willing to cooperate," Chambers concluded.

Only four months previously White sat before a grand jury and openly answered all questions relating to Bentley's and Chambers's charges. He had been interviewed thoroughly by the FBI and put under round-the-clock surveillance for months in 1945-46. They bugged his apartment and tapped his phones and covered his mail. Not a shred of incriminating evidence was discovered.

Soon after taking his oath, White said, "I cannot recollect ever knowing either a Miss Bentley or a Mr. Whittaker Chambers, nor, judging from the pictures I have seen in the press, have I ever met them." White unqualifiedly denied obtaining positions for persons he knew were Communists or knew were engaged in espionage. "There is and can be no basis of fact whatever for such a charge." After reading into the record his creed of patriotic American ideals, White commenced answering questions.

He had, of course, known Lauchlin Currie for many years. They attended Harvard together, and both had taught there. White also knew Abraham George Silverman very well. William Taylor had worked for White and so had Nathan Gregory Silvermaster.

Representative Mundt asked: "Do you believe that a member of the Communist Party can be loyal to the American Government as a public servant in a high, important Government post and a member of the Communist Party at one and the same time?"

"I should not think so," White replied. "I would not have employed anybody I knew or suspected to be a Communist to such a post."

Chairman Thomas wanted to know if White ever gave information "to Mr. Silvermaster concerning the work of your department?"

"We must have talked about the work in my department," but, White qualified, "I would never give him any secret or confidential information."

The committee was most interested in White's relationship with Silvermaster because they knew Silvermaster had been asked to resign from the Board of Economic Warfare (BEW) in 1943 under suspicion that he was a Communist, and they also knew that Harry

Dexter White was instrumental in clearing Silvermaster of the charges. And later, in 1944, White appointed Silvermaster, who spoke Russian, to attend the Bretton Woods Monetary Conference as a translator. However, Silvermaster became ill and could not attend.

White explained that he had known Silvermaster for perhaps ten years; they had visited each other's homes many times and shared numerous conversations on all sorts of topics. He felt certain Silvermaster was not a Communist. White remembered Silvermaster telling him in 1943 about the disloyalty charges at the BEW, and he implored White to assist him in clearing his name. "I said to him," White testified, "well, I was a little taken aback, and I said, 'Well, are you a Communist?' He said, 'No.' I said, 'Well, what is there that you can give me or show me or what charges have been made? I cannot do anything for you unless I know … more….'"

"He subsequently sent me a 10- or 20-page — it was a fairly long — statement, in which there was, prefacing each paragraph, an allegation or a claim or a statement…. I would judge from the paper that he had access to the charge that was made. And then his reply was set up there. After reading the reply it convinced me of the integrity of the man and that he was not a Communist."

White then went to see Herbert Gaston, the Assistant Secretary of the Treasury in 1943 and a member of the Loyalty Board, and in White's view "a fairer and more conscientious man never served the government." He told Gaston that Silvermaster had been asked to resign immediately. In White's opinion Silvermaster should not keep his position if there is the "slightest question of [him] being a Communist. We were at war, and there was no need for that. I said that I was not interested in seeing him get his post back. In fact, I did not think he should." In the end, Silvermaster was cleared by the Board. "That was the only occasion," White testified, "in which there was any question in my mind raised as to any of these men that you mention being a Communist."

Not a man to suffer fools lightly, and on this day he was surrounded by them, White's answers, progressively insouciant and witty, finally provoked the surly Chairman Thomas, who scolded the audience for applauding White's "side remarks." Attempting to embarrass White, Thomas read aloud a private note White had relayed, asking for a five-minute break once an hour because he was recovering from a severe heart attack. White protested the public broadcast of his condition, and Thomas sheepishly backtracked. Harry Dexter White suffered a heart attack on the way home from the hearing that afternoon. Another attack, three days later, was fatal.

Donald Hiss was the last to testify that Friday the thirteenth. Along with his brother Alger and five others, Whittaker Chambers alleged ten days earlier, he was the leader of a cell of a secret apparatus of the American Communist Party for which Chambers was a courier.

When asked if he knew a man by the name of Whittaker Chambers or just "Carl," Donald Hiss brusquely informed inquisitor Stripling: "I want to make it perfectly clear, sir, that I have never known any person by the name of Whittaker Chambers, by Carl, or any other name — the man who testified against me before this committee."

Ten days before, after reading Chambers's public HUAC testimony of August 3, Donald Hiss made a statement to the press denying the charges and forwarded a sworn copy to the committee that was read into the record. Now he denied the charges once again and answered the committee's brief questions, as the hearing was drawing to a close for the week.

"If it develops that Mr. Chambers' testimony is false," Representative Mundt remarked at the end of the session, "then it must also follow ... that some highly impelling motive must have activated a man of such high responsibility, great standing, and who has made a significant success of his career, to launch such charges against people like you and your brother Alger."

Donald Hiss replied, exasperated by the notion of "impelling motive," that "if I am lying I should go to jail and if Mr. Chambers is lying he should go to jail."

CHAPTER V

HUAC Questions Hiss Privately

"I read a lot of Government files from time to time — and I don't say this disparagingly — but I have seen your name for years in Government files as a person suspected of Communist activity. Now, there has to be some basis for the thing." — Robert Stripling (HUAC chief investigator) to Alger Hiss

Alger Hiss found HUAC's telegram when he returned to his apartment after work that Friday the thirteenth. The committee wished to see him again, though in a private session, the following Monday in Washington. As he picked up a few items before catching the train to join his wife and son vacationing in Peacham, Vermont, Hiss felt certain the committee had finally arranged for him to see Whittaker Chambers in the flesh.

Ten days had passed and still Hiss had no inkling who Chambers was, even though the several news photographs he had now seen of him were "not unfamiliar." The week after his public HUAC appearance, as he awaited the committee's next move, Hiss consulted several friends and colleagues, after Dulles had advised him not to approach Chambers at his *Time* office, about what other actions he might take. Should he hire a professional investigator to gather information about Chambers? Should he sue him for libel or slander? No, Hiss was informed, an investigation could wait, and whatever Chambers had said about him to HUAC or any government agency was privileged against suit.

While in Vermont, Hiss called a friend who had recently counseled him and who agreed to accompany him on the train trip from New York to Washington Monday morning. The friend brought several newspaper clippings which appeared over the weekend of accounts of HUAC's "secret" meeting with Chambers the week before; one of the press leaks reported Chambers telling the committee that he had stayed in Hiss's house and driven his car. "This was the item," Hiss later recalled, "that brought George Crosley back to mind."[1]

Yet Hiss could not imagine that the George Crosley he knew for perhaps eighteen months in the mid–1930s, who did not even fit the physical description of Whittaker Chambers, was the actual Whittaker Chambers who was now spreading lies about him. Was it possible, Hiss thought, that Chambers could have known Crosley and from him learned something about Hiss and his family? First of all, the newspaper photographs he had seen of Chambers did not recapture the disheveled, grubby figure Crosley cut in the midst of the Depression. And though Robert Stripling clarified that Chambers had gained a lot of weight in the last decade, the photographs didn't look to Hiss like just an overweight Crosley. The most "arresting feature" of Crosley's that Hiss remembered was the incredibly bad state of his teeth, so disfigured that they averted attention from his other physical traits; but none of the recent photographs of Chambers showed poor teeth, and nothing had been said about Chambers having had severely decayed teeth in the 1930s.

George Crosley was one of many people Hiss met while he was counsel to the Senate Committee Investigating the Munitions Industry, or Nye Committee, on loan from the Department of Agriculture in 1934-35. Headed by Senator Gerald Nye of North Dakota, the hearings attracted broad public attention to, and domestic and foreign press coverage of, the reported activities of arms manufacturers and dealers throughout the world. As a public relations staff member, Hiss allotted much of his time to assisting student researchers, writers and editors, members of peace organizations, among others who remained after the hearings to ask questions or examine transcripts and exhibits. Crosley introduced himself as a freelance writer living in New York who planned to write articles about the munitions inquiries and hoped to sell them to magazines. Hiss believed that Crosley's first visits, concerning the committee's public hearings on overseas sales of American aircraft firms, were at the end of December 1934 or early 1935. He saw Crosley two or three times at the Senate Office Building, and on a couple of other occasions they had a working lunch nearby.

Except for a coincidence, Hiss's acquaintance with Crosley would surely have ended after a few business meetings, but Crosley mentioned during one meeting that he wanted to move his family to Washington for a few months so he could write with less interruption. It so happened that the Hisses were moving in April from an apartment near Wardman Park to a house on P Street, but the lease on the apartment was not up until July 1. Having been resigned to paying double rent through June, he now offered to sublet the apartment to Crosley, who was just as eager to rent it. There was no written contract; it was an informal handshake agreement. At $60 a month there was no profit in it for Hiss, and the utilities were included with the rent.

When Crosley and his wife and their eighteen-month-old daughter arrived from New York to occupy the 28th Street apartment, they instead stopped off at the Hisses' P Street address. Their household belongings, sent to Washington separately by a mover, Crosley maintained, had not yet been delivered. The Hisses had left much of their furniture at the apartment for the time being because the P Street house was leased furnished, but they took with them all the linens, dishes, and kitchen utensils. Hiss knew Crosley was hard up — most everyone was in those years — and could probably not afford a hotel room for the night, and as there were two extra rooms on the top floor of the P Street house the Hisses offered to put the Crosleys up until the expected arrival of their things the next day. Hiss recalled that the mover didn't arrive until two or three days later.

Some weeks before the Crosleys moved in to the apartment Hiss mentioned to Crosley that he was going to drive to New York. Crosley asked for a ride, which Hiss gave him, and it was on this trip, which took several hours and led through Hiss's hometown of Baltimore, that Hiss reminisced with Crosley about his growing up there and about his interest in birds. He believed it was very likely he told Crosley about seeing a prothonotary warbler. He recalled Crosley saying he worked laying railway track in Washington just after the First World War. They rode to New York in a sturdy but tattered 1929 Ford roadster with little resale value that Hiss had owned for years. Later, when occupying the apartment, Crosley borrowed the old car once or twice, and Hiss told him that when he took possession of the new car he was going to buy that summer, instead of trading the roadster in for little more than scrap, Crosley could have it.

Hiss felt sorry for Crosley — but only for his poverty. He remembered Crosley as entertaining and somewhat vain, appearing to know something about most any topic that came up. He spoke with authority on literary matters and publishing; said he had traveled extensively in Europe and knew German literature. Yet Hiss claimed his memory of Crosley was not all that precise or definite. Except for his devastated teeth, Crosley's appearance was not remarkable; he had ordinary features, was short with light brown hair.

Hiss later remarked that he unconsciously identified Crosley with his deceased brother Bosley who had died in 1927, eight years before Hiss met Crosley. There was, of course, the assonance of the two names; they were born in the same year; both were aspiring writers working as journalists; both were bookish and saw themselves as men of letters. Yet consciously, at the time Hiss knew Crosley, he made no connection between the two because they also differed in many respects. Bosley was tall and handsome and lithe, while Crosley was short and plain and slovenly. Bosley spoke with an infectious comic spirit. Crosley was humorless and self-involved. "Yet all this was in line with the image of the writer and the transient intellectual," Hiss said years later, "and I found Crosley more attractive than other writers."[2]

But the brief relationship ended because of money — Hiss believed Crosley had used him. Crosley was unable to pay the apartment rent as he had promised but instead had given Hiss an oriental rug, which Hiss accepted as payment in kind. Also, according to Hiss, Crosley habitually asked for small loans, four or five dollars each time, that he never repaid, and Crosley always waited for Hiss to pay for both their lunches. Moreover, Hiss felt deceived when Crosley failed to produce any of the articles about the Nye Committee's investigations he claimed he was writing. Finally, Hiss realized how gullible he had been. His last contact with Crosley was a telephone conversation sometime in the fall of 1936. He had not heard from Crosley for some time. Again, Crosley called to borrow a few dollars. Hiss refused, reminded Crosley of the unpaid loans, and told him he didn't want to see him again.

At 2 P.M. Monday, August 16, Alger Hiss, without counsel, met in closed session at the Old House Office Building with a HUAC subcommittee comprising Thomas, Nixon, McDowell, and Hébert, along with chief investigator Stripling and five staff members. Chairman Thomas declared to all present that "this is an executive session ... everything is supposed to be right within these four walls."

Nixon began with a statement, directed to Hiss, that the committee felt a responsibility to discover who — either Chambers or Hiss — had given false testimony, and to hold the perjurer to account, if possible. Then, after going back over some of Hiss's August 5 testimony, Nixon informed Hiss that Chambers told the committee on August 7 that Hiss had not known him as Whittaker Chambers but as "Carl," solely as Carl with no last name. Hiss said he knew no such person, and in his mind the possible link with George Crosley now seemed even more remote.

Nixon asked Hiss if he'd ever been to the apartment of Henry Collins, who Chambers alleged had been the treasurer of the underground apparatus. Hiss answered that he'd known Collins for years and had visited him at his home, and that Collins had also been his guest. Hiss could not recall if his brother Donald even knew Henry Collins, and he had no recollection of Lee Pressman, John Abt, Nathan Witt, Charles Kramer, or Victor Perlo — all named by Chambers as Communists and apparatus members — being at Collins's place at the same time he was, adding that he had never met Perlo. Hiss swore he had never given money to Collins (CP dues were paid to Collins by the others, according to Chambers) for any reason whatsoever.

Hiss was shown more pictures of Chambers and was asked if he could "remember that person either as Whittaker Chambers or as Carl or as any other individual you have met." Already growing impatient with this line of questioning, Hiss reminded the committee of his August 5 testimony that he could not swear that he had never seen "the man whose picture was shown me," whose "face has a certain familiarity." He wanted to see Chambers face to face, and he still hoped a meeting would be arranged that very day.

Would his answer be different, Nixon retorted, if the man in the picture had claimed he had "stayed overnight in your house on several occasions?" Again the question seemed to Hiss to preclude Crosley, who had not stayed with the Hisses overnight on "several occasions."

Hiss reiterated: "I do hope I will have an opportunity to actually see the individual." Nixon said a meeting would be arranged, but the committee preferred these private sessions to make certain there was no question of mistaken identity — the very issue a meeting would settle immediately. Moreover, Chambers had assured the committee the week before that there was no mistaken identity. Nixon was hedging because he wanted to feel certain that Hiss, not Chambers, was lying about the relationship and thus not publicly humiliate himself and the committee. (As late as December 1948, *four months* after Chambers's first private HUAC interview, and after many personal conversations with Nixon, an event occurred — recounted later in the narrative — in which Nixon was convinced, for a few hours at any rate, he had been ruined because Chambers had been lying all along.)

Nixon returned to questions previously — and once again — answered in the negative: Had Hiss ever paid CP dues? Ever been a CP member? Ever been connected to any underground organization of the CP?

Then, in the midst of questions, Nixon remarked: "I will say that both you and Mr. Chambers are as convincing witnesses as I have ever seen." But Hiss would have none of that, and he brusquely replied that Chambers "is not capable of telling the truth or does not desire to." Hiss was angered by the committee's attitude of bestowing equal credibility on Chambers's testimony; he was, after all, a confessed former Communist. Also, Hiss believed Chambers had become the committee's proprietary witness. "I have seen newspaper accounts, Mr. Nixon, that you spent the week end ... at Mr. Chambers' farm." Nixon denied it, leaving the false impression he had not seen Chambers privately at all the previous week. But Hiss was now afraid that whatever testimony he gave would get back to Chambers, who would use it against him. "I do not wish to make it easier," Hiss said, "for anyone who, for whatever motive I cannot understand, is apparently endeavoring to destroy me." Nixon took offense at the implication that the committee would coach Chambers "so that he can more or less build a web around you," and he reminded Hiss that all the questions asked him so far concerned facts that could be verified by third parties. Stripling added that he had listened to Chambers for hours the week before and there was certainly "no prearrangement or anything else.... He has either made a study of your life in great detail or he knows you, one or the other, or he is incorrect." And then Stripling brought out yet another, larger, picture of Chambers, taken two weeks earlier — "Does this picture refresh your memory in any way, Mr. Hiss?" Again Hiss swore that the "face is definitely not an unfamiliar face," but he had never known anyone who "had the relationship with me that this man has testified to," and that was the most important point. "This man may have known me, he may have been in my house. I have had literally hundreds of people in my house in the course of the time I lived in Washington." It was becoming clear to Hiss that the committee was building up the implication that if he had known Chambers he must have also been a Communist, and so he attempted to steer them away from that notion. "The issue is not whether this man knew me and I don't remember him. The issue is whether he had a particular conversation that he has said he had with me and which I have denied and whether I am a member of the Communist Party or ever was, which he has said and which I have denied." And for the third time in less than an hour Hiss remarked that if he could see Chambers face to face "I would perhaps have some inkling as to whether he ever had known me personally."

Chairman Thomas then obliviously asked: "Now, here is a man who says he spent a week in your house in the last 15 years. Do you recognize him?" Hiss repeated that he did not recognize Chambers "from that picture," and he hoped the committee would not think he was being unreasonable because he was not prepared to testify on the basis of a photograph. "If the man himself came in here," Thomas asked, "you would be able to say yes or no?" "I think I would, sir," Hiss responded. But whether he had known Chambers or not, Hiss maintained, he never had the sort of conversations with anyone that Chambers claimed he had with Hiss. Stripling then asked, as if to stump or confuse Hiss: "What conversations did he testify he had with you?" "[A]ccording to the record that I read," Hiss replied, "he said that he came to my house and pled with me to break with the Communist Party, and that I refused, and that I had tears in my eyes, and that the reason I gave was something about the Communist Party line."

Nixon explained that the committee would find out from third parties if Chambers had perjured himself by way of checking Hiss's answers of the committee's "completely objective questions." And Nixon said Chambers had been instructed "off the record" before his August 7 testimony that any answer he gave, if false, would subject him to perjury.

Yet before further questions were put to him, Hiss announced that he had "written a name" on a pad in front of him of a man he knew at the time in question, a man who not only "spent some time in my house but sublet my apartment." This man had spent more than a week in the apartment — but not while Hiss was there. However, Hiss did not believe this man was the man in the photographs. He had only thought of the man's name that morning on his way to Washington when he read in the papers that Chambers testified he "knew the inside of my house." Still, Hiss was reluctant to name the man and testify to all he knew about him until he had seen Chambers face to face, to discover if Chambers was this man.

"This man," Nixon inquired, "is still a man with whom you are acquainted?" No, Hiss answered, adding that the man was not named Carl or Whittaker Chambers. But he was hesitant to provide details that Chambers might use against him if the committee leaked his testimony as they had some of Chambers's "secret" testimony. Chairman Thomas broke in — "Questions will be asked and the committee will expect to get very detailed answers to the questions. Let's not ramble all around the lot here.... I want the witness to answer." Without mentioning Crosley's name, Hiss said he sublet an apartment to the man, and the man had spent a day or two in his house just before moving in. And once again Hiss balked, pleading not to be asked these questions because he feared his answers would be used against him. Now Stripling cut in — "Let the record show, Mr. Hiss, you brought up this ex post facto business. Your testimony comes as ex post facto testimony to the testimony of Mr.

Chambers. He is already on record, and I am not inferring that you might know what he testified to." Nixon said that surely it must be obvious that the committee was not going to brief Chambers with facts provided by Hiss. "What we are trying to do is test the credibility of Mr. Chambers, and you are the man who can do it, and you can help us out by answering these questions and, frankly, I must insist." Though Hiss felt he should meet Chambers in person before answering questions, he finally deferred to the committee's wishes: "If you wish to ask me detailed questions and think it is your duty to ask me, it is my duty to answer." But not before another scolding, now from Hébert, the only Democrat (and potential friend) on the subcommittee. "Either you or Mr. Chambers is lying," Hébert declared. "And whichever one of you is lying is the greatest actor that America has ever produced." Hébert had not yet concluded who was the liar; he was trying to find the facts. "Up to a few moments ago you have been very open, very cooperative. Now you have hedged." That Hiss should be confronted with Chambers instead of his photograph was his right, Hébert agreed, "but if I were in your position, I would do everything I humanly could to prove that Chambers is a liar instead of me."

Hébert wondered aloud what Chambers's motive could be. If proven a liar, why would he destroy his name, his reputation as "the respected senior editor of *Time* magazine"? It had rankled Hiss since Chambers first testified that the committee did not seem to distrust Chambers's credibility in the least. "[T]hat you can sit there," Hiss exclaimed to Hébert, "and say to me casually that you have heard that man and you have heard me, and you just have no basis for judging which one is telling the truth." Hébert replied that he had an absolutely open mind: "The fact that Mr. Chambers is a self-confessed traitor — and I admit he is — the fact that he is a self-confessed member of the Communist Party — which I admit he is — has no bearing at all on whether the facts that he told..." "Has no bearing on his credibility?" Hiss interjected. "No," Hébert claimed. "I do know police methods and I know crime a great deal, and you show me a good police force and I will show you the stool pigeon who turned them in.... I am not giving Mr. Chambers any great credit for his previous life. I am trying to find out if he has reformed. Some of the greatest saints in history were pretty bad before they were saints. Are you going to take away their sainthood because of their previous lives?" To which Hiss dejectedly stated: "You have made your position clear."

What assurance did he have, Hiss asked, that some member of the committee wouldn't tell a reporter that he confessed to knowing Chambers if he testified that the man whose name he had written down was the same man as Chambers? Once more Hiss said he was not prepared to testify that he had never seen Chambers in the 1930s.

Nixon and Hébert admitted that the issue "for the record" was whether Chambers "did have the conversation with you," but what they were really interested in was: did Chambers have "*the occasion* to have the conversation with you"? [Emphasis added]. Insinuating that if Hiss, in fact, did know Chambers under any circumstances he was in for a world of trouble, Nixon said: "Whether you are a member of the Communist Party and whether he had a conversation with you individually is something that no third party can corroborate one way or the other."

Chairman Thomas called for a brief recess; the committee met privately while Hiss waited in another room. When they reconvened, Hiss announced the "name of the man I brought in — and he may have no relation to this whole nightmare — is a man named George Crosley." They met, Hiss said, at his office when he worked for the Nye Committee in 1935 or late 1934. Crosley was a writer and hoped to sell articles about the munitions committee to magazines.

In response to the committee's questions, Hiss described Crosley as shortish and blondish, obviously not financially successful but not destitute. He was married, with a baby girl. His wife was "strikingly dark," but Hiss did not think he could recognize her now, as he had never seen much of her. Hiss particularly wanted to see Chambers's teeth because Crosley "had very bad teeth, did not take care of his teeth." Hiss recalled a conversation in which Crosley wished to concentrate on his articles and wanted to bring his family to Washington until he finished them. The Hisses had moved to P Street yet had an apartment on their hands for two months, so Hiss said he sublet the apartment to Crosley at exact cost to himself. "My recollection is that he spent several nights in my house because his furniture van was delayed." Hiss thought Crosley occupied the apartment beginning June 1935 (but it was actually May).

Hiss's credibility with the committee, including the wavering Democrat Hébert, began its precipitous decline after Stripling asked: "What kind of automobile did that fellow have?" Hiss replied that Crosley didn't have one. "I sold him an automobile," but then Hiss immediately qualified, saying, "I threw it in with the apartment and had been trying to trade it in and get rid of it." The car was a dark blue, early Model A Ford Hiss had owned for over five years. Crosley "wanted a way to get around and I said, 'Fine, I want to get rid of it. I have another car, and we kept it for sentimental reasons, not worth a damn.' I let him have it along with the rent."

Nixon asked how many days Crosley stayed with Hiss. Not more than a couple, Hiss believed, adding that Crosley was a deadbeat who "was using me for a soft touch" because he did not pay the rent. Did Hiss remember any conversations with Crosley? "We talked backwards and forward about the Munitions Committee Work," Hiss said. "He told various stories that I recall of his escapades. He purported to be a cross between Jim Tully, the author, and Jack London. He had been everywhere."

"You gave this Ford car to Crosley?" Nixon was curious. Hiss said he threw it in along with the apartment — "charged the rent and threw in the car at the same time." Nixon asked if he added a little to the rent to cover the car, but Hiss did not believe he got any extra compensation. "You just gave him the car?" Stripling snapped. "I think the car just went right in with it," Hiss replied. Was there a bill of sale? Stripling asked. Hiss thought he had simply turned the certificate of title over to Crosley. "No evidence of any transfer?" Stripling asked. "Did he record the title?" Hiss had no idea. It was also determined that the car was equipped with hand-operated windshield wipers, a fact Chambers had mentioned at the August 7 hearing. There will be more about the car later, but suffice it to say here that Hiss's testimony this day did not square with Chambers's of August 7 or even with what Hiss wrote years later, that he had promised the car to Crosley after he bought a new one — which is not to say that either version was correct. Considering the transaction dates, Hiss could not have "thrown in the car with the apartment" because Crosley moved out before July 1, 1935, and Hiss did not possess his new Plymouth until September of that year; the title to the Model A was not signed over by Hiss until July 1936. Moreover, the next owner was not named Crosley or Chambers.

The questioning turned to Hiss's former housekeepers and cooks, family nicknames and children, pets and vacation spots. When Hiss averred that one of his hobbies was "amateur ornithology," McDowell baited the trap. "Did you ever see a prothonotary warbler?" Confirming Chambers's earlier testimony, Hiss enthusiastically replied: "I have right here on the Potomac. Do you know that place?" McDowell had indeed seen one in Arlington, and Hiss added: "Beautiful yellow head, a gorgeous bird."

When Hiss corroborated Chambers's testimony about this obscure little bird, the committee, to a man, was silently jolted. This was the clinching intimate detail they had been waiting for; their minds were made up. "It is one of the great ironies of the Hiss Case," William Howard Moore wrote in *Two Foolish Men* (1987), "that Chambers continually amplified the social relationship he enjoyed with the Hisses while Hiss strove to diminish it, when each man should have been doing the opposite. For the more fully the social aspect was emphasized the more ridiculous the Carl story became, while such an extended social relationship only made more plausible Hiss's story that he had a perfectly open friendship with a harmless writer named George Crosley."

Nixon maintained that the controversy between the two witnesses was going to be difficult to resolve "on the basis of third-party evidence," and that as matters stood it was Hiss's word against Chambers's. Nixon believed it was only natural that Hiss thought his word should be "given greater weight"; however, Nixon added, "Mr. Chambers feels the same way because he feels he volunteered the information."

Hiss testified that he recalled seeing Crosley a few times after he moved from the apartment. "Even though he didn't pay his rent you saw him several times?" Nixon asked. Hiss said Crosley didn't completely skip out on the rent: "He gave me a payment on account once. He brought a rug over which he said some wealthy patron gave him. I have still got the damned thing." On the other hand, Hiss mentioned the small loans which Crosley never repaid. Soon afterwards he never saw Crosley again — "never thought of him again until this morning on the train."

Stripling asked if Hiss thought Crosley and Chambers were the same man. "I think they are not," Hiss said. "That would be my best impression from the photographs."

Nixon once again remarked how convincing both Chambers and Hiss had been before the committee and he wondered if, "under the circumstances for the assistance of the committee," Hiss would be willing to undergo a lie-detector test. And before he answered, Nixon added, he should know that Chambers was asked the same question the week before and agreed to take the test. "Shall I answer now?" Hiss replied. "Yes," Nixon said. Hiss stated that when he practiced law he and his associates had very little confidence in "so-called lie-detector tests." The experts they had consulted believed there was no such thing — the test was an emotion recorder; the FBI even regarded it as unscientific. Before deciding, Hiss wanted to know who would administer the test and what kind of test it would be, and he was surprised that the committee "would want to rely on something that isn't scientific." Nixon allowed that the committee had contacted Leonardo Keeler of Chicago who was probably the foremost expert of the polygraph machine, a broadly accepted method. But Hiss insisted that it depends on who reads the results, and that the machine shows emotion, not truth; "and I am perfectly willing and prepared to say that I am not lacking in emotion about this business." Did the committee have confidence in this device? Hiss inquired. Nixon was confident "that it is a factor which will be helpful in this case ... to be weighed with the other facts in this matter." But Nixon added, as if the truth of the matter would forever be impossible to obtain, "I realize there is no factor which can be conclusive in this case."

Nixon asked if Crosley was a member of the Communist Party. Hiss said they never discussed the Communist Party, and he did not believe Crosley was a Communist. Did Hiss feel Crosley might be Chambers? "I find it difficult to believe," Hiss replied. "I can't identify him from the pictures and can't see any motive."

When Nixon wrote *Six Crises* (the Hiss Case was crisis one) fourteen years later, note that Nixon attributes *his* press leaks of Chambers's secret August 7 testimony to Hiss, and Nixon inverts the forthright nature of Hiss's August 16 testimony — as plainly revealed in the transcript — to fit the myth Nixon helped create. Nixon wrote:

> Now he was twisting, turning, evading, and changing his story to fit the evidence he knew we had. Despite our efforts to keep Chambers' testimony of August 7 secret, Hiss had learned that Chambers had been able to give us intimate details of their association together.... Hiss had spoken with rather strange and uncharacteristic vehemence when we asked him about the car. "It wasn't worth a damn," he had said. And he seemed to have a similar reaction when we spoke of Chambers giving him the rug. "I still have the damn thing," he had exclaimed. Was there something about the car and the rug that especially worried him? Like Lady Macbeth, was he saying, in effect, "Out, damned spot!"

Inquisitor Stripling, pulling no punches, continued the questioning:

> I read a lot of Government files from time to time — and I don't say this disparagingly — but I have seen your name for years in Government files as a person suspected of Communist activity. Now, there has to be some basis for the thing.... I am trying to determine why [Chambers] would come in before a committee of Congress under the penalties of perjury and just out of the blue make up a story and then have that story check almost in every minute detail, according to check, and then have people come in whom we know are Communists and then ask do they know you, and they refuse to answer.

Hiss had no idea why certain witnesses refused to answer certain questions, nor did he know in what context his name appeared in government files. "I can say that I have never had the slightest indication from my superiors that they gave any credence to what you appear to be giving credence to." Stripling backtracked: "Don't misunderstand me. I didn't say I gave credence to that. I said I had seen." And at this point Stripling wanted to talk off the record — but Hiss said, "It can stay on." They went off the record, but Hiss left the room while the committee met in private. On reconvening, Chairman Thomas told Hiss that the committee unanimously decided to conduct a public hearing on August 25, at which time he and Whittaker Chambers would be the witnesses, with the opportunity to confront each other. If Hiss preferred, Nixon remarked, the meeting could be private instead of public — "If you have a public session, it is a show." "[I]t will be ballyhooed into a circus," Stripling concurred. Hiss said a public meeting was fine with him: "I want to be clear that I am not asking for an executive session as opposed to public.... No public show could embarrass me now. I am asking to see this man.... I think I prefer a public session."

CHAPTER VI

Showdown at the Hotel Commodore

"For the man I saw before me was a trapped man — and I am a killer only by extreme necessity." — Whittaker Chambers (*Witness*) on Alger Hiss

The next day, August 17, Whittaker Chambers deliberated whether he should just stay at his Maryland farm or go to his office at Time-Life in New York. Going out into the world was an ordeal for Chambers. He tried to shut his mind off from the storm whirling around him. As his thoughts turned to Alger Hiss, he was not aware that HUAC had met privately with Hiss the day before.

The two first met, Chambers remembered, the summer of 1934 at Hiss's home in Washington, the 28th Street apartment that Chambers and his family would occupy the following spring. Chambers esteemed Alger and Priscilla Hiss as the closest friends he ever knew, and they shared for almost four years unnumbered acts of affection. Yet Chambers felt he failed to see how much Hiss's regard for *him* had been regard for Chambers as a Communist organizer, instead of as a best friend.

Alger Hiss was no "ordinary Communist." He was one of a new breed of middle-class intellectuals who bypassed the open Party and went directly underground. Chambers had learned something of Hiss's background before they actually met from J. Peters and Harold Ware — that he was highly intelligent but without "real Communist experience." Chambers was charged with presenting himself to Hiss as his primary Party contact. Hiss was a member of the Ware Group, a leading committee of seven men, all Communists, who met to discuss policy, organization, personnel, and projects. Some leaders of the Ware Group also headed secret cells. There were four or more such cells, each comprising as many as fifteen members. Chambers estimated there were 75 underground Communists in the Ware Group, most employed by the U.S. government.

J. Peters proposed separating a few of the most promising Ware Group members and placing them in a "parallel apparatus," which would be more rigorously segregated and subdivided. This plan entailed moving "career Communists" out of New Deal agencies, such as the A.A.A. (which the CP could penetrate almost at will), and infiltrating the old-line departments, especially the State Department. Hiss had recently left the A.A.A. to become an assistant counsel for the Senate's Nye Committee, which was investigating munitions contracts, and this change made it imperative to Peters that Hiss should be detached from

54

the Ware Group at once. Thus Hiss was the first man in the new apparatus that Chambers, who had taken the cover name "Carl," was to organize.

Carl was characteristically anxious the night he formally introduced himself to Alger (whom he had briefly met with Ware and Peters) and Priscilla Hiss—and for good reason. He needed to inspire confidence in Hiss and establish an intellectual bond, despite the little they had in common. He had no immediate task or project to assign to Hiss and therefore nothing specific to discuss. Chambers recalled arriving at the Hisses' apartment after dark on a hot Washington night. They sat in the living room and exchanged small talk, but Priscilla took almost no part in the conversation. Chambers wondered impatiently how he could give some direction to their meeting. Knowing that "fastidious" intellectual Communists such as Alger Hiss were fascinated by the image of the proletarian and the working class ethos, Carl told the story of his youthful experience as an unskilled laborer laying rails in Washington. The meeting did not go as well as Chambers wanted, and as he left he felt he had to try again.

Chambers soon visited a second time and was astounded that the Hisses welcomed him with smiles and graciousness. Hiss apologized about the other evening, but at first he had not known what to make of Carl, who didn't seem like a proletarian. But then it dawned on Hiss—"with the knowing air of a man who cannot be deceived," Chambers reflected—that Carl was a European with a remarkable mastery of English. It was his tone of voice, the clipped sentences, and intonations that gave him away.

Alger and Priscilla Hiss took an instant liking to Carl's wife, Lise (pronounced Leeza), who they knew was American—but with her dark complexion and bobbed black hair she looked Russian enough to carry off the illusion of Carl's foreignness. Where Priscilla was brittle and tense, Lise was mature and calm, transparently sincere and forthright, gentle and warm. Chambers later remembered that it was a friendship that was maintained on two discordant planes. One was the conspiratorial relationship that held them together for more than four years in the closed secrecy of the underground. The other plane was totally different: "It was the easy, gay, carefree association of two literate, very happy, fun-loving middle-class families."

The friendship of Carl and Alger was almost entirely one of character and not of the mind. Despite Alger's decided abilities as a lawyer, which Carl was not competent to explore with him, he was not a highly mental man, and ideas for their own sake held no interest for him. Compared to the eclectic and brilliant gemlike minds Chambers had grown up with at Columbia, Hiss was rather on the stuffy side—he didn't even like Shakespeare, so full of "platitudes in blank verse."

The Hisses were continually kind and solicitous to Carl and Lise and their baby girl, for which Chambers remained grateful, though he sometimes wondered how much of Hiss's solicitude was really for them and how much was for Carl, Communist agent. No doubt, Chambers believed, Hiss would prefer to believe that it was the latter, but Chambers remembered the simple pleasure that they all took in just being together, and he preferred to believe still that it was the former.

In Chambers's mind, the outstanding fact about Alger Hiss was an unvarying mildness, a deep considerateness and gracious patience that seemed proof against the petty annoyances and exasperations of daily life. Only rarely did Hiss exhibit a streak of wholly incongruous cruelty. For example, a strange savagery cropped up once in a conversation with Carl and Lise about President Franklin Roosevelt. Most all Communists, Chambers among them, were contemptuous of FDR, regarding him as a dabbler in revolution who understood neither revolution nor history. But Hiss derided the President maliciously, startling Chambers and deeply shocking his wife with the ugly jokes he told of FDR's crippled condition as a symbol of society's general breakdown.

It was Hiss's idea, Chambers always maintained, that Carl and Lise and their eighteen-month-old daughter move into the 28th Street apartment in the spring of 1935, and live there rent-free, simply as a gesture of friendship and goodwill between Communists. Carl had known Hiss for several months before the move, and had been living with his family in Baltimore on St. Paul Street after moving from New York in the summer of 1934. At least once while they lived in Baltimore, Carl invited the Hisses over for dinner. Carl's friendship with Hiss was not favored in underground work for the obvious reasons, but Carl took the chance and relaxed the procedures of concealment. Also, the personal connection with Carl rescued Hiss from his underground isolation. There was a thrill for Hiss in driving to Baltimore to visit a secluded family whose address only he knew, Chambers reflected in his autobiography, and parking his old Ford blocks away and then slowly walking (on the lookout for observers) to an ordinary house which really served as an outpost of the international underground. The underground security procedures had obviously eroded even more by the time Alger and Carl loaded some of the baby's things into Hiss's old Ford and took them to the 28th Street apartment where the lease still had two months to run.

When the lease expired, Chambers claimed, "Carl" decided to move with his family back to New York. His old Columbia friend, Meyer Schapiro, offered to "rent" his Greenwich Village house to Chambers (Schapiro — apparently not as generous as Hiss — knew Chambers was a CP member involved in "secret" work) for part of the summer while the Schapiro family would be away. Once more Alger and Carl loaded the Ford with the few personal belongings they had taken to the 28th Street apartment. Hiss drove with the goods to the Schapiro house in New York. Carl and Lise and the baby took the train.

Later that summer the Chambers family vacationed for a few weeks at a cottage in Smithtown, Pennsylvania, on the Delaware River. Priscilla Hiss joined them there for ten days, Chambers swore, and took care of Carl and Lise's baby while Lise practiced landscape and portrait painting. Priscilla and Lise worked out a plan for housing the latter's family (gratis, of course) after vacation. Though Carl voiced some "tacit reservations," Priscilla was "generously insistent" that the couple and their baby move in with the Hisses at their P Street house in Washington. The Hisses readied the third floor for the young family, and they moved in right after leaving their vacation cottage. It wasn't an unpleasant stay, but the guests did not remain long, perhaps a week. The baby girl required a special formula which Lise had to prepare often. Lise felt she was upsetting the kitchen routine and distressing the maid, and she implored Carl, who was relieved to hear it, to find them a place of their own.

Chambers was often asked years later how it was possible not to meet any of the Hisses' friends during this period. Chambers explained that when the Hisses lived on P Street they had almost no visitors and kept entirely to themselves. Besides, Hiss was cut off from the Ware Group, which had formerly provided much of his social life. It was not until the Hisses moved to 30th Street (Carl's "informal headquarters," Chambers later testified) that they really began to entertain. And the reason Chambers moved so many times — "a kind of organized flight"— especially in 1934 and 1935, was because of orders from his CP superiors to stay in "instant readiness" to leave for London for a proposed special mission, which never materialized.

Sometime later in 1935 the Chambers family resettled for a spell in Baltimore. Until the spring of 1938, by way of Chambers's narrative, Carl and Lise met with the Hisses dozens of times, even taking an overnight trip with them to New Hampshire in 1937. However, no friends or relatives of either family remember seeing the couples together, not even Priscilla's son, Timothy, who was nine years old in 1935 and who lived with Alger and Priscilla through all those years.

In *Witness*, Chambers recounts his last visit with the Hisses around Christmas 1938, attempting, months after his own defection from the Communist Party, to convince a tearful Alger Hiss to follow him. This was the visit in which the Hisses supposedly told him that they knew his real name.

Whittaker Chambers ultimately forced himself to leave his farmstead the morning of August 17 and go to New York. When he reached Baltimore he impulsively decided to go to Washington instead, feeling an anxious need to go and see the Committee, whose members were the few people left in the world with whom he could communicate. But he had nothing to say to them, no purpose at all in seeing them. He arrived at the Old House Office Building around noon, and to avoid loitering newsmen he headed for a side door he had never before entered. As Chambers stepped up to the threshold, Robert Stripling and several committee staffers bolted out, beholding Chambers as an apparition. It so happened that Stripling and his aides had been calling Chambers all morning, frantically trying to reach him at home, in New York and Washington. The fluke encounter stunned Stripling, who remarked, "I believe he must be psychic." No one would tell Chambers why he was wanted, and they all piled into a car and headed for Union Station. On the way a staffer pulled a newspaper out of his pocket and showed Chambers the headline: Harry Dexter White had died of a heart attack the day before. The news reports implied it was brought on (White had a history of heart problems) by his strenuous testimony before the committee the previous Friday. Chambers was swept through Union Station and onto a Pullman. He was going to New York after all, but he still did not know why. At Pennsylvania Station in New York Chambers took a taxi, along with Nixon, McDowell and Stripling, to the Hotel Commodore in midtown.

While Chambers was mulling over staying home or going to work that morning, Alger Hiss received a telephone call from a HUAC staffer in Washington. Would it be possible for him to meet with Representative McDowell for ten or fifteen minutes later that afternoon in New York? The caller did not know whether McDowell's request was for personal or committee-business matters. Hiss said he would be available at his office on Fifth Avenue and 44th Street. McDowell later informed Hiss by wire that he would call around 5:30 but still gave no reason why.

Hiss learned over the course of the day of Harry Dexter White's fatal heart attack; the afternoon papers prominently displayed the news of his death the previous day. But it did not occur to Hiss that McDowell's message and the news of White's death were connected.

McDowell called a few minutes before 5:30. Expecting the congressman to come to his office, Hiss was surprised when McDowell asked to meet instead at the Hotel Commodore, a few blocks away. He added that Nixon and "one other" were with him at room 1400. Hiss now suspected something more than a casual conversation of a few minutes was planned and that McDowell had been deliberately evasive. Distrustful of the committee's latest stratagem, Hiss asked a colleague, Charles Dollard, to accompany him, if for no other reason than to have a friend present who would monitor the event.

Hotel Commodore's sitting room 1400 was in the midst of conversion to an ad hoc hearing room when Hiss and Dollard entered. Nixon, McDowell, Stripling, and a few staff members, including the stenographer, were present. It dawned on Hiss that there might be more than a happenstance connection between this hurried improvisation and White's death. The press reports of White's fatal heart attack demeaned the committee for baiting White and suggesting he had been feigning illness. This was just the sort of brazen maneuver to fend off a critical press that HUAC was notorious for.

McDowell presided as acting chairman, with Nixon sitting next to him at a lamp table that served as podium. Hiss was sworn in and sat a few feet in front of the congressmen, facing them and the window at their rear. Dollard was introduced by Hiss as a friend who worked at the Carnegie Corporation, then stood silently in the background for nearly two hours. Stripling announced that the meeting's purpose was "to continue to determine the truth or falsity of the testimony which has been given by Mr. Whittaker Chambers" before relinquishing the proceedings to Richard Nixon.

"[T]he case is dependent upon the question of identity," Nixon opened, but the attempt to establish Hiss's identification of Chambers through photographs had so far failed. Nixon allowed the possibility, which Hiss had raised the day before, that a third party might be involved, one George Crosley whom Hiss had described at some length. Or it might be that Whittaker Chambers and George Crosley were the same person, and so consequently the committee had also asked Chambers to appear this day so Hiss could "have the opportunity to see him and make up [his] own mind on that point."

But the "question of identity" had been the issue for twelve days. Hiss swore he had never known an individual named Whittaker Chambers. In addition to dismissing Chambers's charges as "complete fabrications" on August 5, Hiss could not recognize photographs of Chambers as anyone he had ever known — but he had hoped to see Chambers face to face that very day. Because Hiss so resolutely denied the charges and any knowledge whatsoever of Chambers, Nixon said for the record on August 5 that in order to avoid another perhaps "useless appearance" of Chambers, "I think in justice to both of these witnesses ... that the witnesses be allowed to confront each other so that any possibility of a mistake in identity may be cleared up." But this was disingenuous because Nixon could have immediately arranged a confrontation for August 7, the day his subcommittee met secretly with Chambers at Foley Square in New York, not far from Hiss's apartment.

Nixon was silent about White's death, and he offered no explanation for moving up the date of the confrontation by eight days. However, Nixon provided some answers fourteen years later when he wrote that ("while plausible") White's death had nothing to do with his decision; rather, he "became convinced that if Hiss had concocted the Crosley story, we would be playing into his hands by delaying the public confrontation until August 25, thus giving him nine more days to make his story fit the facts."

Hiss impatiently interrupted Nixon to point out that this meeting was obviously going to take longer than the ten or fifteen minutes McDowell had asked him for, and therefore he needed to call and cancel a six o'clock appointment. Dollard volunteered to make the call, and Hiss asked to make a statement before Nixon continued.

Hiss wanted the record to show that he was greatly shocked by the news of Harry White's death and he was not in the best mood for testimony, but he did "not for a moment want to miss the opportunity of seeing Mr. Chambers." He added that the committee's "oath of secrecy" promised in the executive session of the day before was insincere because the morning *Herald Tribune* reported that the committee had asked Hiss if he would submit to a lie-detector test. He had read other bits of his testimony in the papers "which could only have come from the committee. They did not come from me." Nixon suggested that

Hiss contact the reporter for the source, but Hiss said he had no reason to — "The assurances I had came from the committee." Yet Nixon insisted that "no member of this committee or no member of the staff" had discussed Hiss's testimony with the press. Nixon then asked a staff investigator to bring in Whittaker Chambers.

Chambers was led in from an adjacent room through an entrance at Hiss's back. As Chambers walked toward a couch he was motioned to, Hiss sat looking straight ahead, at Nixon and McDowell and the window. (One commentator, not present but perhaps apprised by someone who was, characterized Hiss as "looking nearly transfixed.... [H]e did not resemble the man who had been demanding such a confrontation but more like a trapped pigeon well aware that the moment of truth with the hawk had arrived.") Just as Chambers sat down, Nixon asked the two men to stand. They stood facing each other, and Nixon said: "Mr. Hiss, the man standing here is Mr. Whittaker Chambers. I ask you now if you have ever known that man before." Hiss thought he recognized an overweight George Crosley in a rumpled suit, but he wanted to hear Chambers's voice:

"Will you ask him to say something?"

"My name is Whittaker Chambers."

Hiss stepped closer to Chambers and asked him to open his mouth wider. Their eyes did not meet.

"My name is Whittaker Chambers."

"I said, would you open your mouth," Hiss repeated. "You know what I'm referring to, Mr. Nixon. Would you go on talking?"

"I am senior editor of *Time* magazine."

Chambers was pale and perspiring, his voice constrained, tight, shrill. He felt on display, like a farm animal at a fat stock auction. Though Chambers's voice seemed "strangled," Hiss said: "I think he is George Crosley, but I would like to hear him talk a little longer." Nixon grabbed a magazine and asked Chambers to read, but Hiss broke in: "Are you George Crosley?"

"Not to my knowledge," Chambers replied. "You are Alger Hiss, I believe."

"Just one moment," Nixon interposed. "Since some repartee goes on between these two people, I think Mr. Chambers should be sworn."

"That is a good idea," Hiss said.

McDowell swore Chambers in, and Nixon ripped into Hiss: "I suggested that he be sworn, and when I say something like that I want no interruptions from you."

"Mr. Nixon," Hiss snapped, "in view of what happened yesterday, I think there is no occasion for you to use that tone of voice in speaking to me."

Chambers commenced reading aloud from a *Newsweek*, but Hiss soon interrupted:

"The voice sounds a little less resonant than the voice that I recall of the man I knew as George Crosley. The teeth look to me as though either they have been improved upon or that there has been considerable dental work done since I knew George Crosley." Yet Hiss said he would not "take an absolute oath" that Chambers was Crosley "without further checking." Nixon elicited from Chambers that since 1934 he had undergone extensive dental work, including extractions and a plate, by a Dr. Hitchcock of Westminster, Maryland. Hiss wanted the dentist to confirm Chambers's testimony. Nixon turned to Chambers and asked him to describe the condition of his teeth in 1934 — "They were in very bad shape."

"Before we leave the teeth," Nixon added slyly to Hiss, "do you feel that you would have to have the dentist tell you just what he did to the teeth before you could tell anything about this man?" Ignoring the sarcasm, Hiss replied he felt strongly Chambers was Crosley, but "he looks very different in girth and other appearances — hair, forehead, and so on, particularly the jowls."

Nixon abruptly changed focus and asked Hiss the name of Crosley's wife, but he couldn't recall. Nixon followed with questions mostly rehashed from the day before — on the rental agreement of the 28th Street apartment, when the lease expired, the rental value, how he first met Crosley, the duration of the acquaintance.

"Never saw him socially during that period?" Nixon asked.

"Never saw him socially," Hiss replied. "Only in the course of my business."

"And then there was some conversation about a car," Nixon remarked. "What was that?" Hiss recalled Crosley wondering about renting a car so when his family was in Washington while he prepared his articles they could get out on weekends. He told Crosley, Hiss continued, that he would "throw a car in" with the rental because he had been keeping an old car for sentimental reasons, couldn't get anything for it on trade-in or sale, and would be glad if someone could make real use of it. Besides, it had been sitting on the streets because he had purchased a new car.

Then followed an exchange which brought into sharp relief the inquisitorial nature of this closed hearing, where the accused, Alger Hiss, answered the questions, while the accuser, Whittaker Chambers, remained silent.

> NIXON: Then before he moved into the apartment I understand that you allowed him and his wife to stay with you in your home?
> HISS: My recollection of that — and this is repetitious —
> NIXON: We are repeating it for his benefit as well as to see if he can recall this incident.
> HISS: I am glad he has no other way of finding out about it, Mr. Nixon.

And so Hiss obligingly recalled that Crosley didn't want to bring many things to Washington because they were only going to stay for the summer; that several items of furniture were thus left in the apartment for the new tenants; that the Hisses put the Crosleys up for a few nights at their P Street home because the moving van Crosley said he hired had not yet arrived. Hiss believed this was simply a helpful gesture — "You develop a kind of pseudo-friendliness over a transaction of that kind." Crosley, his wife, and their infant stayed with the Hisses at P Street for two or three days. "It may have been 4," Hiss said, "may have been 2. It was more than one night. I imagine my wife would testify it seemed even longer than that."

Crosley subsequently dropped by "once or twice ... because of this establishment of a personal relationship." On one occasion Crosley brought over a rug as partial payment of the rent, which Hiss accepted as such. "He hadn't yet sold his articles," Hiss added, "he was hard up, he was going to make payment." But Hiss didn't remember Crosley ever paying any rent in currency. He also recalled giving Crosley a ride to New York, and perhaps Mrs. Hiss had gone along.

Stripling relieved Nixon, and he thought Hiss had acted strangely by basing his identification purely on what Chambers's "upper teeth might have looked like. Now," Stripling went on, "here is a person that you knew for several months at least. You knew him so well that he was a guest in your home ... gave him an old Ford automobile ... leased him your apartment." And in this "very important confrontation, the only thing that you have to check on is this denture; is that correct?"

Hiss recounted how he had been struck by a certain "familiarity in features" of photographs of Chambers he had seen since August 3, and he reminded Stripling of his reaction to the photograph Stripling had shown him twelve days before — that he could not be sure he had never seen the person in the photograph, and that he wanted to see the actual person, Chambers. "I am not given on important occasions to snap judgments or simple, easy statements. I am confident that George Crosley had notably bad teeth. I would not call George Crosley a guest in my house. I have explained the circumstances. If you choose to call him a guest, that is your affair." Crosley had meant nothing to him, Hiss added, and he saw Crosley at a time when he was seeing hundreds of people. Moreover, he would today have had no difficulty identifying Chambers as Crosley, but Chambers "denied it right here." And earlier, when Hiss attempted to ask questions of Chambers, he was rebuffed by Nixon. "I was denied that right," Hiss asserted. "I have been testifying about George Crosley. Whether he and this man are the same or whether he has means of getting information from George Crosley about my house, I do not know."

The committee then allowed Hiss to question Chambers. Chambers did not object.

HISS: Did you ever go under the name of George Crosley?
CHAMBERS: Not to my knowledge.
HISS: Did you ever sublet an apartment … from me?
CHAMBERS: No; I did not.
HISS: You did not?
CHAMBERS: No.
HISS: Did you ever spend any time with your wife and child in an apartment … in Washington when I was not there because I and my family were living on P Street?
CHAMBERS: I most certainly did.
HISS: You did or did not?
CHAMBERS: I did.
HISS: Would you tell me how you reconcile your negative answers with this affirmative answer?
CHAMBERS: Very easily, Alger. I was a Communist and you were a Communist.
HISS: Would you be responsive and continue with your answer?
CHAMBERS: I do not think it is needed.

Nixon, however, pressed Chambers to explain the circumstances. Chambers merely reiterated his August 3 testimony — that he had been a functionary of the American Communist Party connected with an underground group in Washington of which Hiss was a member. "Mr. Hiss and I became friends. To the best of my knowledge, Mr. Hiss himself suggested that I [take the apartment], and I accepted gratefully."

Hiss declared to the chairman that he did not need to ask Chambers any more questions. "I am now perfectly prepared to identify this man as George Crosley." Hiss repeated his positive identification for Stripling on the basis of what Chambers just said, but Stripling wanted Hiss to produce three people who would swear they knew Chambers as Crosley. He said he would, if possible, but the only people who would have known Crosley other than his wife were those who had been associated with the Nye Committee thirteen years before. Later it transpired that of the Nye Committee staff members Hiss believed might have met Crosley, one was dead, another had no recollection, and a third couldn't be located. HUAC investigators searched the Library of Congress for anything published by a George Crosley or Crossley, but found nothing.

Nixon resumed, making the point clear that Chambers said he and Hiss had been Communists. Did Hiss have reason to believe Crosley had been a Communist? Hiss said he certainly didn't, and even though politics were frequently discussed in those years it wasn't customary to ask people, particularly of the press, if they were Communists. "It was a quite different atmosphere in Washington then than today. I had no reason to suspect George Crosley of being a Communist … or whether that was of any significance to me if he was ... and it was my duty to give him information, as I did any other member of the press."

"I would like to say that to come here and discover that the ass under the lion's skin is Crosley," Hiss continued, "I don't know why your committee didn't pursue this careful method of interrogation at an earlier date before all the publicity."

Hiss then stood and walked toward Chambers, heatedly demanding him to make his charges "out of the presence of this committee without their being privileged for suit for libel. I challenge you to do it, and I hope you will do it damned quickly." One of the committee investigators, thinking Hiss might strike Chambers, stepped between the two and lightly fingered Hiss's jacket sleeve. "I am not going to touch him," Hiss glared. "You are touching me."

Chambers believed, as he later recounted, that all this was "great theater.... I am convinced Alger Hiss was acting from start to finish."

After a brief recess a general discussion ensued, rather academic and pointless, about when statements were privileged under government immunity and when they were actionable. The waning session regained some focus when Stripling said to Hiss: "You are fully aware that the public was led to believe that you had never seen, heard, or laid eyes upon an individual who is this individual, and now you do know him." Hiss replied that Stripling was stating his impression of public impression —"And you may have helped the public impression if it is anywhere near what you describe it as."

If we believe Hiss, it only occurred to him *the day before* that Chambers and Crosley might be the same person. And though Stripling and the entire committee knew about this claim, it was precisely what they couldn't believe. They could not reconcile how Hiss could be so indifferent to and dismissive of a former "acquaintance," one whom, however, he had singled out (or perhaps vice versa) among others interested in the Nye Committee's work, provided this man and his family with an apartment and a car, loaned him money and bought him lunches, and accommodated the "Crosleys" at his home for a few days. Yet Hiss maintained he had only helped someone in need and that Crosley had never been a friend or a guest.

Hiss's testimony revealed most everything he could remember about Crosley, though he diminished their involvement to the status of a business transaction. But Chambers was not even questioned about the relationship. He had supplied the committee ten days before with many homey details about the Hisses and emphasized the closeness of the friendship, but today he was given a free pass. And that was Hiss's fault. Moreover, it was a crucial mistake, one of many devastating blunders yet to follow. Hiss could have questioned Chambers — he had the committee's blessing — about any and all aspects of their putative friendship, specifics of the underground apparatus and the collection of CP dues, details of their first meeting, family particulars, and so on, with all of it transcribed for the record. At the very least Hiss should have asked the committee to repeat some of the questions posed to Chambers on August 7. Though Hiss did briefly question Chambers, his anger threw him off balance when he positively identified Chambers as Crosley, and he consequently ended the cross-examination, abandoning his lawyerly instincts.

Around seven o'clock Nixon suggested adjournment. Hiss and Chambers were instructed to appear again as witnesses before the full committee in public session on August 25 at 10:30 A.M. in the caucus room of the Old House Office Building.

Nixon could hardly wait to get to a telephone and spill the committee's side of the story to the press before their deadlines. Remaining all night at the hotel, Nixon briefed the news outlets for hours. To the Associated Press he said Hiss had identified Chambers as a man he had known under a different name: "The impression given to the public was that [Hiss] had never known this man at all. This identification today is a direct contrast with that impression." Nixon told the *New York Times* that Chambers "did not recall having used the name 'George Crosley,'" and that Chambers had in previous "secret closed sessions ... described furniture, paintings on the walls, and other objects of the Hiss home." The International News Service wrote:

> Alger Hiss, former high State Department official accused of being in the Communist under-ground, admitted lending money from time to time to Whittaker Chambers, his accuser. Hiss acknowledged such loans during his face-to-face meeting with Whittaker Chambers in a New York hotel when he identified Chambers as George Crosley, who occupied his apartment in the Summer of 1935, Richard M. Nixon revealed today.
> When the tardy identification of Chambers by Hiss is reenacted at a public hearing of the House Committee on Un-American Activities on August 25, Chambers, confessed Red courier, will reiterate that any money he received from Hiss was in payment of Communist Party dues, Representative Nixon predicted.

The Hearst papers reported that Nixon said two former friends of Chambers testified that he had not "changed perceptibly" since 1935, and that they could easily have identified him from the same photograph which failed to stir the memory of Hiss. The fact remains, Nixon asserted, that Hiss "told a Congressional Committee he could not recognize the photograph of his accuser as any man he knew under any name and now he records the recognition of him."

Alger Hiss called John Foster Dulles, the Carnegie Endowment's chairman, later that evening from his Eighth Street apartment and recounted his ordeal. He and the committee were "now at war." And he could have added that the committee was winning because soon after a reporter called and informed Hiss of the stories Nixon was feeding the press. Hiss quickly reacted with a post-midnight press conference at his apartment, but it was too little, too late.

CHAPTER VII

"The Truth Doesn't Matter"

"There was such an air of suppressed melodrama about him that I should not have been greatly surprised if one day a Communist gunman had shot him down in one of the office corridors."[1]— T.S. Matthews on Chambers at *Time*

Whittaker Chambers also met with the press after the confrontation, though his was a convivial dinner with Henry Luce, the editor-in-chief of *Time*, *Life*, and *Fortune*, and his employer since 1939 when he was brought on as a book reviewer at *Time*. Chambers maintained it was his first "real job." For almost seven years prior he had lived under a variety of aliases invented not only for himself but also for his wife and children; lived at dozens of different addresses; stolen the identities of others; fraudulently signed leases, passports, checks; and paid no income tax. Luce first noticed Chambers in 1940. He had written a movie review of *The Grapes of Wrath* and rather praised the acting, though not concealing his contempt for the book or author John Steinbeck. Luce saw the movie and read the review, remarking, "It's the best cinema review ever in *Time*." Chambers's biographer, Sam Tanenhaus, wrote that Luce thought Chambers was the best writer *Time* ever hired, meaning Chambers "uniquely mastered the emerging Luce formula, which consisted of portioning out Big Thoughts, bite-size, to readers in a hurry."

A relative of Henry Luce remarked that Luce admired Chambers's trenchant mind, and Chambers's vision of a world polarized by Communism (long before the Cold War) had a uniquely powerful appeal for Luce. John Hersey, a leading World War II correspondent for *Time* and the author of *Hiroshima*, who, like Luce, was a child of missionaries in China, believes Luce underwent a basic change of view about the inevitability of a Communist victory in China after Luce fell under the sway of the obsessively anti–Communist Chambers. The former vice president of Time, Inc., Otto Fuerbringer, told an interviewer that Chambers was *Time*'s expert on Communism —"He treated all the rest of us, even Luce, as innocents."[2]

About three weeks before their dinner engagement Chambers had told Luce: "The years are running out on me.... I think I have something to say and little time to say it.... Has a man who has something to say and the ability to say it any real place at *Time*?" Chambers wanted to resign from *Time* effective January 1949 and write only on a freelance basis. On August 2, the day before his initial public HUAC testimony, Chambers met with Luce to discuss his future — or what he thought was left of it. "It seems to me that you will not want me around here any longer," Chambers said, after telling Luce he had been subpoenaed by HUAC the day before. "Nonsense," Luce replied, "testifying is a simple patriotic duty."[3]

Time magazine was a relatively small editorial operation when Chambers came aboard in 1939 at age 38. Two assistant managing editors edited all the copy before it went to the managing editor, and Luce himself read every word and wrote comments in the margins of every issue for the employees to read. The staff was quite young (Luce was just over forty), and most were fairly new to the organization. Luce preferred sidestepping the managers, according to Peter Drucker, who worked at *Fortune* in 1940, by encouraging backstabbing, secrecy, feuds, and competing cliques. Though the political atmosphere at the magazine was much in concert with the political atmosphere of "youngish informed New York life," wrote former *Time* editor Louis Kronenberger, policy "at the Time Inc. top had already acquired a hard crust." Luce was already a public figure and a publishing dynamo, and a "dislike of *Time*, in educated-minority circles, was by now voluble enough to be judged a public fact."

In 1939 *Time* distributed almost three-quarters of a million copies a week, and within five years the various Time Inc. publications, including the *March of Time* newsreel, reached over a third of the total literate adult population of the United States. Whittaker Chambers believed, so Sam Tanenhaus tells us, that a popular magazine "could be a powerful vehicle of mass enlightenment." And it could also be, in the words of Louis Kronenberger, "the instrument for implanting, emphasizing, proselytizing opinions and beliefs."

Chambers was hired by *Time*'s managing editor, T.S. Matthews, in April 1939 at a salary of one hundred dollars a week. Robert Cantwell, a longtime friend of Chambers and a book reviewer for the magazine who had recently been promoted, recommended Chambers to fill his vacancy. Cantwell likened Chambers to the French novelist André Malraux, and Matthews was impressed after reading one of Chambers's short stories — "It *was* something like Malraux ... shot through with the same murky flashes of rather sinister brilliance." Matthews — having been informed by Cantwell that Chambers was a renegade Communist in fear of assassination and in hiding — arranged an interview with Chambers, who arrived wearing his signature attire: rumpled dark gray suit, soiled white shirt, short black tie, dingy fedora. He looked to Matthews like a lay brother or a Quaker. Kronenberger observed a "stagily drab" quality to Chambers's appearance, "something to make you wonder who would dress like that — a man on call as a pallbearer?" At first glance his face seemed "cornfed and countrified," but at second take his countenance revealed "curiosity, a hint of complexity, intelligence." Chambers spoke little of himself or his circumstances during the interview, Matthews recalled, while he "listened with an air of cynical understanding, and sucked a short pipe." And Matthews suspected that "Whittaker Chambers" might be an alias — "There was such an air of suppressed melodrama about him that I should not have been greatly surprised if one day a Communist gunman had shot him down in one of the office corridors."

Chambers was indeed afraid he might be accosted at work, for he seldom appeared in the corridors. He scurried from the elevator to his office, always closing the door and usually locking it. He kept a loaded revolver handy, and his desk sat at the far side of the room squarely facing the entrance, providing an unobstructed view of anyone who entered. Except to go to the men's room or the elevator, he rarely left his cell.

Chambers's paranoia soon became legendary. His colleagues were amazed at his bizarre mannerisms and gestures — speaking out of the side of his mouth in a deep-voiced drone, looking over his shoulder and casing the room for lurkers, leering at people in a disquieting way. Chambers's first biographer, Meyer Zeligs, was told by several former *Time* employees that Chambers kept a notebook in which he detailed the daily habits and activities of his coworkers. As his position at the magazine became more solid and secure, Kronenberger recalled, Chambers's reputation "became more shadowy and in some quarters quite sinister." He unnerved and scared researchers and junior staff by "going at" them, making them confused and undermining their sense of wellbeing, tactics characterized by Kronenberger as "deliberately conspiratorial" and "a form of self-dramatization."

Suspicious of everyone and blatantly disagreeable, Chambers spurned office social events, parties, group lunches, drinks after work. He always displayed, one colleague recalled, "the gaucheness of someone who decidedly lacked a social sense."[4] However, in addition to Luce and Matthews, there were admirers and supporters of Chambers who early on befriended him. One who sought his company for lunch — but was usually told he was too busy or not hungry — was Duncan Norton-Taylor, a conservative writer in the National Affairs section who later became managing editor of *Fortune* and eventually a close friend who compiled and edited Chambers's papers for *Cold Friday*, published after Chambers's death. But Norton-Taylor persisted and finally won Chambers over for a lunch date. He followed Chambers from the building into the subway where they took the downtown train for two stops, got off, crossed over to the uptown side, rode to Times Square and then entered an Automat on Broadway. Chambers sat in the rear where he could monitor all the entrances.

Sam Welles, who worked in Books with Chambers, and later became a faithful Chambers ally and advocate, asked Chambers several times out for lunch but was invariably rebuffed. Sometime after, apparently convinced Welles wasn't an assassin, Chambers himself extended an invitation. Welles's initiating noontime adventure entailed a subway ride to 34th Street where they entered Macy's and walked its entire block length to an escalator at the opposite end, went up a floor and hiked back the same block through hordes of shoppers, making their way ultimately out to the street and over to the Empire State Building for a sandwich at Longchamps. Chambers confided to Welles that he never trusted another's timing or direction, and restaurants were especially perilous because food could easily be poisoned by an enemy with an accomplice.

Within three years Chambers advanced to editor of almost a dozen back-of-the-magazine sections, such as Art, Books, Religion, and Medicine. He worked at a fiendish, suicidal clip; *Time*'s five-day week was too short for his compulsive, self-destructive energies. Chambers began the habit of working thirty-six hours at a stretch without sleep, a killing routine he followed — until he inevitably collapsed — throughout his years at *Time*. Yet often following these torturous sedentary marathons he disappeared from the office for days, incommunicado, so that not even the managing editor could reach him. Chambers lured into his deadly schedule an unfortunate assistant, Calvin Fixx, his best friend at *Time*. Routinely he and Fixx ended their week just before dawn after having worked a day and a half nonstop, stimulating themselves with six packs of cigarettes and a continual stream of coffee. Fixx was the first to collapse.

A few weeks later severe chest pains forced Chambers to see a doctor, who ordered immediate and sustained bed rest. Chambers later claimed that the diagnosis was angina pectoris, but his primary physician and a consultant believed he suffered what is commonly called a nervous breakdown, caused by emotional strain and physical neglect, incapacitating Chambers for over six months. Dr. E. Reese Wilkens, who attended Chambers from October 1942 to May 1943, noted: "The angina-like sensations which he had ... were probably not true angina. There was no detectable aftereffect on the heart muscle or on any other cardiac component as judged either by examination or by electrocardiography. I believe there is ample explanation for this illness on the ground of extreme exhaustion, worry, overstrain of every nerve and quite insufficient sleep." Dr. E.W. Bridgman, a consulting specialist, concurred that Chambers did not have angina but emphasized his anguished emotional state — he was "very disturbed about the future of the world," a constant lament of Chambers, the apostate Communist with the premonition (tragic but true, he believed) that he had escaped the winning side of imminent global Communism to join the ranks of free God-fearing losers.[5]

In his early years at *Time* Chambers was occasionally assigned Russian news to write, but his editors, especially managing editor Matthews, were put off by his references to Stalin and the Soviets as cynical and treacherous enemies, not friendly allies, and they habitually killed his copy. His anti–Communist bias, which in a few years would be shared by most Americans, was in the first years of the war "embarrassingly peculiar" to Chambers, Matthews believed. His exclusion from writing news stories about Communism exasperated Chambers because he believed no one at *Time* knew anything about the subject — other than Communists. But Chambers resigned himself to the prohibition and came to see that his attitude had been shallow after all. So he took the high road, and if there was a sinister aspect to Chambers he could also manifest (at least in his autobiography) an angelic quality. It was his calling, he felt, to point out the religious and moral positions making Communism evil. And he would accomplish this mission as a book reviewer. The Books section, the last section in the magazine, would become his pulpit and *Time*'s editorial page. He would explain to millions why the Enlightenment was an error and why secularism is wrong and religious faith is right, why the Christians are right and the heathen are wrong.

This change of approach and outlook effected an almost miraculous transformation in relations with his colleagues. "Now a truly wonderful thing began to happen to me," Chambers recalled. "[L]ittle by little people began to open my office door at *Time* which in my own need few had ever opened." They confided to him all sorts of personal problems, desperate confessions. "They came from people at all levels of the organization, from top to bottom. Men and women have both burst into tears in my office while I rose to snap the lock on the door."

Chambers recounts in *Witness* his first wrenching months at *Time* when he grappled with the "*Time* curve," a learning process whereby most writers (and Chambers included himself) discover that writing naturally is not enough and that something extra is required. Attempting to write "*Time* style" only results in parody because the style is a tight form of expression, not a game using peculiar words and vague phrases. The writer becomes trapped in a squirrel cage of parody. His copy isn't publishable and must be rewritten again and again. He feels frantically insecure as a writer and an employee, and nobody offers guidance or advice. Chambers wondered why they didn't fire him, but he couldn't quit.

But T.S. Matthews, the managing editor who became a good friend of Chambers and supported his rise at the magazine, remembered Chambers from the outset as a truculent and exceedingly confident writer and editor, not the self-effacing amateur portrayed in *Witness*. Matthews wrote in 1985:

> Almost all *Time* writers had to resign themselves to having their copy cut and also to being hacked about ("edited") and often largely rewritten by an editor. From the very first, Chambers made it quite clear that he objected violently to this convention and would never resign himself to it.

Whenever I edited his copy, if I cut a sentence or altered a word, I could always expect his protesting presence or, more effectively, an eloquently despairing note ... to the general effect that his story was now ruined and, if these indicated changes were made, completely senseless and not worth publishing. In these and other ways he let it be known that he did not feel himself among his intellectual superiors or even equals.[6]

Such was Chambers's proficiency and self-assurance that in his first or second week at *Time* he was assigned a *cover story*, the feature article which was almost always given to a writer with long tenure at the magazine. The piece, about James Joyce and the recent publication of his novel *Finnegans Wake*, perhaps forever the most "difficult" English language masterpiece, was part biographical sketch, part classroom appreciation, part cribbing salute to critic Edmund Wilson for working out the most intelligible interpretation of the book.

Another early notable article by Chambers, "The Revolt of the Intellectuals" (January 1941), sneered at leftists and "literary liberals," now "ex–fellow travelers," who had jumped off the "Red Express." (Chambers himself had never been a mere liberal or even a socialist. He traversed the political spectrum in great strides, from reactionary to Communist to reactionary, with no trepidation and no stations along the way in which he displayed the least compassion or empathy for his fellow humans — no appeals to civil rights or economic equality, no soup kitchen duty, no helping the disadvantaged in any way. One year he'd be a staunch supporter of Republican governor Calvin Coolidge whom Chambers admired for the way he quashed the 1919 Boston Police Strike; another year he'd be composing revolutionary poetry; and finally, in his darkest year of the Communist underground, God's design was revealed to him through the delicate contours of his infant daughter's ear as she ate her morning porridge.)

Chambers wrote:

The Depression came to them as a refreshing change. Fundamentally skeptical, maladjusted, defeatist, the intellectuals felt thoroughly at home in the chaos and misery of the '30s. Fundamentally benevolent and humane, they loved their fellow countrymen in distress far more than they could ever love them in prosperity. And they particularly enjoyed life when applause began to greet their berating of the robber barons, president makers, economic royalists, malefactors of great wealth.

From this it was but a step to supporting the Communist Party, especially when Marxists pointed out that while under capitalism, a writer is either a wretched hack or a vulgar best seller, under Communism he is a privileged employee of the State.

Also noteworthy about this piece of mockery is that one of the subjects, writer Malcolm Cowley, kept notes of Chambers's confounding interview with him a month earlier. "He gave me a lot of dope on the CP underground," Cowley recorded in his journal on Friday the 13th of December 1940. "He said that it had its people all through the government service.... Sayre, the high commissioner to the Philippines, is also connected with the underground movement." Intriguingly, Francis B. Sayre, the son-in-law of Woodrow Wilson and a former Assistant Secretary of State, had been Alger Hiss's boss from 1936 to 1939. According to Chambers, Hiss had been his best friend and underground confederate during most of those years, yet Chambers did not even cite Hiss's name to Cowley. And strangely enough, there is no record that Chambers ever again mentioned Sayre (other than twice to Cowley) as connected in any way to the Communist underground or CP. Cowley's journal entry continues:

Chambers boasts that he tried to disrupt every underground activity that he knew about after leaving the party, and although he wants me to keep the information quiet he has turned it over to the proper sources.

He is fighting now for "the Christian democratic counter revolution." He has joined the Episcopal Church. When I expressed some wonder, considering the formal and rather neutral quality of that church, he explained that it contained the worst enemies of the Comintern. There is utter sincerity in his hatred.

In spite of having a good job, he dresses rather badly. He is a short, stout, broad man with an apparently amiable soft face, and with very bad teeth — one of them only a metal bar from which the porcelain has been chipped. His eyes shift and he laughs on the right side of his mouth. He believes that conspiracies, traitors and spies surround us on every side and he is determined to wipe them out.... At the same time, in his hatred, he gives you an impression of force and malign power.

By the summer of 1944, T.S. Matthews came around to the opinion that Chambers was completely right about the ruthlessness of Stalinist Russia, even though Matthews remained wary of Chambers's vague melodramatic pronouncements of international Soviet conspiracies. When the sitting Foreign News editor, John Osborne, went abroad to cover the war, Luce and Matthews chose Chambers to temporarily head the section. The injunction against Chambers writing or editing Soviet or Communist news was finally lifted, and he instantly became *Time*'s most contentious and infamous editor. Chambers felt vindicated — and elated. "I have spent some 15 years of my life actively preparing for FN," he told Luce. "Some of those years were spent close to the central dynamo that powers the politics of our time. In fact, I can say: I was there, I saw it...."

At a time when the public was encouraged by the government and much of the press to view the Soviets as an heroic ally, Chambers reversed *Time*'s news policy (by asserting his editorial slant) toward the U.S.S.R., making it plain that the Soviet Union was an enemy, not a friend, who was using World War II as a staging ground for World War III, and that China was vital to geopolitics: to lose China to Communism was to risk losing World War III.

"My assignment sent a shiver through most of *Time*'s staff," Chambers recalled, where his views were very well known and denounced vociferously. Yet without the indisputable backing of Luce and Matthews he wouldn't have lasted a month. For Chambers, it was more than just a fight for control of a seven-page section of a magazine, it was a battle to decide whether millions of Americans were going to get the facts about Soviet aggression, or whether those facts were going to be distorted or suppressed. Many writers under Chambers in the New York office soon transferred out of the department, or, failing that, tried to obstruct or sabotage his operation, but Chambers would work around the clock and do their work as well as his own. In Chambers's inimitable mind he ranked his colleagues — they knew little of the forces shaping history — into three disparate orders: fools, knaves, and little children ("knowing and clever little children, but knowing and clever chiefly about trifling things").

The recurring grievance against Chambers concerned his ingrained *dishonesty*. No doubt Chambers was an artful polemicist, but he was not a principled journalist. Lael Tucker Wertenbaker, who reported to him, remarked that Chambers's "interest in reportorial on-the-scene truth was limited to what served his 'greater truth,' which was whatever he conceived it to be. His conviction that ends justified means did not change when he lost faith in Communism. To report to him was quite useless unless it served his purposes."[7]

Filmore Calhoun, *Life*'s cable editor, said he was amazed to see that Chambers misinterpreted, left unprinted, or "weaseled around to one man's way of thinking [about]"[8] incoming cables. From Paris, Charles Wertenbaker protested Chambers's story of "Red riots," which had replaced his cable describing France's orderly new local governments. Stoyan Pribichevich's reports of the slaughter of partisans in Yugoslavia never saw print, and neither did the dispatches of Richard Lauterbach, Percy Knauth, Walter Graebner, and C.D. Jackson which related the emergence of popular governments backed by partisans who had fought Hitler. Annalee Jacoby, who co-authored *Thunder Out of China* (1946) with Theodore H. White, claimed Chambers fabricated a large part of her interview with Nationalist leader Generalissimo Chiang Kai-shek, published "with questions I did not ask and answers Chiang did not give."[9] So many of John Hersey's stories from Russia were suppressed by Chambers's "monotony of paranoia" that he stopped sending in political news.

When Stephen Laird, chief of correspondents for *Time* and *Life*, admonished Chambers for ignoring the cables, which he often immediately trashed, Chambers sloughed him off with the rationalization that his own sources were more accurate. He provided senior researchers with phony lists of scheduled stories and refused to coordinate Foreign News copy with other departments. Fact checkers protested the inaccuracy of his stories, but Chambers routinely replied: "Truth doesn't matter."[10] One editor maintained that Chambers drew from "his own private cache of material. Much of it came from fanatic right-wing magazines full of reports of Communist intrigue, some of them true, some false, and most unverifiable."[11]

Theodore H. White, *Time*'s star correspondent in China, bitterly complained that Chambers disfigured his long cable on the controversial recall of top American general Joseph Stilwell. White also denounced his friend Henry Luce, who "let the story of the crisis be edited into a lie, an entirely dishonorable story."[12] White's cable chronicled the chaos, decay, misery, and dissolution in the country — conditions which he blamed on Chiang Kai-shek's corrupt regime. But the cover story as edited by Chambers, which ran on November 13, 1944, argued that Chiang was "ruling high-handedly in order to safeguard the last vestiges of democratic principles in China," while at the same time the Kuomintang military "was locked in a life & death struggle with Japan." And if Chiang "were compelled to collaborate" with the Chinese Communists on their terms, then the Communists might soon replace him, thus "a Communist China (with its 450 million people) would turn to Russia (with its 200 million people) rather than to the U.S. (with its 130 million) as an international collaborator."

In 1939, at age 24, White became the first reporter in *Time*'s history to earn a byline, reporting behind enemy lines of Japanese atrocities. He soon became chief of the China bureau and a favorite correspondent of Luce. Before his views altered under the sway of General Stilwell, White had written flattering accounts of Chiang as China's indispensable man and a leader of great intelligence, with a deep understanding of the people. But in reality Chiang Kai-shek was the supreme warlord who presided over semi-independent provincial warlords and orchestrated a massive expropriation and military conscription racket. The Kuomintang (KMT) devised a quota system for army recruits in which local warlords eventually collected fourteen million men to serve unlimited terms, resulting in a military far too large to support effectively. Conscripts were forced to live off the land and walk great distances. They were always guarded and often tied together, with their clothes taken away at night to prevent escape. Suffering from all sorts of disease, these starving masses drifted like plagues through KMT-controlled areas where Communists had never been, stealing from peasants and billeting in their homes. The warlords colluded with landowning elites, local bankers, and merchants, and were only interested in maintaining their power. And since Chiang was certain the United States was going to defeat Japan, he saw no reason to discontinue his schemes. Senior U.S. officials in China were outraged by Chiang's corrupt preoccupations, none more so than General Joseph Stilwell.

Stilwell had served three tours in China between the wars and was fluent in Chinese. President Roosevelt selected him to coordinate the KMT forces in the war against Japan, and he became Chiang's chief of staff. But the generalissimo and the general were at odds from the start. Stilwell pressed Chiang to engage the enemy, but Chiang preferred a defensive posture for political reasons, or he would demand extraordinarily vast supplies before agreeing to fight. Moreover, Chiang wanted to keep Nationalist forces prepared to fight the Communists when the war with Japan was over. Convinced the U.S. was being swindled by gangsters, Stilwell sought to deny China further Lend-Lease aid, and he demanded from Washington sole command of the Chinese forces. But Chiang prevailed in the climactic political battle, and Stilwell was sent packing by FDR in October.

White got the exclusive *Time* story from Stilwell himself, and his detailed report was smuggled past Chiang's censors on Stilwell's flight back to the States. However, White also learned a political lesson — from the man Chiang Kai-shek called China's "single most powerful friend in America," Henry Luce. The malevolent dirty work was left to the Manichean Whittaker Chambers. Luce then punished White's outcry by barring any more political reporting from China. The next year Theodore White resigned. The "inaccuracy, stupidity, deceit," White wrote years later about Luce, Chambers, and the Stilwell cover story, "was the worst bit of journalism I have ever seen in America."[13]

All of *Time*'s European correspondents angrily protested to Matthews the mutilations and perversions of their dispatches by Foreign News editor Chambers — and they wanted Chambers ousted. It was a tricky situation for Matthews: his FN editor despised his correspondents as fools or worse, and an enraged corps of reporters considered the FN editor "insane or crooked or both." Matthews's job was to get the magazine out, but he was also responsible for *Time*'s reputation, which he knew to be biased. He had a choice to make: side with Communist-policy-is-cynical Chambers or with the Communist-policy-is-humanitarian correspondents. "My choice was to uphold Chambers." It was the correspondents who should have resigned, Matthews reflected triumphantly years later, because by late 1944 both he and Luce were "convinced that Chambers knew what he was talking about, and that they didn't."

However, Allen Grover, one of Luce's principal aides, took seriously the "real danger of an explosion, breaking up the staff,"[14] and he even suggested in a note to Luce that a lot of money could be saved by replacing the correspondents if Chambers continued to ignore them, though "I'm not saying what I think would happen to the magazine if we did." Grover, whom Luce occasionally called on to mediate problems with reporters, later said that Luce kept Chambers in authority (in fact, Luce was the "*only* reason" Chambers was still employed) because "he so *desperately* wanted ... to believe that [Chambers] was right in his violent anti–Communist views."[15] Luce responded to Grover's memo: "Yes, yes, of course I know all this. But what is needed is not just reiteration of the point but *constructive* action based on painstaking analysis." Luce ordered his editorial director, John Shaw Billings, to investigate the correspondents' complaints. Billings sent them surveys to evaluate Chambers's editing. The replies were unanimous; not one approved of Chambers. Their indictments ranged from unfair to vicious.

Caught between the revolt of his best reporters and his idealization of Chambers as an anti–Communist oracle, Luce was forced to brazen out a plan to placate much of the news staff while extolling Chambers for having butchered their dispatches. In a bewildering memo circulated to the home office editors and the overseas protesters in January 1945, Luce wrote:

In my opinion the correspondents did a fine job.... It is also my opinion that the Foreign News Department under Chambers did a fine job.... In general ... the Senior Correspondents wished to convey the information that the rulers of the world ... are well-meaning people who are trying to do their best for their own countries and the world. In general ... the Foreign News Department wished to convey the information that ... things are not going very well. The posture of events in January 1945 seems to have confirmed Editor Chambers about as fully as a news editor is ever confirmed.

To back up his observations, Luce noted the obvious Soviet military occupation of Eastern Europe and Communist encroachment in China. Chambers may have, Luce added, "given a disproportionate amount of space and emphasis to the problem of Russia." *Yet—* "Overemphasis may rightly be criticized but there were good reasons for erring in this direction...."

But behind the scenes, and before Henry Luce even wrote that memo, a compromise was worked out which eviscerated much of Chambers's command and control of Foreign News. First of all, John Osborne was still the official FN editor; Chambers had only been filling in since August while Osborne was overseas. Until mid–December 1944, Chambers carried the title Back-of-the-Book editor and was paid $12,000 a year; but on December 18, according to his personnel file, he received a $2,800 raise and a new job title: Editor of Foreign News, *Canada and Latin America*.[16] John Osborne, meanwhile, was slated to head up a new section called "International," which, as *Time*'s Robert Elson later wrote, would "be free to take over all stories on international relations from both the U.S. at War and Foreign News sections." Luce let it be known that dispatches could now be skirted around Chambers and directed to the new International department, which debuted in February. Osborne subsequently wrote: "I took the job only when I got Luce's promise ... that Chambers would never again replace me in any job or that he never again would be put in a position to misuse and distort the reports of *Time*'s foreign correspondents."[17]

In his panegyrical biography of Chambers, Sam Tanenhaus distorts this episode, choosing to falsely glorify his hero: "Luce's memo dealt a blow to the correspondents, as he had known it would. As a sop, he created a supplement to Foreign News, International, which provided a home for stories Chambers would not print.... FN remained Chambers's preserve, at Luce's insistence."

Former *Time* editor Thomas Griffith recalled that Chambers was indeed "judged to be the winner" of Luce's memo, but the "victory came to seem less clear-cut.... Readers may have been baffled by two sections seeming to cover the same territory, but the International section enabled correspondents to get stories into the magazine without being subjected to Chambers's whims and biases."

And Allen Weinstein, who generously provided his research to Tanenhaus (who chose to ignore this), wrote in *Perjury, the Hiss-Chambers Case*: "Despite his genial defense of Chambers, Luce moved to curb his authority over handling foreign news.... Chambers clearly had won the battle for Luce's approval, but had lost the war for control of *Time*'s foreign-news output."

Chambers remained a FN editor, but now he was assigning stories to himself as well as editing them because many correspondents refused to work with him. He remonstrated that no other editor "would have stood for a week the insubordination, hostility and insulting behavior to which certain members of my staff treated me." That many of the best minds at *Time* appeared to him to believe the Soviet Union must be conciliated to avert World War III infuriated Chambers. It was "willful historical self-delusion" by those who had just fiercely supported a war in which their great outcry had been against appeasement. The news from day to day seemed to prove Chambers's point, but few other than Luce and Matthews believed him. Yet ultimately Chambers proved to be the opposite of a Cassandra whose accurate predictions no one believed; he was a false prophet whose conjectures never materialized, but his credibility became almost universally accepted well into the 21st century. He foresaw "history" racing towards a denouement. "I am forecasting a world," Chambers wrote, "in which Communism may have so far extended its power that the U.S. will be islanded and outnumbered so that the questions of the day will be whether the last fringe war is to be fought in the U.S. and how to avoid it. That is where I am assuming the socialist beachheads come in. They will provide the mediating forces with Communism."[18]

Moreover, Chambers was by turns malicious and clever — and pathologically vindictive. John Osborne recalled that in 1945 Chambers had "cited as evidence of Communist influence on *Time* the fact that I had edited and published a favorable story about Hiss in his role as secretary general of the founding United Nations conference.... Chambers didn't know that Henry Luce, who attended the conference, was impressed by Hiss and ordered me to have the story written and printed." Yet in 1949, during Alger Hiss's first perjury trial, Chambers was questioned about that same flattering Hiss story *Time* ran in May 1945. "You remember that?" Hiss's attorney Lloyd Stryker asked. "I believe I wrote that," Chambers testified. And only a few months before Chambers relieved Osborne as FN editor in the summer of 1944, he wrote an article on foreign policy for the *American Mercury* magazine under the pen name "John Land," praising the State Department for its cautious and astute relations with the Soviets — while at the same time he was vilifying senior State Department officials as Communists. This inscrutable behavior, psychoanalyst Meyer Zeligs contended, "seems explicable only in terms of Chambers' private necessity to repeat the endless cycle of doing and undoing, sinning and repenting." "He was always playing a role," Allen Grover recalled. "He thought of himself as the savior of the world — an anti–Communist Christ."[19]

By the summer of 1945 Chambers was again habitually working two days at a stretch without sleep, overeating, swilling too much coffee, and (though having quit cigarettes) constantly smoking a pipe. On August 23 he briefly blacked out on the train from Baltimore to New York and arrived at the office trembling. He had broken down again from exhaustion, nerves, and overindulgence. It is uncertain whether Chambers asked for a week off to rest or if Matthews insisted, but his file shows that he was out of the office for two weeks, until September 6 when he returned for a week and was then off again for an undisclosed duration. In any event he was forthwith reassigned from Editor of Foreign News, Canada and Latin America, to Editor of Books. Both Weinstein and Tanenhaus claimed that Chambers soon after asked for his FN job back, but Chambers says nothing in *Witness* about wanting to return. In addition, Grover later said that he and two editors (whom Grover did not identify) wanted Chambers permanently removed from the news side of the business, and they gave Luce an ultimatum — either they go or Chambers goes. Grover recollected that Chambers was "sent off on compassionate leave" that day.

"Harry Luce was certainly wrong to let Chambers disfigure the magazine (and its credibility) with his twisted personal view," Grover wrote in 1969, "but Harry and Whit were both right in the sense that they saw the Russian threat ... and were willing to take an unpopular stand at a time when many Americans really believed we could be buddies with Moscow for no better reason than we had all got drunk together when the Armies met."

Such were the harrowing milestones which marked an interval of Whittaker Chambers's life at *Time* magazine, a period he chronicles without irony in his autobiography as "The Tranquil Years."

Chapter VIII

Wall Street Lawyer

"Alger had no street smarts — and for a man who'd seen so much of the world, I thought at the time that this was a little strange. And in retrospect I find it even stranger. I don't think he ever realized the strength of the forces that had been released against him."[1] — Kenneth Simon, former Hiss attorney, 2001

Was Alger Hiss ever a dues-paying Communist? This question was never addressed in any depth throughout the entire Hiss Case, which included Congressional hearings, grand jury proceedings, a libel suit, and two long trials after Hiss had been indicted for perjury. Though rumors (initiated, as we shall later see, by Chambers and the influential anti–Communist writer-editor Isaac Don Levine) had circulated around Washington for years, it was Whittaker Chambers who solely and publicly — under oath and subject to prosecution for perjury — asserted that Alger Hiss had been and perhaps still was a secret member of the Communist Party who had infiltrated the U.S. government. Chambers maintained that Hiss's wife, Priscilla, and his younger brother Donald, were also secret members. Both Alger and Donald immediately denied the charges publicly before HUAC, where Chambers made the charges. For reasons inexplicable other than Alger's more prominent government service during the New Deal, thus providing conservatives with a weightier liberal villain, HUAC dropped its investigation of Donald Hiss and others accused by Chambers and focused only on Alger. Chambers stepped up the import of his charges when he provided details (though most were either embellished or false) of a close friendship with Hiss to Nixon and his subcommittee in a private session. In a subsequent private meeting with HUAC, Hiss continued to deny ever knowing anyone named Whittaker Chambers and could not identify various photographs of Chambers as anyone he had known under any name, though Hiss always qualified the denials by saying that the photos of Chambers looked "not unfamiliar." When the two men were confronted in yet another executive HUAC session, Hiss was able to identify Chambers as a freelance writer (but named George Crosley) he had known in the mid–1930s. But, Hiss claimed, the relationship was an official one, related to his work at the time on Senator Nye's committee. Yet Chambers/Crosley (or just "Carl," according to Chambers) lived in Hiss's former apartment for two months in 1935 and drove Hiss's car on occasion, and, Hiss volunteered, Crosley and his wife and infant daughter stayed with the Hisses for a few days before moving in to the apartment. These were simply goodwill gestures, in Hiss's view, made to a struggling family who sublet his apartment during the Depression, and other than that there was no social relationship — and certainly no Communist conspiracy — between them.

And that is where this narrative now stands. To fast forward for a moment, a televised HUAC hearing on the Hiss-Chambers affair, examined in the next chapter, was held on August 25, 1948, in which Hiss fared poorly, and from then on public opinion was squarely against him. But then Hiss turned to the legal system, where he felt confident of vindication. He filed a $75,000 civil suit against Chambers for defamation of character. Chambers was deposed in early November by Hiss's attorney, who requested that Chambers provide evidence to support his charges, and two weeks later Chambers produced copies, typed and handwritten, of State Department documents which he said Hiss had given him. But now Chambers significantly changed the story he had previously fed to HUAC and the public. In the initial version he pronounced himself a former functionary of the American Communist Party with no ties to the U.S.S.R. and no knowledge of espionage, and that he had quit the CP and denounced its ideology in 1937. In fact, he accepted a Federal relief job under the name Chambers in October 1937. Now Chambers swore he had been a courier for Soviet intelligence and that Hiss gave him the documents for delivery to Russia. Hiss admitted that he wrote the handwritten notes but denied giving them or any other papers to Chambers. The typewritten copies, according to an FBI documents examiner, were typed on the same machine used to type Hiss household letters found from the 1930s. (The actual typewriter used to write those letters was given away by the Hisses in late 1937 or early 1938 to the family of their former maid, yet it was Hiss who later recovered the machine — or one very similar — before his first trial in 1949 and presented it as evidence.) The typed documents were all dated within the first four months of 1938, obliging Chambers to fudge the date of his defection from 1937 to mid–April 1938. These documents were turned over to the Justice Department for investigation in November 1948. However, in early December Chambers turned over more evidence of espionage to HUAC. He had hidden a quantity of 35mm film in a hollowed-out pumpkin on his farm (the "pumpkin papers"), and a few of the frames of those photographed State Department documents revealed Alger Hiss's initials.

As ominous as the situation portended for Alger Hiss, Chambers too was in deep trouble with the grand jury because he swore to them in October without qualification that he knew nothing about espionage, and now he recanted. Ultimately, their vote to indict only Hiss for perjury on December 15 was not unanimous.

Throughout the two long trials (the first ended with the jury undecided) the prosecution never asked their chief witness, Chambers, about the Communist dues he allegedly collected from Hiss or how he knew Hiss had really been a Communist. When questioned earlier by HUAC in August 1948 how he knew Hiss was a Communist, Chambers sidestepped the question by saying Hiss merely "submitted" himself as such, and Chambers presented HUAC with three separate and conflicting accounts of how Hiss supposedly paid party dues. On August 3 he testified that he did not collect the dues, they were handed over to him by Henry Collins, the Ware Group's treasurer who collected dues from the "whole apparatus." Four days later Chambers swore that all dues were "collected individually," and that he personally obtained Hiss's (and his wife's) party dues once a month for two or three years, "as long as I knew him." Then on August 25 Chambers testified he collected dues from Hiss "at least on one occasion, and I would think on at least three occasions." Chambers remarked several times that Hiss paid ten percent of his salary to the Communist Party, and he was pious about paying regularly. No member of HUAC questioned Chambers's contradictory statements, conspicuous in the printed record, and Chambers could not substantiate any of them. Furthermore, in a March 1946 interview with the FBI, Chambers stated that he had "absolutely no information ... that Hiss ... was an actual dues paying member of the Communist Party." Sixty years later still not a shred of evidence has appeared incriminating Alger Hiss, Priscilla Hiss, or Donald Hiss as members of the Communist Party at any time.

Alger Hiss's extensive legal and investigative files have been open without restriction for over fifty years to scholars, journalists, and historians. Two comprehensive biographies of Hiss appeared in his lifetime, and more are in progress. For decades he openly answered all questions from interviewers. Hiss pursued vindication by the courts, if not by public opinion, for thirty years after his perjury conviction, and he wrote a book about his case in 1957 and a memoir in 1988. His friends and relatives rejected — and continue to reject — the very notion that he had ever been a Communist or a Soviet agent; there was nothing in his nature or family background suggesting such radicalism or betrayal of his professed values. Even the malignantly credulous G. Edward White, author of *Alger Hiss's Looking-Glass Wars* (2004), a factually distorted psychobiography of Hiss, replete with specious theories about why he became a Commie spy, reluctantly admitted at the outset that "there is no evidentiary smoking gun revealing Alger Hiss's motivation." "Alger Hiss," White wrote, "as he turned 30, may have been attracted to the secret life of an underground espionage agent. The life of an agent offered opportunities to exercise one's intellect.... So, over time, Hiss found that by being a spy, and keeping others from knowing that, he could find a deep sense of satisfaction, even a kind of inner peace." That sort of speculation and license-taking, though common among those who despise Alger Hiss for political reasons, does not qualify as plausible biographical interpretation.

Born in 1904 and raised along with two sisters and two brothers in a solidly middle-class section of Baltimore, Alger Hiss's childhood memories were "of a lively and cheerful household, full of the bustle of constant comings and goings.... Dinner in the evening was noisy, full of animated talk and much laughter. It took little to make us laugh." They were a religious household; the family regularly went to the neighborhood Episcopal Church, and the children attended Sunday school. Hiss remained a faithful Episcopalian all his life, including the years when he knew Chambers/Crosley, who quixotically insisted Hiss had been forbidden to worship by his Communist superiors.

In his youth and early manhood Hiss manifested a judicious and conservative temperament. His moral code, prominent throughout his life, consisted of "honor, loyalty, pride, an aversion to exploitation of others, and independence." Yet Hiss self-deprecatingly characterized his life up to the early 1930s as "The Progress of a Prig." During college at Johns Hopkins in the mid–1920s where he majored in history and Romance languages, Hiss complacently scorned politics as demeaning scut work performed by a parasitic class of citizen-politicians, and the Russian Revolution was rarely if ever mentioned in classes. Hiss's congenial classmates shared his negative attitude toward politics, reflecting the conventional wisdom of their elders who also thought of politics as dirty business. Their natural hero was the cynical critic H.L. Mencken who wrote in those years for the Baltimore *Sun* papers.

Business as a future livelihood was also distasteful to Hiss. He was chiefly interested in the intellectual currents of the day — wit and iconoclasm, and to his friends he was nothing if not a dandy.

But Alger shed his provincial conservatism during his years at Harvard Law School, from September 1926 to June 1929. Early on he discovered that lawyers took politics seriously; to ignore politics was to default to others control of major affairs of one's life. Political trends often determined court decisions, regulations, and legislation. Moreover, the entire complex of laws and the Constitution itself were produced by a highly sophisticated and evolving political philosophy. Issues involving management and labor, government and labor, and labor's point of view especially interested Hiss. For the *Harvard Law Review* he wrote on the constitutionality of yellow-dog contracts in which employees promise not to join a union, or face dismissal if they do, and he contributed a lengthy piece on federal jurisdiction over foreign corporations. Remembered by one of his classmates as "the most distinguished man in our class," Alger was appointed to the editorial board of the *Law Review* in his second year, serving with Lee Pressman (who a few years later joined the Communist Party and the Ware Group — admitting so in 1950, which confirmed Chambers's 1948 accusation of his involvement), and Edward McLean and Harold Rosenwald, both of whom later represented Hiss during his perjury trials.

An altruist with a deep desire to serve, Hiss encountered at Cambridge the doctrine of disinterested, dedicated public service. And it wasn't just a high-flown tenet of the lecture hall but was exemplified by the professors, particularly Felix Frankfurter, already prominent nationally as a friend of leaders throughout the country and who served in various federal agencies during World War I. Frankfurter advised New York Governor Franklin D. Roosevelt in 1930 and 1931, became a member of the New Deal brain trust, and was later appointed to the Supreme Court by FDR. Indisputably the most combative and contentious teacher on campus, Frankfurter was not very popular with his students or the faculty, though often surrounded by a clique of admiring pupils, Hiss among them, while he laid down the law in his didactic style. He was a brash and outspoken polemicist, and the leader of the faculty liberals at a time when most of his colleagues and even most of the students were politically conservative. As one of Frankfurter's top students, Hiss was invited to the professor's seminars on law, government, and social philosophy, and Hiss frequently visited the Frankfurter home where he socialized with students, teachers, and local writers and lawyers.

In his final year at Harvard Law, Alger Hiss received a handwritten note from Supreme Court justice Oliver Wendell Holmes, Jr., informing him that on the recommendation of Frankfurter, the Justice had chosen him as his clerk ("private secretary" in those days) for the following term, beginning October 1929. The 88-year-old Holmes, appointed to the high court in 1902 by Theodore Roosevelt, presently became the most important influence of Hiss's life.

Holmes too had studied at Harvard Law School and graduated in 1866 after his Civil War service, where he had been wounded several times and once left for dead on the battlefield. He later practiced law in Boston and taught law courses at Harvard College. Since his appointment to the Supreme Court he employed a new secretary/clerk each year, and these working relationships were necessarily informal. Alger, like the clerks before him, became part of the household, taking lunch and tea there and dining with Holmes if Court was not in session. But Hiss distinguished himself from his predecessors and drew even closer to the philosopher-judge by reading aloud to him after working hours, a pleasure for both, though it took some initial persuading on Hiss's part because Holmes felt it might be awkward and too personal. However, the reading sessions delighted the judge, and Hiss's successors, including his brother Donald, continued the trend even after Holmes retired from the bench in 1932.

Thirty years after the judge's death in 1935, Hiss told an interviewer he had keenly admired Holmes's

wit and gift of language, his vast reading and incisive opinions in philosophy and general literature, including the classics (he read Greek, Latin, German, and French), his taste in art, his
knowledge of history and world culture, his courtliness and graciousness of manner, his high
standards in intellectual matters and in character and personal conduct. He referred often to
the lessons in democracy he had gained from his army experience, which tempered his patrician
youthful outlook and gave him an appreciation of the worth of individuals from less privileged
origins — their courage, honesty, manliness, dignity.[2]

However, Holmes believed the doctrines of socialism and communism were ludicrous
and muddleheaded. (And there is no evidence that Alger Hiss believed differently, about
communism at any rate.) He was convinced that most initiatives in support of the working
class were futile (though here Hiss did not agree), since (as the judge once expounded) "the
crowd now has substantially all there is." Holmes's "personal sympathies," Louis Menand
wrote in *The Metaphysical Club* (2001), "were entirely with the capitalists. He not only considered them virtuous engines of social wealth; he had a kind of schoolboy's respect for their
energy and willpower." Indeed, Holmes sided with J.P. Morgan in his first notable dissent
in 1904 as a Supreme Court justice, enraging the trustbusting Teddy Roosevelt who had
appointed him to the Court two years earlier. When Holmes later emerged, Menand noted,
"as a consistent judicial defender of economic reform and of free speech, he became a hero
to progressives and civil libertarians."

If Alger Hiss was a secret underground Communist by 1934, as Whittaker Chambers
claimed, he evinced not a scintilla of radicalism or revolutionary zeal by the close of 1930.
And notwithstanding the liberalizing influences of Harvard Law, Felix Frankfurter, and Justice Holmes, Alger Hiss was no more politically engaged or willing to dedicate himself to
public service than he was in 1926. Upon completion of his government service in the
employ of Justice Holmes, he immediately began a career as a corporate lawyer.

Another alleged politically radicalizing influence on Alger Hiss was Priscilla Fansler
Hobson, whom he married in December 1929, two months into his clerkship with Holmes.
They met in 1924 but were not romantically involved until 1929. A year older than Alger
and a Bryn Mawr graduate, she entered Yale University as a graduate student in literature
when Alger was a junior at Johns Hopkins. While visiting family friends of the Hisses in
Baltimore in the spring of 1925, Priscilla announced to a stunned Alger (who was obviously
falling in love with her) and a few friends on their way to a local dance that she was engaged
to marry Thayer Hobson, a fellow graduate student at Yale she had recently met. But their
subsequent marriage failed and they separated not long after their son, Timothy, was born
in September 1926. Priscilla took a job as a copy editor and office supervisor, and in the
fall of 1928 attended Columbia University where she was awarded a Master's degree in literature the following summer. Alger, meanwhile, wrote to Priscilla after hearing of her
divorce, and they were reunited in New York in the spring of 1929. As for Priscilla's "extremist" political views during those years, her ex-husband Thayer Hobson (they were divorced
in January 1929) remarked years later: "Priscilla was an impractical idealist, interested primarily in art, literature, and music. It was just that oil and water don't mix, and we never
should have married."[3]

After completing his year as Holmes's law clerk in October 1930, Hiss joined Choate,
Hall and Stewart, a venerable Boston law firm. He worked chiefly as an assistant to one of
the partners on a prolonged case involving the Gillette Safety Razor Co. Hiss would have
been content to remain indefinitely at the firm, but Priscilla did not like living in Boston
and could not find suitable work or activity. She applied for, and was awarded, a research

grant for a study of fine arts from the Carnegie Corporation, but the work required moving to New York City. The couple decided to relocate. However, Alger remained in Boston for a few more months to complete his legal work while Priscilla and Timothy went ahead, renting an apartment near Columbia University.

In the spring of 1932 Hiss was hired by the Wall Street law firm Cotton, Franklin, Wright and Gordon. Committed to his work as a corporate attorney, he had given little thought to the worsening social conditions brought on by the stock market crash and the Depression, but when he moved to New York the growing unemployment and massive economic distress were brought into sharp relief. "I became acutely aware of the shallowness of my conventional concern for the welfare of others," Hiss later wrote. "I saw daily the growing breadlines and soup kitchens, the shanty towns in parks and vacant lots, the beggars along with men who masked their appeal for alms by 'selling' an apple."

Priscilla, in the weeks before Alger joined her and Timothy in New York, occasionally volunteered her time after her studies at a Socialist Party feeding station near her apartment, and she chipped in to pay for the sandwiches and coffee. She registered to vote in 1932 as a Socialist, was a member of the Party from 1930 to 1932, and she and Alger sometimes attended Socialist Party meetings on Claremont Avenue. Alger was never a member, and when they moved to Central Park West in the spring of 1932, away from the Upper Broadway feeding station, Priscilla gave up her association with the Socialist Party.

Alger, too, wanted to help the victims of the Depression and do something "constructive in a private capacity," he later remarked. He offered his legal expertise to a small group of young, like-minded New York lawyers who had formed an association, the International Juridical Association, and issued bulletins for labor lawyers and those representing struggling farmers. Without realizing it, they were part of the grass roots of the New Deal. In the winter of 1932-33 Hiss attended a few meetings of contributors, wrote two or three articles, and gave a speech at one gathering concerning foreclosures of farm mortgages. The group was composed of other corporate lawyers interested, as Hiss was, in social reform and economic justice for workers and sharecroppers, and in steering the legal system to the needs of these often helpless people. Also members were Hiss's Harvard Law contemporaries Lee Pressman and Nathan Witt. One member, Jerome Hellerstein, years later recalled that in 1932 the Association was certainly "liberal." "Some few of them were probably out and out Communists.... However, there were many other liberals who were not Communists.... Lee Pressman and Nat Witt also were active in the group. They were not Communists, at least at that time." Hellerstein claimed he had not been a member of either the Socialist or Communist Party.

By President Franklin Roosevelt's inauguration on March 4, 1933, Alger Hiss was completing his first year as a Wall Street lawyer, working on antitrust cases for clients such as AT&T, GE, and RCA. He had a promising future with a solid firm — while the country was experiencing an economic catastrophe.

As FDR took office, unemployment exceeded twenty-five percent; thousand of banks had failed and most states had shut all their banks; the New York Stock Exchange and the Chicago Board of Trade were closed; United States Steel was idle, having laid off all its full-time workers; industrial production had fallen more than fifteen percent in the past year alone and more than fifty percent since 1929; GNP had declined by thirty percent in four years; millions of farmers were devastated by falling prices while mountains of unsold grain accumulated in the open.

Roosevelt immediately called a special session of Congress and a nationwide "holiday" for banks. In a single day Congress passed the Emergency Banking Law, and in his first "fireside chat," only a few days into his administration, Roosevelt assured the public that their money could safely be returned to the banks. When banks opened the following day, deposits far exceeded withdrawals, and the trend continued. The jitters subsided and the banking crisis, if not the Depression, had bottomed out.

Another national crisis crying out for immediate legislation was the despairing plight of tens of millions of American farmers caught in a double bind of overproduction and low prices. The profits and markets farmers enjoyed, particularly during World War I and its aftermath, were long gone. Jerome Frank, head of the legal division of the Department of Agriculture, drafted the bill to create the Agricultural Adjustment Administration (AAA), which the Senate was resisting. So by late March, only weeks into FDR's first term, Frank urgently needed a staff of lawyers to write compromise amendments right away if the bill was to become law before the planting season was too far along. Provided with the names of a few first rate young lawyers by FDR's friend and adviser Felix Frankfurter, Jerome Frank called Alger Hiss.

Hiss considered the offer but turned Frank down, just as he had previously spurned an opportunity to join the Justice Department in the Hoover Administration. Hiss wanted to make a career in private legal practice. Moreover, he was in the midst of two important cases, and had established warm and friendly relations with his associates. And though joining the New Deal was alluring, Hiss felt an obligation to his employer and could not leave suddenly. He informed Frank that he wasn't in a position to even ask them — the firm's partners certainly weren't Roosevelt supporters, and they wouldn't approve.

In early April, as the AAA bill made its way to the full Senate for debate, Hiss received a peremptory telegram from the scrappy Felix Frankfurter himself. "On the basis of national emergency," the wire implored, he must accept Jerome Frank's offer. A summons from a major player like Frankfurter couldn't be rejected ("I accepted on the basis of conscience and civic duty," Hiss wrote fifty-five years later, "It was like enlisting in time of war"), and Hiss was grateful that Cotton Franklin didn't disapprove after all. In fact, the firm hoped Hiss would eventually return after the crisis, bringing his experience and contacts back with him.

Though he ultimately changed his mind about remaining in the private sector and joined the New Deal, Hiss had been conscious for years "of the shallowness of my conventional concern for the welfare of others." He was now convinced by his own observations (and the lessons of Frankfurter) that only massive government intervention could meliorate the economic devastation of the Depression. Hiss later wrote:

> My becoming a New Dealer had not been a matter of course. Like many of my contemporaries, I had found that my social and political values were tested and altered by the Great Depression. That vast misery resulting from the economic dislocation it caused during its first several years forced my sense of social responsibility to become more concrete, where it had once been abstract. The seriousness of my new social commitment in turn required changed political beliefs. The threat of a breakdown in our democratic social order aroused my sense of patriotism and hastened my readiness for true political commitment.

The Agricultural Adjustment Administration, created by the Agricultural Adjustment Act of May 1933, was integrated into the Department of Agriculture, already a vast bureaucracy with forty thousand employees. The AAA's basic purpose was contracting with farmers, wholesalers, and food processors to reduce production. Jerome Frank, an impassioned liberal who later became a Securities and Exchange Commission officer and a federal judge, was

appointed general counsel for the agency. Frank deputized two assistant general counsels —
Alger Hiss and none other than Lee Pressman, Hiss's law school friend whose involvement
with radicalism and the Communist Party would later haunt Hiss's nightmare confrontations
with HUAC and Whittaker Chambers. Hiss was put in charge of twenty-five lawyers who
drafted contracts for paying farmers to reduce their output. At the age of twenty-eight Hiss
had taken on major responsibility and authority years before he could ever have expected
such power in private practice.

There soon developed within the AAA feuding factions; the old-line pragmatic agrar-
ians were at loggerheads with Jerome Frank and Alger Hiss and the other young "shock
troops" and social reformers of the legal section. It was a fight over what the New Deal was
really supposed to be. As the reformers saw it, their charge was to overhaul a crisis-ridden
and corrupt system which included agribusiness, the Farm Bureau, and even agricultural
colleges. The pragmatists, though not fundamentally opposed to social reform, believed the
AAA's priority was to rescue farmers from the ongoing crisis, and if that meant compromise
with the farming establishment — the powerful congressional committees, the slaughter-
houses, the distributors, the Farm Bureau — then so be it; nothing could be accomplished
otherwise.

Both sides believed only they represented Secretary Henry A. Wallace's aims. The agrar-
ians laid claim to Wallace by virtue of his family's longstanding affiliation with land grant
colleges, and his bona fides as a plant scientist and editor of farm journals. But the reformers
saw Wallace as their mirror image — young, idealistic, and determined to mitigate the economic injustices inherent in the agricultural market system. In fact, Wallace was part of
both camps, and managed to stay in the good graces of each and rise above the fray by
leaving the daily administrative duties to assistants while traveling around the country pro-
moting the New Deal and its innovative farm program.

Wallace blamed such disputes on the leadership style of President Roosevelt. "In this
administration," Wallace later said, "the objectives were experimental and not clearly stated.
Therefore, there was certain to be, from the White House down, a certain amount of what
seemed to be intrigue. I did not think that this situation would be remedied until the president abandoned to a considerable extent his experimental and somewhat concealed
approach."[4]

The inevitable showdown occurred in early 1935. The aggressive Jerome Frank, head
of the legal division, led the reformers. Chester Davis, the mild-mannered agrarian who
had replaced George Peek as chief of the AAA, commanded the opposing pragmatists. As
John C. Culver and John Hyde recount in their biography of Wallace:

> Davis had about had his fill of Frank and the young lawyers. The legal division's "sharp tricks" —
> its delays, its hidden agenda disguised in legalistic language, its leaks to reporters — were enough
> to make Davis talk about leaving government altogether. The liberals, in turn, saw Davis as ...
> all too ready to do business with the big corporations and plantation owners who stood on the
> necks of consumers and farm laborers.

The final eruption was over tenant cotton farmers in Arkansas. Some tenants worked
for wages, but almost half of them were "sharecroppers" who received a fraction of the crop
in lieu of wages and lived in shacks provided by the landlord, and even bought marked-up
groceries from the owner's store. Their hardships were exacerbated, the liberals argued, by
the AAA program itself. Though the AAA contracts obliged plantation owners to share government subsidies with sharecroppers, the injunction was seldom enforced, or the landlords
imposed onerous new conditions on the tenants, sometimes evicting them off the farm.

After an absentee landowner in Arkansas evicted some forty tenant families, share-croppers organized the Southern Tenant Farmers Union, an association which fought for their economic and political rights in the courts, in the press, through lobbying agricultural institutions, and by popular public opinion. The landlords, however, fought back with political muscle, economic intimidation, and violence. The AAA liberals were not so naïve as to think the sharecropping system could be dismantled, but they sought to close a loophole in the law that created the AAA, an "insofar as possible" clause defining benefits to tenants, to which the plantation owners resorted to default on payments. By eliminating the law's ambiguity, the legal reformers could provide the Southern Tenant Farmers Union with sanc-tions for fighting the owners in court. A "reinterpretation" of the statute was drafted by Alger Hiss, Frank's top lieutenant on cotton issues.

Jerome Frank knew that Chester Davis would never approve the reinterpretation, so he waited until the AAA director was out of town before attempting to bluff it through. Frank cajoled Victor Christgau, second in command at the agency and a liberal former con-gressman, into unveiling the change by way of telegram to local AAA offices; and Christgau, doing his part, induced a top Department of Agriculture official to send the telegram in the name of Henry Wallace.

Because the reinterpretation completely changed the basis on which cotton contracts had been enforced since the inception of the AAA, the telegram provoked an immediate backlash. An Arkansas congressman and the head of his state's Farm Bureau were in Wallace's office denouncing the reversal before Wallace even knew anything about the telegram. And when a highly agitated Davis returned to Washington, he gave Wallace an ultimatum: either the legal department liberals would be fired or he would quit. Wallace gave Davis complete authority to handle the situation as he wished because Wallace was convinced that from a legal viewpoint the reformers/liberals had nothing to stand on. "[T]hey allowed their social preconceptions," Wallace later said, "to lead them to something which was not only inde-fensible from a practical, agricultural point of view, but also bad law."

What became known as the "purge of the liberals" commenced the following day. Davis fired Jerome Frank, telling him he was "an outright revolutionary, whether you realize it or not." Assistant counsel Lee Pressman was next to go, followed by Gardner Jackson of the consumer affairs office and Francis Shea, head of legal's opinions section. Victor Christgau was reprimanded and demoted, but he remained in the AAA. Yet Alger Hiss, who drafted the explosive reinterpretation, was not fired. Later that day those terminated demanded a meeting with Wallace. Believing that Davis was attempting to engineer a coup against Wal-lace himself, they wanted to hear what Wallace had to say. The Secretary agreed to see them, but only two of them, so the group chose Frank and Hiss as their representatives. Wallace's account of the session was later recorded in his diary: "I indicated that I believed Frank and Hiss had been loyal to me at all times, but it was necessary to clear up an administrative situation and that I agreed with Davis. They wanted to hear it direct from the horse's mouth."

So why wasn't Alger Hiss fired? First of all, Chester Davis — and literally all of Hiss's colleagues throughout his years of government service — did not adjudge him as a radical or a revolutionary. He was a New Deal liberal, certainly, but in the political context of the time a liberal was not considered a watered-down socialist or a useful idiot for Soviet Com-munism; those equations would only later become commonplace rants of withering con-servatives and reactionaries who invariably mistake all social and economic redress, regardless of need, as misguided if not evil statism. Secondly, Hiss drafted the reinterpretation at

Frank's behest while on loan to a Senate committee for much of the previous six months and was not involved in the legal department's "sharp tricks" that so infuriated Davis. But with Frank gone and his other work now a fulltime commitment, Hiss formally resigned from the AAA in March 1935. The program was declared unconstitutional by the Supreme Court on January 6, 1936.

In the summer of 1934 Republican Senator Gerald Nye of North Dakota asked the AAA for the loan of Hiss's services, and so Hiss took on a second job as counsel to the Senate Committee to Investigate the Munitions Industry. The Nye Committee, as it was known, was established a few months earlier in response to the country's growing isolationism and resentment of corporate profiteering from weapons sales. Many hearings explored the massive loans by U.S. bankers to the Allied Powers prior to America's entry into World War I. The committee believed the loans gave the bankers undue influence and interest in seeing that the Allies were victorious and repaid the loans, even if it entailed lobbying the U.S. government to enter the war.

In the latter months of 1934 (the exact date is uncertain) Whittaker Chambers arrived in Washington and entered the life of Alger Hiss in the guise, according to Hiss, of a freelance writer named George Crosley, an alias that Chambers later admitted he may have used when he knew Hiss, though usually when Chambers retold his story he insisted that his underground confederates, including Hiss, knew him only as Carl. Hiss remembered their initial meeting as occurring about the winter of 1934-35, while Chambers recounted in *Witness* that his first visit to the Hisses' home was a sultry summer night. Hiss's work as counsel to the Nye Committee included providing students, researchers, and writers — such as Crosley — information about the committee's investigations and hearings. But Chambers maintained that Hiss was already a secret member of the Communist Party who belonged to the Ware Group, an underground unit in Washington, and that not long before his first call at the Hiss household he had met briefly with Hiss in the presence of J. Peters, the head of the American CP underground, and Harold Ware, a Communist and agricultural expert whose secret unit was composed mostly of Department of Agriculture lawyers and economists. Peters and Ware decided that Chambers would be in charge of transferring Hiss from the unit's "Apparatus A" to a parallel "Apparatus B."

Chambers testified publicly before HUAC on August 3, 1948, that the "head of the underground group at the time I knew it was Nathan Witt, an attorney for the National Labor Relations Board. Later, John Abt became the leader. Lee Pressman was also a member of this group, as was Alger Hiss." Chambers also named Donald Hiss, Charles Kramer, Henry Collins, and Victor Perlo as members. Alger and Donald Hiss immediately denied Chambers's charges, but all the others asserted their right not to answer most of HUAC's questions.

But on August 28, 1950, seven months after Alger Hiss had been convicted of perjury and sentenced to prison for five years, Lee Pressman once again appeared before HUAC, this time testifying without exercising his constitutional privileges.

The Un-American Activities Committee had learned through the public press that Pressman had recently resigned from the American Labor Party (not long after the outbreak of the Korean War) because he believed the organization was controlled by Communists. The committee felt that Pressman's testimony might reveal that his repudiation of Communist associations had been complete and that his action was taken in good faith. However, the committee informed Pressman that they would "not be satisfied with a mere perfunctory repudiation of the Communist Party." He was expected to name names and expose subversive activities. Pressman agreed to answer their questions, and also to expose distortions in HUAC's record regarding his past activities.

Pressman recalled for the committee that in the spring of 1933 he was offered employment in the legal division of the AAA by Jerome Frank, who had offered a similar position to Alger Hiss. Pressman accepted the job, but, he told the committee, he was not responsible for getting Alger Hiss a job in AAA, as some people believed; nor did Hiss help him get a job there. In his desire to see improvements in the domestic economy and the destruction of "Hitlerism" abroad, Pressman joined a Communist group in Washington sometime in 1934. He remained active in the group for about a year, until he was fired from the AAA and subsequently left Washington for private practice in New York City. "And at that time," Pressman swore, "I discontinued any further participation in the group from that date until the present."

He was asked to join the Communist Party by Harold Ware, Pressman continued, and was assigned to a group composed of himself and three others — John Abt, Nathan Witt, and Charles Kramer — all employees of AAA. They met once or twice a month to discuss Communist literature, books and magazines mostly, provided by Ware. After Ware was killed in an automobile accident in the summer of 1935, the study materials were delivered at least once by a man named Peters. Party dues were paid to Harold Ware or, after his death, to Peters.

Pressman stated that Donald Hiss was not a member of his group and he had no information concerning his political views. "I have no knowledge regarding the political beliefs or affiliations of Alger Hiss," Pressman added. "And when I say I have no knowledge, I am not endeavoring to quibble with this committee.... I do know, I can state as a matter of knowledge, that for the period of my participation in that group, which is the only basis on which I can say I have knowledge, Alger Hiss was not a member of the group."

Richard Nixon, still a HUAC member until he won a senate seat in November 1950, asked if Pressman knew Whittaker Chambers. Pressman replied:

> I have absolutely no recollection of having met Whittaker Chambers in Washington in connection with my participation with the group. I have searched [HUAC's] record to find out whether or not Mr. Whittaker Chambers states anywhere that he met me in connection with that group, and I have not found any such reference. I did find a reference in the record that Mr. Whittaker Chambers ... put me in Washington in the Federal Government in 1936.... There was always the inference he knew of us as a group, but not that he met me at the meetings.

Chambers had testified two years earlier that in 1936 some of the group's members "were going places in the Government," including Lee Pressman. But, of course, Pressman didn't make it very far because he had been fired from the AAA in February 1935, and by the end of that year he was living and working in New York.

Yet Pressman recalled one brief meeting with Chambers at his private law office in New York City sometime in 1936. Chambers had introduced himself using another name, but Pressman said he couldn't remember the name or find it in his files. But he knew it was Chambers because of all the pictures that had appeared in the press since the summer of 1948. Pressman explained:

> He looked quite different from when I saw him, but I recognized him.... He came in with another individual. Whittaker Chambers, by whatever name he appeared at that time, stated that he knew of me through mutual friends, without identifying them, and was bringing to me this second person as a potential client.... I have not seen Whittaker Chambers since the day that he appeared in my office at that time.

The other person was one J. Eckhart, a representative of the Spanish Republican Government whom Pressman subsequently represented and accompanied on a brief trip to Mexico.

In January 1952 lawyers for Alger Hiss filed a motion for a new trial (his second perjury trial ended in a guilty verdict two years earlier), citing Lee Pressman's August 1950 HUAC testimony. And the following month the U.S. government entered a rebuttal before the Senate Committee on Internal Security. Nathaniel Weyl, a freelance writer of articles and books who had been employed by the AAA in 1933-34, swore on his oath before the committee that he had been a member of the Ware Group along with Alger Hiss, and he had seen Hiss pay CP dues.

Weyl testified that he belonged to the Communist Party at the time he joined the AAA as an economist in Washington in 1933 at age 22. He was soon approached by Harold Ware and ordered to join Ware's unit. The unit "was engaged," Weyl said, "purely in study, that is, Marxist study," and the members, in addition to himself, included Alger Hiss, Lee Pressman, Charles Kramer, Henry Collins, John Abt, Nathan Witt, and Victor Perlo. Except for leaving out the name Donald Hiss (whom Weyl said he had never encountered), these were exactly the names Whittaker Chambers had named in August 1948. Weyl had never known Whittaker Chambers under any alias; he assumed Chambers had arrived on the scene just after he left in the summer of 1934.

When asked by the committee's counsel how he knew Alger Hiss had been a member of Ware's cell, Weyl replied, "Well, I only know that ... because I saw him there on, let us say, more than two occasions, because nobody was in that unit who was not a Communist party member, and I saw him pay dues." (Eleven months later, in an interview with *U.S. News & World Report*, Weyl said he saw Alger Hiss at those meetings "35 to 40 times, a rough estimate.")

"Prior to Alger Hiss's trials [in 1949]," Senator Homer Ferguson inquired, "were you approached to try to get this testimony?"

"No, Senator, I was not," Weyl replied.

"However, Mr. Weyl," committee counsel Robert Morris interjected, "you were called before the House Committee [HUAC] in 1942 [actually 1943] were you not?"

Weyl said that was correct, but he did not give the same testimony at that time. He had no way of knowing then, Weyl continued, that Hiss and the others he had met in Ware's "study group" in 1933-34 were still Communists—"So I remained silent about them.... I told the committee that I had been ... a Communist, and I offered to the committee, into evidence, writings subsequent to 1939 showing them that I was now an anti–Communist."

Two days later Weyl was back on the stand before the Senate committee to "correct" his previous testimony. His "recollection was in error" when he told the Senators that he testified to HUAC in 1943 and told them he had been a Communist. "I stated falsely before the House committee in 1943 that I had never formally been a member of the Communist party."

But why did Weyl remain silent after Whittaker Chambers testified before HUAC in August 1948? Why did he remain a mute bystander through two long trials, especially after the first trial ended in a hung jury? No one on the senate committee was asking such questions.

Even more astonishing — Weyl's audacity was eclipsed only by the committee's failure to conduct even a cursory background check — is that *after* the Hiss trials Weyl published a book called *Treason* in 1950, a historical compendium of treasonable acts. In the chapter devoted to the Hiss case, Weyl wrote:

If he was a secret Communist, he hid the fact superbly. Former spy courier Elizabeth Bentley testified against Assistant Secretary of the Treasury Harry D. White, but offered nothing detrimental concerning Hiss. Julian Wadleigh, the Soviet espionage agent who worked in the same division of the State Department as Hiss, thought him "a very moderate New Dealer with strongly conservative instincts."

In another passage, summarizing how Hiss distinguished himself in court, Weyl continues:

> Throughout the two arduous trials he underwent, Hiss cut an impressive figure. His open countenance, forthright denials and distinguished record told heavily against the dark, labyrinthine past of his assailant. Alger Hiss avoided testimony with intellectual overtones. His mind seemed simple in its basic processes, sure and practical. To him, apparently, every former Communist was "a traitor." There were no shadings.

Is it conceivable that those considerate words, supportive of Hiss, were written by a man who later claimed that he witnessed Alger Hiss paying dues at secret Communist meetings in the 1930s? By the 1970s even mythmaker Allen Weinstein, in an unusual moment of scholarly integrity and astute interpretation of character, questioned the credibility of Nathaniel Weyl. But in the 1950s Weyl's contradictions escaped scrutiny. When Alger Hiss's motion for a new trial was denied in 1952, Judge Henry Goddard (who also presided over Hiss's second trial) referred to Weyl's Senate testimony, oblivious of any discrepancy. In January 1953, *U.S. News & World Report* published an eighteen-page interview with Weyl in which he claimed he was interrogated by the entire editorial staff. The editors lobbed questions typical of this:

> *To what extent would you say the liberals of the country — the professors, intellectuals, artists — who were not themselves Communists and who don't believe in Communism at all are the victims of, or the dupes of, the strategy of Communist sympathizers or operators in this country?*

In October 1957, an editorial in *The Saturday Evening Post* championed Weyl as the "Missing Witness" in the Hiss case who had "kept his knowledge to himself. His subsequent testimony might have saved much mental anguish among Hiss's many zealous defenders." The magazine sourced Weyl's Senate testimony but gave no inkling that Weyl lied under oath to congress in 1943, nor did they quote from his book *Treason*.

Fred J. Cook, an investigative journalist who authored *The Unfinished Story of Alger Hiss* (1958) and several articles on the case, was the first reporter with the courage and decency to unmask the lies of Nathaniel Weyl. In an unflinching indictment of American journalism's posture on the Hiss case, Cook wrote in 1958:

> Whatever one may conclude from the writings and the testimony of Nathaniel Weyl, it would seem that the partisan reception given one portion of his testimony, the virtual news blackout concerning the other, indicates that there are powerful segments of American society more concerned with the permanent condemnation of Alger Hiss as the symbol of a liberal New Deal past than with a question of justice. At the very least, it would seem that Nathaniel Weyl's testimony, and even more the manner in which it has been treated, has effectively exposed the intellectual dishonesty of those who cite the last segment of it, standing in isolation, as the irrefutable proof of the guilt of Alger Hiss.

Nathaniel Weyl continued to lie to the very end. He died at age 94 in 2005, and in 2003 he wrote his final words on the Hiss case in his book *Encounters with Communism*. Probably the truest, most revealing words appear on page 9: "Since I have not kept papers or correspondence from that period ... there may be errors in this account." In other words:

no corroboration, no documentation, no proof. As pathological liars always embellish, Weyl capped his lying life with this preposterous tale:

> He [FBI Special Agent Bert Zander] added the interesting news that the hotel room in which the Hisses stayed in during the second trial had been bugged by a government agency which he did not identify. The wire tap revealed that Alger said to his wife that the situation was hopeless and he had decided to change his plea to guilty. Priscilla Hiss did everything in her power to persuade him to stand firm. She brought Lee Pressman into the discussion and these two zealous Communists made him decide to bite the bullet, that is to say to continue lying.

Setting aside the commonsensical and psychological impossibility of such an episode ever occurring, one a child wouldn't believe, why would the Hisses have stayed in a hotel when their Greenwich Village apartment was less than two miles from the courthouse? According to their son Tony, they were at home each night during both trials.

Nathaniel Weyl was certain that he, along with Alger Hiss and a few other AAA employees, attended the first meeting of the Ware Group sometime in the summer of 1933. Yet only a few months earlier Alger Hiss was reluctant to leave his corporate clients on Wall Street. Was it possible he was now a concealed Communist planning who-knows-what villainy with his newfound confederates in anticipation of the glorious revolution, and tithing ten percent of his government salary to the Communist Party? No, it wasn't possible, but that doesn't necessarily mean people don't believe it to this day. Especially now, when the two chief obfuscators are otherwise credible and highly credentialed members of American mainstream society and culture: Allen Weinstein, former Archivist of the United States as of 2008 and author of *Perjury, the Hiss-Chambers Case* (1978, updated 1997); and Sam Tanenhaus, former editor of the *New York Times* Sunday Book Review, whose biography of Whittaker Chambers was published in 1997. Both books were widely reviewed and praised, though even some positive reviewers believed Weinstein did not provide sufficient political context, and Tanenhaus was politely faulted for timidity and idealization. But the historical value of both books is greatly diminished by factual distortions and suppressions — all to the benefit of Whittaker Chambers. Both drew heavily upon (and accepted for the most part as factual) Chambers's *Witness*, a tome near the top of every list of America's great autobiographies — and surely the most fraudulent of them all.

Chambers wrote that in the first weeks of their friendship he rescued Hiss from isolation and loneliness. Now that Hiss had been transferred to Apparatus B, Chambers would have us believe, his only social contacts — former Ware Group comrades — were severed. But the facts and the evidence provided by others who knew Hiss well in the years 1934 and 1935 testify otherwise.

Constance Ducey, Hiss's secretary at the AAA, told biographer Zeligs: "Mr. Hiss worked night and day to do the tasks given him to do, although he tried to read one night a week to Justice Holmes while the Justice was still alive; and also saved an afternoon for his stepson when he could. He had to work many Sundays."

Hiss's colleague Charles Horsky, who worked closely with Hiss for a year beginning in the summer of 1935 said, "I would see Alger Hiss every day and night too…. Sometimes we'd work till 4 or 5 A.M. against a deadline…. We worked long hours and we worked holidays."[5]

Alger and Priscilla Hiss often attended Sunday-evening supper parties organized by Roy Veatch, a State Department economist, and Hiss belonged to the Foreign Policy Association, which held regular dinner meetings featuring speakers and general discussion.

Whittaker Chambers's motives for ingratiating himself with Alger Hiss at the latter's place of employment in 1934 will never fully be known. However, it appears certain that Chambers needed unwitting scapegoats, innocent others he might try to implicate if his crimes were exposed. That Chambers zeroed in on Hiss rather than some other official may have been simply an on-the-spot decision, but Hiss later believed Chambers may have been stalking him.

The *American Magazine* published an article about youthful New Dealers in February 1934. Alger Hiss was mentioned in the piece, written by Beverly Waugh Smith, who had known Hiss for years, and a photograph of Hiss was included. Some months later, Hiss recalled, Chambers introduced himself as George Crosley, a freelance writer working on articles about the Nye Committee's hearings for the *American Magazine.*

As for Harold Ware and his group, Chambers, a magpie gossip and scandalmonger, knew only what he had learned second hand. Upon that tenuous armature he embroidered successive lies and was never held to account for them — for beginning with his first public testimony in August 1948 he swore he never knew Harold Ware.

In April 1935 the Hisses moved from their 28th Street apartment, about two months before the lease expired, to a larger rental, a furnished house on P Street. Within a month of the Hisses' relocation, Chambers and his wife and baby daughter moved into the mostly furnished apartment (the Hisses left some furniture for the new tenants to use, as they were also moving into a furnished place) and stayed until a day or two before the lease was up on July 1. These are unquestioned facts. According to Chambers, Hiss invited him and his family to live in the vacant apartment as a favor from one comrade to another. Hiss contended that he sublet the place to George Crosley for about sixty dollars a month.

Perhaps the most bewildering paradox of the Hiss-Chambers affair is that Hiss could not recognize Chambers in 1948 as anyone he had ever known until he saw him in the flesh, and then he was certain he had known Chambers as George Crosley; but Chambers, though he obviously recognized Hiss and knew him by his given name, was not quite certain by what name Hiss had known *him*, despite his assertion that Hiss had been his best friend for four years. When Chambers initially made public his accusations, he insisted that Hiss and the other underground CP members knew him only as "Carl." But soon after Chambers began hedging and backtracking because someone else had come forward who had also known him as George Crosley.

Samuel Roth, a New York writer and publisher of erotica, had followed the HUAC hearings with interest, and when he heard the August 25, 1948, broadcast of Chambers swearing that he had never used the alias George Crosley, Roth knew that Chambers was lying and Hiss was telling the truth. Roth had seen Whittaker Chambers several times in 1926 and 1927 when Roth was publishing the magazines *Two Worlds Quarterly, Two Worlds Monthly,* and *Secret Memoirs.* Roth swore in an affidavit to Hiss's attorney only days after the public HUAC hearing that during those years he met Chambers on at least six occasions, most of them at his office, but he believed Chambers had also visited his home. In 1926, Roth said, Chambers submitted several poems to him for publication under his own name, two of which Roth paid for and published. The next year Chambers submitted more poems, attaching a letter requesting Roth to publish the poems under the name "George Crosley." Roth could not decide whether to publish the poems, and he held them for about a year, until Chambers asked Roth to return them by mail to an address in Long Island. A careful search was made for Chambers's initial letter, Roth added, but he had not been able to find it. "However," Roth continued, "I remember clearly that Mr. Chambers submitted to me the poems referred to above for publication under the pseudonym 'George Crosley.' My memory is fortified by reason of the fact that I held the poems for a long period of time and by the further fact that one of the poems was of particular interest to me."

Samuel Roth could have been a valuable witness for Alger Hiss at his perjury trials the following year, but Hiss and his legal team, in one of the worst of their many bad decisions, never called him because of Roth's criminal past. He had been imprisoned three times since 1928 — once for three months in New York for selling Boccaccio's *Blank and Madonna*; two months in Philadelphia in 1929 for selling James Joyce's *Ulysses*; and almost three years in Lewisburg, Pennsylvania, for transmitting obscene material through the postal system in 1936.

Another telltale sign pointing toward Chambers's use of the alias George Crosley was proffered by Chambers himself. On July 6, 1935, about a week after moving from Hiss's 28th Street apartment, Chambers wrote a typically self-absorbed letter to his old friend Meyer Schapiro. The letter was signed "George."[6]

In *Witness*, Chambers said he moved to Schapiro's place in New York just after leaving Hiss's 28th Street apartment in Washington, and that the Hisses delivered the few personal items Chambers and his family took with them to Shapiro's doorstep.

And that lie is compounded by another lie Chambers told about four years before *Witness* was published. In the fall of 1948 Hiss sued Chambers for calling him a Communist at the HUAC hearings and on the popular radio program *Meet the Press*. In the course of the subsequent lawsuit deposition, Chambers was asked to provide corroboration of friendship with Hiss during the years in question. Other than his wife, Esther, Chambers could not produce another witness who had seen him and Hiss together, nor could he supply personal letters or inscribed books or gifts received from the Hisses. However, Chambers said Hiss had given him several items of furniture from the 28th Street apartment that Chambers took upon leaving the apartment, and he still possessed these objects: table, rug, wing chair, child's rocker, chest-of-drawers, loveseat, and child's table and chair.

Though the Hisses could not remember what happened to the furniture they left in the 28th Street apartment, it seems highly unlikely they would have given any furniture to George Crosley, who had failed to pay the rent for two months. Moreover, when Edward McLean, an attorney for Hiss, visited Chambers at his home in Westminster prior to Hiss's trials to see firsthand the furniture Chambers claimed Hiss had given him, all Chambers could show him was an old, neatly folded section of cloth. It was the fabric, Chambers attested, which once upholstered Hiss's wing chair. Chambers had carefully removed and dry cleaned the covering and preserved it for thirteen years. Though he offered no explanation to McLean why he kept it so long, the cloth represented (in Chambers's fantastic way of thinking at any rate) a keepsake of his former best friend, or what psychology defines as a fetish — a material object substitute for the absent loved one.

After Hiss pressed the libel suit against Chambers in the fall of 1948, Chambers felt compelled to manipulate, embellish, or completely change aspects of his previously concocted story about his relationship with Hiss. Before HUAC in August, Chambers provided a variety of homey details about the Hisses, many of which were utter fabrications, but Chambers assured Nixon's subcommittee that he had *never taken overnight trips or vacations* with the Hisses, only a couple of day trips by car to New York and Pennsylvania. But three months later, flagging under the biting and belittling questioning of Hiss's libel attorney, William Marbury, Chambers invented yet another adventure, retold (and much enhanced) in *Witness*, to play up his close friendship with the Hisses:

Chambers decided to give up the Schapiro house, as the summer was very hot in Greenwich Village, and move with Maxim Lieber to the country for the summer. They found a furnished cottage near the Delaware River at Smithtown, Pennsylvania, and lived there during the late summer of 1935.

Chambers maintained that Priscilla Hiss visited them and looked after his daughter while his wife painted landscapes. Priscilla was supposedly at Smithtown for perhaps ten days.

Chambers curiously also claimed that because Maxim Lieber knew of Priscilla's visit, he could have made an important witness later in the Hiss Case, but the Hiss defense never called him to the stand.

If this tale were true, one wonders instead why the *prosecution* never called Maxim Lieber, a New York literary agent, to the stand. In his November 1948 libel deposition, Chambers told Marbury that Lieber was his associate in the Communist underground and "was very much impressed with Mrs. Hiss."

But when interviewed in April 1951 by Chester Lane, Hiss's attorney, Maxim Lieber said Chambers had never even mentioned the Hisses' names to him throughout their acquaintance, and that his story was fiction. "I wouldn't know Mrs. Hiss," Lieber exclaimed, "if she were to come in this office and spit in my tea!"

In 1978, Maxim Lieber told Victor Navasky, editor of *The Nation*, that he had been a Communist in the 1930s and had known Chambers; however, "I was never a member of any underground and I never worked with Chambers on any underground project." As for the Hisses, Lieber remarked, "I never met or saw Priscilla or Alger Hiss or even knew about them until the trial."

Indeed, Chambers and his wife were vacationing with Maxim Lieber at Smithtown for two or three months the summer of 1935. They were known as Mr. and Mrs. Breen, Chambers said, and even their toddler daughter was issued a cover name—Ursula. Esther Chambers agreed completely with her husband's court testimony, and recalled that she gave Priscilla Hiss a landscape she had painted and then later saw the painting hanging in the Hisses' 30th Street house. Priscilla, she said, called her "Lise," and when their vacation concluded Alger Hiss drove them all back to Washington.

Lieber and Chambers rented the Smithtown cottage from Joseph Boucot, who occupied an adjacent cottage less than 50 yards away. Chambers testified he had met Boucot on many occasions, adding that Boucot and his sister, Ms. Brown, had met Priscilla there often during their stay. Yet Boucot and Brown swore they had never seen Priscilla Hiss. At Hiss's second trial Chambers equivocated, saying he couldn't remember if Boucot and his sister had actually met Priscilla, but Esther Chambers was still certain that they had because Boucot "used to come in for coffee quite frequently."

Priscilla Hiss testified she had never been in any Smithtown cottage in her life. On cross-examination she was asked no questions about it.

Precisely on August 9, 1937—at least nine months after Alger Hiss swore he had last seen or heard from George Crosley—Whittaker Chambers testified (twelve years later) that he commenced a journey with the Hisses, in their car, to Peterborough, New Hampshire. That this trip ever happened was demolished beyond any reasonable doubt in court, but, as was his wont, Chambers reprised the legend in his autobiography.

He explained that while talking to Hiss casually in early August 1937, he said he had to go to Peterborough, but he didn't tell Hiss who he was going to see there or why. Harry

Dexter White was at his summer home near Peterborough, and Chambers urgently needed to see White to direct him to produce a financial plan for Soviet Russia!

So on a whim, Chambers elaborated, he and Alger and Priscilla decided to make an outing of it and drive to New Hampshire by way of a favorite route of Priscilla's which avoided the cities and meandered through the countryside. That trip, Chambers asserted, became important in the Hiss perjury trials (though Chambers previously swore he had never taken overnight trips with the Hisses or even Hiss alone). It was one incident he believed would support his story of his secret association with Hiss.

Harry Dexter White was safely in his grave by the time Chambers first told this story, so he couldn't dispute it or corroborate it, though he had sworn to HUAC that he had never laid eyes on Chambers.

As Peterborough was about 500 miles from Washington, Chambers recalled that they stopped over at a tourist home, arriving after dark, in Thomaston, Connecticut. The next day, August 10, they reached their destination.

Chambers stated that he never told the Hisses the purpose of this road trip and never mentioned Harry Dexter White (who knew Hiss) on the drive to New Hampshire or on the way back. Alger Hiss, the alleged driver, was instructed by Chambers to pull off the main highway and then stop near a lane leading to White's residence, which couldn't be seen from where Hiss parked. Chambers got out of the car, walked toward the house, and saw Harry White playing with his children in the yard. Chambers and White talked for some twenty minutes, and then Chambers returned to the car and they left.

The evening of the 10th, according to Chambers, they saw Oliver Goldsmith's comedy *She Stoops to Conquer*, performed by the Peterborough Players. Chambers was proud of this trivial fact, which for him was fraught with significance because the FBI later established that *She Stoops* had been presented only once by the Peterborough Players, on the night of August 10, 1937, "and never before or after."

They spent the night at a bed-and-breakfast called Bleak House, Chambers taking one room and the Hisses another. The next day they drove about 350 miles to New York City. Chambers was unsure why he wanted to go to New York, but he recalled the Hisses telling him they wanted to revisit the little hotel where they spent their honeymoon.

Alger and Priscilla Hiss maintained it was all a cock-and-bull story, including the honeymoon they never celebrated in New York. The Hisses, in fact, had been on vacation at Chestertown on the eastern shore of Chesapeake Bay the month of August 1937. Alger Hiss was there until about the 15th, when he returned to work in Washington. Priscilla's son Timothy, and her two nieces, Ruth and Cynthia Fansler, were at summer camp there. Priscilla visited the children every day in August and was not away from Chestertown for a single night all month. J. Kellogg-Smith and his wife Margaret, who supervised the camp, testified at Hiss's trials and supported the Hisses' account. Thomas Fansler, Ruth's father, testified that he visited his daughter at Chestertown on August 6, and on August 9, the day Chambers said they set out for New Hampshire, the Hisses drove Fansler to Wilmington, about 50 miles from Chestertown, where he caught a train.

Lucy Elliott Davis, who managed Bleak House, testified she had never seen the Hisses or Chambers before the trial, and her guest register was produced in evidence. Davis had opened the fourteen-bedroom guesthouse on August 1, 1937, and had registered only a few guests prior to August 10, none of whom fit the descriptions of Chambers or the Hiss couple. Davis lived on the premises and seldom left the place. And Chambers, who believed the New Hampshire trip would yield evidence to corroborate his story, was unable to recognize

Ms. Davis at trial. Never one to let the truth stand in his way, Chambers reflected in *Witness*: "Obviously, if I had been lying, I would have taken care to contrive a better story, since there was no need to invent any story at all."

Yet invent stories Chambers certainly did, scarcely dreaming them up only until the moment of need, such as the incident he had "forgotten" until about a month before Hiss's second trial. It's a vague and dreamlike account, but one perfectly representative of the method of his madness, blending a few facts and a lot of fantasy.

Chambers couldn't recollect the purpose of this trip, but he and Hiss left Washington on the Saturday before Easter 1935 and drove to Erwinna, Pennsylvania. They stayed that night at a tourist house near Center Square, Pennsylvania, but Chambers couldn't recall the name of the place or the location. He felt sure they registered and were checked in by a Polish proprietor. And he plainly remembered that on Easter Sunday he and Hiss watched a policeman carrying an Easter lily, a sight that Chambers thought greatly pleased Hiss.

But the one circumstance in which Chambers could have early on proven even a slender documentary trail and thereby magnify the probability of his putative "close relationship" with Hiss, Chambers failed to mention voluntarily. Only after the tabloid press published the sensational story did Chambers elaborate. But, as usual, Chambers embellished the details, rendering his version only partially true when compared with the documented facts.

On August 27, 1948, just two days after the dramatic HUAC hearing in which Hiss and Chambers confronted each other before television cameras, the *Baltimore News-Post* reported that the house and property Chambers purchased in 1937 had almost been sold to Hiss in 1936! Edward Case, a Carroll County, Maryland, realtor who handled both transactions separately, told the *News-Post*: "It was one of the oddest deals I ever had. The house was run down. It was five miles off a paved road. Yet here were two important men, both apparently anxious to buy it." The deals were about a year apart, and Case had seen no connection between the two buyers. "But now, since reading about the hearings and the stuff about whether they knew each other — well, I'm not so sure." The article included photographs of the property and of letters to Case from both Hiss and Chambers.

HUAC summoned Chambers to an emergency private session the evening of the 27th. Chambers testified:

> As well as I can remember, Mr. Hiss and I had talked about how much each of us would like to have a small place in the country somewhere, but particularly I would like to have a small place in the country.
> Some time after such conversation, I think it was he who unearthed an advertisement of Mr. Case's.... The advertisement was for this property and at a very low price.... There was also included a little, ramshackle barn. Mr. Hiss then got in touch with Mr. Case and made a down payment or deposit of some kind.

When asked how he knew that, Chambers said: "He must have told me.... He then at sometime took Mrs. Hiss up there, and Mrs. Hiss did not like the place and did not like the countryside. I heard her say this.... Some such expression like 'a nasty, narrow valley'.... Then, Hiss called off his arrangement with the realtor.... I left out an important thing — I made one trip up there with Alger Hiss."

In *Witness* Chambers expressed that he and Hiss had planned to buy this property *together*. Hiss had shown him Case's advertisement and proposed that they drive to Westminster and look at the place, and, if suitable, buy it. Then Chambers and his family could spend the summer there, the Hisses could visit them, and the families could be together without always trying to avoid being seen, as was the case in Baltimore and Washington.

But Chambers's earlier testimony of the 27th leaves no such impression:

> So [Chambers swore], I made one trip up there with him and saw this place. It was after that that he called off this arrangement and then still later ... that I came into the picture.
>
> I also [later] left the deposit with the agent. Now there is a point that has to be clarified. Hiss did not know that I was in the picture then. I did not want him to know it, because I bought the house under my name, and didn't want him to know my real name. As far as I know he never knew I had that place, nor did I want him to. I had two compartments, Whittaker Chambers on one side, which is my more or less private compartment, and Carl in these [Communist] groups here, and I did not want to make any bridge between them.

But his relationship with Hiss was obviously an exception; the bridge was already in place. Chambers tells us time and again of the affections shared between them and their families. When Chambers purchased the Westminster property in February 1937, he was allegedly visiting the Hisses regularly at their 30th Street house, Carl's "informal headquarters." Yet at the same time he was living in Baltimore using the name Chambers. Also, the Westminster place was not "bought" under his name; his wife was the legal owner. Moreover, by the end of 1938, according to Chambers, the Hisses knew his real name anyway. If all we had to go on was what Chambers said and wrote and testified to, our understanding of the truth would never obtain satisfaction.

Alger Hiss denied that Chambers ever went with him to inspect the Westminster property. Hiss was still seeing George Crosley from time to time until the fall of 1936, and Hiss believes he must have mentioned the property to him or, more likely, shown him the advertisement which provided the information Chambers would later need to locate and buy the place himself. Priscilla Hiss did not recall the transaction at all. She told this to a lawyer in 1948, who noted that Priscilla and Alger "had frequently looked at old farms in various parts of the country but never bought any. She does not recall signing the contract to buy this one but recognized the picture of her signature on the contract in the newspaper."

The first letter to Edward Case inquiring about the property was written by Priscilla on November 5, 1935. The realtor's files revealed that Case met with Alger for the first time on April 4, 1936. Nine days later, after more correspondence, Hiss visited the property again, this time with Priscilla. They made a $20 deposit on the place and later that day Hiss wrote Case, attaching a $100 check for down payment and a signed contract to purchase the property for $650. Later that month Case informed Hiss that the trustee of the estate who owned the land refused to sell for less than $850. Hiss was unable to negotiate a better deal; he wrote Case on May 13 asking for the deposit back, and his last letter on May 26 asked Case again to return the money and "terminate the negotiations completely."

Edward Case swore in an affidavit that he never saw Chambers with Hiss at the property. Case's business neighbor, Calvin Zepp, also recalled Hiss's visit and said Chambers was not with him.

"If Chambers did visit the farm with Hiss," Allen Weinstein wrote in *Perjury*, "it would have been sometime in mid–April." And Sam Tanenhaus noted in his biography of Chambers: "Eventually Hiss had backed out of the deal because Priscilla disliked the area." But both authors' interpretations are logically senseless and dishonest. If one accepts Tanenhaus's view — which simply parrots Chambers's gratuitous swipe at Priscilla — then why would Hiss take Chambers to visit the property *after* Priscilla had been there? She allegedly said it was "a nasty, narrow valley" and refused to have it. But she obviously said no such thing —

and Weinstein and Tanenhaus must have known it — because it was only after she visited the place with Alger that they put down a deposit and offered to buy it. There was nothing in the Hiss correspondence with Case about Priscilla not liking the location. The deal was broken off only because they couldn't agree on the price.

The following February Whittaker Chambers wrote to Edward Case inquiring about the same property. He signed the letter "J.W. Chambers," with a return address in care of his wife's brother, an attorney. Chambers soon after bought the place and eventually moved in. He lived there the rest of his life.

Meyer Zeligs, a San Francisco psychoanalyst who became enthralled with the Hiss-Chambers story in the 1950s, wrote an analysis of Chambers and Hiss titled *Friendship and Fratricide* (1967). Reviews of the book were mixed. Much of the negative criticism came from New York Jewish literary intellectuals, Freudians all. Even twenty-five years after its publication, Diana Trilling, for instance, disingenuously wrote: "Zeligs had no acquaintance with Chambers. To analyze him without knowing him violated a fundamental premise of his profession, but on the ground of his presumed analytic into character and unconscious motivation, he put together an elaborate defense of Hiss and extended indictment of Chambers." To attempt to provide *therapy* without knowing the person might surely be a violation of Zeligs's profession, but *analysis* is quite something else. Literary critics, historians, and biographers commonly practice a sort of analysis based on what their subjects said or wrote, or what others said or wrote about them — a living person who lies on the couch, free associates, and is led through the Greek circle of myths is not required. Zeligs was not attempting to "psychoanalyze" Chambers (who was, of course, dead in 1967 and beyond any need of insight or therapy) as he would an actual patient who came in for help. Zeligs's psychological interpretations may be dismissed as subjective or irrelevant, such as the Freudianism that Chambers suffered from an "infantile neurosis," but his lasting contribution to other historians is the extensive research he conducted, including interviews with everyone related to the story who agreed to talk. Whittaker Chambers was still living when Zeligs commenced research in the late 1950s — but Chambers refused to talk or correspond with him (or anyone else, *ever*, about the Hiss case).

Alger Hiss, however, never refused an interview with Zeligs and never refused to answer any question. "Indeed," Zeligs wrote, "from a close study of [Hiss] as a person one senses a lack of those very attributes of character — shrewdness and cunning — which characterize his public image. In his need to seek out the good in people, he unconsciously prevents himself from recognizing guile and deceit." Or, as Kenneth Simon (an attorney who once worked for Hiss) put it in a 2001 interview: "Alger had no street smarts — and for a man who'd seen so much of the world, I thought at the time that this was a little strange. And in retrospect I find it even stranger. I don't think he ever realized the strength of the forces that had been released against him."

In the guise of George Crosley, Whittaker Chambers, a master of intrigue and ingratiation, built up Hiss's interest and expectations, all the while exploiting and deceiving him. It took Hiss well over a year to see through the fog of his gullibility.

By September 1936, when Alger Hiss joined the State Department, George Crosley had disappeared from his life. Though Chambers would claim in 1948 that he saw Hiss often during 1937 and early 1938 there is no independent evidence of it, only the documents which Hiss allegedly gave him and which Chambers himself provided as corroboration.

Also, Chambers was ignorant of all the significant events (which all of the Hisses' genuine friends knew about) in the life of the Hiss family during 1937-38, such as Timothy Hobson's serious accident in February 1937 and other incidents mentioned previously.

Alger Hiss's most important work for the State Department began with his transfer in 1943 to the division responsible for postwar planning and the creation of the United Nations. He resigned as legal counsel for the Nye Committee in the fall of 1935 and joined the Justice Department's Office of Solicitor General. There Hiss was involved in litigation concerning the constitutionality of the AAA and the Trade Agreements Act. Francis B. Sayre, Assistant Secretary of State for Economic Affairs and Hiss's former law school professor, offered Hiss a job in the State Department as his personal assistant in the fall of 1936, which Hiss accepted. When Sayre became increasingly enmeshed in preparations for granting independence to the Philippines and went there as the U.S. High Commissioner in late 1939, Hiss became an assistant to Stanley K. Hornbeck.

Hornbeck was an Adviser on Political Relations to Secretary of State Cordell Hull. From 1928 to 1937 he was chief of the State Department's Division of Far Eastern Affairs and played a powerful role in shaping policies in the region. One official policy, toward China, which Alger Hiss also supported, was to provide aid only to Chiang Kai-shek and the Kuomintang. The Chinese Communists were left to fend for themselves or get what they needed from the Soviet Union. Those who resisted this policy, arguing that the Communists were fighting more successfully against the Japanese and deserved all the aid we could give them, were opposed by Hiss and Hornbeck, as they had hopes and plans for a postwar China under Chiang's regime. Ultimately the policy failed, and, ironically, Hiss and the administrations of Roosevelt and Truman generally, who shored up the gangster Chiang to the end, were bitterly denounced by the Right for "losing China" to the Communists.

Hornbeck became ambassador to the Netherlands in 1944, and Hiss, in April of that year, was appointed deputy director of the Office of Special Political Affairs, a new division headed by Cordell Hull's assistant Leo Pasvolsky. From August to October Hiss served as secretary of the Dumbarton Oaks Conversations, a conference in Washington of the major Allied powers — the United States, Great Britain, and the Soviet Union — on the formation of the proposed United Nations. Hiss was not a United States delegate but rather the executive secretary who arranged transportation, recorded the official minutes, and distributed documents. In addition, Hiss was an adviser to the U.S. delegation and attended meetings as Pasvolsky's chief aide. At Dumbarton Oaks the Allies agreed on most of the major points of the proposed United Nations, and all of the remaining open issues were resolved at Yalta four months later.

Alger Hiss was a member of the American civilian delegation at Yalta, formally called the Crimea Conference, in February 1945. And those facts are about all that the conspiracy theory myths and the reality have in common. The typical myth declaims Soviet agent Hiss was an influential adviser to an ailing President Roosevelt, who gave away Eastern Europe to Stalin at Yalta. But the truth is that Hiss's role was minor, and it was only by accident that he even attended at all because he was not initially chosen by the Secretary of State to go. Furthermore, the U.S. requested much from Russia at Yalta and gave little in return.

Hiss was a last minute substitute for James C. Dunn, the director of an office in charge of European affairs in the State Department, whom Roosevelt struck from Secretary Edward Stettinius's list of proposed aides because of Dunn's frequent and open opposition to FDR's liberal policies and programs. The President told Stettinius he didn't care who else was named, but Dunn wasn't going to Yalta. So Hiss was chosen in consideration of his service at Dumbarton Oaks and his efforts on the projected United Nations.

Yalta was the only joint meeting of the military chiefs of the U.S., the U.K, and the U.S.S.R. during the war. Allied success was now certain in Europe, but Germany's military strength was still formidable, as demonstrated at the recent Battle of the Bulge, and plans were required for a final Allied onslaught. Thus the military realities on the western front and in Japan eclipsed the political and ideological differences of the three great powers.

In coming to Yalta President Roosevelt wanted to attain political as well as military commitments from the Soviets — and he got them. Stalin agreed to support the U.S. and declare war against Japan three months after Germany's surrender. Politically, accord was reached on terms of the future peace in Europe and the structure of the United Nations. Stalin reluctantly accepted French involvement in the control of occupied Germany, a measure he had previously strongly opposed, and he agreed to U.S. drafts on the Declaration for a Liberated Europe and on German reparations. Stalin accepted without change America's proposal for Security Council voting procedures of the United Nations, which provided for the veto power of the permanent members. Only Poland's Soviet-controlled regime was not negotiable. But the Soviets occupied most of Poland and would soon occupy it totally, leaving the United States and England little to bargain with. It was the Western powers who sought concessions and commitments from the Soviets, not the opposite. Except for the Russian demand for reparations, all the requests came from the United States. And all U.S. demands were granted on their terms except for liberalizing the Polish government. Russia was granted concessions of their own for agreeing to join the war against Japan, but this too was a U.S. initiative and a major objective of the Joint Chiefs of Staff. At a time when Soviet military glory was never greater, and with a vast credit of casualties, Stalin played a conservative hand at Yalta and granted more that he asked in return.

Yalta was an encouraging and inspiring event for the United States. "We really believed in our hearts that this was the dawn of the new day we had all been praying for and talking about for so many years," FDR's adviser Harry Hopkins wrote. "We were absolutely certain that we had won the first great victory of the peace.... The Russians had proved that they could be reasonable and farseeing and there wasn't any doubt in the minds of the President or any of us that we could live with them."

The Allied military personnel attending Yalta numbered almost seven hundred, while the civilian delegates, including Alger Hiss, totaled no more than eighty. On the morning of February 3, Hiss arrived with the American delegation at Saki airport in the Crimea. Then there was a cold, exhausting eight-hour drive over war-torn roads to Yalta. The first plenary session was held the following afternoon at Livadia Palace, once the summer residence of the former Tsar and more recently occupied and looted by the Nazis.

"For me," Hiss later wrote of the meetings, "Roosevelt had by far the greatest presence. His easy grace and charm were combined with serenity and inner assurance. His posture at the great round table where the participants sat at plenary sessions was one of regal composure. He radiated goodwill, purpose, leadership, and personal magnetism." Yet the photographs of FDR the day he arrived depict a very weary and perhaps seriously ill old man. Roosevelt died ten weeks later, and his detractors pointed to those photographs as proof that he was not wholly competent and consequently the U.S. suffered a diplomatic defeat at Yalta. But Alger Hiss recalled that Roosevelt never lost his natural buoyancy and playfulness, and had regained his color and vitality within a day or so. "All of us at Yalta had no doubt that he was in full command of his faculties, and all of us left Yalta pleased with the results of our diplomatic efforts."

Stalin also made a striking impression on Hiss. For a leader the Americans and British "knew to have been a vicious dictator," Hiss recalled, Stalin surprised them by his "geniality as host and ... conciliatory attitude as negotiator." He was calm and restrained, courteous and soft-spoken, well-prepared and seldom read from notes. "He was always alert to the discussion and reacted quickly to what he considered a weakness or inconsistency on our part.... He was a skilled and adroit negotiator who could be decisive or delaying, as suited his point." The U.S. and British civilian delegation could only speculate as to the reason Stalin was more gracious and flexible and agreeable at Yalta than he was at the earlier Teheran Conference or the later Potsdam Conference. After all, it was the Western powers, not the Soviets, who came to Yalta bearing requests.

Hiss was primarily responsible for issues related to the United Nations, one of the most important topics of the conference. The main objective, soon achieved, was obtaining agreement on Security Council voting procedures and veto power of the permanent members. There was debate over which Latin American countries should be invited to the first U.N. conference. The Russians wanted only those actually at war with the Axis, but the U.S. wanted all of them invited and eventually won Soviet agreement. Hiss was *opposed* to the extra Assembly votes allotted to the Soviet Republics Ukraine and Byelorussia (a bizarre position to take if Hiss was a Soviet agent, as the myth has it) but was unable to prevent them. As Secretary of State Stettinius later explained:

> Hiss, our representative on the subcommittee, told me as the [plenary] meeting was coming to order that he had just asked Eden [Anthony Eden, British foreign secretary] for a copy of the report drafted by the subcommittee, which the British representative had agreed to have typed. When Eden had somewhat reluctantly handed him a copy, Hiss noticed that it expressed American support for the extra votes, which had not been in the draft which he as the American representative on the subcommittee had approved. He protested to Eden that the United States had not approved the extra votes, but Eden replied, "You don't know what has taken place." It was obvious from Eden's remark that the President had had a private talk with the British after the subcommittee had adjourned and before the plenary session had convened.

Furthermore, Stettinius did not just assume that his subordinates, Hiss included, were completely reliable and loyal Americans. In October 1943, as Under Secretary of State, Stettinius brought in the FBI — with the approval of President Roosevelt and Secretary of State Cordell Hull, and with Assistant Secretary of State G. Howland Shaw as the FBI liaison — to conduct a security examination of the State Department. Later, after Whittaker Chambers publicly accused Hiss of being a Communist, Stettinius published his book *Roosevelt and the Russians* (1949) and remarked: "I never heard of any questioning of Mr. Hiss's loyalty from anyone inside or outside of the State Department or from the FBI during my time of service in the Department." The FBI, however, knew of Chambers's accusation of Hiss in 1942, a year before the bureau investigated State Department officials. After interviewing Chambers extensively, the FBI's New York office sent Hoover a special eight-page report in which Alger and Donald Hiss, among others, were accused of Communist activity. But Hoover dismissed Chambers's account, concluding that "most of his information is either history, hypothesis, or deduction."

As for Hiss's influence on Roosevelt during the conference, there is simply no evidence of it. One of FDR's top advisers at Yalta, James F. Byrnes, who succeeded Stettinius as Secretary of State in the summer of 1945, wrote about the Yalta Conference in two volumes of his memoirs. In the first book, *Speaking Frankly* (1947), Hiss is not mentioned at all. But in the second, *All in One Lifetime* (1958), published eight years after Hiss's perjury conviction, Byrnes reflects on Alger Hiss:

> I have previously expressed my doubt that at Yalta Hiss exercised any influence directly upon President Roosevelt in the decisions he and Churchill made on the Far East.... Whether Hiss, through Hopkins and Stettinius, influenced the President on any matters other than the United Nations proposals is pure speculation and a point upon which partisan opinion will never agree.

All parties at Yalta agreed, however, that the draft of the U.N. Charter would be written beginning April 25, 1945, at San Francisco, and because he "performed brilliantly throughout the Dumbarton Oaks Conversations [and] the Yalta Conference," Alger Hiss was named by Stettinius and Roosevelt as Secretary-General.

President Roosevelt was working on his speech for the opening U.N. ceremonies when he died on April 12. Soon after, the elated "Spirit of Yalta," and the hopes and illusions of Americans, died with him. The conservative State Department shunned the more liberal aspects of FDR's policies; they were more confrontational with the Russians and less willing to negotiate. Moreover, the alliance between the U.S. and the Soviets was never political; it was a military coalition, and now that the end of the war was near, the exigencies of genuine compromise were also coming to an end.

Harry Truman, FDR's accidental and unprepared successor, was even less conciliatory than the State Department toward the Russians. He was perturbed at the Soviets because they insisted — for their western border security — on controlling the Polish government. When Soviet foreign minister V.M. Molotov, en route to the San Francisco conference, made a ceremonious stopover at the White House, Truman spoke bluntly, in his characteristic coarse and pugnacious style, intent on getting tough with the Russians. Molotov was deeply offended and protested that he had never been talked to so harshly. Truman retorted that if the U.S.S.R. would keep its agreements, he would not be talked to in that manner. The Cold War had begun. Secretary of State Stettinius witnessed the unpleasant meeting, and the next morning he told Alger Hiss that the tension was great and that he had expected Molotov would return to Moscow, an event which Stettinius believed would have aborted the initial United Nations conference.

Molotov, however, led the Soviet delegation at San Francisco and was one of the conference's four presidents — the others representing the U.S., the U.K., and China. As leader of the secretariat, Alger Hiss sat at the rostrum in plenary sessions next to the president of the day, and he later described Molotov as unapproachable, "churlish and rude," stiff and gruff in manner, and that his "ever-present interpreter set him off even more from his fellow delegates and from us of the secretariat." The Polish issue and the Security Council veto became key points of conflict. Molotov was unbending in his refusal to liberalize Poland's regime, and he wanted veto power (but didn't get it) over not only Security Council resolutions but also to squelch unwanted discussion in the general assembly.

When Alger Hiss left Yalta — promoted to director of the Office of Special Political Affairs — he concluded that the scope of agreements reached there portended the genuine possibility of what diplomats call a "correct" relationship between major powers with clashing values and priorities; but less than three months later the cooperative spirit of Yalta was largely absent at San Francisco. Roosevelt had been passionate about creating a world organization to maintain peace and order. His death and Truman's blatantly suspicious approach toward the Soviets were the paramount reasons for the less trusting change in attitudes.

When the San Francisco conference concluded, Hiss — whose responsibilities for the conference's daily operations were similar to those he performed at Dumbarton Oaks, only greatly expanded — was disappointed that the event had not been the diplomatic success he believed it would be.

War historian Gabriel Kolko wrote:

> The United Nations was born without illusions and without sacrifices on the part of the United States. The new organization failed before it began, for Washington conceived it with exceptions and loopholes, in an atmosphere of suspicion and manipulation, not as a forum for agreement, but as an instrument in the Great Power conflict. The voting structure of the organization prejudged the outcome of its future decisions, and it was obvious to all that the Great Powers would proceed on a more realistic basis in attaining and protecting their vital interests.

World War II was a tragic error to the U.S. government, Kolko believed, "in that even before the war was over it understood that perhaps a less imperialist Germany and Japan would be preferable to the U.S.S.R. as allies in the future."

After the San Francisco conference Alger Hiss thought of leaving government service to re-enter private law practice. Both corporate firms he had worked for in the 1930s wanted him to return, and he was also offered teaching jobs at Harvard and Yale. But Edward Stettinius urged Hiss to remain at State until the U.N.'s bylaws and procedural rules were drafted. Stettinius had resigned as secretary of state soon after Truman assumed office and was appointed U.S. representative and principal adviser to the U.N. Preparatory Commission, scheduled to meet for its organizational meeting in London in January 1946. Hiss agreed to stay and coordinate the documentary materials outlining the State Department's positions for the delegates.

Three months before Hiss sailed to London for the U.N. meeting, a Soviet espionage network was discovered by the authorities in Canada and the U.S. A Russian code clerk named Igor Gouzenko, who worked at the Soviet Embassy in Ottawa, Canada, defected in September 1945 and provided documents revealing an extensive Soviet spy network in North America. According to a November 1945 FBI memo, Gouzenko told Canadian security officers and an FBI agent the month before: "That he had been informed by Lieutenant Kulakov in the office of the Soviet military attaché that the Soviets had an agent in the United States in May 1945 who was an assistant to the then Secretary of State, Edward R. Stettinius."[7]

The FBI's only clue about who this "assistant" could possibly be had been provided by Whittaker Chambers in two interviews prior to September 1945. Director Hoover had then dismissed Chambers's information as unimportant, but now Hoover was taking a closer look. Chambers had mentioned in those interviews (May 1942 and May 1945) that State Department officials Alger Hiss and Donald Hiss had been members of an underground group in the 1930s organized by a communist named Harold Ware. But Chambers never told the FBI he had been a Soviet agent, and he never mentioned espionage; he specifically denied that the Hisses and others he accused of communist sympathies were spies — their alleged mission was only to mess up government policy. Donald Hiss had left the State Department in March 1944, but Alger Hiss remained there until the end of 1946, and in May 1945 his position could very well be described as an "assistant" to Secretary Stettinius.

According to a memo by Hoover dated August 18, 1948, the FBI "first learned of Whittaker Chambers through Ludwig Lore 8/3/41.... Chambers first interviewed by FBI 5/13/42. At this interview Chambers advised that he gave all info in his possession to [Adolf] Berle of State Dept in Sept 1939."[8] Berle's sketchy notes of his meeting with Chambers were turned over to the FBI in June 1943, but the FBI made nothing of them and never even discussed them with Berle, an oversight which later dismayed Hoover. An FBI memo of September 1948 states that Berle's notes "should have been discussed with him at least for the purpose of determining whether the individuals in the Department of State whose names appeared in the notes were still employed by the Department of State." In a later chapter of this book the 1939 meeting between Adolf Berle and Whittaker Chambers (writer/editor Isaac Don Levine was also there) will be explored in detail — without suppressions and distortions common to most accounts — from the perspective of all three participants.

In a third FBI interview in March 1946, Chambers told the agents he had lost all contact with Alger Hiss after 1937 and could provide no further details. Chambers stated, according to the FBI report, "he has absolutely no information that would conclusively prove that HISS held a membership card in the Communist Party or that he was an actual dues paying member of the Communist Party even while he [Chambers] was active prior to 1937. He volunteered that he knew that in 1937 HISS was favorably impressed with the Communist movement."[9]

State Department security official Raymond Murphy also interviewed Chambers in 1945 and 1946 but learned nothing new. Chambers continued to insist that Hiss had not been involved in a spy ring. However, Chambers revealingly embellished his relationship with Hiss in an interview with Murphy on August 28, 1946. By then Hiss was a fairly well-known national name due to the publicity and praise for his work as Secretary General at the U.N.'s San Francisco Conference. Now, instead of merely mentioning Hiss's name along with a list of others, Hiss had become Chambers's former close personal friend. Murphy wrote in his report: "My informant [Chambers] asked Alger Hiss personally to break with the Party in early 1938, but Hiss refused with tears in his eyes and said he would remain loyal to the Party."[10]

Secretary of State James F. Byrnes, who succeeded Stettinius in June 1945, assigned Under Secretary Dean Acheson to discuss "developments in the Canadian case" and Gouzenko's hearsay evidence about a spy in the State Department with J. Edgar Hoover. Hoover came to Acheson's office on October 9 and was asked about possible suspects. According to the FBI report:

> The Director told Acheson we had not been able to definitely establish the identity of this man. He [Acheson] inquired as to whether the Director had any suspects. The Director said we had one party in mind as a possible suspect, though there was no direct evidence to sustain this suspicion. He [Acheson] inquired as to who this was and the Director told him Alger Hiss, but the Director did not feel it was the time to make any accusation in this matter as there was no direct proof of the same.... Acheson stated the Secretary of State was greatly concerned about the matter and it was desired that every effort be made to ascertain definitely the identity of the person referred to.[11]

Acheson had known Alger Hiss since 1929 when Hiss became Justice Holmes's law clerk, but he had had no close association with Hiss until April or May 1946, months *after* his conference with Hoover. "Alger Hiss had been an officer of the Department most of the time I served there," Acheson wrote in his 1969 memoir. "We had become friends and remained friends.... Donald Hiss had been my assistant when I was Assistant Secretary of State, had served me and the country with complete fidelity and loyalty, and [later] was my partner in the practice of law ... with everything that that relationship implies."[12]

Also, in August 1945, Elizabeth Bentley "defected," and in a fog of fear, loneliness, and inherent mental chaos began enumerating to the FBI a tangled web of espionage tales, implicating dozens of government officials. By the end of the year more than seventy FBI agents were chasing her lies to dead ends. During her almost constant interviews with the FBI in November she was asked repeatedly about Alger Hiss. In her signed statement earlier that month Bentley never mentioned his name, but by the end of November she had finally come up with a "Eugene" Hiss who worked, she claimed, for Dean Acheson at the State Department and had recruited two or three others in government to work for the Soviets. An FBI telegram from New York to bureau headquarters stated that Bentley "admitted that the information concerning Hiss was vague, and because of this was reluctant to make any definitive statements as far as Eugene Hiss's activities were concerned."[13] Donald Hiss, in fact, worked for Dean Acheson from 1941 to 1944, and Acheson was Alger Hiss's superior at State, but only after April 1946. Hoover could have just as easily hectored the guiltless Donald Hiss, but for reasons soon to be shown, Hoover was hidebound in his pursuit to capture Alger Hiss.

With the flimsiest of evidence — a Soviet defector's second-hand rumor that an assistant to the U.S. secretary of state in May 1945 was a Russian agent; Bentley's "recollection," after a month of FBI coaching, of a man named Eugene Hiss, a State Department official who allegedly recruited others for espionage work; and Whittaker Chambers's several statements to both State Department security officials and the FBI that Alger Hiss and Donald Hiss were secret Communists positioned to influence government policy but never to recruit or spy — Hoover requested permission from Attorney General Tom Clark to conduct technical surveillance (wiretap) on Alger Hiss. "In connection with this Bureau's investigation of Soviet espionage activity," Hoover wrote — and lied — to the attorney general on November 28, "it has been reported that Alger Hiss ... has been engaged in espionage for the Soviet Secret Intelligence (NKVD). I recommend authorization of a technical surveillance on Hiss to determine the extent of his activities on behalf of the Soviets and for the additional purpose of identifying espionage agents."[14]

When government documents concerning FBI investigative techniques were released to Alger Hiss in the 1970s by way of the Freedom of Information Act (FOIA), no written authorization from the attorney general for a wiretap was among them. Nevertheless, a "technical surveillance" was placed on the Hisses' home telephone for twenty-one months, from December 13, 1945, to September 13, 1947, when the Hisses moved from Washington D.C. to New York City. The logs of this wiretap comprise twenty-nine volumes of FBI serials, about 2,500 pages containing a vast amount of information about the Hisses' personal lives, habits, and relationships with friends and colleagues. The FBI obtained long-distance telephone records from the Hiss residence going back to 1943, intercepted telegrams to Hiss in September 1945, and put a mail cover on their mail. Continuous twenty-four-hour physical surveillance of Alger Hiss commenced in late November 1945 but was discontinued on December 14. Physical surveillance of Hiss was continued frequently thereafter until September 1947.

The FOIA documents confirm what Hiss attorney William Marbury had been told in 1948 by an FBI agent: that Hiss's phone had been tapped for years, and the FBI transcripts filled three cabinets — but nothing derogatory or incriminating had been found. And, more importantly, the documents show that information gathered through the exploitation of unlawful wiretaps and other illegal surveillance was used during Hiss's perjury trials. This information was the source for much of the testimony of the "intimate knowledge" details of the Hisses' life that the government asserted as corroborating Whittaker Chambers's allegations.

J. Edgar Hoover harbored ulterior motives in menacing Alger Hiss. If Hoover had been sincere in the conduct of the FBI's investigation of Hiss — was he *in fact* a Soviet agent or even a Communist? — Hoover would not have lied about the "evidence" against Hiss to his superiors. Hiss believed that Hoover's motives "included a large measure of personal vindictiveness against me because I had been one of the early New Dealers who had complained of his disloyalty to Roosevelt's policies, for which I believed he should have been forced out of office."[15] When Hiss was assistant general counsel at the AAA in the early 1930s he learned that FBI field agents harassed members of farm organizations who supported AAA programs and sided with conservative critics of the agency's efforts. Hiss and his colleagues were appalled that the FBI locals were hindering, not assisting the AAA's officials and supporters; and they knew of the exacting control Hoover had over his agents and felt certain that their coercive actions met with the director's approval. Hiss's views, along with those of his associates and superiors, were common knowledge. "It was a badge of honor for me and my colleagues," Hiss wrote years later, "openly to characterize Hoover's uncurbed lust for personal power as a national disgrace." FDR was aware of Hoover's disloyalty but "had enough fights on his hands" and did not want to take on Hoover, who had by now established solid Congressional support. So the FBI's dishonorable if not illegal tactics continued unabated. Hiss's contempt for Hoover never ceased. Even in 1946, as Hoover was maneuvering to have Hiss fired, Senator Arthur Vandenberg (Republican, Michigan) remarked: "Alger, why don't you New Dealers stop trying to get rid of J. Edgar Hoover. He has a dossier on every member of Congress."

Hoover addressed a long report on "Soviet Espionage in the United States" to President Truman in late November 1945, summarizing the allegations and devoting several pages to his suspicions of Alger Hiss. Secretary of State Byrnes and his security officers also received copies, the first of many similar FBI memos which falsely branded Hiss a Soviet agent.

In March 1946 a top aide to Byrnes alerted the FBI "that Alger Hiss was on the Secretary of State's 'pending' list, and that Hiss was to be given no further consideration for promotion or assignment of responsible duties in the State Department, and that a study should be made of his case to determine if he could be dismissed summarily under Civil Service regulations." Attorney General Clark informed Hoover that Byrnes wanted to fire Hiss but had learned that he couldn't without a Civil Service hearing. Hoover replied that he "did not think a hearing would be wise as the material against Hiss was confidential and if it were not used there would not be enough evidence against him." Hoover suggested that Clark tell Byrnes to transfer Hiss to "an innocuous position where he would understand the situation and resign."[16]

Byrnes, in turn, proposed informing Hiss that complaints about his loyalty had come to his attention, but Hoover was against possibly alerting Hiss to the nature of the FBI's information and thus ruining an important espionage investigation. Hoover offered to "contact several key men in the House and Senate and explain [the] predicament to them," so that the FBI and Secretary Byrnes could both avoid future criticism (and political damage) from the legislature, while Byrnes could tell Hiss that Congress was the source of the denunciations. This stratagem was acceptable to Byrnes, and he even agreed to phone a few legislators himself.

On March 21, after Hiss's return from London, Byrnes told Hiss that "two separate committees 'on the Hill'" were threatening to make speeches condemning him as a Communist because a former FBI agent who worked for one of the committees claimed Hiss's name appeared on several lists of subversives. The Secretary advised Hiss to arrange an appointment with Hoover and get to the bottom of the matter. Byrnes then informed Hoover of his talk with Hiss. But Hoover instructed Assistant Director Ladd that when Hiss called for an interview, Ladd (not Hoover) would give him one, but he should not "disclose information on current cases" to Hiss nor mention the name Whittaker Chambers. Hiss "was going to do the talking," Hoover remarked to Attorney General Clark, "and we would do the listening."[17]

Hiss arrived at FBI headquarters on March 25 and spoke with Assistant Director Ladd. Ladd did not reveal who was calling him a Communist or why, but instead asked Hiss to make a statement. Hiss could only speculate about where the rumors were coming from. Byrnes had asked about his involvement over the years with Lee Pressman. "Hiss stated that he told Mr. Byrnes," Ladd wrote, "that he used to know Pressman very well but had had no contacts with him recently." Hiss acknowledged that he had met Pressman at Harvard, they worked on labor law cases together at the International Juridical Association (IJA) for a few months in 1932, and they both served under Jerome Frank in the AAA from 1933 to 1935. The IJA had been taken over by the National Lawyers' Guild after Hiss left it. Some Guild members were Communists, and the IJA had been considered a subversive organization by the FBI. "Ladd asked me a number of questions which seemed to me rather perfunctory," Hiss later recalled. "He asked me whether I knew various people, some of whom I did not and some of whom had been New Deal colleagues. He seemed satisfied with my answers, and I believed I had settled the matter." Hiss recounted to Byrnes his discussion with Ladd, adding that he wanted the FBI to make a full inquiry to get to the root of the innuendos.

"Declassified State Department memos," Allen Weinstein wrote in *Perjury*,

> show that by the spring of 1946 almost all of the Department's security staff thought Hiss had been involved in some form of undercover Communist work. Not only was his future at State placed in a departmental holding pattern — with consideration for promotion or for confidential assignments ruled out by orders from Secretary Byrnes's office — but Hiss's daily work and associates came under the closest scrutiny. By August, even his desk calendar was being monitored, its appointments list duly noted for future investigation.

But by September the FBI and State Department security had still not obtained concrete evidence of Hiss's disloyalty. Hoover had expected Byrnes to fire Hiss or at least force him out of government, but it didn't happen. So Hoover commenced another round of leaks and slanders to his supporters in Congress and the media. Walter Winchell, the celebrity gossipmonger who was always accommodating to the Master of Deceit, announced on September 29, in an obvious reference to Hiss: "It can be categorically stated that the question of the loyalty and integrity of one high American official has been called to the attention of the President."

Rumors of Communist associations actually led Alger Hiss to remain at the State Department longer than he had planned. "I did not wish to appear to be leaving under fire," Hiss wrote in his memoir. "The cold war had already led me to conclude that we would make little use of the UN, and I had therefore decided that my position as coordinator of our policies toward the UN would no longer be rewarding. But I stayed on for another year, by the end of which I felt confident that the FBI story had been laid to rest."

A year before Hiss left government service, while aboard the *Queen Elizabeth* en route to London for the U.N.'s premier meeting of the General Assembly in January 1946, John Foster Dulles, a member of the delegation, asked Hiss if he intended to remain indefinitely at State. When Hiss indicated he did not, Dulles inquired if he would be interested in succeeding Nicholas Butler as president of the Carnegie Endowment. Initially Hiss was not "seriously tempted," and Dulles could not make a commitment because his own election as chairman of the board of trustees of the Endowment was not scheduled until May. Yet Dulles thought Hiss a top candidate because he had met him at the San Francisco conference and admired Hiss and his accomplishments there.

Dulles was probably unaware that he had been recommended in early 1945 as an adviser to the U.N. delegation by Hiss and Stettinius, despite the protest of President Roosevelt who felt Dulles would not be in sympathy with FDR's foreign policies. But for domestic political reasons Hiss and Stettinius prevailed upon Roosevelt to accept Dulles, who was in the unique position of advising two potential Republican presidential candidates—New York governor Thomas Dewey and Senator Vandenberg of Michigan—on foreign policy. As the senator was one of the delegates, it was important to give a prominent role to someone who had Dewey's confidence as well, and only Dulles met this requirement. Moreover, Dulles's appointment would promote the bipartisanship so vital in assuring wide public support for the U.N.

Dulles agreed in 1945 to become chairman of the board of trustees of the Carnegie Endowment on the condition that he could appoint a fulltime president to handle all the administrative duties. His high regard for Alger Hiss was reinforced by the recommendations of journalists to whom Dulles had mentioned the opening while on board ship, most notably Bert Andrews, Washington bureau chief of the *New York Herald Tribune*, and James Reston of *The New York Times*. Dulles's idea of reforming the Endowment to focus its agenda in support of the U.N. appealed to Hiss, who thought the U.N. should be an essential component of U.S. foreign policy.

Dulles reported his proposal and conversation with Hiss in a letter to John W. Davis, chairman of the executive committee of the Endowment, convinced that Hiss "was the right man for the job" and that Hiss "seemed quite interested in the idea of the Carnegie Endowment. Although he feels that he probably ought not to leave the State Department for three or four months, he wanted me to talk to Jim Byrnes to get the Secretary's ideas as to how soon he could leave the Department without embarrassment."

Dulles followed up with Byrnes, who asked Dulles to postpone Hiss's appointment—provided Hiss remained interested—until December because Hiss was needed at State for the time being. According to Hiss, Dulles renewed the offer in May or June, but Hiss said he "was not prepared to leave the Department because of the conversation I had with Mr. Byrnes in March, which might make it look as though I were leaving under fire."[18]

In November Hiss told Dulles he was "very much interested" in the presidency of the Endowment and that he would discuss the matter with Acheson and Byrnes to see if he could resign "without injury to the work of the Department." Hiss then asked Acheson, his immediate superior at State since May, to meet with Byrnes and determine "whether he did not think that I would no longer be in a position of resigning under fire." Acheson recounted his talk with Hiss to the Senate Foreign Relations Committee in January 1949, a month after Hiss had been indicted on two counts of perjury. Hiss met with him, Acheson said, wanting advice about the Endowment's offer, remarking "that he did not want to leave the Government while he was subject to this criticism. He thought that ought to be cleared up, and did I have any advice for him.

"I said yes, I had. I said, 'My advice to you is to take this job. This is the kind of thing which rarely, if ever, gets cleared up. The Government has to protect its sources of information; there is no way of having any final adjudication of this matter. People will continue to raise these doubts about you so long as you are in a position where you are subject to this sort of attack, and if I were you, I would just leave and go to New York.' He followed that advice."

Alger Hiss was elected president by the trustees of the Carnegie Endowment for International Peace on December 9, 1946. The next day he resigned from the State Department.

When the *Christian Science Monitor* reported Hiss's resignation on December 14, Acheson dispelled rumors that Hiss was leaving under fire:

> Acting Secretary of State Dean Acheson announced with evident regret this week the resignation of Alger Hiss, able chief of the Department's Office of Special Political Affairs, to become President of the Carnegie Endowment for International Peace....
>
> "Mr. Hiss," Acheson remarked, "it can be said positively, is not retiring because of any pressure or criticism of him for leftist leanings. That he was the subject of much propaganda on that score is public knowledge. More than one Congressman, whenever the subject of leftist activity in the State Department was mentioned, pulled out a list of suspects that was invariably headed by Mr. Hiss."[19]

Yet even after Hiss's departure from government the hounding continued. On December 23 Dulles received a letter from Larry S. Davidow, a representative of the American Unitarian Association, concerning Hiss's new role as president of the Carnegie Endowment. "The information we have," Davidow wrote, "would indicate that Mr. Hiss has a provable Communist record," according to "reliable individuals in Washington." He implored Dulles "to become familiar with the facts" and avoid "substantial embarrassment."[20] But Dulles, defending Hiss, responded to Davidow three days later:

> I have heard of the reports which you refer to, but I am confident that there is no reason to doubt Mr. Hiss's complete loyalty to our American institutions.... I have myself in the past ... been victim of the so-called "documentary proof" that I was various things that I was not. Under the circumstances, I feel a little skeptical about information which seems inconsistent with all that I personally know and what is the judgment of reliable friends and associates in Washington.

In a related exchange soon after, Alfred Kolhberg, a wealthy importer and financier of the reactionary anti–Communist magazine *Plain Talk* (edited by Isaac Don Levine, enabler of Whittaker Chambers), and an acquaintance of Endowment trustee General David P. Barrows, told Dulles of hearsay reports that Hiss was a Communist. Dulles wanted proof, which Kolhberg could not, of course, provide. Later, in a February 24, 1947, letter to Dulles, Kolhberg allowed that the information was "uncorroborated except, I am informed, by the files of the FBI."[21] Kolhberg then asked Levine if he could persuade Chambers to meet with Dulles and tell his story, but Levine was certain Chambers had no documents or other evidence, so the whimsical notion was dropped.

Arthur Schlesinger, Jr., one of America's most respected historians, claimed he had seen "documentary" evidence that Alger Hiss was a Communist. But what Schlesinger had in fact seen was one of Chambers's many FBI statements shown to the historian by an agent during an interview for a *Life* magazine article on "Communists in Government," published in July 1946. Barbara Kerr, a researcher for Time, Inc. who assisted Schlesinger on the piece, interviewed Chambers at his *Time* office. In his peerless paranoid style, Chambers made an ineradicable impression on Kerr, insisting that none of the names mentioned as Communist conspirators be used in the story, and he even beseeched her to remove her notes from the building lest they be stolen. She was especially intrigued by Chambers's naming Alger Hiss a Communist because Hiss once interviewed her for a State Department job — but she wasn't hired. Chambers feared, Kerr recalled, that the Communists would kill him if he told all he knew; he had made a pact with them — he wouldn't talk if they would let him live. Kerr was certain everything Chambers said was true. His fear was palpable, and she felt he had no reason to lie. But she promised Chambers she wouldn't repeat the names, and when Schlesinger's article appeared, neither Chambers nor Hiss nor any others accused by Chambers were mentioned.

J. Edgar Hoover knew beyond the shadow of any doubt in early 1947, after Alger Hiss resigned from public office, that Hiss's fourteen years in government were served with exemplary dedication and loyalty to his country. The FBI had conducted too many investigations *not to know* Hiss's record was spotless, and that his rectitude was beyond question to his associates and superiors. Yet, on June 2, 1947, FBI agents descended simultaneously on Alger Hiss at his office and Priscilla Hiss at home. This time the FBI was doing most of the talking because many names were mentioned, including, for the first time, the name Whittaker Chambers, and they wanted to know the extent of Hiss's association with them. Hiss recounted his relationship over the years with Lee Pressman, and when asked if he knew Whittaker Chambers or Nathan Gregory Silvermaster, Hiss said he did not know either one. The agents wrote up a summary of the interrogation, which Hiss read and signed.

The questioning of Priscilla Hiss was somewhat more blunt and direct. The FBI report states Priscilla

> was informed that the Bureau had information to the effect that her husband, Alger Hiss, had, while employed by the Federal Government, collected and secured information from the files of the government agency and turned this information over to a third party who was not authorized to receive same. She was also informed that her husband was allegedly a member of a ring which was formed for the purpose of ... delivering such information through appropriate channels to the Soviet Union. Mrs. Hiss immediately commented that the aforementioned allegation was "absolutely false."

This "information" was obviously a reference to the hearsay evidence of Bentley and Gouzenko, and had nothing to do with Chambers. Chambers had never once mentioned espionage to the FBI or anyone else, according to his own confessions, until November 1948 — after Hiss sued Chambers for merely calling him a Communist.

When Priscilla was asked about Whittaker Chambers, the agents referred to him only as an apostate Communist, not a Soviet agent. The report continued:

> Mrs. Hiss was questioned at length concerning Whittaker Chambers. She immediately denied ever hearing of the name and elaborated by saying that she "knows no such person." It was pointed out to her that Chambers was a former member of the Communist Party who renounced his affiliation and subsequently entered the newspaper field and that Chambers was well known. It was also mentioned that Chambers allegedly knew Mr. and Mrs. Hiss intimately and on occasion was a guest in the Hiss home. Mrs. Hiss steadfastly denied being acquainted with him or knowing his identity.

One of the last accusatory letters John Foster Dulles received about Alger Hiss was from conservative Congressman Walter Judd, who suggested that Dulles check with security officer John Peurifoy of the State Department whom Judd believed held information of Hiss's disloyalty. Peurifoy replied to Dulles that while the FBI mentioned Hiss in their files, the State Department security officials were "convinced of [Hiss's] complete loyalty to the United States and, in fact, thought of him as more conservative than many in the State Department." Peurifoy also asked Dulles to relay to Judd that "he had never intended to suggest to the Congressman that Hiss was disloyal." In his reply to Judd, Dulles championed

Hiss as a strong supporter of American foreign policies, including the Marshall Plan, which was, Dulles wrote, "the phase of our foreign policy which the Communists are fighting most bitterly."[22]

"You can't prove a negative" is a hollow cliché because proof is incumbent upon those who make positive assertions. Beyond reasonable doubt it has been revealed here that Alger Hiss was not a Soviet agent nor a Communist nor even a liar. Yet it remains to be shown exactly *how* Alger Hiss was finally trapped and captured.

CHAPTER IX

Confrontation Under Klieg Lights

"How many cars have you given away in your life, Mr. Hiss?" — Richard Nixon

"[I]n this sadistic age," British journalist and author Alistair Cooke lamented in 1950, "something very like a seventeenth-century religious war," it was almost irresistible because of outside pressures "to swallow whole the Hiss story or the Chambers story, and to join one or other of the entailed crusades." By August 25, 1948, just three weeks after Chambers's first HUAC appearance, when the committee held its public confrontation between the two men, it was obvious to all who followed the news that either Whittaker Chambers or Alger Hiss was on a lying binge; the contradictions were so gross between the two that people, according to Cooke's reporting, "had simply to decide whether Chambers's story was a wholesale fabrication or whether Hiss was making a blanket denial of an experience it would have been fatal to admit in part." All HUAC members were now righteously in Chambers's camp; they were inclined to believe the worst about an unrepentant New Dealer like Hiss anyway, and they could not imagine that Chambers, who held a high position in journalism and stood to lose at least his job at *Time* if found lying, was making it all up. What motive could he possibly have?

Nixon and the committee succeeded in mutating the conflicting narratives of Chambers and Hiss into a referendum on the New Deal. HUAC had been fattening its files since 1938 with the New Deal's calculated flirtations with Communism. Republicans won control of Congress in 1946 largely because of their anti–Communist posturing, and now the White House too looked to be theirs for the taking in November. "Those who were for Hiss or against him," Cooke explained in *A Generation on Trial*, "felt their own pride and past political judgment to be at stake. Many Democrats and old New Dealers felt that Hiss was a gallant protagonist of the younger liberal crowd that went to Washington in the New Deal's first crusade."

For many conservative Democrats and Republicans of the "Eastern establishment," Alger Hiss represented the graceful breeding and high-mindedness of a diminishing New England culture — and was thus easily forgivable. On the other hand, Chambers, the renegade Communist with a vagabond past, exemplified, in Cooke's words, "the old threat of the great unwashed against the genteel tradition." Yet Cooke also noted many youthful onlookers who self-consciously spurned that attitude, especially lawyers and newsmen whom he characterized as belonging to the "fast-ripening American breed of the unfooled, the chronically unconvinced, the man who before the appeal of conflicting certainties keeps up a hardboiled neutrality."

Hiss had demanded a public confrontation with Chambers at the conclusion of his meeting with the committee on August 16, and now, nine days later, it was just what Nixon and Stripling warned him it would be: a show ballyhooed into a circus. More than 1,000 spectators filled the spacious caucus room of the Old House Office Building, and another 300 waited outside in the sticky summer heat. Dozens of reporters were allowed in, along with radio broadcasters, newsreels, Klieg lights and newfangled television cameras — a first for a major congressional hearing.

Having consulted with several lawyers since Chambers's initial charges, Hiss was accompanied by attorney John F. Davis. Another lawyer and friend, Max Lowenthal, had advised him to prepare a retaliatory statement to read into the record, in effect appealing for public support directly because Hiss had lost all hope of changing HUAC's collective mind. The statement was written in the form of a letter and released to the press before the hearing, as Hiss anticipated that Chairman Thomas would not let him read it at the outset.

Chambers, however, arrived at the Capitol alone and without prepared remarks. And even though he appeared as HUAC's star witness, he was obviously very distressed. "As I took my place," Chambers later recalled, "a cold wave of aversion and hostility swelled out toward me from the spectators.... A little girl about seven years old was sitting next to me. She had come with her father, mother and a woman whom I took to be her grandmother.... When I sat down, the father got up and changed places with his daughter so that the child would not have to sit beside me."

In the week leading up to the public confrontation, Richard Nixon later recalled that "we drove our staff at an even harder pace" in attempting to find evidence that would support either Chambers's or Hiss's version of their relationship. That there had been some sort of association between the two men was, of course, no longer in question. However, it is also apparent, more than sixty years after the fact, that HUAC did not conduct much of an investigation of either man. There were no background checks or interviews with their families, colleagues, or friends. Chambers was simply more believable to them than Hiss, and HUAC just assumed that Hiss had concealed any other Communist affiliations so well that it would be futile to search for them.

Nixon and the committee believed that if Hiss was found to be lying on some questions, his credibility on other issues was not trustworthy. HUAC had already discovered that Hiss had known Chambers, a fact Hiss initially denied — with the qualification that Chambers's photo looked familiar. Now the question was how well he had known Chambers and whether he knew him as a Communist. But HUAC's attention was myopically focused on trapping Hiss with his equivocations, if not lies, not on revealing his alleged Communist activities.

"The critical piece of evidence in the case," Nixon wrote, "was Hiss's 1929 Ford roadster." (A car Chambers had on occasion driven in 1935, which he claimed Hiss had later donated to the Communist Party for use by a "poor organizer in the West or somewhere" after Hiss had purchased a new Plymouth. Hiss insisted that he had given the old Ford to Chambers/Crosley — but his testimony was contradictory on this point, as he also said he sold Crosley the car and then said he had thrown the car in with the sublease to the Crosleys of the 28th Street apartment.) "Here our staff seemed to have reached a dead end," Nixon added. "They searched the records of the Department of Motor Vehicles for all automobile transfers in the District for the year 1935 and came up with a blank. Finally I suggested that they might be checking the wrong year and that they extend their search to include both 1934 and 1936. On August 23, two days before the public confrontation, they hit pay dirt. We had found what we were looking for."

Just after 10:30 A.M. on "Confrontation Day," Chairman J. Parnell Thomas read a short statement to the assembly, a summary of appearances before HUAC to date of Whittaker Chambers and Alger Hiss.

On August 3 the committee publicly heard testimony from Chambers regarding government infiltration of an underground Communist apparatus during 1934 to 1937, and that Alger Hiss was one of the members. Two days later, again in open session, Alger Hiss testified at his own request and categorically denied Chambers's accusations, and stated he had never known a man named Whittaker Chambers and could not identify photographs of Chambers as anyone he had ever known.

In an effort to determine the facts, paraphrasing Thomas, a subcommittee headed by Nixon interviewed Chambers privately in New York City on August 7. Chambers furnished many personal details and information about the Hiss family during the period in question, and the committee concluded that the two men must have been closely associated. Then, on August 16, Alger Hiss was questioned for the second time at a closed meeting in Washington. Again Hiss was unable to identify Chambers from photographs. However, Hiss recalled for the committee an individual named George Crosley, a man Hiss had known in the mid–1930s. Hiss believed Crosley could have passed on personal information about the Hisses to Chambers, but Hiss was doubtful that Crosley was actually Chambers. Yet the following day, August 17, when the committee arranged a surprise confrontation between the two at another closed session at the Commodore Hotel in New York City, Hiss was able to make a positive identification of Whittaker Chambers as the individual he once knew named George Crosley.

While the testimony of Whittaker Chambers, Chairman Thomas noted, did not directly involve espionage, as had been alleged by Elizabeth Bentley at the opening session of the "spy hearings," the committee continued its investigations in an effort to determine the true facts. "As a result of this hearing," Thomas concluded, "certainly one of these witnesses will be tried for perjury. The Congress and the American people are entitled to the truth on this important matter."

Alger Hiss was first to testify, and he repeated the circumstances under which he had known Chambers as George Crosley, commencing in the winter of 1934-35. Crosley had presented himself as a freelance writer preparing articles about the Nye Committee's munitions investigations, and one of Hiss's duties was providing information from the record to researchers, students, and writers such as Crosley.

HUAC counsel Robert Stripling followed with questions concerning Hiss's residences in Washington D.C. since the early 1930s, particularly the 28th Street apartment Hiss allegedly sublet to the Crosleys (Chambers agreed that his family had lived there, though rent free, as a favor from one Communist to another) for two months in 1935. Hiss was unable to remember exact dates of when the various premises were rented. But Stripling had statements ready from landlords giving the record dates, and it was plain that Stripling was asking Hiss these questions not to seek information but to elicit errors of recollection, as if to discredit his testimony. In the case of the 28th Street apartment it was established that Hiss made an application in May 1934 for tenancy to begin on July 1, 1934. The apartment was vacated on June 28, 1935 (the Hisses moved to P Street in April; the apartment was then occupied by Chambers and his family from May until June 28, but there was no record of a sublease), and was unoccupied during July. On August 1, 1935, it was rented to a Mr. Isemann. However, according to the building manager, the old leases had all been destroyed.

Hiss objected to "housekeeping" questions as unimportant compared to the real issue of whether he was or ever had been a Communist. Nixon interjected that the "issue in this hearing today is whether or not Mr. Hiss or Mr. Chambers has committed perjury before this committee, as well as whether Mr. Hiss is a Communist." Nixon added that it wasn't the intention of the committee to hold Hiss to exact details on matters which occurred years before, but it was their intention to question Hiss and Chambers very closely about their former acquaintanceship, "because it is on that issue that the truth or falsity of the statements" of either man will stand or fall. Nixon reminded Hiss of the "standard instruction which is given to the jury on cases of credibility of witnesses"—that a witness's entire credibility is suspect if he is found to be telling an untruth on any material issue.

The questioning then turned to Hiss's former 1929 Ford roadster. The committee learned of the car when interrogating Chambers privately on August 7. Chambers recalled driving Hiss's dilapidated Ford not long after he met him, but Hiss later got rid of it and bought a new Plymouth. Chambers added that Hiss disposed of the car through a Communist who owned or managed a service station or a car lot in D.C. "I never knew who this was or where it was," Chambers said. "It was against all the rules of underground organization for Hiss to do anything with his old car but trade it in … but Hiss insisted that he wanted the car turned over to the open party.... Much against my better judgment and much against Peters' better judgment, he finally got us to permit him to do this thing.... I should think the records of that transfer would be traceable."

When Hiss was interviewed privately on August 16, Stripling asked: "What kind of automobile did that fellow have?" Hiss testified that Crosley didn't have a car—"I sold him an automobile." But Hiss quickly changed his mind: "I threw it in with the apartment and had been trying to trade it in and get rid of it." Crosley "wanted a way to get around and I said, 'Fine, I want to get rid of it. I have another car, and we kept it for sentimental reasons, not worth a damn.' I let him have it along with the rent."

The committee was mildly astonished that Hiss would so nonchalantly give a car away. "You just gave him the car?" Stripling had asked on the 16th. "Was there a bill of sale? No evidence of any transfer? Did he record the title?" Hiss couldn't remember.

In the week between the 16th and the 25th, HUAC investigators "hit pay dirt" with the discovery of two vital facts concerning Hiss's former automobiles. The title to the 1929 Ford was signed by Hiss, notarized, and turned over to an auto dealership on July 23, 1936, more than a year after Crosley had moved out of the 28th Street apartment and ostensibly many months after Hiss had broken off with Crosley, whom he characterized as a deadbeat for not paying the rent or repaying small loans. So Hiss obviously couldn't have (legally) given the car to Crosley at the time of the sublease. And why would he have given the car to Crosley a year later, after Hiss claimed to have brushed him off as a freeloader? Moreover, the title to the Ford was eventually passed to a man named Rosen, not Crosley (or Chambers or one of his many aliases). As for Hiss's 1935 Plymouth, the title certificate was dated September 7, 1935, fully two months after Crosley moved out of the apartment. Hiss could have had the car before the date on the title, but if not, then it was impossible for him to have had those two cars at the time Crosley lived in the apartment, and it did not seem likely that Hiss would have given Crosley the only car he then owned, the 1929 Ford. With these facts in hand, HUAC grilled Alger Hiss for several hours on August 25. A few testy exchanges will suffice:

NIXON: Mr. Hiss, your recollection is still that you gave the car to Crosley as part of the apartment deal; is that correct?

HISS: My recollection is as definite as it can be after this lapse of time, Mr. Nixon, that as I was able to give him the use of the apartment, I also and simultaneously, I think, although it could have possibly have been a little later, gave him the use of the Model A 1929 old Ford. That is my best recollection.

NIXON: Well, there were facts, as I recall, just checking through the record, 18 occasions in which you were asked the specific question, specifically about this on Monday and Tuesday [August 16 and 17] in the record, as to whether you had given him the car, sold him the car, threw it in, given him the title, and as to whether it was part of the apartment deal, and in each case you said, "Yes," and at that time you did not qualify your answers with "to the best of my recollection."

NIXON: Now returning to the automobile, did you give Crosley a car?

HISS: I gave Crosley, according to my best recollection —

NIXON: Well, now, just a moment on that point. I do not want to interrupt you on that "to the best of my recollection," but you certainly can testify, "Yes" or "No" as to whether you gave Crosley a car. How many cars have you given away in your life, Mr. Hiss? That is a serious question.

HISS: I have only had one old car of a financial value of $25 in my life. That is the car that I let Crosley have the use of.

NIXON: Well, now, is your testimony this morning then that you did not give Crosley the car, that you gave him the use of the car?

HISS: Mr. Nixon, I have testified, and I repeat it, that my best recollection is that I gave Crosley the use of the car. Whether I gave him the car outright, whether the car came back, I don't know.

NIXON: You do not know whether you had the possession of this car after Crosley left you?

HISS: That, I am afraid, I cannot recall. I do recall having a Plymouth and a Ford at the same time for some months, not just a few days. I do recall the Ford sitting around because it was not being used, the tires going down because it was just sitting on the street.

NIXON: In fact, you have testified that that is the reason you gave Crosley the car, because you did have the two cars.

HISS: I testified that that was the reason, I believe, the car was of no financial consideration to me, Mr. Nixon, during the period we are talking about.

NIXON: All right. Now, your testimony is that you did give Crosley the car for a period of 2 months. When did that occur?

HISS: My best recollection is that it coincided with the sublease. I am not positive that it occurred then, rather than in the fall or some other time.

NIXON: Just a moment. Mr. Hiss, it is not likely that you would have given the car to Crosley after he failed to pay the rent, is it?

HISS: I do not recall the details of when I concluded he was a fourflusher.

NIXON: Your testimony was that you had seen Mr. Crosley after he failed to pay the rent.

HISS: Yes; I feel quite confident I saw him some time after the sublease transaction.

NIXON: Now, do I understand you to say that you might have loaned Crosley a car for a couple of months after he failed to pay the rent?

HISS: I might have, if I had considered that his reasons for not paying were as plausible as his reasons had been for not paying back small loans, because the rent was not a major consideration in my mind. Of that I feel quite confident.

NIXON: Well, didn't you ask him for the rent?

HISS: Mr. Nixon, I don't recall at any time his ever refusing, ever saying, "I just am not going to pay." Quite the contrary, he was always going to pay at some time.

NIXON: How long after he moved out of [your] apartment did you decide he was a deadbeat?

HISS: Mr. Nixon, I am not able to testify with exactness on that.

NIXON: But you think it is possible that you loaned him a car or gave him a car after he failed to pay the rent?

HISS: I may very well have given him the use of the car even though he had not paid the rent at that particular time.

Read into HUAC's record was the fact that the title certificate to Hiss's Plymouth sedan was dated September 7, 1935 (more than 60 days *after* Crosley and family had vacated Hiss's 28th Street apartment). And the title to Hiss's 1929 Ford was signed over by Hiss on July 23, 1936, to the Cherner Motor Company and purchased on the same day for an undisclosed amount (the document indicated a chattel mortgage of $25) by William Rosen of Washington D.C.

NIXON: Your testimony is that you could have given [Crosley] the car before, during, or after the subleasing transaction?

HISS: To the best of my recollection I would not be able to be sure.

NIXON: At the time you gave him the car did you have your new car?

HISS: Again my recollection, Mr. Nixon, is that I had a Plymouth and the Ford at the same time. Of that I feel very confident.

NIXON: In any event, Crosley had the car according to your recollection for a period of say 2 months?

HISS: A period of time, that is correct.

NIXON: If he had the car for 2 months, it would seem quite obvious that you must have had another car at that time.

HISS: It may or may not be obvious.

NIXON: Do I understand you to say that you might have loaned the car to Crosley for 2 months and you didn't have a car during that period?

HISS: Mr. Nixon, if during that particular period I for some reason had no need of a car, either because someone had loaned me a car which was better than that one or because I was on a vacation when the car was of no use to me, there are many possibilities. I don't feel I have exhausted all the possibilities.

NIXON: Then you wish to change the testimony that you gave on Monday and Tuesday [August 16 and 17] that at the time you gave the car to Crosley you had your new car. Is that correct?

HISS: Mr. Nixon, so far as I am aware I am not changing any testimony. I am doing my best to amplify my testimony, to continue to answer questions asked by this committee.

CHAIRMAN THOMAS: Was the car in your name?

HISS: The evidence before this —

CHAIRMAN THOMAS: Never mind the evidence. You know whether the car was in your name or not. Was the car in your name?

HISS: I do not know for certain, Mr. Chairman. I am testifying on the basis of the evidence that has been submitted here today.

NIXON: Mr. Hiss, you are an attorney. You realize that under the law that if the title of the car was in your name, you would have been liable for damages in the event this man had an accident. It is rather amazing to me that a man who stood extremely high in his class at Harvard Law School could say that he had gone through law school and would know that when the title to a car was in his own name, that in the event an accident occurred to that car that he would be liable for damages. You are not testifying to that, are you?

HISS: Mr. Nixon, I would like to testify right now that as of the present moment I really do not have a firm opinion as to what the law would be if someone were driving a car registered in my name and were guilty of negligence causing the injury of someone else. I am slightly surprised at your implication that that would automatically make me as the registered owner of the car liable. Even now at this minute.

NIXON: Mr. Hiss, how much did you get from the Cherner Motor Co. when you transferred the car?

HISS: I have testified that I have no recollection of transferring the car to the Cherner Motor
Co. and I certainly have no recollection of receiving any payment.

NIXON: It was also established in checking the records that no transfer of any type of an automobile was recorded to Mr. Crosley from Mr. Hiss, either of the '29 Ford or of any other
automobile, and it was established through the records that in July of 1936, one year after
Mr. Hiss testified that he had given the car to Crosley and transferred the car to Crosley, one
year later, he had transferred the car to Cherner Motor Co. Also that the Cherner Motor Co.
the same day had transferred it to one William Rosen who had given an address which, as
the result of the committee's investigation so far, is a false address.

"We endeavored to trace the path of the Ford," Robert Stripling wrote in 1949, "without
too much success. It remained something of a mystery." But within a year of the hearing
some facts emerged about William Rosen and the disposition of the Ford. Rosen refused
to testify before HUAC, but on March 9, 1949, Rosen's attorney, Emmanuel Bloch (who
later represented Julius and Ethel Rosenberg), spoke with Edward C. McLean, Hiss's principal lawyer. McLean noted for the files what Bloch told him:

> Rosen does not know Hiss. Rosen did lend himself to a dummy transaction concerning the
> Ford car. Apparently Rosen did not sign the title certificate dated July 23, 1936. It is not clear
> whether Rosen knew at that time that his name would be used in this transaction. However, at
> some later date, a man came to see Rosen and told him that the title certificate to the Ford was
> in Rosen's name and asked Rosen to sign an assignment of it to some other person. Rosen did
> this. The man who came to see Rosen is a very high Communist. His name would be a sensa-
> tion in this case. The man who ultimately got the car is also a Communist. Bloch implied that
> Rosen was a Communist too but did not say so expressly.[1]

Hiss was never able to recall with certainty what he had actually done with the old
Ford. Beyond question it was his signature on the title transfer, which was notarized by W.
Marvin Smith, Hiss's colleague in the Solicitor General's Office, in July 1936. The Ford was
signed over to the Cherner Motor Company, the largest Ford dealer in D.C.— not a "service
station" or a "car lot," as Chambers claimed. The Ford was immediately resold to Rosen,
subject to a lien of $25. So the car was not given away to some poor CP organizer, as Cham-
bers also maintained, and its value — basically junk — was what Hiss had testified it was.

When asked by an interviewer years later why the Ford title *had not* been transferred
to Crosley as Hiss had implied when he testified he had given or sold it to Crosley, Hiss
said he assumed that Crosley would keep the Ford as long as it was useable. "I took no
thought then of his wishing to sell it. Consequently, when I handed over the certificate of
title to him, its sole function was to establish his right to possession. It never occurred to
me to fill out on the back of the certificate the form printed there for use in sale." Hiss
further assumed that Crosley, having retained the car for a period of time, simply sent a
messenger to his office with the certificate of title, which Hiss signed "in the midst of a busy
day." If Chambers indeed disposed of the Ford in this manner he could later say with confidence, as he did, that the transaction records were on file in the District of Columbia, which
they were.

Hiss also concluded that the 1935 Plymouth was in his possession at least weeks before
September 7, 1935, the date on the title, because he remembered driving it with dealer's
plates earlier that summer. Amazingly, Chambers corroborated Hiss when he testified at
Hiss's second perjury trial that he thought Hiss had the Plymouth *as early as Easter 1935*—
which would mean that Hiss could very well have "thrown in" the Ford along with the 28th
Street apartment sublease, just as he initially told HUAC.

Nixon's interrogation of Hiss about the cars finally gave way to general questions about Hiss's acquaintance with Crosley. Hiss allowed that he had probably seen Crosley six or seven times before Crosley moved into the 28th Street apartment, and that they had lunch together a few times at the Senate Office Building when he worked for the Nye Committee. But Hiss could not recall if anyone else on the staff knew Crosley or had met him, though he was checking with former staffers and friends who may have remembered him visiting his office or home. As it turned out, Hiss never found anyone who saw the two men together, except for his wife. (Hiss's stepson, Timothy Hobson, who lived with Alger and Priscilla in those years, has always denied ever seeing Chambers, though he does remember seeing Chambers's wife on at least one occasion.) Nevertheless, Chambers always emphasized the closeness — the family lovingness — of his relationship with the Hisses, while Hiss and his wife could scarcely remember the Crosleys and never with fondness, rendering their alleged generosity toward the Crosleys unusual if not suspect. This was the dissonant note which played to Chambers's favor with HUAC — his emotional warmth toward Hiss and his family won them over.

As Representative Mundt observed near the end of Hiss's testimony:

> You knew this man; you knew him very well ... so well that you even trusted him with your apartment; you let him use your furniture; you let him use or gave him your automobile. You think you probably took him to New York. You bought him lunches in the Senate Restaurant. You had him staying in your home when it was inconvenient for him to stay in the apartment, and made him a series of small loans.
>
> [Chambers was] a Communist functionary.
>
> The important thing to me, Mr. Hiss, is that he was living in your home, that you were associating with him, that you were taking him out in the car, that you were letting him use your car, that you were letting him use your apartment, and making him loans and having associations with him of that nature.
>
> We proceed[ed] on the conclusion that if either one of you is telling the truth on the verifiable data, that you are telling the truth on all of it. And if either one of you is concealing the truth from the committee on verifiable data, it points out that you are concealing from us the truth on obviously the points that we cannot prove.

But Hiss replied that he had not seen Chambers's previous secret testimony which Mundt characterized as standing up in verifiable details. "I am very anxious to see that testimony to see how verifiable they are.... The time has been very short," Hiss said. "If this man actually was a Communist at the time, as he testifies — and, so far as I know, you have only his unsupported testimony for that particular allegation."

After Alger Hiss's six hours on the witness stand, Whittaker Chambers was called to testify. He told Stripling he had been a member of the Communist Party from 1924 until about 1937 or early 1938, and was involved in the CP underground from "1932, roughly, through 1937." During that period he met Alger Hiss, "introduced to Mr. Hiss by Harold Ware and J. Peters" (though on August 3 Chambers swore to HUAC that he never knew Harold Ware) at a restaurant in Washington, and continued to know Hiss until leaving the CP in early 1938. Chambers added that he saw Hiss once again toward the end of 1938.

Chambers testified that he did not represent himself to Hiss with the name George Crosley and had never met Hiss at the offices of the Nye Committee in the Senate Office Building in 1934 or 1935. Hiss knew him only as "Carl," Chambers said, and always called him by that name. However, Chambers said that during those underground years, in which he lived in Baltimore or New York, among other places, he was known by, and lived under, the name of Chambers, only his Washington Communist contacts knew him as Carl.

"How do you know that [Hiss] was a Communist?" Nixon asked.

CHAMBERS: The assumption was in the whole set-up. J. Peters was the organizer of the underground section of the Communist Party. He was dealing with party comrades, and these were dues-paying members of the Communist Party.

NIXON: Do you have any other information on which to base your statement that Mr. Hiss was a member of the Communist Party, other than J. Peters told you he was?

CHAMBERS: Mr. Hiss obeyed party discipline in every respect.

NIXON: Did you yourself have occasion at any time to take dues from Mr. Hiss for the Communist Party?

CHAMBERS: I did.

Chambers assured Nixon that there was no rental agreement with Hiss on the 28th Street apartment he lived in with his wife and baby daughter for two months in 1935 — "Because Mr. Hiss and I were Communists, and that was a comradely way of treating one another." He did not buy or borrow Hiss's old Ford, Chambers maintained.

NIXON: Now, did you see Mr. Hiss any time after 1935?

CHAMBERS: Yes; I saw Mr. Hiss constantly through 1937, until I broke with the Communist Party.

NIXON: Well, how many times?

CHAMBERS: By constantly, I mean at least once a week.

NIXON: Did you ever stay overnight in his home?

CHAMBERS: I stayed overnight frequently in his home.

NIXON: When you say "frequently," do you mean twice or more than that?

CHAMBERS: I mean that I made his home a kind of headquarters.

NIXON: What arrangement was made for paying Mr. Hiss at the time of staying overnight?

CHAMBERS: There was no question of payment involved at any time.

NIXON: What is the reason for that?

CHAMBERS: Mr. Hiss considered it a privilege to have a superior in the Communist organization in his home.

NIXON: You were very fond of Mr. Hiss?

CHAMBERS: Indeed I was; perhaps my closest friend.

NIXON: Mr. Hiss was your closest friend?

CHAMBERS: Mr. Hiss was certainly the closest friend I ever had in the Communist Party.

NIXON: Mr. Chambers, can you search your memory now to see what motive you can have for accusing Mr. Hiss of being a Communist at the present time?

CHAMBERS: What motive I can have?

NIXON: Yes. I mean. Do you — is there any grudge that you have against Mr. Hiss over anything that he has done to you?

CHAMBERS: The story has spread that in testifying against Mr. Hiss I am working out some old grudge, or motives of revenge or hatred. I do not hate Mr. Hiss. We were close friends, but we are caught in a tragedy of history. Mr. Hiss represents the concealed enemy against which we are all fighting, and I am fighting.

I have testified against him with remorse and pity, but in a moment of history in which this Nation now stands, so help me God, I could not do otherwise.

Three days later HUAC released an interim report on the "spy" hearings, noting its opinion that Hiss had "changed his position on the car and testified in a manner which to the Committee seemed vague and evasive ... [and] raises a doubt as to other portions of his testimony.... Chambers, on the other hand, was for the most part forthright and emphatic in his answers."

"The confrontation was over," Richard Nixon wrote years later. "The tide of public opinion which had run so high in favor of Hiss just three weeks before had now turned against him. Critics who had condemned the Committee for putting Chambers on the stand now congratulated us for our perseverance in digging out the truth."

Indeed, the contrast between Hiss's first HUAC appearance on August 5 and his final one twenty days later was, according to journalist and historian William A. Reuben, "so enormous as to be almost beyond recognition. At his first appearance, he had been forthright and direct and indignant. At his August 25 appearance, he seemed cautious, hedging, careful."[2]

"But more damning still to Hiss's reputation," Alistair Cooke observed,

> or the hope of retrieving the respect he had in earlier sessions, was the persuasive psychological force of a hearing that had taken on the sound and appearance of a cross-examination in court. Hiss assisted this powerful deception by abruptly adopting the vocabulary of a trial session, evidently determined at last to fortify a legal case against any possible thrust of a perjury charge. One hundred and ninety-eight times, by the Committee's count, Hiss had qualified his replies with some such phrase as "According to my best recollection." The spectator had to shake himself from time to time out of this trance to appreciate that he was not in a court of law, that Hiss was not a defendant, that there was no right of rebuttal, no cross-examination of the accuser, that, in a word, it was the heyday of the public prosecutor (and in the wrong place).

Chambers, on the other hand, "was ready with answers without hesitation," Reuben recalled, "able to supply all sorts of pinpointed details for all his responses. On the basis of what anyone could *see*— including the fact that, unlike Hiss, Chambers seemingly had no need for counsel — the accuser, Chambers, was infinitely more impressive and convincing."

Whittaker Chambers left the August 25 hearing with the conviction that Alger Hiss was still an active Communist, and through him Chambers was at war with the Communist Party in its fullest extent.

CHAPTER X

Libel: Hiss v. Chambers

> "I had reasoned that once Alger Hiss made the gesture of suing me, there was an outside possibility that he would postpone the action, on one pretext or another, until people lost interest." — Whittaker Chambers, *Witness*

Chambers soon accepted Hiss's challenge to repeat his charges in public, beyond the protection of a congressional committee, so Hiss could sue for libel. On August 27, only two days after HUAC's televised hearing, Chambers appeared on *Meet the Press*, then a popular radio program hosted by Lawrence Spivak. He did not want to be sued — "the very idea of a lawsuit was alien and repugnant; nor did I believe that Hiss could want a suit" — and after accepting the invitation Chambers wired Spivak and canceled. But Spivak protested, and Chambers realized there was really no choice but to go through with it. And he delivered the actionable words.

> MTP: Are you prepared at this time to say that Alger Hiss was anything more than, in your opinion, a Communist? Did he do anything wrong? Did he commit any overt act? Has he been disloyal to his country?
>
> CHAMBERS: I am only prepared at this time to say that he was a Communist.
>
> MTP: Would you be prepared, for instance, to put on the record the testimony that you gave during three or four interrogations by the FBI?
>
> CHAMBERS: The gist of that testimony is already on the record in the Un-American Committee.
>
> MTP: Are you willing to put on the record, so that it can be tested in the courts under the laws of evidence, that this man did something wrong?
>
> CHAMBERS: I think that what needs clarification is the purpose for which that group was set up to which Mr. Hiss belonged. That was a group, not, as I think is in the back of your mind, for the purpose of espionage, but for the purpose of infiltrating government policy by getting Communists in key places.
>
> MTP: It was not, then, by definition, conspiracy?
>
> CHAMBERS: No, it was not.

The editorial pages of three major newspapers usually critical of HUAC — *The New York Times*, *The Washington Post*, and the *New York Herald Tribune* — all now agreed that the House Committee's Communist hearings had raised important though still unanswered questions. A Gallup poll in September revealed that eighty percent of Americans surveyed approved of HUAC's spy hearings and believed they should continue.

Many observers felt Hiss's public reputation was now completely shattered. John Foster Dulles said in so many words that Hiss should resign the presidency of the Carnegie Endowment. But Hiss was certain the courts would vindicate him if he sued Chambers, that to resign now would be fatal to his case, and Dulles reluctantly acquiesced. Nixon, meanwhile, sent Dulles a letter in early September reiterating HUAC's position on Hiss's veracity:

> I have come to the conclusion that at the very least Hiss deliberately misled the committee in several important respects during his appearances before it. Whether he was guilty of technical perjury or whether it has been established definitely that he was a member of the Communist Party are issues which may still be open to debate, but there is no longer any doubt in my mind that for reasons only he can give, he was trying to keep the committee from learning the truth in regard to his relationship with Chambers.[1]

Dulles had staunchly defended Hiss the year before, but to side with him now could be political suicide; Republican nominee Dewey was likely to win in November and Dulles expected to be his secretary of state. Therefore, he thanked Nixon for "setting out so carefully your conclusions," which he circulated among several of the Endowment's trustees, leaving Hiss to twist in the wind this time.

Outlandish rumors also began to surface in early September. According to the account in Weinstein's *Perjury*, "Government security officers speculated wildly that Alger Hiss planned to flee the country." The Central Intelligence Agency was informed by Naval Intelligence, who probably initiated the fiction, that Hiss "may be preparing to leave the United States, possibly for the Far East." The CIA then alerted the State Department about the "unconfirmed report," requesting that the Agency "be notified ... of Mr. Hiss's destination, if and when a passport is granted him."

HUAC investigators lit on the rumor and immediately leaked it to the *Chicago Tribune*. Under the scare headline "HISS PREPARING TO QUIT COUNTRY, PROBERS ADVISED," the article alleged that Hiss "has been taking a series of inoculations ... of a type which would indicate that Hiss planned to go to the southwest Pacific or to the Soviet Union." "Hiss has not sued Chambers for libel or slander," the report added, "although the latter waived immunity of his testimony before the congressional committee by openly charging Hiss was a member of the pre-war Communist underground in the capital."

Chambers, meanwhile, was more terrified of being shot than sued. "Once more he feared assassination," his biographer Tanenhaus wrote. "At home he kept his gun within easy reach and placed bullets in every one of the thirteen rooms."[2]

Alger Hiss always maintained that his reaction from the outset to Chambers's accusations was that of an innocent man defending his good name. Though he was cautioned by colleagues, most of them lawyers, not to testify before HUAC, he ignored their advice. And now he was snared in a nightmare from which he believed the courts would extricate him. Yet even after Chambers repeated the charges on *Meet the Press*, Hiss's chief lawyer, Edward McLean, discouraged Hiss from suing him. Hiss's lifelong friend, attorney William L. Marbury, however, adamantly disagreed with McLean. Marbury had silently accompanied Hiss at his first HUAC appearance on August 5, but had left for Europe on business later in August. Marbury was in Geneva when he was stunned by the news that HUAC had reopened public hearings on the 25th, that Hiss had been confronted by Chambers, and that Hiss had supposedly equivocated as to their past relationship. "As time passed," Marbury recalled, "more and more ominous reports began to come in about the progress of the investigation and even the Swiss newspapers carried articles on the subject." Marbury wrote to Hiss from Geneva, apologizing for deserting him in his time of trouble.[3]

Hiss, in turn, sent a letter to Marbury's Baltimore office informing him that in his absence he had employed Edward McLean of New York to represent him, and that he wanted to bring a libel suit against Chambers. Hiss asked Marbury to call him as soon as he returned.

Marbury returned from Geneva on September 12 and immediately went to Cambridge for a meeting of the Harvard Corporation. That evening he talked about the Hiss case with Harvard president James Bryant Conant and Grenville Clark, a senior member of the corporation. Both Conant and Clark felt that Hiss had no alternative save bringing a libel suit against Chambers promptly. Hiss's failure to do so "had already been taken as an admission of the truth of Chambers' charges," Marbury wrote, "and they feared that a flood of similar charges against political and academic figures would soon follow, which would have a very serious impact on our foreign policy and on academic freedom generally."

The next day Marbury phoned Hiss, who asked him to come to New York to discuss the libel suit matter with McLean and other attorneys that were ambivalent about suing. Marbury interviewed Alger and Priscilla all day at their New York apartment, warning them that if either had skeletons in the closet they would certainly be exposed if suit were filed. Both assured him there was no need to worry. Later, Marbury attempted to persuade McLean and company to withdraw their objections. McLean worried that the suit would not be heard in New York until it was too late to do any good. Marbury pointed out that Chambers only worked in New York but lived with his family in Maryland, conferring jurisdiction on the federal District Court in Baltimore, which would try any case within sixty days unless the parties sought delay. Furthermore, Marbury reckoned Chambers was not in a position to raise any postponing technical issues and was bound to defend his statements as being true.

The ultimate decision was up to Hiss. At a meeting in Marbury's office on September 22, Hiss announced that he wanted to proceed with the suit immediately. "I again warned about skeletons in the closet," Marbury recalled, "but Alger brushed this aside, saying that he had nothing to hide." Edward McLean offered to draft the complaint and continue his services, while Marbury and his partner Charles Evans would file in Baltimore and assume primary responsibility for the trial.

Though the burden of proof of Maryland libel law was not incumbent upon the plaintiff, Marbury believed that the only way a jury would find for Hiss, considering the damage the HUAC hearings and negative public opinion had already inflicted upon his reputation, was to prove that Hiss's character and conduct throughout his life were entirely at odds with Chambers's story, and that Chambers was unworthy of belief. On the one hand, Marbury proposed to show that Hiss had earned the trust of many of the country's most respected leaders, and that he had often opposed on principle the tenets and policies of the Communist Party and the Soviet Union. And on the other hand, he would prove that Chambers made false statements under oath to HUAC, and that his character and conduct throughout his life rendered his testimony suspect. Marbury hoped to frame the issue before the jury as one of "veracity between a valuable public servant of spotless reputation and a renegade Communist who, on his record, could not be believed under oath."

Hiss and Marbury agreed to seek damages of fifty thousand dollars, a sum large enough to hurt Chambers but probably not bankrupt him. Hiss wanted vindication, not money, and Marbury felt that a jury would likely hesitate to impose a heavy judgment anyway, so better not to risk asking for a huge sum and defeat the purpose of the suit if a small verdict was returned.

The suit was filed on September 27 in the U.S. District Court for the district of Maryland. On hearing the news, Chambers told the Associated Press: "I welcome Mr. Hiss's daring suit. I do not minimize the audacity or the ferocity of the forces which work through him." His statement seemed clearly libelous to Marbury, who filed a supplementary complaint asking for additional damages of twenty-five thousand dollars.

Time magazine came to the aid of Chambers, Luce's favorite senior editor, and took a stake in the outcome by volunteering to pay for his legal defense; while Hiss received public support of his integrity from dozens of prominent individuals, Republicans and Democrats, whom he had worked with in government, including three former secretaries of state, two senators, a sitting supreme court justice, and Eleanor Roosevelt, with whom Hiss had served at United Nations conferences.

As first pointed out by John Chabot Smith, a reporter for the *Herald Tribune* who covered events as they unfolded (and later wrote a book about the case), an "entirely new situation had now been created." What began as a Republican Party election-year ploy by HUAC—to put the heat on Harry Truman by charging there were Communists in government going back to the early New Deal—had evolved into a libel suit which would attempt to prove that Whittaker Chambers was a liar and a fraud. Now HUAC could no longer shield its star witness, and the survival of the committee might very well depend on the outcome of the trial—and especially so if Truman won and the Democrats regained control of the House and Senate, precisely what happened only two days before Chambers sat for his first deposition. Finally Hiss was getting a break, and no one was more aware of it than Chambers, who realized the tables were turning.

More good news for Hiss was published by *The New York Times* on October 15. The Justice Department informed the paper that after a six-week study of HUAC's transcripts there was insufficient evidence to prosecute either Hiss or Chambers on perjury charges for their conflicting testimony. "Consequently," the report read, "unless new facts become available, it appeared there would be no action to carry out the [HUAC's] prediction ... that one of the two would 'certainly' be tried for perjury."

Weeks before Hiss's final decision to proceed with the suit, McLean had already hired private detectives to collect background information on Chambers. They were particularly interested in discovering if Chambers had ever used the alias George Crosley and if he had ever been treated for mental disorders, having heard that Chambers had allegedly once been committed to a psychiatric hospital. By October, Hiss's investigators were hearing rumors that Chambers was a homosexual, and Marbury received a written report in early October that, according to John Cowles, publisher and chairman of the Minneapolis Star and Tribune Company, "the gossip among newspapermen was that Chambers was a homosexual." Rumors were also beginning to fly that Hiss and Chambers had been lovers, or that Chambers and Priscilla Hiss had been lovers, or that Chambers had sexually molested Hiss's ten-year-old stepson Timothy in 1936—but these rumors would remain unfounded.

Chambers's alleged homosexuality was a subject Marbury "definitely did not intend to get into" in the upcoming oral deposition of Chambers, scheduled for early November, but Marbury did bring the subject up with Hiss, who told him in strict confidence that Timothy, now 22 years old, had been discharged from the navy in 1945 because of a homosexual episode. Hiss felt certain that HUAC knew this and would not hesitate to broadcast it if the rumored homosexuality of Chambers was brought up. Timothy was eager to testify that he had never seen Chambers at any of the Hiss residences in the 1930s, but both his mother and Hiss would not allow him to be involved.

Chambers confessed to numerous homosexual encounters over a five-year period in the 1930s to the FBI a few months later, in February 1949. "I actively sought out the opportunities for homosexual relationships," Chambers stated in a handwritten note, "continuing up to the year 1938," the year of his Communist underground "defection." He used assumed names, and the assignations usually took place at hotels in New York and Washington. "In 1938, I managed to break myself of my homosexual tendencies," Chambers wrote,

and ... for years I have lived a blameless and devoted life as husband and father. It will be noted that three things of some great importance happened during the year 1938. First my cessation of my homosexual activities, my final break with the Communist Party, and my embracing for the first time, religion. I do not believe that the cessation of my homosexual activities and my break with the Communist Party were in any way connected with each other.... I tell it now, only because in this case I stand for truth. Having testified mercilessly against others, it has become my function to testify mercilessly against myself.... I have said before that I am consciously destroying myself. This is not from love of self-destruction, but because only if we are consciously prepared to destroy ourselves, in the struggle, can we fight the thing, can the thing we are fighting be destroyed.

But Chambers was "telling it now" only because, as he told the FBI, Hiss "obviously intends to press the charge that I have had homosexual relations with certain individuals." Chambers had learned that a man whom he had sexually *assaulted* in 1932 had recently told his story to Hiss investigators.

Leon Herald first met Chambers in the winter of 1926-27 at the 42nd Street Library in New York. He moved to Chicago in 1930, and in 1932 was a delegate at the John Reed Club convention held in Chicago. Chambers also attended as a delegate from New York. Herald recalled:

At the first session the Chicago delegates were asked to find lodging for the outside delegates. Having known [Chambers], I took it upon myself to get him a room in the same lodging house where I myself lived.

I took him along with me to our place at Chicago's near North Side. The hour was late, and we being quite tired after the day's work, I bade him good night and went to my room.

In the middle of the night I suddenly awoke in the midst of having an orgasm. When I saw him laboring at my penis still in his mouth, I pushed him aside, while moving myself away from him. My shock was so great that I could not say a word.... Since I was completely dumbfounded, he started asking me to do the same thing to him. This was too much. The only words I could manage to speak were: "You get out of here...." He left immediately.... Nor did I ever see him from then on.[4]

Chambers was never confronted in court with those revelations, nor did he acknowledge homosexual encounters in his autobiography; they weren't made public until Meyer Zeligs's biography of Chambers was published in 1967 and the FBI reports were released through the Freedom of Information Act in the 1970s. Chambers, who often contemplated suicide, was terrified that his homosexual past would be publicized by the "Hiss forces," and had his shame been exposed he would likely have killed himself. His emotional state at the time was remorselessly expressed in a macabre letter to his friend Ralph de Toledano years later:

It occurred during the first Hiss trial, when it looked as if we should be borne down and destroyed, and could not dream of leaving our children in a world where such things were possible. We used to get up before dawn, in those days, to milk. One morning, my wife and I sat together, drinking coffee in the pre-dawn, and, somehow, I explained to her that it might be necessary for us soon to kill, first our children, and then ourselves. Somehow, she told me that she had reached the same conclusion. Then she placed on my hand her own hand which was as cold as if she were already dead. That is the kind of woman I am married to. That is the kind of people we are: we plan to kill our children, but not to let them fall to the mercy of the enemy world.

On November 4 and 5, 1948, Whittaker Chambers testified in the pretrial deposition at the law offices of Marbury, Miller and Evans in Baltimore. He was accompanied by defense lawyers Richard F. Cleveland and William D. MacMillan of the firm of Semmes, Bowen and Semmes, and Harold Medina, Jr., an attorney who worked for Time, Inc.

Chambers was confounded by the suit; he really didn't believe Hiss would go through with it. After all, Chambers had rarely been held to account for his impulsive allegations and devious actions over the years. Henry Luce even encouraged Chambers's distortions and fabrications on an international scale. When his colleagues at *Time* threatened to revolt, Chambers, the Foreign News editor in late 1944, told them, "The truth doesn't matter." If others wouldn't bend to his will, he'd suspect Communists were plotting against him. "I had reasoned that," Chambers wrote in *Witness*, "once Alger Hiss made the gesture of suing me, there was an outside possibility that he would postpone the action, on one pretext or another, until people lost interest." However, Chambers said in his autobiography, Hiss's lawyers summoned him immediately to a pre-trial deposition in Baltimore. Chambers now had no doubt that the Communist Party intended to destroy him with the libel suit. But, in fact, Chambers was not "summoned ... almost at once"; he met with his lawyers daily for *six weeks* in preparation for questioning.

In his testimony before HUAC throughout the previous August, Chambers swore he had been a paid functionary of the Communist Party from 1924 to 1937, that Alger Hiss had been his best friend in the Party from the time they met in 1934 until Chambers defected, and that he personally collected Party dues from Hiss and used Hiss's home as an "informal headquarters." Along with their wives, Chambers maintained, they had met socially numerous times. Yet after two days of interrogation by Marbury, Chambers was unable to substantiate any of it, including any proof that he himself had been a member of the Communist Party. "What about a Communist Party card?" Marbury inquired. "That I do not have," Chambers replied. At the end of the first day of questioning — Chambers, of course, arrived without corroborating documentation — Marbury demanded that he produce the next day any correspondence, if he had any, from any member of the Hiss family which he had received at any time. The next morning Chambers turned up again empty handed. He had not yet "explored all of the sources where some conceivable data might be," Chambers's attorney conceded.

The only verifiable information Chambers provided about his past had nothing at all to do with the Communist Party. He once worked at the New York Public Library as a clerk in the newspaper division for "about a year or a year and a half," until sometime "in the fall of 1924." This was "perhaps six months" after he had joined the Communist Party, Chambers said. Why did he leave this job? Marbury asked. "My locker was forced open in my absence," Chambers explained, "and in it were found a number of Communist hand-bills, and I believe also evidence that there was a Communist cell working in the library."

The employment files of the New York Public Library confirm that Chambers had been a clerk at the 42nd Street branch. But their records, obtained by Hiss's investigators, show that Chambers was employed there for *three and a half years*, from September 1923 until April 1927 when he was fired — not because of anything to do with the Communist Party but because he had stolen 63 library books.

During his years at the library, Chambers declared to Marbury, he had submitted poetry to publisher Samuel Roth, who, two months earlier, in September 1948, swore in an affidavit that Chambers had once sent him poems for consideration under the name "George Crosley." Chambers indifferently admitted he may have used the alias. But had he conceded as much before HUAC in August it would have destroyed his credibility.

After the library job Chambers said he was a sales clerk for Morris Zukofsky's book store on Fourth Avenue in New York. Chambers recalled working there for perhaps six months or a year in 1924–1925. Louis Zukofsky, a brother of the owner, knew Chambers well during the 1920s and early '30s and confirmed that he worked at the book store for about a year beginning in 1927 — which squares with the correct date Chambers left the library — not in 1924.

During his employment at the library and the book store, Chambers told Marbury, he had also been active in the Communist Party "in the small ways novice Communists operate," such as collecting unsold copies of the *Daily Worker* at newsstands around Manhattan and returning them to the paper's office. But it wasn't until after his brother's suicide, a devastating emotional shock to Chambers, that he became a fulltime resolute Communist. "Now, you say that after the period of several months following your brother's death," Marbury asked, "that you decided the best way to snap out of it, so to speak, was to throw yourself actively in the work of the Party. Now, will you tell us what you did?"

"I went to the *Daily Worker* and began to write for it," Chambers replied.

"You mean as an employee, or just voluntarily?"

"I believe first voluntarily," Chambers added, "and then later I was taken on the staff."

However, here again the facts and dates render Chambers's account impossible. Chambers testified that his brother committed suicide at age twenty-one in 1925 and that several months following his death Chambers began writing for the *Daily Worker*. But his brother, Richard, who gassed himself in a kitchen oven, died in September 1926, two weeks before his twenty-third birthday. Chambers was employed at the library until the following April and then at the book store well into 1928. Furthermore, he was unable to substantiate that he had at any time worked for the *Daily Worker*. As revealed by the research of William A. Reuben, Chambers contributed nothing to the *Daily Worker* during the 1920s except a single poem published in July 1927.

Chambers's "phenomenal memory," so characterized by Richard Nixon after their many interviews and meetings in August, was found after his deposition with Marbury to be in error about even the most significant life events. He testified that he graduated high school in 1918, though the correct date was 1919; that he left Columbia University the first time in the spring of 1921, but it was actually 1922; that he visited Europe in the summer of 1921, but in fact he went two years later; that his father died of a heart attack in 1927, though he died in 1929 of hepatitis; that his mother was a homemaker who had never worked, yet she had been employed fulltime for twenty years (1921–1941) as an investigator for the Board of Child Welfare of the City of New York, qualifying for the job by lying about living in Manhattan while she resided in Long Island; that he and his wife, Esther, were married in 1930, but it was really 1931.

His steel-trap memory also failed him when questioned about translating books — Chambers's *actual* major vocation during much of the period when he otherwise fancied himself a fully committed American Bolshevik. Chambers swore to HUAC in August that after his defection from the Party in 1937 and joining *Time* magazine in 1939, he "translated a book." Nixon asked if he had translated just that one book, and Chambers replied: "I do not recall any others." But three months later Chambers testified to William Marbury that he had translated a book prior to 1929. Chambers maintained that the only other income besides the ten-dollars-a-week salary from the Communist Party he received up through 1929 was two hundred and fifty dollars paid by publisher Simon & Schuster for translating Felix Salten's *Bambi*.

"Did you publish any other translations during this period?" Marbury inquired.

"No," Chambers said, "I don't think that I did."

It should scarcely be shocking at this point to learn that between 1928 and 1940 Whittaker Chambers was the English-language translator of *seventeen* German and French books, four of them translated before the end of 1929, six translated in 1930, three in 1931, two in 1932, and one each in 1938 and 1940. *Bambi*, his first translation, was a Book-of-the-Month Club selection. Simon & Schuster published six of his translations, and many were widely reviewed.

And there was more, much more, money obtained by Chambers in these years which had nothing at all to do with the Communist Party. Reuben's investigations, which continued over many decades in the Hiss-Chambers affair, also reveal that Chambers inherited nearly $9,000 from the estates of his father and both grandmothers between February 1930 and September 1933. This was a substantial amount of money in the early 1930s, considering that the average annual salary in 1934 was merely $1,400. And this was in addition to his income as a translator and his wife's income through 1933 as a clerk and typist.

To Marbury's astonishment, Chambers then swore that he had been out of the Communist Party altogether from 1929 until 1932, further reducing his putative thirteen-year tenure as a Communist functionary to something like five years — and we shall see that his purported "underground" activities of even those five years stretch credulity to the limit. Chambers said that by 1929 he had become the "editor of the *Daily Worker*" but had quit the paper and the Communist Party that year after becoming involved in the Party's factional intrigues, which culminated in the expulsion of hundreds of followers of Jay Lovestone, an "oppositionist" who had neglected Moscow's dogmas.

"You had diverted, I take it," Marbury inquired, "from the Party line?"

"It is not only that," Chambers explained, "but I was working with the oppositionists, which is also a sin in the eyes of the official Party." And for the next three years, Chambers remarked, his erstwhile comrades who remained faithful denounced him as "an enemy of the Communist Party," and he only associated with "people who had been expelled from the Party." He was not so malevolent as to be tagged a "diversionist wrecker," but he was definitely "in disgrace." As Chambers elaborated in *Witness*, he was on the outside of the CP but not out of it. He claimed the Party never expelled him, and he still believed he was a Communist. The break was over differences in strategy and tactics, not theory.

However, Chambers's interests were manifestly literary, not political, Communist or otherwise, and by early 1931 he was writing proletarian short stories for the Soviet-leaning *New Masses* magazine. The stories received glowing reviews and were praised by the Russian press. In May 1932 the name Whittaker Chambers appeared for the first time on the masthead of the *New Masses*, along with eight other editors. But his good fortune soon changed because, as he testified before Marbury, he only held his editorial position for two months before being "ordered" underground.

Chambers's underground life, what few true facts are known of it, will be explored in subsequent chapters. The account he gave to Marbury is dreamlike, incoherent, and aimless; a series of meetings with men continually on the move without declared purpose or last names. Marbury asked Chambers what he did during his first underground project, which Chambers claimed lasted two years, from 1932 to 1934, in New York City.

"Very little that I can recall," Chambers replied. "There were occasional days I think I did not do anything at all."

"Well, what did you do, just sit around the house?"

"Stayed home," Chambers said, "or would go into the city and go to a movie."

Chambers commenced working with the Washington, D.C., apparatus of the Communist Party, he told Marbury, in "the early spring" of 1934, after J. Peters had introduced him to Harold Ware (whom, it bears repeating, Chambers swore to HUAC he never knew), a Communist who oversaw the apparatus. Chambers's "mission" was to go to Washington and "look over the possibility of setting up a parallel apparatus."

"What I had to do," Chambers testified, "was look over the possibilities for taking people out of the apparatus that existed and perhaps drawing other people in, if they could be suitable for the purpose." The government officials comprising Ware's group knew nothing about Chambers, who was supposedly introduced to them only as "Carl." Why these sophisticated officials, most of them lawyers, would confer faith in a nameless stranger, losing their careers if exposed, Chambers doesn't say, except "that he was a man who could be trusted," and they were committed to the robotic notion of "Communist discipline."

When the questioning turned to Alger Hiss, Chambers said he met him in late 1934 or "sometime" in 1935. "In other words," Marbury remarked, fishing for something more precise from the illusive witness, "you had been in Washington some six months before you met him?"

"No. If I had been in Washington six months, I had met him earlier than that."

"Now, you said yesterday that your first visit to Washington you thought was paid around June, or in fact in the spring."

"That is possible."

"Well, now, where did you meet him?"

"Apparently in a restaurant of some kind."

"Why do you say apparently?"

"Because my recollection is not very clear about it." Chambers was nothing if not unclear, but he recalled that Harold Ware and J. Peters were also present, "and I have some kind of memory of a restaurant."

"Now," Marbury continued, "what was the gist of the conversation on that occasion?"

"The gist of the conversation was, or the purpose of the meeting was to introduce me, and the gist of the conversation was that we wanted to begin to separate Mr. Hiss from his own [apparatus]."

"What was the function of that group?"

"The function of that group, I presume — I took part in very little of its affairs — was to consider their general work in Washington, the organization of the cells and certain policy matters with respect to work in the government."

"Well, now," Marbury asked, "what did you learn about them when you were introduced to them, what were you told?"

"That this was a group of Communists, most of them government workers, who were involved in certain party activities in Washington." But Chambers no sooner said this than he testified that Hiss "was supposed to keep himself as far removed from any Communist activities or suspicion of communism as possible, and advance as far in the government as possible."

"In other words," Marbury summarized, "he was to behave himself like a man who is not a Communist, but to try to get ahead in the government, and separate himself from the other Communists — in other words, he was to behave exactly like a man who was not a Communist?"

"Yes, of course."

Marbury pressed Chambers for specific actions by Hiss that might indicate he was a Communist. Chambers retold the tale about Hiss's 1929 Ford; how Hiss had given it away to the Communist Party, much against Chambers's better judgment because the transaction might be traceable. Another incident, Chambers recalled in testimony for the first time, which had "caused a considerable stir," involved Hiss obtaining "certain special documents" from the State Department while he was counsel for Senator Nye's Committee in 1935. The documents were not passed to the Communist Party; Chambers simply wanted to satisfy himself that Hiss could procure them if they were demanded. Chambers added, also for the first time, that Hiss "occasionally gave the Communist Party bits of information which he thought might be useful to them," and that he sought the Party's approval before joining the State Department in 1936.

"I frequently read State Department documents in Mr. Hiss's house," Chambers maintained. "Mr. Hiss very often brought a briefcase with documents home, and I used to read those that were interesting. They were not very interesting, most of them. I think they were chiefly on trade agreements, and one thing and another.... I simply read most of them out of curiosity, to see what kind of things were written about in such places."

Nevertheless, Chambers swore that such documents were of no interest to the Communist Party and that he had never relayed them or any other official documents from Alger Hiss to the Communist Party.

After two full days of testimony Chambers's deposition was adjourned for eleven days, until November 16. Marbury later wrote that "it was apparent that in the absence of some written evidence which would corroborate Chambers' story, no jury would ever believe it." A week before the examination resumed, Marbury told a Boston friend: "Chambers not only confirmed everything which we had heard which was derogatory to him but testified to other matters of which we had had no previous knowledge. I should add, however, that we have received no confirmation of the fact that Chambers has ever been confined to a mental hospital or treated for a mental disease.... That is only one of the surprising aspects of this amazing case."

CHAPTER XI

Comrade Carl

"For I had come to believe that the world we live in was dying, that only surgery could now save the wreckage of mankind, and that the Communist Party was history's surgeon." — Whittaker Chambers, *Witness*

In the Jazz Age year 1925, amidst boundless opportunity, dazzling economic expansion, and unparalleled national optimism, Whittaker Chambers, a forlorn 23-year-old provincial from Long Island and recent dropout from Columbia University, joined the Communist Party, composed then mainly of alienated foreigners who couldn't speak English.

Chambers possessed a mind that ran to chimerical extremes. When he began at Columbia a few years before joining the CP, he was conservative in his view of life and politics, and undergoing a religious experience. By the time he left he was no longer a conservative and no longer a believer. Chambers entered college, he remarked to FBI agents in a 1949 interview, "much against my will." He was living at home in Long Island and commuting daily to Columbia. "At that time," Chambers reflected on his youthful political views, "I was a staunch supporter of Calvin Coolidge, who had just put down the Boston Police Strike." However, Whittaker Chambers was a born student, an omnivorous reader who taught himself many foreign languages as a child, so it would seem Columbia was ideal for him.

His parents, the highbrows of Lynbrook, assuredly encouraged their two sons to go to college. Whittaker was born in 1901 (as Jay Vivian Chambers on his birth certificate, adopting Whittaker, his mother's maiden name, after he left high school), followed by his brother almost three years later. He was a pensive, self-conscious, awkward boy, indulged by his homemaker mother yet virtually ignored by his father, a commercial artist. "Not once in our whole lives," Chambers recalled, "did he ever play with me. He was uncommunicative to the point of seeming mute." On occasion his father took him to his Manhattan studio or an art museum, but they never exchanged a word.

His father insisted that the boys call him Jay, not Dad or Papa, and he invented the nickname "Beadle" for Whittaker, who hated it worse than his given name, Vivian, by which his mother addressed him. There was never any outright abuse or yelling in the home; decorum was scrupulously controlled. "The voices around me," Chambers remembered, "were all gentle voices." And each evening when his father came home from his office in the city, Vivian and his little brother "had to meet him at the door and kiss him."

Soon after graduating high school — with mediocre grades and few friends — in 1919, Chambers ran away from home and worked as an unskilled laborer in Washington, D.C., and New Orleans for several weeks before going broke. He wrote home for money and was sent a ticket back to Long Island. He used aliases such, as Charles Adams and Charles Whittaker, on his working road trip, a name-changing bent which he employed often in his secret agent underground years — and even after he defected.

The next year Chambers matriculated at Columbia and thus began what he called "my intellectual pulverization." His faculty advisor and English teacher was Mark Van Doren, a poet and critic who won the Pulitzer Prize for poetry twenty years later. Van Doren, whom Chambers labeled a "liberal rationalist," admired and promoted Chambers's poetry, except for his religious verse, which Van Doren politely told him contained "pathological" fallacies, such as God operating in nature. His classmates — "young zealots" — lectured him continually on Marxist ideas, inflaming "long and violent arguments." But the impressionable Chambers soon capitulated — the very thought of God was now an embarrassment — and forthwith he became the most radical man on campus, writing for the school magazine in the current nihilistic style of profanism and publishing an explosive atheistic play mocking the resurrection of Jesus. The short blasphemous script infuriated many students and was prominently denounced by several New York City newspapers. Chambers was forced to resign from the magazine's staff, and not long after, in the spring of 1922, he quit Columbia but returned in September 1924, only to leave again after three months. In February 1925 he joined the Communist Party.

His friends, well-acquainted with Chambers's furtive histrionics, regarded the decision as impulsive and weird, but also predictable. Former Columbia classmates, especially the apolitical literary intellectuals, mocked his folly: "Is there still a Communist Party?" asked Clifton Fadiman, later a *New Yorker* book review editor and Book-of-the-Month Club judge for more than fifty years. "Do you drill in a cellar with machine guns?"[1] Meyer Schapiro, a close friend of Chambers for many years who became a full professor at Columbia and a distinguished art historian, surmised that the CP's new recruit was acting out yet another "mystification." Schapiro later testified that Chambers displayed no interest whatever in socialism or communism during their three-month tour of Europe in 1923.

Chambers recalled portentously: "For I had come to believe that the world we live in was dying, that only surgery could now save the wreckage of mankind, and that the Communist Party was history's surgeon." The CP issued him a little red book with his membership number, but Chambers rarely attended meetings. Party meetings, he complained, were quarrelsome and unbearable, and it was impossible to avoid factional disputes. Sam Krieger, an erstwhile comrade and tutor, remarked years later that the Communist exploits Chambers confessed to the world "could not have happened." "Chambers's claims constitute one of the biggest hoaxes ever perpetrated on the American people." Moreover, Krieger said, "by my own personal knowledge ... he was actually in the party for only about two years. Also ... he was a politically very unreliable individual and the last person in the world to have been entrusted with any kind of official responsibility."[2]

After Chambers was fired for stealing books as a library clerk, and after a stint as a salesman at Zukofsky's bookstore, he joined the editorial staff of the *Daily Worker* in 1927 — not 1925 as a "Communist functionary," as he often later testified. Chambers was teaching a rudimentary English course at the Workers' School, which in 1927-28 was under the direction of Bertram D. Wolfe. Along with friends Michael Intrator and Sender Garlin, Chambers asked Wolfe "how they could serve the Communist movement and learn to write well." Wolfe explained that one learns to write by writing, and "if they could tolerate being directed and given orders by a fool [Robert Minor]," Wolfe could "get them on the *Daily Worker*." "Working under Robert Minor," Wolfe said forty years later, "disillusioned all three of them, in spite of my warning."[3]

Chambers held minor positions at the paper until he left in 1929; he never became "the editor," as his self-myth professes. At the office he was a scheming interloper, repeatedly meddling in others' disputes, gossiping about superiors, and belittling CP leaders. "He was always very mysterious and secretive," said co-worker Sender Garlin. Chambers would vanish for several days at a stretch, as he did at *Time* magazine more than a decade later, but would not tell Garlin where he went, as though he'd been on a classified mission.[4] (Garlin believed that the relationship between Chambers and Michael Intrator—"insepa-rables," Bertram Wolfe called them—was homosexual, a belief shared by others who knew them. In his personal relations with men, Schapiro recalled, Chambers could be "tender as a young, sweet girl."[5] Garlin remarked how surprised Chambers's friends were when he married Esther.) It wasn't long, however, before his conspiratorial office hijinks brought trouble from Party officials. The phone call, Chambers recounted in *Witness*, came from Charles A. Dirba, the chairman of the Central Control Commission, who demanded a meeting with Chambers that night. But Chambers remarked that he would offer no apologies or excuses or confessions. He never returned to the *Daily Worker* office. He now fancied himself an independent Communist oppositionist.

For the next two years Chambers was busy with literary translations, staying in Lyn-brook with his mother most of that time. He recalled a hitchhiking trip to the western states during this period, and he applied for a job with the Atlas Stores Corporation in February 1931 but wasn't hired. In April 1931 he married Esther. Most significantly, four of his short stories were published by *New Masses* in 1931.

His pro-communist fictional proletarian narratives were enthusiastically reviewed by the Russian magazine *International Literature*. Surprised and altogether flattered, Chambers remarked that Moscow—the voice of real authority—reacted favorably to the stories imme-diately. So he thought that his quarrel wasn't with Stalin or Moscow but with the stupidity and pettiness of the American Communist Party.

On the critical and popular success of his stories, Chambers maintained that the Amer-ican CP offered him the editorship of *New Masses* at a salary of fifteen dollars a week. Though he had (so he said) broken away from the party in 1929, he eagerly wanted the job. But first, Chambers recalled, he would have to make amends with the Party. He paid a friendly visit to Alexander Trachtenberg, a member of the Central Control Commission and the party's "cultural commissar," who was the head of International Publishers and had *New Masses* and the John Reed Clubs "under his wing." Trachtenberg arranged for Chambers an equally friendly talk with Charles A. Dirba, the Control Commission chairman. "In fifteen minutes," Chambers wrote, "I was back in the Communist Party without ever having, officially, been out of it. I was also the editor of the *New Masses*."

Both Trachtenberg and Dirba were interviewed twenty-five years later about this pur-ported episode in the life and autobiography of Whittaker Chambers. The notes of William A. Reuben, indefatigable researcher and leading expert on the Hiss-Chambers case until his death in 2004, reveal that Trachtenberg did not know that Chambers had *ever* been a Party member. His firm, International Publishers, did reprint a short story by Chambers which had appeared in *New Masses*, but Trachtenberg was not personally involved in the transaction. He knew who Chambers was and recalled "seeing him around," but his only encounters with him occurred in the mid–1920s at the 42nd Street Library. Trachtenberg often read foreign-language newspapers there when Chambers was employed by the library, and they occasionally exchanged small talk in German. His "one vivid memory" of Chambers was "his utter and complete slovenliness and sloppiness ... his clothes were always so dirty and sweaty and soily." Trachtenberg denied without qualification that he had anything at all to do with Chambers and the CP's Central Control Commission—"no such incident ever occurred."[6]

Charles A. Dirba also could not recall the two contacts he supposedly had with Chambers as described in *Witness*. First of all, Dirba clarified, he had been *secretary* of the Control Commission, not its chairman. Matters of reinstatement, Dirba said of Chambers's account, "were dealt with in formal hearings in which everything was done in writing and subject to careful review"; they were acted upon by all members of the Commission and under no circumstances by Dirba alone. Thus, Dirba concurred with Trachtenberg that Chambers's yarn of friendly meetings resulting in his re–entry to the CP in fifteen minutes was patently impossible.

In fact, thanks to the research and findings of Svetlana Chervonnaya, a Moscow-based independent historian of American studies, Chambers *was* officially expelled from the Communist Party in 1930, and reinstated in March 1932. Meeting minutes of the Central Control Commission reveal that Chambers had not responded to several notices to appear and disclose "information pertaining to frictions in the *Daily Worker* editorial staff." Chambers was suspended on February 6, 1930, until he complied with the CCC's demands, which Chambers continued to ignore. In July he was expelled: "Chambers shall stand stricken from membership rolls of the Party." The order was signed by Secretary Dirba. Nearly two years later Chambers formally applied for reinstatement. Whittaker Chambers, the minutes read, "has now applied for readmission stating that he recognizes the erroneousness of his action for which he was expelled, that he has not had and does not have the slightest political differences with the Party and that he will unreservedly obey its discipline." Chambers was readmitted, with the provision that he contribute "direct mass organization work" in addition to his literary work. After August 1932, Chambers is never mentioned again in CP files.

Yet there remains another kernel of truth to Chambers's far-fetched tale (a smokescreen for what's soon to follow): Chambers indeed joined *New Masses* in early 1932. But there's no evidence he was hired as, or became, chief editor; and in any event he did not require permission from the Communist Party—many contributing editors were not even sympathetic to the CP. Chambers's name appeared on the magazine's masthead for the first time in May 1932, along with eight others, but from 1931 to 1933 only Michael Gold or Walt Carmon were listed as "editor."

Then, abruptly, in June 1932, while he was editing his third issue of *New Masses*, Chambers said he received a telephone call from Comrade Bedacht who wanted to see him immediately. Max Bedacht ordered Chambers to his office, Party Headquarters on 12th Street, immediately. Chambers went and was told he had been chosen for underground work. Bedacht did not explain the nature of the work, and when Chambers asked for time to think it over Bedacht gave him until the next morning. Chambers's wife was adamantly opposed to the assignment, and Chambers turned Bedacht down the following day. But Bedacht informed him that he had no choice, and that he must also quit the magazine and separate himself from the open Communist Party.

Chambers was determined to never leave the CP again no matter what; he would buckle under and accept Party discipline, whether he believed it or not. Asked years later by a grand juror to illustrate what he meant by "discipline," Chambers said: "Every Communist exists under what is known as Party discipline. Party discipline means, in effect, that every Communist is at the complete disposal of the higher organs of the Communist Party. Now, I don't mean to imply that that works arbitrarily. In most cases, the human factor is considered and acted upon; but if the Party decides that a man is to do a certain job for the Communist Party, the decision is binding on that Communist."[7] Or he risks expulsion from the Party.

It is quite an irregular turn of events; Chambers had been an enemy of the CP, "in disgrace," for two years or more, and suddenly he's not only back in the fold but also hand-picked for secret, perhaps momentous and dangerous work. Nevertheless, others corroborated at least parts of his story in various ways.

Felix Morrow, a leading figure of American Trotskyism in the early 1930s, wrote years later that Chambers played a minor role in the Communist underground in the 1930s — and that he was *forced* to accept it. Morrow added that Trachtenberg introduced Chambers to the underground, but, as noted above, Trachtenberg denied it. Robert Cantwell, a close friend of Chambers in those years, believed Chambers was removed from his position at *New Masses* and thrust into "an ineffectual, menial job as a courier in the underground" because of the Party's penchant to "kill off their good men, lest they become too forceful."[8] Chambers was, after all, renowned as a "revolutionary poet" par excellence; and he was highly respected for his knowledge of literature and languages, his talent as a writer, and his hard-driving work ethic.

Other friends thought Chambers appeared proud of his new role. "He had found valuable work," Meyer Schapiro recollected, "and had regained a sense of dignity." Cantwell recalled that after a short time in the underground Chambers proclaimed "that he was working in a highly confidential function for the Communist Party" and asked Cantwell to join him. Cantwell refused: "I told him that I did not believe that he was what he said he was, and that it seemed to me the secrecy of the operation was not very secret. The truth is that I thought it was some sort of complicated gag."[9] Chambers mentioned to other friends and acquaintances that he was doing "highly secretive work" but refused to disclose any details.

Chambers himself was very pleased with his new dispensation. He felt elated that an efficient organization within the Party selected him to work for it, and that he could not have been simply chosen at random; therefore, "they" must have been clandestinely watching him for some time.

Yet there are more complications and confusions to this *New Masses*/underground episode. Max Bedacht (to whom we'll soon return) commanded Chambers to quit his job at *New Masses*—Chambers recalled that he submitted a letter of resignation—and dissociate himself from the open CP. Still, the name Whittaker Chambers, in large upper-case letters, appeared on the masthead of *New Masses* as a member of the editorial board; and he and his wife, Esther Shemitz, were also listed as contributors through September 1933, fifteen months after Bedacht's ultimatum to cut all ties. However, there's no indication that Chambers was active as a *New Masses* editor or contributor after July 1932.

In a letter to Nathan Adler, a young colleague on the magazine, Chambers wrote in July 1932, on *New Masses* stationery:

> I have asked for, and have been granted a release, and am leaving *New Masses* at once. In fact, chronologically speaking, I have already gone. My work is finished here. Certain problems have been settled and, I believe, certain rudiments of policy and conduct laid down.
>
> I shall return to my writing, which is where I belong or at least where I seem to function best.[10]

Adler, interviewed years later, said that after Chambers's surprising departure from the magazine, the office gossip — very hush-hush — was that Chambers was working for the Soviets. A year or so later Adler saw Chambers walking down Fifth Avenue all dressed up in a too-baggy dark suit and fedora. "He had a roving eye, a paranoid look," and Adler suspected he was "making a drop somewhere.... One would assume that if people were involved in a conspiracy," Adler explained, "they'd be quiet about it. The whole atmosphere at that time, however, was one where the legal and illegal organizations were not hidden from each other. It was a kind of open secret."

Another friend remarked that

> during the period he was in "special work," [Chambers was] theatrically mysterious, so wrapped up in a cloak-and-dagger pose, looking over his shoulder, convinced he was being followed, that I got the idea something was strange and it got so I didn't like to have him around. I began to feel he was a little peculiar. As a matter of fact, that role suited him to perfection. Even *before* he got conspiratorial, he was conspiratorial, if you know what I mean.

Grace Hutchins, a friend of Chambers and Esther, who was present as a witness at their wedding in 1931, recalled Chambers appearing at her New York office in late 1932 or early 1933 and saying he was involved in "highly special underground work." Hutchins, an author of books on labor, women, and children, and a Communist Party member who ran for state office in the late 1930s, said Chambers was thoroughly convincing and she didn't question him. But the actual purpose of his visit was to ask for a loan of fifty dollars so he could get his rotten teeth fixed. The importance of his special work, Chambers told her, demanded a respectable appearance. Fifty dollars was a lot of cash for Hutchins in those years when she survived on a modest allowance from her family, but she loaned Chambers the money. He never made any attempt to repay Hutchins, and his teeth remained blackened and broken until the 1940s.

Another witness of Chambers's unusually secretive behavior — and his political radicalism — was Matthew Josephson, author of several books on literature and history, most notably *The Robber Barons* (1934). Josephson had met Chambers only once, for about two hours, the day before Franklin D. Roosevelt's inauguration in March 1933, "under circumstances rather particular" and unforgettable, and he described the encounter to biographer and psychoanalyst Meyer Zeligs thirty years later. At the time, he told Zeligs, he lived in the country but rented a room for one or two days a week in New York at the apartment of his friend Robert Cantwell. "All the banks were closing before Roosevelt's inauguration," Josephson recalled, "and I came down to raise some cash for my family needs in the country, so I remember that time of crisis very distinctly."

> As I knocked at the door, Cantwell came, but strangely delayed opening it, calling out to someone: "It's all right, it's Matty Josephson." I had given my name. This was unusual. Then he opened and I went in. Chambers then came out from the room I rented — which he had been using during my absence — to which he had retreated at my knock. He had gone back to hide himself, and looked embarrassed as he came out to meet me.
> Cantwell had (laughingly) mentioned this odd acquaintance once or twice as a "half-baked" young writer for the *New Masses*, who dramatized himself as a desperate sort of secret agent, carried a big revolver with him and told everyone that U.S. secret service agents (FBI men) were forever trailing him from place to place.
> He was shabby and frowsy, with eyes red-rimmed as if he slept badly, bony of figure, though short, and hardly prepossessing. Our talk for an hour or two hours ran on the economic crisis and banking panic. Chambers and Cantwell questioned me, because I was supposed to be knowledgeable in this field, and argued that The Revolution had begun in America. "This is

it!" Chambers exclaimed. "The whole financial system has broken down.... Barricades in Union Square this week!" I opposed this idea, saying: probably no revolution, but reform measures by incoming administration, and money-inflation such as I had seen in Germany after the war. Chambers exploded with anger at me, and began shouting me down, calling me a "bourgeois" or a "stooge" for the capitalists. He sounded as if I were snatching his "baby," the Revolution. As he became abusive, I grew angry also and raised my fists; Cantwell intervened and asked Chambers to leave, also apologizing for Chambers' behavior to me.

Ella Winter, author of *Red Virtue* (1933), whose first husband was the muckraking journalist Lincoln Steffens, told interviewers in the 1960s and 1970s that Chambers had asked her to steal documents from the State Department. She said they first met in late 1932 or early 1933, while she was staying at Hotel Winthrop in New York City. Chambers was using an alias, Harry Phillips, and Winter (who later learned who he really was) recalled that he was a brilliant and fascinating talker, but often spoke in a conspiratorial parlance which seemed fantastic to her. Winter was an enthusiastic fellow traveler of the first rank (if not an actual CP member), with entree to several government officials who were friends, and Chambers, aiming to exploit her as a conduit for his own access, hounded Winter for months, with little success.

Winter traveled to Washington, D.C., to congratulate her friend William C. Bullitt after his appointment as ambassador to the Soviet Union in 1933. Prior to the visit, Winter recalled to John Lowenthal in 1969, Chambers asked if she would steal documents from the Japanese Desk of the State Department. All she had to do, Chambers suggested, was make an appointment with the appropriate official, and if he left the room for whatever reason during the meeting she could take papers from his desktop — it didn't matter what type of documents, only that they concerned Japan. Winter refused to steal anything, but she believed she may have given Chambers a detailed report of her trip. Winter also remarked to Lowenthal that Chambers wanted to give her one hundred dollars in cash, making it clear that the money was for her own use "as a member of the underground." But again she refused him.

Ella Winter wasn't the only woman with vulnerabilities that Chambers tried to manipulate for his own nefarious purposes. Diana Trilling, essayist and literary intellectual who was married to Lionel Trilling, eminent cultural critic and venerable professor of English at Columbia, confessed in her 1993 memoir:

> Whittaker Chambers came to see me [in early 1933]. He came to ask me to help him with his spying operation for the Soviet Union. Lionel had been casually acquainted with Chambers at college, but this was not a visit to Lionel; it was a visit to me. He had been watching for Lionel to leave the house. Chambers promptly stated the business on which he had come to see me: he wanted me to receive mail for him. In spy language, he was asking me to be his "drop." Today, as I look back on this visit from the distance of more than half a century, a passage of time in which we witnessed not only the apotheosis but also the total dissolution of Soviet power, what most impresses me about Chambers's request is the emotion with which I received his invitation to be a spy or at least an accomplice in his spying. From the start of our conversation, I knew that I was not going to do what he asked of me. Yet I was enormously flattered that he thought me capable of such an assignment and I was ashamed to refuse him. With good reason, I regarded myself as preternaturally fearful, yet here was this man of the world, this man of two worlds, who believed me to be enough courageous to be a semi-spy. I felt greatly complimented.

At the time Chambers was summoned into the depths of Communism, he only knew of Max Bedacht as a fatherly Communist who had eight kids and was a member of the

Central Committee and head of the International Workers Order, an insurance and benefit program run by the CP. Chambers's descent underground and his initial subterranean adventures are surely overblown (assuming there is any truth to them at all) as he recounts them in his autobiography, but he told an earlier, less grandiloquent, version to the FBI in early 1949, after Hiss had been indicted for perjury but before the first trial. The significance of the story he told the Feds — not that it's any more credible than *Witness* — is that Chambers dictated the account and then later proofread, edited, and corrected the typescript. (The statement was purposely left unsigned so as to bypass sharing it with the defense in court and to avoid probable complications — such as a contradictory and hence unreliable chief witness — for the prosecution at Hiss's later trials. By way of a Freedom of Information Act request, Hiss obtained the statement — but only part of it — twenty-seven years later.)[11]

Bedacht led him out of his office to the street, Chambers told the FBI, and on to the subway at 14th Street where they met John Sherman, whom Chambers had worked with at *Daily Worker*. Bedacht then left the two alone. "You're in the underground now," Chambers recalled Sherman saying, "where I ask questions, but don't answer them, and you answer questions, but don't ask them." Chambers's statement continues:

> SHERMAN and I then walked to Riverside Drive, where parked just south of Grant's Tomb, headed downtown, was a large, black automobile. At the wheel was sitting a man whom I presently knew by the aliases of HERBERT and CARL, and who was a Russian. HERBERT, SHERMAN and I then drove downtown in New York City. HERBERT questioned me very closely about my political background in the Communist Party, about my break with the Communist Party in 1929, and my present ideological position within the Communist Party. He seemed satisfied with my answers.... HERBERT gave me no indication of the nature of the underground activity in which I was to engage. I believe that it was decided in the course of this ride that my underground alias was to be "BOB." My instructions in preparation for underground work were to separate myself completely from the Communist Party and to have nothing to do with Communist Party members regardless of whether they treated me as a renegade or not. I was forced to give up my job as editor of *New Masses*....
>
> HERBERT had been Commander of Tanks in the Leningrad Area and had been lent to the underground organization.... HERBERT had been an anarchist during the Civil War and on one occasion had been captured by the White Russians, but had escaped. I also heard that HERBERT was a very prodigious eater, on occasions consuming twelve eggs for breakfast.... HERBERT once owned a movie house in New Haven, Connecticut.
>
> At the time of my contact with HERBERT and SHERMAN, I was dressed like an "average Communist" in a shirt and a pair of pants. SHERMAN gave me $50.00 and told me to buy myself some more suitable clothes when next I saw him. SHERMAN explained to me that my functions in the underground would be to act as liaison man between the underground and the American Communist Party in the person of MAX BEDACHT.
>
> During the first month of my operations in the underground, SHERMAN introduced me to an individual who I knew only as ULRICH....
>
> It was my understanding from talking with ULRICH that at one time he was employed in the shipyards at Nikolaev [Mykolayiv], Russia; that at other times he was employed as a stoker on Russian vessels, both before and after the Revolution in Russia. He was not a Communist but as I understand a Left Socialist Revolutionary.
>
> Again referring to my first introduction to ULRICH by SHERMAN, I recall that the latter informed me that ULRICH, from that time on, would be my superior and that he, SHERMAN, would no longer contact me....
>
> After my first introduction to ULRICH ... I would meet ULRICH by prearrangement at some designated place in New York City and during the first period of our meetings we had nothing of importance to discuss....
>
> As I previously stated, nothing of importance happened insofar as my work with the appa-

ratus was concerned during the first few months. I was, of course, seeing ULRICH and MAX BEDACHT regularly and it is highly possible that on occasions I delivered messages to BEDACHT from ULRICH and vice versa, although I cannot place any particular importance to them at this time.

Another incident, which I particularly recall ... involved a visit by ULRICH to the house of MAX BEDACHT. I recollect that ULRICH expressed to me a desire to go to BEDACHT'S and wanted me to introduce him to BEDACHT....

After introducing ULRICH to BEDACHT, I stayed with them during the first part of their conversation which was purely social.... I recall that as ULRICH and I were leaving the BEDACHT home, ULRICH pressed into BEDACHT'S hand a sizable roll of bills, but no conversation relative to this money was had between the two at that time.

This passing of bills between ULRICH and BEDACHT, in my presence was not good underground technique but ULRICH was sometimes careless in such matters....

Sometime probably in early 1934, or late 1933, ULRICH began to indicate to me that the apparatus was going to disband and suspend operations.... It was my understanding that ULRICH and ELAINE [Ulrich's wife] were to return to Russia. I recall that when ULRICH parted from me, he indicated that there should be no future correspondence between him and me....

I remember that ULRICH'S last words to me were spoken in a semi-humorous, slightly sinister manner, and were to the effect that "Remember, BOB, you can be shot by them or you can be shot by us."

My association with MAX BEDACHT continued until sometime in 1933, when he went away, either on a vacation or a mission. At that time, he left J. PETERS in his place as my contact. However, this situation did not last for long and BEDACHT returned. After his return, however, I began seeing both he and J. PETERS for a short period. However, before my next problem arose, BEDACHT passed out of the picture. I do not recall any of the details of the cessation of my contacts with BEDACHT.

I also recall that J. PETERS once indicated that he was interested in the possibility of holding up banks in order to secure necessary funds for the operation of the Communist Party.

He [PETERS] dropped hints to the effect that he had something extremely interesting operating in Washington, D.C.

Chambers's rehearsed recital to the FBI, one he checked and rechecked, is nevertheless characteristically vacuous, desultory, and senseless. Bedacht hands him off to John Sherman and then leaves; Chambers and Sherman walk and then join a man in a car, a Russian who goes by only Herbert and Carl, a former Commander of Tanks in the Leningrad area with a gross appetite for eggs; Sherman defers to Herbert, who instructs Chambers to drop his Communist Party associations, a command already made by Bedacht; Sherman gives Chambers fifty dollars to buy suitable clothes, and informs him that he will be the liaison between the underground and Max Bedacht, who represents the American CP; Sherman then passes Chambers over to Ulrich, another Russian but *not* a Communist; Sherman then goes away; Chambers meets Ulrich from time to time, but they have nothing of importance to discuss; Ulrich, surprisingly, has never met Max Bedacht, so Chambers takes Ulrich to Bedacht's home where Chambers sees Ulrich give Bedacht a wad of money; by early 1934, Ulrich goes back to Russia and Bedacht also leaves the picture, having transferred Chambers once again, this time to J. Peters, who entertains the idea of robbing banks to provide cash for the Communist Party.

In January 1949, as Chambers dictated his life story to FBI agents, Max Bedacht testified openly and answered all questions before the New York grand jury — whose records were unsealed in 1999. Bedacht had been expelled from the Communist Party in 1947 and was living on a small farm in New Jersey. He was born in Germany, became a U.S. citizen at age 32 in 1915, worked as a barber and then editor of a German weekly newspaper, and became a member of the Communist Party when it formed in the United States in 1919. He then edited a Communist magazine and was a paid functionary of the Party until 1932, when he was hired as General Organizer for the International Workers Order (IWO), a fraternal benefit society. Bedacht remained with the IWO until he left the CP because of policy disagreements in 1947.

When asked by the grand jury if he knew Whittaker Chambers, Bedacht replied, "I don't know whether I do, but I think I do," and remarked that photographs of Chambers looked familiar. He knew Chambers by sight and by name only, Bedacht maintained, and if he ever met him it was when the IWO placed advertisements in *New Masses* during the period Chambers was working there. Bedacht insisted repeatedly that he had never been connected with any intelligence gathering while a CP member, and he denied the existence of a Communist "underground" which ostensibly undertook espionage.[12] A few years later Bedacht told an interviewer: "I certainly never had at any time any underground contact with any country in the world, whether American, Russian, or whatever. I had no occasion to carry or convey any information. I was opposed to connecting legal work with illegal work. It is common sense not to connect the two."

In his unpublished memoir, written years after Chambers's bestselling autobiography came out, Bedacht continued to defend himself against Chambers's lies. "He never worked with me," Bedacht wrote, "he never worked under and most certainly never worked for me, nor did I ever work for him." In *Witness*, Chambers recounts the visit he and Ulrich made to Bedacht's home — where the eight little Bedacht children were running about. But there were really just four Bedacht children, and only two (the youngest was 14) living at home in 1932. Chambers's account of Bedacht ordering him to his office at CP headquarters on 12th Street was also factually impossible. "First," Bedacht continued, "the Workers' Center was located on Union Square near 17th Street, while the National Office of the Party was located on 13th Street. Second, in 1932 I had no office in Party headquarters. Third, I was elected to the position of General Secretary of the IWO only in the summer of 1933 and therefore could not have been the head of that organization when the teller of tales claims to have received a summons from that head."

J. Peters was a leading player in Chambers's narrative of his underground years, but once more there is little if any evidence to support his narrative. Peters (actually Jozsef Peter — and those who knew him in the U.S. CP, such as Bedacht, knew him as Peter, not Peters) wielded great influence within the global Communist movement, according to ex–Communist and professional government witness Louis Budenz. He held high office as an organizer in the open Communist Party in America, and he wrote *The Communist Party: A Manual on Organization* (1934), a widely circulated booklet.

Jozsef Peter was arrested in the United States by the FBI in October 1947. He subsequently refused to answer most questions before HUAC in August 1948, and was finally deported to Hungary as "persona non grata for subversive activity" in May 1949.

Allen Weinstein interviewed Jozsef Peter in Budapest in 1975. The Hiss trials were by then ancient history, Chambers had been dead for more than a decade, and Peter was in his eighties and perhaps willing to tell all he knew. But Weinstein, pursuing corroboration of Chambers's story, came away disappointed. Peter, Weinstein wrote in *Perjury*, "insisted to me that he served in the United States only as an ordinary CP functionary and was never involved in 'secret work.' He said he never met Whittaker Chambers except possibly once early in the 1930s at the *New Masses* office. He also denied having been involved in Communist espionage in the United States, either as head of the entire underground or in any other capacity."

Returning to Chambers's long statement to the FBI, he spoke of another Soviet agent with whom he had been associated in the years 1934 through 1936, while also working with J. Peters in Washington, D.C. Chambers knew him only as "Bill," and they were introduced by a Communist dentist soon after Ulrich left the country. Bill informed Chambers that he was going to London to head up a Soviet apparatus. He invited Chambers to join him but suggested that Chambers provide a suitable cover, such as representing a legitimate American business. Chambers discussed the proposition with J. Peters, who, "after some thought," brought Chambers together with Maxim Lieber, a New York literary agent and member of the open Communist Party. Chambers told the FBI that he and Lieber had previously met as members of the John Reed Club. He detailed for Lieber how the apparatus would finance the London branch of Lieber's agency. Chambers would be chief editor there and actually see authors and prepare manuscripts received from Britons. However, arrangements to launch the operation dragged along.

In the meantime, Chambers continued, Bill wanted him to meet and help a man who had an important and special problem. The man in question was John Sherman, who Chambers already knew. Sherman too was going to set up a Soviet apparatus, in Tokyo, and he too needed a legitimate cover for his enterprise. Seeing that the London campaign had stalled, Chambers broached the idea to Bill of employing Lieber's firm as a cover for Sherman in Japan. Bill agreed, and Chambers introduced Sherman to Lieber. It was Sherman's inspiration, Chambers recalled, to set up an organization called the American Feature Writers Syndicate under the business umbrella of Maxim Lieber. Correspondents would be dispatched around the world and supply copy for the syndicate, and Sherman would be their man in Tokyo.

After Sherman had been in Japan for about eight months, Chambers said Bill notified him of Sherman's arrest there. Bill then ordered Chambers to close down the American Feature Writers Syndicate. Chambers destroyed the stationery, closed out the bank account, and removed the syndicate's name from Lieber's door. But the next day Bill informed Chambers that Sherman had not been arrested after all; somehow communications had gone haywire. Nevertheless, the syndicate remained out of business, and Sherman, the syndicate's first and only correspondent/apparatus operative, returned to the States.

Chambers never explained why he and his underground confederates believed that a business owned by a declared member of the open Communist Party, Maxim Lieber, would bestow legitimate cover for a clandestine Soviet apparatus in a foreign country. And why shutter the American Feature Writers Syndicate in the U.S., even removing the name from Lieber's New York office door, because of Sherman's alleged arrest in Japan? And why would Maxim Lieber get involved in this nonsense in the first place? Like all Chambers's stories, this one is ludicrous and illogical, but there's a grain of truth to it, enough to have implicated Maxim Lieber (Chambers's *real* motive) and destroyed his livelihood.

The FBI interviewed Maxim Lieber, and he subsequently appeared before the grand jury, in February 1949, shortly after Chambers informed on him. On advice of counsel, Lieber refused to answer nearly every question. He was born in Poland in 1897 and arrived in the U.S. in 1907, lived in the Bronx and went to New York City schools, joined the army after World War I and later worked in literary publishing. He testified that he owned a farm in Pennsylvania but refused to answer questions about the American Feature Writers Syndicate or Whittaker Chambers or Alger Hiss or J. Peters or espionage, among many other questions. FBI agents hectored Lieber's clients, telling them that their gentleman literary agent worked for the Soviets. It became impossible for Lieber to earn a living. He eventually found work as an editor in Poland and did not return to the United States for nearly twenty years.

In June 1969, in New York City, Maxim Lieber was interviewed by William Reuben about his relationship with Whittaker Chambers in the 1930s. Lieber said his friendship with Chambers (he always knew Chambers by his real name) was casual, not close. They met in early 1932, Lieber was certain, when Chambers was an editor of *New Masses*, one of the magazines that published his clients. He denied Chambers's claim that they had known each other earlier as members of the John Reed Club. And the last time he saw him was sometime prior to Chambers joining *Time* magazine in 1939. Lieber insisted that he had never been involved in any sort of underground and never worked with Chambers on any underground project, though he freely admitted to having been in the CP and to have represented Party authors. The American Feature Writers Syndicate had really existed, Lieber confirmed, but it was completely his invention and design, created to sell the works of his clients — notably Erskine Caldwell and Josephine Herbst — overseas.

Chambers was only a social acquaintance, Lieber remarked, and (until Chambers made his accusations) Lieber had been impressed with Chambers's positive qualities. "He was witty, charming, intelligent, extremely well-read," Lieber told Reuben. "He could hold you spellbound with his stories. He could captivate any audience." Yet, "That man ruined my life," and Lieber believed Chambers must have been mentally unbalanced to have turned on him as he did in the late 1940s. However, if that was the case, Lieber said he never saw any evidence of mental instability in Chambers's behavior when he was around him in the 1930s.

Why Whittaker Chambers rejoined the Communist Party in 1932 and went underground for over five years, whether it was the Communist underground or an underground of his own devising, historians have never been able to say with convincing authority. And Chambers wasn't certain himself. "A force greater than myself," he wrote in *Witness*, after twenty years of reflection, "had picked me up and was disposing of me — a force that, in the end, it would all but cost me my life to break away from." At the time, Chambers "disposed" of much that had been most important in his life, such as moving from his comfortable home in the countryside he loved to a city which he hated and likened to a grave; giving up a recently-acquired distinguished editorial position and a promising career in journalism; even forsaking his own creative writing and translation projects. Also at the time, newly married, his homosexual urges — of which he was intensely ashamed and kept utterly secret — became irrepressible and remained so for five years, the exact duration of his underground life (by his own admission to the FBI). As for money to survive, for there's no evidence to support his claim that the Soviets or the CP paid him, Chambers could have financed these five lost years with the cash he inherited in the early 1930s, enough funds to last that long considering the places and circumstances under which he and his wife said they lived. However, this is, of course, only informed speculation, even if a likely possibility.

"But if the historical determinants are cloudy," Meyer Zeligs wrote in 1967 on why Chambers went underground, "the psychic determinants are clear — and at least as important." In plain language, what are some of the most cogent psychological explanations for Chambers's actions, not only for his role as an underground espionage agent but also for his later role as a renegade and informer?

Zeligs noted that Chambers was incapable of telling the "whole" truth and thus wove his fabrications around "certain provable facts and actual experiences." Zeligs adds:

> There is a psychological as well as a material reality in the legal interpretation of documentary evidence when used as evidence by a witness. The laws of evidence insist that partial truths are not enough; for testimony to be valid it must be the *whole* truth. Wholeness of truth (credibility) from a human witness is dependent upon the psychic motivation that determines his state of mind. Hidden motives from inner recesses may thus govern the factual reliability of his memory and the validity of any documentary evidence he may produce.
>
> Careful analysis of his specialized mode of identity manipulation not only sheds light on the symbolic meaning of Chambers' acting out but explains *the function of the lie* in his bizarre behavior [emphasis added]. On the surface he was (or posed as) a secret agent for the Communist underground. But in his own private world he was the omnipotent one. Chambers exploited the Communist Party, its technical resources and unique structure, for conspiratorial acting out. In this setting the Communist Party, like J. Peters, served as a private, secret "agent" for *him*.

Dr. Carl Binger, a practicing psychoanalyst and associate professor at Cornell Medical College's department of clinical psychiatry at the time of Alger Hiss's second perjury trial in early 1950, testified as an expert for the defense that Chambers exhibited many traits of a psychopathic personality, based on his observation of Chambers's courtroom behavior and testimony, transcripts of previous sworn testimony, and Chambers's writings. The psychopath is quite aware of what he is doing, Binger expounded, but he doesn't always know why he does it, and his acts are frequently impulsive and often bizarre, making little sense to the casual observer who does not understand the particular fantasy or imagination behind these acts. Psychopaths, Binger testified, "have a conviction of the truth and validity of their own imaginations and their own fantasies without respect to outer reality: so that they play a part in life, play a role ... and on the basis of such imaginations, they will claim friendships which were nonexistent, just as they will make accusations which have no basis in fact ... because they have a constant need to make their imaginations come true by behaving as if the outer world were actually in accord with their own imaginations."

Admittedly, Dr. Binger was a somewhat imperious witness, and his testimony was mocked during cross-examination by prosecutor Thomas Murphy to great effect on a jury (and general public) skeptical of psychological interpretations to begin with.

Another psychology expert, Dr. Henry A. Murray, former director of the Harvard Psychological Clinic and a pioneer in the development of personality theory, testified in a secondary role and agreed completely with Binger. Years later, after having read *Witness*, in addition to Chambers's other writings and transcripts of his various testimonies, Murray wrote in an unpublished letter that

> Chambers *could not be depended on* to distinguish *at all times* between fantasy and reality. In other words, in many instances but not in all instances, it would be more difficult for Chambers than for most people to give an accurate account of an event, because of the fusion in his mind between fact and fantasy. On other occasions he might *be able* to make the distinction but *be disinclined* to do so, his dream of it being more appealing to him than the actuality. In other situations he could distinguish perfectly clearly between the actuality and the make-believe but for one reason or another he would choose to tell a lie.... There is a stage of development in childhood when uncertainty exists as to whether something was dreamt or whether it actually happened. In most cases the time comes when a child can inspect its own thought processes or its own speeches and reject what is not true. The psychopathic personality is retarded insofar as the operation of this internal censor is concerned: what is false in his memories is not deleted.[13] [Emphases appear in original.]

To the independent/skeptical historian, Chambers's acknowledged behavior, testimony, and writings often appear shallow and obvious — comic masquerades. But artless impostures are the norm in clinical psychology. "The investigation of even a few instances of imposture," Dr. Phyllis Greenacre, a former president of the American Psychoanalytic Association, wrote in an essay on imposters in 1971, "is sufficient to show how crude though clever many imposters are, how very faulty any scheming is, and how often, in fact, the element of shrewdness is lacking. Rather a quality of showmanship is involved, with its reliance entirely on the response of an audience to illusions."

Chambers's impostures were successful not only because many people believed in him but also because they encompassed a social element — disturbed political times such as the early 1930s when he fancied himself an American Lenin performing special work for Communism, man's promise for the future, and then again in the late 1940s he exemplified the Communist renegade, exploiting the public's anxieties and fear of Soviet infiltration. "In some of the most celebrated instances of imposture," Greenacre continues,

> it indeed appears that the fraud was successful only because many others as well as the perpetrator had a hunger to believe in the fraud and that any success of such fraudulence depended in fact on strong social as well as individual factors.... To this extent those on whom the fraudulence is imposed are not only victims but unconscious conspirators. *Its success too is partly a matter of timing. Such combinations of imposturous talent and a peculiar susceptibility of the times to believe in the swindler, who presents the deceptive means of salvation, may account for the great impostures of history*[14] [emphasis added].

Chambers confessed to the FBI that though he never held a regular job during his underground years he sometimes passed himself off as a freelance writer or journalist. It is significant that Alger Hiss (and a few others, such as George Silverman) claimed that Chambers said he was a freelance writer — in other words, presenting himself to Hiss as his ordinary "other self." But Chambers's impostured character was to himself so much more interesting and fulfilling that one is inclined to say that he was his own work of art.

CHAPTER XII

Saint Whittaker

"I felt a surging release and a sense of freedom, like a man who bursts at last gasp out of a drowning sea."—Whittaker Chambers, *Witness*

Whittaker Chambers's re-emergence from the underground and his decisive rupture with Communism transpired in a fog of mystery and absurdity which had also marked his earlier headlong embrace of Stalinism and "secret special work." That special work, particularly his reputed document-stealing partnership with Alger Hiss, will be examined closely in the next chapter, but here Chambers's rationale for returning "back into the world of free men" will be considered.

Chambers's political odyssey from Stalinist left to reactionary religious right in only a matter of months in 1937 was frenziedly abrupt compared with the familiar story of the Trotskyite of the early 1930s who by the 1980s became a neoconservative. Chambers's contemporary, Sidney Hook, an assistant professor of philosophy at New York University, for instance, wrote in 1933: "It seems to me that only communism can save the world from its social evils," though Hook was opposed to Stalinism and the Communist Party as it then existed. Twenty years later, in 1953, now a full professor who considered himself a socialist, Hook wrote that "communism ... is the greatest menace to human freedom in the world today." In 1968 Hook campaigned for Richard Nixon, and in 1980 he eagerly voted for Ronald Reagan. "Remarkably," Alan M. Wald wrote in *The New York Intellectuals* (1987), "most individuals [of the anti–Stalinist left] made this shift in a staggered sequence — each denouncing the others for their apostasies before themselves following suit." Philip Rahv and Dwight Macdonald labeled this phenomenon "cultural amnesia," in which the "victim" is simply oblivious of "the most elementary truths from his past experience."

As an unwavering Stalinist, Chambers "resolved to obey absolutely its harshest, most fantastic and irrational demands ... provided only that Communism would let me collaborate in its central effort. For I found in Communism a rational and dedicated purpose." He acclaimed "terror [as] an instrument of policy, right if the Communist vision is right, justified by history." Moreover, Chambers celebrated Stalinism as "the least hypocritical in announcing its purpose and forcibly removing the obstacles to it." He chose the party line, and its cult of personality and discipline, even over the pleading emotional objections of his wife.

However, after only a few years of "intensive Communist experience," Chambers wrote, "inflamed by the great Russian Purge and Show-trials," in addition to a religious re-awakening, compelled him to completely re-examine his Communist belief. Leaving aside for a moment the matter of his renewed faith in God, it is questionable just how "Communist" or even "intensive" Chambers's underground experience actually was. His activities were never political, only conspiratorial, and by his own admission he often did not "do" anything. And the Soviet purges and show trials initially compelled Chambers to stridently defend Stalin, not to re-examine his Communist belief.

As recounted by Allen Weinstein in *Perjury*, Chambers paid a visit to his close friend Meyer Schapiro (whom Weinstein interviewed) in December 1936. In the early 1930s Schapiro was sympathetic to the CP but now was an anti–Stalinist who actively supported the Committee for the Defense of Leon Trotsky. The first Moscow Trials had begun a few months earlier. They were Stalin's treacherous means of eliminating potential challenges to his authority. The ghastly outcomes were predetermined; confessions were extracted by way of torture. Yet many Western observers who attended the show trials believed they had been conducted fairly, with the defendants being justly convicted. In the United States, hardcore Stalinists such as Chambers denounced criticism of the sham verdicts. At their December meeting, Weinstein wrote, Chambers and Schapiro "argued over the question of Stalinist repression." Chambers "castigated Schapiro as a Trotskyite and an enemy of the … revolution," and "stormed out of Schapiro's home." The two men did not meet again for months.

In April 1937 a "Commission of Inquiry," led by philosopher-educator John Dewey, held a series of hearings at the Mexico home of Leon Trotsky to investigate the charges of the Moscow Trials against Trotsky and others. The Commission's findings were published the following September, clearing those accused and exposing the vast fraudulence of the trials. By then Chambers was compelled — mostly by the prodding of his old Columbia friends, particularly Schapiro and Herbert Solow — to face the facts of Stalin's brutality. But there was no "rigorous re-examination" of Communism on Chambers's part, just a second round of "intellectual pulverization" by a few of his former classmates — one of whom, Lionel Trilling, best summed up Chambers's mind as: "though certainly not without force, … easily seduced into equating portentous utterance with truth."[1]

Chambers was a determined Stalinist revolutionary one day, an equally unflinching counterrevolutionary the next. "I left the Communist Party to fight it," Chambers declared. "I was already fighting it when I left it." He told the FBI in 1949: "Sometime during 1937, I entered upon a period of questioning and stress which culminated in my decision that Communism was a false and evil doctrine. I decided on a complete break with the Communists." But Chambers lied when he told the Feds that he "reached this decision reluctantly over a considerable period of time." His "philosophical" break with Stalinism and Communism was quite sudden, not at all prolonged. Now, indeed, it was several more months before he fully extricated himself from illegal underground activities, but that was a carefully contrived plan *after* his decision to split.

Chambers reflected that during his underground years, though he wouldn't even read a book critical of Communism, the thought that something was missing often crossed his mind. "What is our lack?" he wondered. Succumbing to despair, he asked if it could be God. He associated God with limited or closed minds. How could it be God? He was astonished that he could even consider such a thought. Nevertheless, Chambers took up the wholesome habit of prayer, and as he continued to "pray raggedly," the act ceased to be self-conscious and awkward; it became a daily need to which he looked forward. In his auto-biography Chambers would have us believe that his spiritual-mystical awakening was a long, drawn-out affair (subconsciously, he qualifies, yet he remembered it well enough when he wrote his book years later); and that his essential goodness and morality were always there, lurking just below the surface of his squalid life. He fixed the date of his break via a common occurrence. It was a quotidian family scene, at breakfast, in the spring of 1935, more than two years before his actual break. Chambers was watching his baby daughter eating in her high chair, his gaze transfixed on the delicate contours of her tiny ears — "those intricate, perfect ears. The thought passed through my mind: 'No, those ears were not created by any chance coming together of atoms in nature (the Communist view). They could have been created only by immense design.'" It was an involuntary, unwanted thought that he crowded out of his mind but never forgot. "I did not then know that," Chambers revealed, "at that moment, the finger of God was first laid upon my forehead." Another sit-uation along the course of his "long break" with Communism occurred even earlier, in Jan-uary 1933, only months after Chambers re-affirmed his dedication to Stalinism and supposedly went underground. The news of Esther's first pregnancy briefly gave Chambers a physical jolt of joy and pride, but his "special secret work" obviously precluded domestic normality. Thus an abortion was assumed; they were so mired in the sordid life of the underground that the thought of having a baby was only a fleeting desire, succeeded by an equally fleeting sadness that they would not have the child. But, miraculously, they somehow chose life; the righteous couple was destined to be blessed with a daughter, and three years later a son.

In his quest to become one with the almighty, Chambers — and now having no truck with half-measures — became one with himself. The deep unconscious values of his life, which had been lost so long in the emptiness of modernity, suddenly emerged. The almighty "mind" and its ability to plan for humanity's salvation was merely hubris.

By rejecting *only* Communism, Chambers believed, he would be spurning merely one political expression of the modern mind, albeit the most logical, persuasive, and brutal "in enforcing the myth of man's material perfectibility." An extremist without modulations (no matter what he might choose to believe), Chambers determined that "the Enlightenment and its fruits were a wrong turning in man's history." Beastliness and folly inhered in Com-munism, Chambers maintained, and were inseparable from it. They were inevitable man-ifestations when people explicitly reject God and seek to organize life in terms of their own faulty thinking. The problem of Communism, Chambers now believed, is not a problem of economics but instead a problem of atheism.

This quick-shifting fanaticism epitomized the "Nonsense" of Whittaker Chambers, critic Philip Rahv noted in a perspicacious review of *Witness*. For Chambers the only germane issue is atheism. Wrote Rahv:

> It is futile to expect religion to undertake the radical task of reorganizing the world. Its insti-
> tutional practices are remote from such aims, and its doctrines have hardened in the mold of
> otherworldliness. In truth, we have nothing to go on but the rational disciplines of the secular
> mind as, alone and imperiled, it confronts its freedom in a universe stripped of supernatural
> sanctions. Chambers' melodramatic formula — God or Stalin? — is of no help to us in our mod-
> ern predicament.... There is no substitute for politics, just as for those who must have it there
> is no substitute for religion. It is true that religious believers have every reason to be hostile to
> Communism; yet the motive of belief forms but one strand in a complex of motives. Believers,
> like all men, live in the real world of varied and pressing needs and interests.

Rahv concluded that Chambers was "essentially a mystic swept into the world of parties and movements by the crazy pressures of the age" and oblivious to "politics in its hard empirical aspects."[2]

Thus, sometime in 1937, probably only three or four months after he rationalized and condoned Stalin's malevolent policies in an angry dispute with Meyer Schapiro in December 1936, Chambers summarily reversed course, deciding that he would rather die than live under Communism. And he warned his long-suffering yet enabling wife of the long-term penalty she and the children must pay for the decision he was making. He meant that he was choosing the side that would probably be defeated in the revolutionary conflict of the 20th century. In addition to scuppering his identity as an underground Communist revolutionary, Chambers was also financially strapped, having by now spent all the money inherited from his father and grandmothers, and increasingly harried with guilt over cruising for men in parks and movie houses — inconvenient facts he chose not to mention when testifying a decade later, or in his autobiography.

Time and again Chambers swore that his only income during his underground years (with one exception near the end) was the cash payments from Communist superiors: one hundred and sixty five dollars a month plus expenses for telephone, rent, medical care, even entertainment. He said he submitted expense reports each month before his salary and expenses were paid. Needless to say, he never retained a copy for himself or posterity, and there's no evidence that the Communist Party, the Soviets, or anyone else ever paid him a cent for his purported services as an "underground agent."

The one exception to his problematic underground income was a legitimate job he held for only a few months, government relief work with the WPA, a fully documented episode which Chambers could not deny, though he later certainly distorted the real reason he took the job, explaining his motives with the usual sinister Communist twist. But at the time he landed it, in October 1937, he was "greatly relieved," according to his friend Robert Cantwell, because Chambers told him he was "out of work and out of funds."[3]

Chambers got the job through Abraham George Silverman, a Washington, D.C. acquaintance who was research director of the Railroad Retirement Board. Silverman, in testimony before the grand jury in December 1948, recalled Chambers visiting his D.C. office in late 1936 and introducing himself as David Chambers, a freelance writer seeking information about the Railroad Retirement Act. Silverman swore he had never been a Communist and did not know Chambers had ever been one. Chambers continued to see Silverman occasionally during the following year, and they often talked about music, art, and politics, but Silverman could not remember (ten years after) details of any particular conversation. He liked Chambers and enjoyed their intellectually stimulating talks. Silverman remarked that Chambers was always hard up for money and that he loaned Chambers small amounts on several occasions, as Alger Hiss claimed he had done, totaling perhaps seventy-five dollars. He added that Chambers attempted to pay him back by selling him two oriental carpets, in which Silverman's cash loans were deducted from the asking price of the expensive rugs. Ultimately, Silverman helped Chambers get a job at the WPA's National Research Project as a report editor, where Chambers compiled an index of the nation's railroads at a salary of two thousand dollars a year. Government documents indicate that Silverman submitted a requisition for a research assistant on September 30, 1937, and Chambers soon applied for the position under the name of Jay V. David Chambers. He was officially approved for the job on October 15 and began working three days later. He remained employed for fifteen weeks, until January 31, 1938, when he was furloughed because of lack of work.

In Chambers's telling of the story, events are naturally more ominous and conspiratorial. "I planned my break cautiously and gradually," Chambers informed FBI agents in 1949, "for I felt sure an effort would be made to kill me and perhaps my family. One of the first things I did was to have the Communist Party get me a job in the United States Government." There might come a day, Chambers gathered, when he would be compelled to confess the lurid tales of his underground life to the authorities, and the practicality of informing had its appeal — after all, it would scarcely be worth the Party's while to kill him *after* he told all; the only guarantee of his silence was death. But first Chambers felt it was important to have some proof that he had worked for the Communist Party in Washington, for the government no less. This job would ostensibly serve two other purposes: provide extra money for his break, and by working under his own name it would help restore his long-lost identity and establish the fact that a man named Chambers worked in Washington in 1937-38.

In the dissembling mind of Whittaker Chambers, George Silverman wasn't simply a government bureaucrat and dilettante of the arts, but a member of the underground and a dues-paying Communist. In *Witness*, Chambers claimed he instructed Silverman (one of his "apparatus" men) to get him a job in the U.S. Government. His pretext was a need for a "cover." According to Chambers, Silverman never loaned him money, and the oriental carpets were actually gifts of gratitude from the Soviet people. Several rugs were delivered to Silverman's home and distributed to likewise loyal and productive comrades, Chambers boasted, such as State Department official Alger Hiss and Harry Dexter White of the Treasury Department.

Chambers asserted that he held the job only long enough to establish he had worked in Washington and then gave it up. But his Federal employment file plainly refutes him.

And what did Chambers's Communist superiors think of his taking a common relief job under his own name? In *Witness*, Chambers said he did not inform his boss, but a few years prior to the book's publication he told the Feds a different story: "I got this job by going to J. PETERS and telling him that I could no longer knock around Washington without some apparent occupation. He agreed. I proposed the Party get me a job in the Government." But his chiefs would have pointed out the obvious conflicts between the job and his responsibilities as a clandestine courier. Besides, Chambers also wrote and testified that during 1937 through early 1938 he was swamped with underground duties: frequent meetings with sources who provided classified documents, managing photography operations in Baltimore and Washington, weekly trips to New York to deliver microfilm. There would have been no time for a mundane make-work Federal job. However, that job was *real*. The "underground" is comprehensible only in terms of Chambers's "private belief system," as Meyer Zeligs would say.

One of the reasons Whittaker Chambers offered for taking the government job was that he needed to re-establish a "visible identity" as himself— as Chambers, an identity he believed had been all but lost for five or six years of underground anonymity. If he suddenly vanished, he feared no one would notice. Typical of his contorted logic, Chambers believed the Communists would consider it much easier and less dangerous to kill a man who didn't exist than to kill one who did. But Chambers and his wife and two children had been settled — and known, even their telephone number was listed — in Baltimore as "Chambers" for more than six months before he took the job, so the notion of feeling he didn't exist was simply more bamboozlement, or a gratuitous lie, or a delusion of a paranoid mind.

Though Chambers occasionally used aliases and misrepresented himself to new acquaintances and landlords after leaving his *New Masses* job in 1932, he used his real name at many places he lived. He, of course, lived under his real name when he commuted to New York City from Glen Gardner, New Jersey, until he moved to New York City in the summer of 1932. For a few months in 1933 he and his wife lived on Staten Island as Mr. and Mrs. Arthur Dwyer. They lived on Long Island with Chambers's mother after their daughter was born in October 1933. In August 1934 the couple moved to Baltimore and lived in an apartment on St. Paul Street, perhaps using the name Cantwell. During May and June 1935 they lived in a 28th Street apartment in Washington, D.C. which had previously been occupied by Alger and Priscilla Hiss and Timothy Hobson. Hiss maintained (in 1948) that he sublet the apartment to a George Crosley. Chambers insisted that he stayed there as a guest, as a favor from one Communist to another. He initially denied (in 1948) living there as Crosley but soon after said it was quite possible that he had used that name. In July 1935 Chambers claimed he stayed at Meyer Schapiro's West 4th Street home in New York. From August to October 1935 Chambers lived in Pennsylvania, also as Chambers. Chambers rented a house for six months on Eutaw Street in Baltimore, probably using the name Cantwell again, from October 1935 to April 1936. They moved to Long Island for a short time in 1936, living under their real name, and from the summer of 1936 until April 1937 they lived again in Pennsylvania under the name Chambers. They returned to Baltimore, as the Chambers family, in April 1937, renting an apartment at Auchentoroly Terrace. They moved to another Baltimore address, at Mount Royal Terrace, in December 1937, again as the Chambers family. This was Chambers's address when he completely "broke" from the Communist underground in April 1938, meaning he never showed up for a scheduled appointment with his superior — and that is when Chambers said he went into hiding, staying awake at night with a gun at the ready. Yet in July 1938 Chambers *bought* a house in Baltimore, in the 2600 block of St. Paul Street.

Far from being invisible in the years 1932 through 1938, Chambers was nearly ubiquitous. In New York he was a storied character, not only as the well-known Whittaker Chambers, but also in his persona as secret and special agent for the Communists (no matter what alias he hid behind), which was hardly a secret. He was often in touch with his old Columbia mates, and he frequently wrote letters to Meyer Schapiro, who preserved them. Had he disappeared, he would not have gone unnoticed. Other friends, such as Robert Cantwell and Maxim Lieber, would also certainly have missed him, not to mention his own mother.

To facilitate his final rupture and flight from the Communists, Chambers enumerated crucial "needs," including a gun, a hideout, a fast car, an identity, an authentic record that a man named Chambers had worked in D.C. in 1937 and 1938, and, most tellingly, "*a life preserver, in the form of copies of official documents stolen by the apparatus, which, should the party move against my life, I might have an outside chance of using as a dissuader*" [emphasis added].

If, as Chambers often claimed, it would scarcely be worth the party's effort to kill him if he informed, then why didn't he head for the authorities as soon as he "defected"? Because, in fact, Chambers was not worried about the party or anyone else moving against his life, he was terrified of being arrested for those stolen "copies of official documents," some of which he stashed away as his "life preserver." Indisputably, Chambers received stolen classified and restricted documents in 1938 from at least one government official, though not from Alger Hiss — an assertion that will be proven beyond any reasonable doubt. After his break, Chambers undeniably had an intriguing story (really a collection of lies) to tell, and he attempted to publish at least some of it. But he refused to name real names, which doomed his prospects; no editor would consider it. Chambers implored two editors, Herbert Solow and Isaac Don Levine, to arrange for him a meeting with the President of the United States; and if granted immunity, Chambers would tell his story in full — but only to Roosevelt himself. In *Witness*, Chambers flatly denied ever asking for immunity, even "by a hint or a whisper."

Though a deadbeat and a parasite who always gained some immediate advantage from those who entered his orbit during most of the 1930s, Whittaker Chambers still favorably impressed most everyone who knew him, such was the intensity and persuasiveness of his personality, notwithstanding the revulsion he projected with his rotten teeth and filthy clothes. But beyond using people in the moment, Meyer Zeligs noted:

> Chambers secretly appraised and tagged them for possible future use as well. In his conspiratorial way Chambers collected and created suspects. In the event that he himself might be caught (either by the "secret police" or his own guilty conscience) and forced to confess, he would have stored away some kernel of fact or idea which had the potential of wringing confessions (true or false) from others.

Chambers told so many conflicting tales about his traumatic final break from the Communists that had they all come to light during Hiss's perjury trial the charges against Hiss would surely have been thrown out. Invariably, after Chambers told one version, some immoveable fact would then crop up, obliging him to embellish or bob-and-weave or flat out make up a new story. Before HUAC on August 30, 1948, Chambers swore that very shortly after he left his government job on January 31, 1938, perhaps only two or three weeks later, he had completely severed ties with the Communists. In other words, by the end of February 1938 he would have been back in the world of free men. But that HUAC testimony was three months *before* Chambers confessed to criminal activity (receiving stolen government documents for transmission to Communists) as late as April 1938. The *only* reason Chambers confessed, it bears repeating, is because Alger Hiss sued him for saying publicly that Hiss had merely been a secret dues-paying Communist who had infiltrated the government, an astonishingly suicidal act by Hiss if he had been the one stealing the documents and giving them to Chambers. But this is exactly what Chambers swore Hiss did, and to prove it Chambers claimed to have hidden some of them for more than ten years, his life preservers. But many of the documents were dated March or April 1938, a month or more after he supposedly defected.

Chambers then changed the date of his break to no earlier than April 15, due to the dates of the papers and film he had squirreled away. The family remained at the Mount Royal Terrace residence, Chambers testified, until he had collected his life preserving material and defected. They then immediately moved to a cramped rented room in a house on Old Court Road near Baltimore to hide out just before Chambers failed to show up for a pre-arranged meeting with his Communist manager. However, Esther Chambers recalled to the FBI that it was February or March when they moved to Old Court Road, contradicting Chambers's date of mid–April.

In need of money now, Chambers sought translation work, employing Schapiro as an intermediary with publishers. While living in fear and seclusion on Old Court Road, "Dr. Meyer Schapiro," Chambers told the FBI in 1949, "recommended me to one Paul Willert, an Englishman who was an officer in the Oxford University Press. Willert was described by Schapiro as an absolutely reliable non–Communist. Willert got me a translation job." But two years later, after Hiss's trials and conviction, correspondence about details of the translation dated *March* 1938 between Willert and Chambers was discovered, and Willert later told interviewers he believed he began negotiations with Chambers (whom Willert characterized as vociferously anti–Communist) in *December 1937*—yet more evidence belying Chambers's revisions. Weinstein discovered letters from Chambers to Schapiro dated March 1938 that also mention Chambers's translation efforts, and Weinstein himself believed Chambers began the work for Willert in February 1938.

Another indication that Chambers defected in 1937 and not 1938 was revealed by Grace Hutchins, the CP woman Chambers swindled fifty dollars from in 1932. Chambers apprised the FBI, and later enhanced the account in his autobiography, that after his defection Hutchins had been dispatched by Communist superiors to find Chambers and issue an ultimatum. Unable to locate him, Hutchins went to the New York law firm of Reuben Shemitz, Esther Chambers's brother, and left a note. Chambers maintained that he never saw the note; his brother-in-law never showed it to him but later gave it to the FBI. A few days later, having received no reply, Hutchins allegedly returned to attorney Shemitz. At Shemitz's office Hutchins issued an ultimatum, so Chambers claimed. If he agreed to turn Chambers over to the CP, his sister and the children would not be harmed. And if Chambers did not show by a certain date, he would be killed.

To interviewers in the 1950s, Grace Hutchins depicted a markedly different scenario at attorney Shemitz's office. Hutchins knew Chambers through Esther, with whom she had worked in the early 1920s, and in 1931 she attended the couple's wedding. Hutchins had not seen Esther or Chambers for several years. Wanting to collect on her fifty-dollar loan, and wondering where the Chamberses were, Hutchins indeed visited Reuben Shemitz, but attempted only to get her money back. She insisted that she visited his office only *once*, and she wasn't certain she even left a note. "When the FBI came to me and questioned me about it," Hutchins recalled, "they said they had a note I left. I asked if I might see it. I was not even sure if I had left a note, and wanted to see if it were my handwriting and what it contained. They said they didn't have it with them. They never showed me the note. There is something funny about that note. Clearly they did not want me to see it."

"I am almost certain," Hutchins said of her visit to Shemitz, "that this was in 1937.... If I could see that note, it might be that it had a date on it, and that the date would prove that it was 1937, not 1938, that he made what he described as his break with the Communist Party."[4]

In his chronicle, Chambers engaged a logic uniquely his own as he retraced the steps of breaking away. He planned to defect from the Communist Party merely by not showing up at the next scheduled meeting with his underground chief. He supposed that the Communists would expect him to leave Baltimore immediately and go far away. But Chambers doesn't say why, just because he didn't show up for a meeting, the Communists would jump to the conclusion that he had defected, or why they would expect him to leave Baltimore if they had suspected his defection. After all, he'd been living under his own name there for a year, his family was settled in, and he was known — and truly existed — as Chambers.

Nevertheless, in his mind he anticipated the Communists by not leaving and instead digging in with his wife and two young children in one room of a house on Old Court Road. Yet within a month the family was a bundle of raw, vibrating nerves. They all needed a complete change, and tactically, Chambers rationalized, the time was ripe to escape Baltimore. So they went on a working vacation to Florida. Chambers rented an isolated cottage near Daytona Beach, where he worked nights translating a book while he slept during the day, his wife on the lookout for Communist assassins. They stayed in Florida about a month and returned to Baltimore. Chambers decided that hiding out had served its purpose — to baffle the CP in its automatic reaction to kill him — and that now he would live openly under his own name. He even bought a small house in Baltimore. But, of course, it has already been established that by this time, around July 1938, Chambers had been out in the open for over a year. The truth of his "break" and collection of "life preservers" is clear: he had stolen and fabricated documents for the sole purpose of implicating others, in the event he was arrested, months *after* he dropped all outward pretense of being a Communist.

Whittaker Chambers did not "defect" from Communism in the usual sense of the word. Undoubtedly, Chambers suffered a psychological "break" of an emotionally distraught, tormented soul. Virtually his entire life, in Zeligs's words, "must be viewed as one prolonged span of psychic conflict." But there were no evil Communists poised to assassinate him if he deserted; no underground superiors to whom he had genuflected with unquestioned discipline; no monthly paydays for five years from the Soviets or the CP; no cells or units of treasonous government officials subservient to his commands. What Chambers was involved in during his criminal years of theft and impersonation was a racket, not an ideology; plus, the "underground" furnished a sheltering milieu for his cruising.

In the later months of 1938, when Chambers was inquiring after honest work and outwardly professing a life of Christian virtue, he and his wife applied for retail credit using information from the personnel file of another Jay Chambers, a Treasury Department employee whose government dossier, it was later discovered, had been stolen. Esther Chambers filled out the credit application, listing her husband as Jay Chambers, "Senior Administrative Officer, Treasury Department," and her own occupation as a volunteer teacher at the Park School. She provided private information from the stolen file of Jay Chambers, such as former home addresses and previous employment. And the fraud most likely went beyond stealing another's identity in order to establish a good credit rating, because the real Jay Chambers of the Treasury Department was soon billed by Washington and Baltimore department stores for items he never purchased.[5]

Whittaker Chambers's most willing victim was his wife, Esther Shemitz Chambers, whom he held unconditionally under the sway of his domineering personality. She believed that he was a great man, under any circumstances. She testified under oath that she sympathized with everything Chambers ever did, never asked him what he was doing, happily accepted any task he might assign, and obeyed his every word without question. When at Hiss's second perjury trial the prosecutor asked her: "If he [Chambers] told you that starting tomorrow we are going to Ypsilanti and your name was Hogan...." She interrupted, "We would go to Ypsilanti and we would be Hogans." Yet Esther Chambers was no helpless child bride; she was thirty when she married Chambers and had led a very independent life for a woman in the 1920s, championing radical causes, pacifism, civil rights, and feminism. She was idealistic, romantic, and liberal — the type most responsive to Chambers's siren songs.

The break Chambers desired most desperately was from homosexual encounters, his "darkest personal secret," which he had never confessed to his wife or attorneys or even a minister. Only to the FBI did Chambers confide that in 1938 he had "managed to break myself of my homosexual tendencies and since that time I have been a model husband and father." He had abstained, Chambers said, with "God's help," after "embracing, for the first time, religion."

However, Allen Weinstein wrote in *Perjury*, "Chambers's memory may have tricked him on this point," noting that his formal affiliation with Episcopalianism "came several years later and his 1937–39 letters do not indicate interest in religion." Weinstein maintained that "Chambers persisted in forming casual homosexual attachments after he broke with Communism when ... he made a number of brief, sometimes puzzling trips to New York City, ostensibly in connection with efforts to obtain money and translating jobs." It is possible that Chambers finally broke "all ties with his only remaining underground activity, that restless 'cruising' of the city streets for male partners," Weinstein concluded, only after he joined *Time* in 1939 and formed close (but nonsexual) friendships with a few religious colleagues.

With financial help from his mother, Chambers purchased a modest house in Baltimore in July 1938, but by August the family was again in urgent need of money, so Chambers sought out in New York City another Columbia friend, Herbert Solow, an anti–Stalinist political journalist for the *New York Sun* and other publications who later became one of the senior editors of *Fortune*. Chambers was working on articles about the Communist underground that he hoped Solow would market for him. "He needed help," Solow recalled, "and he wanted me to arrange a meeting with the President of the United States in order to make a deal with the President in which he would reveal secret information of a very important nature, the possession of which could get him in trouble, in exchange for which he wanted immunity."

Solow never knew what to make of Chambers's alleged underground ventures. "Had I been asked to prove that he was engaged in underground activities," Solow remarked, "I would have been unable to do so. Either he was engaged in underground activities or he wished he was." Solow told Chambers that if he really was an ex–Soviet agent who had defected, then he should make a public statement. But Chambers refused to go public, telling Solow he "felt he was safe from the [Communists]." And though he was living openly in Baltimore, he insisted that his Communist enemies "could not find him." Chambers evaded Solow's questions, relating nothing concrete about himself or his former underground work, suggesting only that he had been "engaged in important secret work" and could reveal information "terribly damaging" to the Communist Party and Soviet intelligence.[6]

In late October Chambers delivered a manuscript to Solow for his comments. The narrative obscurely sketched Soviet passport racketeering in America; names and other various facts were disguised, although the article was signed "Carl," a dead giveaway to *his* identity, for Carl, as he was wont to broadcast, was his primary underground moniker.

Solow advised Chambers to rewrite the piece (and other writings Chambers brought for review) with more detail and factual density and real names. Chambers agreed to revise the work, and he returned to Baltimore with a two-hundred-dollar loan from Solow.

Chambers blustered in *Witness* that the day he quit the Communist Party he would go to the police, but certainly not if *he* was going to be the one locked up. In a letter to Solow, who had consulted an attorney about Chambers's legal liabilities as a favor, Chambers inquired if the lawyer could secure, "and if so how, an unconditional pardon for past sins?"[7]

When the two men met again in late November 1938, Chambers for the first time opened up, and, according to Solow, named some of the "people involved in his work either as agents, fronts, sources or what not." However, Chambers did not mention either Alger Hiss or Donald Hiss. Solow recorded his talks with Chambers on more than a dozen typewritten pages, which include statements such as:

> Chambers has broken but fears he may be shot. He would like to make his knowledge public.
> But fears the U.S. government. He wants to make a deal with the police. If he can't get a prom-

ise of executive clemency in advance, he will take his chances with the GPU, figuring that he can keep moving and escape them. In the meantime, he refuses to make any public statement of repudiation of the CP; he claims that will only "anger" them and speed their work of pursuing him. He has very few friends to trust, is in dire need [of money].

Ultimately, Herbert Solow was personally unable to help Chambers except for loaning him money. Yet it was Solow who, on Chambers's behalf, made the fateful telephone call to Isaac Don Levine, the indomitable anti–Communist writer/editor whose subsequent pernicious alliance with Whittaker Chambers would prove almost as deadly to former State Department official Alger Hiss as the evil teamwork of the seventeenth-century imposters Titus Oates and Israel Tonge was to the English Catholic courtier Edward Colman.

Russian-born Isaac Don Levine became a U.S. citizen in 1918 at age 26. He had arrived seven years earlier, completed high school in Missouri, freelanced for a variety of newspapers in Kansas City, Chicago, and New York, and wrote his first book in 1917, on the Russian Revolution. He returned to Russia in early 1919 as a correspondent, and for several years thereafter wrote for the Hearst papers. By the mid–1920s he was also writing and editing books about Lenin, Stalin, and the Revolution. Levine's most renowned — and most lushly profitable — collaboration was with Soviet intelligence defector Walter Krivitsky, for whom Levine ghostwrote a series of espionage articles in the spring of 1939.

Walter Krivitsky sailed to America from France with his wife and young son in November 1938. He was 39 years old and, according to his biographer Gary Kern, "claimed to have directed Soviet military intelligence through all of Western Europe" before his defection in France in 1937. Curiously, the details of Krivitsky's defection are unknown because French security purportedly lost the files. He soon determined that his life was in danger there and that the United States was the only country in which he could feel safe — though he later told friends that the U.S. was deeply penetrated by Soviet agents. Constantly in fear of assassination, he was apprehensive that whatever he confided should be held in utmost secrecy.

The U.S. Immigration Board denied Krivitsky (he told American and French authorities his real name was Samuel Ginsberg) and his family official admission to the United States because they were, in fact, "immigrants not in possession of immigration visas." Krivitsky appealed, posted bond, and was issued a visitor's visa good for four months, though he later obtained an extension.[8]

In 1939 Krivitsky proffered his expert knowledge, particularly of how the Soviets counterfeited passports, to the State Department, and later that year testified before HUAC. In July 1939 he was interviewed by the FBI, but the bureau later said they were not interested in Krivitsky himself, only a case they thought he knew about.

In February 1941 Krivitsky was found dead in a Washington, D.C. hotel, an apparent suicide from a gunshot through the temple. He had recently purchased the weapon, and some friends believed he had been noticeably depressed. Discovered in his locked hotel room were three suicide notes in different languages to his family and friends.

Isaac Don Levine was introduced to Krivitsky in early 1939 by an editor of a Yiddish newspaper in New York. After a week of riveting nightly conversations with the Soviet defector, Levine made a deal with the *Saturday Evening Post*, on the basis of a small sheet of paper with eight scribbled chapter headings and a few notes about Soviet machinations in Europe, for forty thousand dollars to write a series of articles. Levine ghosted the narrative to earn his twenty grand, the other half went to Krivitsky. The *Post* editors never even cared to meet Krivitsky; they merely wanted to peruse the first installment.

Whittaker Chambers read Krivitsky's first articles in the *Post* with keen interest, and he implored Solow to introduce him to Isaac Don Levine. Chambers wasn't alone in his appreciation of the marketability of spy stories, as Levine was now being approached by several ex–Communists looking to cash in on the novelty. But Chambers had Solow in his corner, a heavyweight political writer whom Levine respected. Levine got Solow's call in late April 1939 informing Levine in highest confidence of a former important Soviet operative in Washington, an American Krivitsky, who wanted to know if Levine was willing to sell *his* story to the *Saturday Evening Post*.

Chambers soon met Levine in Manhattan, at the latter's East 64th Street office. Levine recalled that Chambers "was an exceptionally suspicious and fear-ridden man ... living with his wife and children in hideout quarters," who "slept with a rifle at his side." He was "in dire straits financially" and "had broken with the Communist underground a year or two before."[9] Actually, Chambers was now working as a *Time* book reviewer at five thousand a year, and he lived in cheap New York hotel rooms most of the week, while his wife and children tended their farm property in Maryland where they had recently moved. And even though Herbert Solow had disclosed Chambers's name to Levine, Chambers inanely insisted that Levine call him "Carl."

Initially Levine found it difficult to "develop a flowing exchange of views" with Chambers, and his appearance was unprepossessing, looking as haggard as a denizen of the Bowery — rumpled dirty clothes, unsightly teeth, and a leg injury that caused him to limp. As the two men walked to a neighborhood restaurant, Chambers suspiciously scrutinized every passerby, Levine noted, and then leered at every customer in the eatery. All of which made a bizarre impression on Levine, who was astonished that an American, for he knew Chambers was a native, could actually be afraid to go to lunch in one of Manhattan's finest districts. "He was as scared as any hunted animal," Levine said, "and it was unbelievable to me that [Chambers] should fear his own shadow in the daylight ... in the center of the city."[10]

Chambers's dread and distrust extended to Levine as well. Levine tried to probe, as was his right and responsibility because Chambers desired to sell articles to the *Saturday Evening Post*, but Chambers suspected he was being conned somehow. Yet they presently overcame their doubts and developed a friendship.

At that first meeting Chambers gave Levine a long manuscript of more than fifty pages for consideration, but he must have known that Levine would reject it because the work was just as nebulous as that shown to Solow. Levine kept the manuscript for several days, read it carefully, and was impressed by Chambers's stylish literary gifts. "And my conclusion was that his story," Levine recalled, "the way it was told, was not marketable, that I could not take it to an editor of any magazine ... because there were no names, there were no dates, places were disguised...." Moreover, Levine told an interviewer in the 1960s, Chambers did not offer any secrets or information important to national security, and the manuscript was not written out of patriotism or deep loyalty to the United States.

Nevertheless, Levine beseeched Chambers "for more meat, more meat in the story." But Chambers persisted in refusing to write the account the way Levine wanted, feigning fear for the safety of his wife and children. "But he did not," Levine recalled, "shut the door. Neither did I, because I wanted to hold on to this prize." Thus it was Levine who, with or without realizing it, encouraged Chambers to make false accusations, as Chambers soon would to an assistant secretary of state for security matters.

And it was Levine who arranged a meeting with Chambers and Krivitsky, on the one hand in the hope that Chambers would open up, and on the other to learn more about

Krivitsky, because Levine obviously did not completely trust either, though longing to exploit both. "I was anxious to have Mr. Chambers meet Krivitsky," Levine testified a decade later, "so as to check on the veracity of both of them and so as to accumulate the kind of evidence I thought the American people should have."[11] Wary of a concealed trap, both Chambers and Krivitsky at first balked at the idea of a face-to-face encounter. Levine believed Krivitsky was the most reluctant because Krivitsky doubted Chambers was on the up-and-up, even if he had once been a Soviet agent; Chambers's story, as related to Krivitsky by Levine, was just too vague. Though after a bit of cajoling, Levine brought the two men together at his place for dinner. The trio chatted until past midnight when Levine retired, leaving the two counterrevolutionaries with a pot of coffee, which they were still swilling in the midst of absorbing conversation — from totalitarianism to Soviet agents in America — when Levine awoke eight hours later. Some of Krivitsky's revelations to Chambers that night (and on meetings to follow) were repeated, as we shall see, by Chambers in sworn testimony years later as knowledge based on his own experiences.

Whittaker Chambers never published any of the accounts shown to Solow or Levine of his alleged underground exploits. By July 1939 Chambers had solidly established himself as one of *Time*'s most erudite and prolific writers. For the next nine years he lived a passably settled life in the ritualized routine of business and domesticity. Indeed, in his autobiography Chambers yearningly recalls this period as "The Tranquil Years," even though they were punctuated by suicidal marathons of work and nervous breakdowns.

If not for the shocking news of the nonaggression pact between Germany and Russia on August 24, 1939, leading to a prolonged chain reaction of events in which Chambers played a part — and culminating, in the triumphal pronouncement of Isaac Don Levine, in "America's greatest espionage saga" — Whittaker Chambers would perhaps at best be memorialized today as the translator of *Bambi*.

News of the Soviet-Nazi pact galvanized Levine, and from his many talks with Krivitsky he was convinced that Russia had obtained U.S. codes — that the Soviets were "getting a torrent of information from numerous Government bureaus in the United States," vital data now likely to fall into Nazi hands also. Levine immediately sought out Chambers at his *Time* office in Rockefeller Center and urged him to reveal to Federal authorities the real names of Communist conspirators he had so far kept secret. "When I pressed Chambers that it was his duty to go to Washington and tell all," Levine wrote in his memoir, "he blurted out: 'The statute of limitations has not yet run out in my case. How would *you* like to face a fifteen- to twenty-year jail sentence if you were in my boots, with a wife and two children, and without any savings?'"

Levine replied that he would secure for Chambers a promise of immunity from prosecution.

"That would be fine," Chambers said, "but who can give it to me? In my condition, I wouldn't trust anybody's word but that of President Roosevelt himself."

Then he would go to the White House and try to arrange it, Levine assured Chambers. "If you could take me to the President of the United States," Chambers vouched, "it wouldn't take any time with the evidence in my possession to crack this case wide open."[12]

Levine once met President Roosevelt in 1936 during a brief off-the-record conversation, and FDR's appointment secretary, Marvin McIntyre, knew Levine and the story of his collaboration with Krivitsky, and was easily accessible. McIntyre listened attentively to Levine's agitated account of his "discovery of a former Soviet agent who had for years tapped the secrets of the State Department" and was "willing to tell all only to the President himself if guaranteed immunity by him." McIntyre explained that a meeting with FDR on such short notice was simply not possible, but he suggested that Levine talk with Roosevelt's assistant secretary of state for internal security, Adolf A. Berle, whose office was next door in the old State Department Building.

Fortunately for Levine, he also knew Adolf Berle fairly well, and he met with the assistant secretary of state immediately after his session with McIntyre. "I sketched the whole case for Berle," Levine wrote, "telling him that my informant had an intimate knowledge of the inner workings of the State Department and could not be brought to his office lest he be recognized by some member of the ring with which he had been connected. I made it clear that he would talk only on one condition — that he should not be turned over to the Department of Justice for prosecution. Berle assured me not to worry on that score."

Berle reacted to Levine's report with grave concern — they had previously discussed the Krivitsky case at length — and invited Levine to bring Chambers (though Levine initially withheld Chambers's name "for fear that some leak might disrupt the rendezvous") to his home for dinner on September 2, just a few days later.

Levine returned to New York worried that Chambers might refuse to meet with Berle as a surrogate for Roosevelt. Very few people, Levine explained, knew that Berle, though an early member of the New Deal, was solidly anti–Communist, critical of the Soviets and their zealots in the U.S. And there was no question, Berle promised, of Chambers being prosecuted. To Levine's great relief Chambers said: "Berle's word is as good as Roosevelt's." But Chambers was distressed by the very prospect of confessing crimes to a government security official, and he only agreed to go because he felt a commitment to Levine. Levine told an interviewer years later that Chambers was "reluctant" and had to be taken "by the arm" to Berle's home, while Levine eagerly anticipated another huge *Saturday Evening Post* windfall.

In the Hiss-Chambers saga the conflict between myth and history begins with the sharply clashing versions of what happened at that remarkable meeting the day after the Second World War erupted in Europe. Chambers, Levine, and Berle all left written accounts of various types, and testified before congressional committees and grand juries about what Chambers said (or did not say) that night. For the first time in a single narrative their accounts — without suppressions or distortions — are now brought together. The author is confident that readers will find the truth amongst the lies for themselves.

In *Witness*, Chambers took artistic license, unabashedly confuting Levine: "And so I went to see Adolf Berle.... I never asked for immunity. Nor did anyone at any time ever offer me immunity, even by a hint or a whisper."

Levine and Chambers arrived at Woodley House, the historic estate the Berles were renting from Henry L. Stimson (appointed Secretary of War the following year) Saturday evening, September 2, 1939. Chambers did not bring along "the evidence in my possession" which he had promised would "crack this case wide open." Levine introduced the mystery guest, "the American Krivitsky," as who he really was, Whittaker Chambers, an editor of *Time* magazine.

After dinner the three men conversed and drank cocktails outside on the lawn. Chambers did most of the talking. As recounted in *Witness*, it was a "rambling talk." Chambers couldn't recall many details, but he had drawn a general outline of Communist infiltration of the FDR Administration. Chambers said the three of them were drinking heavily, and he wasn't surprised if anyone didn't remember clearly just what was said on the lawn.

Around midnight they went inside. Chambers recapitulated his story and Berle took notes in longhand. He wrote quickly, Chambers added, at a late hour after too many drinks.

"At no time in our conversation," Chambers added, "can I remember anyone's mentioning the ugly word espionage." However, he immediately qualified that statement, saying paradoxically they all knew espionage had actually been discussed. When Chambers first publicly commented and testified about his experiences as an underground Communist, before HUAC in August and September 1948, he stressed many times that he had no knowledge of espionage and had never been involved with Russia, only the American Communist Party.

In late 1948 and early 1949, three years before *Witness* was published, Chambers was questioned about the Berle meeting by a grand jury particularly interested in whether espionage had been discussed.

> GRAND JURY: Now, in the course of the Grand Jury questioning, Mr. Chambers, you were asked whether this was an espionage group back there, and you said it was not an espionage group; is that correct?
>
> CHAMBERS: Probably yes, that's correct.
>
> GRAND JURY: Mr. Chambers, at the time you talked to Mr. Berle, or at the time you talked to any other individuals with reference to this apparatus, did you tell anybody that you yourself were engaged in espionage, and that you had transmitted information...?
>
> CHAMBERS: I did not, but it was so strongly implied that I need scarcely have added much more.
>
> GRAND JURY: [Y]ou did not tell him [Berle] anything about espionage — is that correct?
>
> CHAMBERS: The word was never used.
>
> GRAND JURY: And ... nothing was said about the transmittal of documents?
>
> CHAMBERS: That is technically true, also.
>
> GRAND JURY: Did you tell Mr. Isaac Levine that you had confidential State Department documents in your possession?
>
> CHAMBERS: I am not sure at this date whether I did or not. I may have implied it strongly, but I am not sure whether I told him.
>
> GRAND JURY: You have testified previously, I think, with reference to these matters, but [we] would like to have any testimony you have on these points repeated, particularly with reference to whether any statements were made by you to Mr. Berle in that meeting at his home in 1939, that documents had been taken out of the State Department and that microfilms had been made and that espionage activities had been going on in the State Department.
>
> CHAMBERS: I ... told Mr. Berle the nature of the underground apparatus ... and gave him, I believe, a complete list of the people involved in that apparatus. Now, the sum total of what I told Mr. Berle of course added up to a picture of espionage. Now, that word, I'm sure, was never used during the conversation. I'm equally sure that everyone present understood, of course, what was implied.
>
> GRAND JURY: Now, was there any discussion about microfilms?
>
> CHAMBERS: I do not recall that we talked about microfilms.
>
> GRAND JURY: Was there any mention of the transmission of documents?
>
> CHAMBERS: I don't recall that there was.
>
> GRAND JURY: Wouldn't you have to explain something about the transmission of documents and the photographing of them, in explaining the nature of the apparatus? I mean, it wouldn't be in general terms but it would have to be rather specific, wouldn't it?
>
> CHAMBERS: We did not use the word "espionage" as nearly as I can recall, and therefore —
>
> GRAND JURY: No, I don't mean that you described what happened; what you did.
>
> CHAMBERS: I did not describe, as far as I can recall, describe the transmission of documents.
>
> GRAND JURY: Was there any reference to Alger Hiss in the conversation?
>
> CHAMBERS: Yes.
>
> GRAND JURY: [I]n connection with his taking documents out of the State Department and giving them to you?
>
> CHAMBERS: I do not believe so.

Levine's first recorded remarks about the Berle meeting were taken by HUAC during their 1948 "spy hearings."

"I think probably between a half dozen and 10 sheets of notes," Levine testified, "were made by Mr. Berle while Mr. Chambers was opening up the insides of the State Department and various other departments in Washington where he had underground contacts who supplied him with documentary and confidential information for transmission to the Soviet Government."

> HUAC: Can you tell us whether the name of Alger Hiss was mentioned in that conversation with Mr. Berle.
> LEVINE: Both Hiss brothers were mentioned. The name of Alger Hiss and the name of the other Hiss.
> HUAC: There is no question that those names were mentioned?
> LEVINE: There isn't any question....

Significantly, Levine's above testimony (in private session) of August 18, 1948, in which he swore that Chambers said to Berle that he received documents from government officials and transferred them to the Soviets, directly contradicted Chambers's testimony in several appearances before HUAC prior to August 18, in which he swore time and again that he had no knowledge whatsoever of espionage. Moreover, two months *after* Levine's HUAC appearance Chambers swore again before a grand jury that he knew nothing, ever, of espionage activities. So why did HUAC not publicize or investigate Levine's shocking revelations? After all, in the frantic summer of 1948 they were virtually in the sensation-and-spectacle business. "Nixon had let it pass," Sam Tanenhaus wrote in his sympathetic biography of Chambers. "Possibly he doubted Levine's credibility. (He would not have been alone. The FBI also thought Levine an unreliable witness.)"

In February 1949, Levine again testified about the Berle meeting before the New York grand jury.

> GRAND JURY: You made it rather clear, I think, and it can be presumed that there could have been no mistake on the part of Mr. Berle that Chambers was talking about espionage, is that correct?
> LEVINE: Yes, sir.
> GRAND JURY: In other words, you say that he mentioned documents, obtaining documents and microfilms and things of that sort?
> LEVINE: Yes, sir.
> GRAND JURY: So there could be no mistake that Mr. Berle knew there was espionage and it was beyond a doubt a fact that these were Communists?
> LEVINE: Not to the best of my recollection except for the fact that Mr. Berle was a very tired man that night, but he did make some notes. I never saw them.
> GRAND JURY: Was there any question at that time, Mr. Levine, about immunity for Chambers?
> LEVINE: Not in Chambers' presence. But the question was raised between Mr. Berle and myself when the arrangements were made for dinner.
> GRAND JURY: With reference to the name of Alger Hiss in that conversation in Mr. Berle's home, did Whittaker Chambers indicate in that conversation that Alger Hiss was actually taking material out of the State Department for the purpose of photographing it?
> LEVINE: To the best of my recollection, Mr. Chambers indicated that material was being taken out of the State Department. I cannot tie up Mr. Alger Hiss with that operation.

But in Levine's memoir, published in 1973, two years after Adolf Berle died, he felt free to revise his story somewhat, particularly regarding Alger Hiss:

The general picture drawn by Chambers that night was of two Soviet undercover "centers" or rings which, according to his firsthand knowledge, had operated in Washington for many years. One was concerned with infiltrating unionized labor and getting Communists into the federal service; the other, with political and military affairs. Both groups were gathering and supplying confidential data to Moscow.

Most of the time important papers would be microfilmed and replaced before they had been missed, and the material would be delivered to Soviet couriers, operating under aliases, for transmission to Russia.

It was clear that Chambers knew his way about official Washington, and he exhibited unusual familiarity with the inside of the State Department. He named six of its officials as having knowingly furnished confidential data to Soviet undercover agents. Mr. Berle and I were shocked by the list, which included the Hiss brothers, then in minor positions.

Adolf Augustus Berle, Jr., assistant secretary of state from 1938 to 1944 and author of a seminal work on the modern corporation, was a Columbia Law professor when he testified privately about the 1939 meeting with Chambers before HUAC in August 1948, two weeks after Levine's testimony:

Mr. Chambers stated that he wanted to disclose certain information about Communist activities in Washington. He related a story to me that he had been a member of the undercover Communist group from 1934 to end of 1937, as nearly as I can recall; that at that time, and apparently as a result of the purge activities which had been going on, he had decided to cut clear of the whole thing. He stated that he had then lived in hiding for a year or more under various names. He appeared to be even then in fear of some sort of reprisal and was obviously under some emotional strain.

He said that in addition to the New York core, the party policy, the Communist Party policy, had been to try to develop a group of sympathizers who might be of use to them later in the United States Government.

This was not, as he put it, any question of espionage. There was no espionage involved in it. He stated that their hope merely was to get some people who would be sympathetic to their point of view.

[Among others, Chambers] mentioned Alger Hiss, Donald Hiss, Nathan Witt, and [Lee] Pressman. He said that these men, it was hoped, would go, as they called it, "underground"; that is to say, that they would not appear as part of the well-known or open Communist group, but that they would simply be there and be sympathetic.

In one respect, what he told me omitted something that he has told you. He did not make the direct statement that any of these men were members of the Communist Party. They were apparently, from what I then gathered, men who were sympathetic to their general point of view and to whom they might have access and perhaps a sympathetic approach in case anybody brought a request there.

I asked whether he had given this information to the FBI, whether they already had that information either from him or secondarily through some other source ... and I asked whether he would come forward and state that or whether this was merely an oral communication. He said that he did not want to appear in the transaction at that time; that he tried to cut all his connections.... [H]e wanted to tell the story, and then he wanted to disappear from the proceedings and not do anything further about it.

I said that this was a pretty grave matter, if true, but that we needed something more than a mere ex parte statement without somebody who was prepared to do something or at least bear witness; that it was difficult to bring charges or otherwise tackle the question unless somebody at least were prepared to stand to the facts stated. He said, yes, that was true, and all he could do was to give the warning.

Berle's testimony before the grand jury four months later was essentially the same except he believed that Chambers may have told him in 1939 that of the government officials he named as CP sympathizers only Donald Hiss was actually a member of the Communist Party. And Berle could not recall Levine's presence at the 1939 meeting in his account to HUAC, but to the grand jury he said, "I don't distinctly remember it but my impression is that Mr. Levine was with [Chambers]. Mr. Levine took no part in the discussion."

GRAND JURY: When Chambers talked to you did he indicate that he had any tangible evidence to back it up with?

BERLE: Not a thing. Not a thing. That was one of the difficulties. There was always the fair possibility this was a straight screwball. Mr. Chambers gave evidence of having been through some deep emotional strain, and that could have been his separation from the Communist Party or it could have been merely mental disturbance.

GRAND JURY: Did Mr. Chambers tell you he had come from the underground or [was he] just a Communist? Did he tell you he was from the underground? Because if such was the case, all of these things would be done underground; they wouldn't be done aboveboard.

BERLE: Mr. Chambers' story was that he had been a Communist and, as I recall it, that he had been in a position to see certain of the underground reports, that he in New York was in a position to see certain reports coming from Washington. He did not make himself out in any sense a principal.

GRAND JURY: But by the same token, he was talking about people in your department who were in this cell or in this apparatus and they probably, by his word, were working in the underground with him. By deduction you could get that.

BERLE: Well, as he told it to me, this would be hearsay on hearsay. The one thing that he did not indicate was his own connection with what was going on.

GRAND JURY: I say, if he hadn't mentioned any names, I could understand that. But actually naming the people for you to be on guard against was something like a sort of red light.

BERLE: Well, of course, you could get into the position of the police state where people stick communications into the mouth of the lion and something happens, but you are apt to be in trouble if you do.

In March 1952, as the *Saturday Evening Post* serialized Chambers's *Witness* prior to the book's publication in May, Adolf Berle reflected on the articles in his diary:

The fact, of course, was that he did not state anything he told me as personal knowledge — but as something he had heard about while in the Communist Party in New York. He did not even remotely indicate that he personally had been engaged in the operation. He did not charge individuals with espionage — they were merely "sympathizers" who would be hauled out later when the great day came. He would not take his story to the FBI. He would not even stand to it himself — he would not himself verify or stick to the story. He really wanted to see the President.

Further, under some cross-examination, he qualified everything to the point of substantial withdrawal. He also told of having fled the Party, and having been in fear of his life, spending a long time in flight and fearing armed attack, and so on. I thought I was dealing with a man who thought he was telling the truth but was probably afflicted with a neurosis.

The aftermath of the Berle-Chambers-Levine meeting — in other words, what action, or lack of it, Adolf Berle took concerning Chambers's revelations — was rife with confusion and speculation in the minds of Chambers and Levine. Though when Allen Weinstein, who is generally credited as having published the definitive account of the Hiss-Chambers affair, wrote four decades later about Berle's motives and conduct subsequent to the meeting, he resorted to straightforward lies and distortions, as we'll see.

Chambers later wrote that he and Levine left Berle's place after midnight. They both supposed Berle, on the telephone even before his guests were out the door, was calling the White House. Always spooked by the police or the legal system in general, Chambers now believed he would probably be arrested, such was the absurdity of his paranoia. But nothing happened. Weeks later he met a "dejected Levine," who said Berle had taken Chambers's information immediately to Roosevelt. "The President had laughed."

To the grand jury in February 1949, Chambers swore that "I left Mr. Berle in a highly agitated condition. I myself returned to New York, expecting that a full-scale investigation would begin at once and, of course, that I would make a complete statement of the whole picture." But Chambers heard nothing.

Once again Chambers repaired to his prosaic existence as a Maryland farmer and New York City magazine editor. Yet years prior to his first public appearance before HUAC on August 3, 1948, Chambers was visited several times by FBI agents in the early to mid 1940s. The FBI first heard of Chambers in 1941, not from Adolf Berle but from Ludwig Lore, a former friend of Chambers.[13] Chambers apprised the first agents who visited him of his 1939 meeting with Berle, and in 1943 the FBI requested from Berle his notes of that meeting. However, Chambers never admitted to any FBI agent in those years that he had been involved in espionage, and he stressed that the government officials he had dealt with in the underground were "too important" for mere espionage. But ever the serial accuser, Chambers stepped up his charges to the FBI: two culpable names he *deliberately* omitted from his conversation with Berle were those of Harry Dexter White, one of the world's leading economists, and George Silverman, who had so generously helped Chambers with loans and a job in 1937.

Ironically, Isaac Don Levine wrote in his memoir that Chambers *had* named Harry Dexter White to Berle and that Berle was incredulous: "But I know Harry Dexter White very well, and I cannot believe it!" If White's name was mentioned, Berle failed to record it in his notes. (See Appendix for a copy of Berle's handwritten notes.)

Levine jotted down the names he could recall from the meeting after retiring to his hotel room. "My notes," he informed the grand jury in 1949, "I want to emphasize here, dealt only with names, not with circumstances or operations." Levine confidently expected "that the explosive Chambers story would be laid before the President and that drastic action would follow." But when he called on Berle two weeks later, the assistant secretary of state told him that FDR had "given him the cold shoulder" after hearing his account of Chambers's disclosures.

Levine had relished the thought that Berle would report back with the results of a damning investigation, or, better yet, inform him that some of the government officials accused by Chambers had been at least dismissed. Then Levine and Chambers could collaborate on an explosive (and rewarding) article or two, Chambers remaining anonymous as "Carl" or Mr. X, the renegade underground Communist who informed to President Roosevelt's chief security agent, Adolf A. Berle. Levine confirmed his crass intentions a decade later to HUAC. Chambers, Levine avowed, "felt that having taken the matter up with [Berle] had gone far enough in his perilous position and he knew that I was hammering away, trying to find an opening ... in the public mind ... for the Chambers story.... I kept in touch with Miss Adelaide Neall, senior editor of the *Saturday Evening Post* at that time.... She was excited; she wanted to know all the developments. I figured that this story would break and that ... I might have a scoop. Nothing happened."

But Levine was not easily deflected from his mission. He soon repeated his version of the Berle meeting to other high government officers and politicians, including Loy Henderson, Russian Section chief of the State Department; Republican senator Warren R. Austin; and Ambassador William Bullitt, who also took Levine's story to the White House but was rebuffed. Levine always carefully avoided mentioning Chambers's name to anyone while consistently identifying those Chambers had slandered, such as Alger Hiss.

In March 1940, Levine talked to Representative Martin Dies and his staff of the temporary Special House Committee on Un-American Activities, hoping "to interest them in employing a dozen ace investigators" to pursue Chambers's charges. Dies, though, outfoxed the predatory journalist, calling a press conference two days later to announce, Weinstein wrote, "that *he* was hot on the trail of several Soviet spy rings in the United States." Moreover, the artful Dies, in a maneuver worthy of Levine himself, also used Levine's story to obtain a large advance from *Cosmopolitan*— for a piece which was never written.[14]

At wit's end, Levine finally descended to telling tales to gossip columnist Walter Winchell, a former Naval Intelligence officer who knew President Roosevelt well. "When Mr. Isaac Don Levine came to me with the story that top Roosevelt people didn't want to hear," Winchell wrote in a 1969 letter to William Reuben, "I decided to bring it to the President in person — since FDR ... had long before ordered me to see him personally about anything that concerned him and our country.

"Imagine my shock and embarrassment when he stopped me cold in his office at the White House and angrily said, 'I do not want to hear one word about it. I'm tired of it. It just isn't true!'"

When Chambers swore to HUAC in early August 1948 that nothing officially was ever done about his revelations to Berle in 1939, reporters clamored for Berle's reaction. "I confirmed to the newspapers that Chambers had talked to me in 1939," Berle noted in his diary, "though we did a great deal about it."

Berle told his side of the story to HUAC a few weeks later.

> HUAC: Did you subsequently do anything officially or unofficially about [Chambers's] information?
> BERLE: Yes; I did a great deal. I was disturbed a good deal.... I looked into the then position of the two Hiss boys, first. According to my recollection, neither of them had any position that amounted to very much in the State Department. My recollection is that at that time Alger Hiss was doing some relatively unimportant work in, I think, the legal department, and I have forgotten what Donald Hiss was doing, but neither was in any position where he either had access to confidential information or where he had much to do with policy, so for the moment there was no immediate danger.
>
> Further, the idea that the two Hiss boys and Nat Witt were going to take over the United States Government didn't strike me as any immediate danger. What was interesting was that the Communist Party was really trying an undercover lobbying operation ... and that worried me and two or three people I talked to.
>
> I checked on the two Hiss boys. Specifically, I checked with Dean Acheson, and later I checked when Acheson became Assistant Secretary of State and Alger Hiss became his executive assistant. That, to the best of my knowledge, was the first time when Hiss would have been in a position to do anything effectively.
>
> Acheson said that he had known the family and these two boys from childhood and he could vouch for them absolutely. I further checked and found that Mr. Justice Frankfurter would give them an exactly similar endorsement. You had, therefore, a chain of endorsements by the men for whom they worked, but reputable men, whether you agree with their point of view or not, and this seemed to negative any immediate danger.
>
> Schematically, however, I believed that Chambers was telling the truth as he saw it, so I caused the Department to establish very close relations with the Federal Bureau of Investigation. We likewise established a weekly liaison meeting with the FBI at which we exchanged

information.... We accordingly caused to be written the Foreign Agents Registration Act, and that act in due time was passed by the Congress.

HUAC: Were you ever at any time suspicious of Mr. Hiss?

BERLE: A better way of saying it is: I was worried.

Berle explained that by the fall of 1944 there was a difference of opinion in the State Department regarding the Soviet Union, and he did not believe the Russians were going to be cooperative and sympathetic when the war ended. Victory was assured but not yet complete, and the intelligence reports in Berle's charge indicated a very aggressive Soviet policy not at all in line with the cooperation which many had anticipated and hoped for. Berle said he pressed for a clean-cut showdown at that time when the U.S. position was the strongest, but others, including Alger Hiss, took "what we would call today the pro–Russian point of view." Berle conceded that Hiss's view (shared by American military leaders) was also U.S. policy during the war, but Berle disagreed with it.

"You have in mind that when Mr. Chambers talked to me in 1939," Berle added, "he was talking about something that was then two years old at the time when there was no strain on relations. A man might be very much interested in Russia, and most people in the State Department were. I was myself, so far as that is concerned ... so that is all you had to go on."

Four months after his HUAC appearance Berle was questioned by the grand jury, specifically about what actions he took after the meeting with Chambers.

GRAND JURY: Mr. Chambers has made the point that he disclosed all of this information back in 1939 to yourself, and he can't understand why you never did anything about it. That's the thing the jury wants to know.

BERLE: I don't like to disagree with Mr. Chambers, but there is nothing in any recollection that I have which suggests that espionage was mentioned. In fact, I rather recall the exact negative impression was given.

GRAND JURY: Did Mr. Chambers tell you at that time that officials in the State Department were supplying State Department data to the Russian underground?

BERLE: He certainly did not. What he said was that one interview which had been had in the State Department had been reported rapidly to Moscow [see page 4 of Berle's notes, Appendix].... At that time, since there was virtually no security limitation on Washington and anybody could talk about anything, and usually did, the wonder would be whether everything that went on in any department didn't leak as rapidly to any foreign government as it did to every Washington newspaper.... The Washington columnists, in my experience, appeared to have access to pretty nearly everything at that time. It was a very wide open, loose system. And there is a very serious question raised there. Except as the war controls finally came on, you — almost anything was available to almost anybody. It was not a system, a security system, that commanded any particular respect. I think you have to say that, sir. It was wide open.

Berle told the jurors that a day or so after his talk with Chambers he met with McIntyre, FDR's secretary, who had directed Levine to his office, and they decided to let Chambers's allegations "run through regular channels," particularly because Chambers "had made it clear," Berle testified, "that he did not want his name to appear in it." Berle then soon made an oral report to the FBI, providing the substance of Chambers's story. The FBI learned of the Berle-Chambers meeting in May 1942 from Chambers himself. He informed the agents that everything he knew about Communist infiltration of the United States government he already told Berle in September 1939. Nevertheless, the FBI did not request a copy of Berle's meeting notes until June 1943, more than a year later.

Allen Weinstein, the *Perjury* author who Victor Navasky aptly designated the "opinion trustee" for a new generation of readers unfamiliar with the facts of the Hiss-Chambers case, knew the truth about the Berle-Chambers meeting yet tortured the facts into lies. "Berle chose to ignore Chambers's allegations of Communist involvements by various officials, including Alger Hiss," Weinstein wrote. Of Berle's testimony before HUAC in August 1948, Weinstein asserted that "Berle, the New Deal partisan, either evaded answering or distorted [Chambers's and Levine's previous] testimony when confronting the subcommittee," and that "Berle's recollections of his 1939 meeting with Chambers and its aftermath were surprisingly inaccurate." And Berle's "failure to check on any of Chambers's leads, not simply those involving the Hiss brothers, is particularly surprising, considering his role as Roosevelt's chief adviser on internal-security matters in 1939."

Finally, there is the evidence of Berle's actual notes of that momentous meeting. "At no time in our conversation," Chambers professed in *Witness*, "can I remember anyone's mentioning the ugly word espionage. But how well we understood what we were talking about, Berle was to make a matter of record. For when, four years after that memorable conversation, his notes were finally taken out of a secret file and turned over to the F.B.I., it was found that Adolf Berle himself had headed them: *Underground Espionage Agent.*"

But Adolf Berle did no such thing. A copy typed by the FBI makes it appear as if Berle titled his notes "Underground Espionage Agent," the "heading" obviously referring to Chambers. However, Berle's notes clearly show that the sinister appellation is not about Chambers.

Since at least 1948 Adolf Berle believed his original notes were lost; to the end of his life he was never able to find them. But the author of this book found them in May 2009 at the Franklin D. Roosevelt Presidential Library and Museum, which houses Berle's papers. Archivist Bob Clark retrieved them in less than a day.

In June 1943 Berle provided the FBI, at their request, his penciled notes, along with a typed copy for clarity. The FBI typed a set for their files and returned Berle's original and typed copy — which remained at large in a random packing box for decades until the FDR Library filed them.

These are the first lines of the first page of Berle's notes:

> *London*— Underground Espionage Agent
> 1) Dr. *Philip Rosenbliett*— Formerly of...

This is the FBI's transcription of those lines:

> LONDON   Underground Espionage Agent
> (1) Dr. Philip Rosenbliett — Formerly of...

Berle's notes comprise more than thirty names, including Donald Hiss, Alger Hiss, and Priscilla Hiss. The descriptive entries are abbreviated but decipherable, with notations such as CP and underground. Philip Rosenbliett is the only underground espionage agent mentioned. The others are sympathizers, Communists, fellow travelers, or infiltrators.

One gets the impression from the notes, as Berle testified in 1948, that Chambers had not been directly involved but was just passing along information. Even more significant is what Chambers chose *not* to say. He said nothing to Berle, as he did to HUAC a decade later, about collecting Communist Party dues from the Hisses or others. He doesn't mention Henry Collins, the alleged treasurer of the Ware group; nor Max Bedacht, who supposedly summoned Chambers into the "crypts of the underground"; nor Boris Bykov, Chambers's last underground chief, whose name had been revealed to Chambers by Krivitsky only a few months before the Berle meeting.

There are, in fact, discrepancies between Berle's notes and his testimony nine years later before the House Committee on Un-American Activities. But Berle maintained that his disclosures to HUAC accurately reflected the sum of his "conversation as a whole," whereas his notes, which he took as Chambers talked, rather than carefully preparing afterwards, "merely reflect statements which Chambers made at one point or another but then failed to stand to."

CHAPTER **XIII**

Suicide Watch

"I have expected for several days to pick up the paper in the morning and read that Mr. Chambers has jumped out the window." — Alexander Campbell, assistant attorney general, December 14, 1948

Whittaker Chambers was despondent when he left William Marbury's Baltimore law office the evening of November 5, 1948, the second day of an onerous and relentless deposition in preparation for a libel trial. Hiss had Chambers on the ropes with the defamation suit, and it now looked certain Chambers would not only have to pay a $75,000 judgment but might also be prosecuted for perjury. Even more depressing, no satisfactory options were open to him, and he was contemplating suicide. His "life preserver," a miscellany of stolen government documents which Chambers squirreled away in 1938, could possibly squelch the libel suit, but he would have to change his story and confess to espionage and admit he'd been lying all along. That very day he swore to Marbury that Hiss had never passed government documents to him. And only three weeks earlier, on October 14 and 15, he avowed to the grand jury that he never obtained any information from anyone for transmission to the American Communist Party — Chambers had always denied any connection to the Soviets. One juror asked: "Could you give one name of anybody, who, in your opinion, was positively guilty of espionage against the United States? Yes or No." Chambers asked for a day to think it over and the next day replied, "No." Even the friendly members of the House Committee on Un-American Activities were liable to turn against Chambers and demand that the Justice Department prosecute him for repeated denials of spying, which he would now have to recant.

Chambers had not gone to look for his life preserver, which his wife's nephew had hidden for him a decade ago, because he didn't believe it was important. As he noted in *Witness*, he was overcome with lethargy, and the very thought of traveling to New York City to reclaim old scraps of paper seemed an unendurable task. But his lawyers warned that the case was lost without corroborating evidence.

According to his nephew-in-law, Nathan Levine, Chambers was in "morbid fear of his life" when he gave Nathan, an attorney, a large sealed envelope for safekeeping sometime in 1938 or 1939. The Communists were stalking him, Chambers told Nathan, and if he were to be killed or disappear, Nathan should give the parcel to his Aunt Esther who would know what to do. Nathan never knew what was in the envelope but assumed it contained "innocent papers," maybe just Chambers's discourses about his Communist experiences in the 1930s. Perhaps Levine was only too familiar with his uncle's melodramatic personality and didn't take him seriously, but, oddly enough for a seasoned lawyer, he didn't put the envelope away in a locked safe in his law office as one would expect. Instead he hid it in his mother's house in Brooklyn "where kids couldn't get at it."[1] Chambers himself did not know where Nathan had put his "life preserver" and had never inquired about it until November 1948, a decade later. If Nathan Levine had unexpectedly died, the package may never have been found.

On November 12 Chambers called Nathan, telling him he was coming to New York, and asked if he would have his "things" ready for him, reminding Nathan of the package he left a decade before. Two days later, on Sunday, November 14, Nathan led Chambers up to the second floor of his mother's house in Brooklyn where, over the tub in the bathroom, a window opened into what used to be a dumbwaiter shaft that was now partly a closet of an adjacent room. Above the top partition, next to the abandoned pulleys, was the treasure. Nathan stood on the bathtub rim, opened the false window and half disappeared into the shaft. He reappeared with the prize, laden with dust and cobwebs, and handed it to Chambers. While Nathan swept up, Chambers opened the envelope and quickly closed it. Nathan never saw its contents.

Later that Sunday, while alone at his Westminster, Maryland, farm, Chambers examined for the first time, so he said, all the items in the envelope. "I forgot I had put [them] by," he later remarked. "I thought I had destroyed them. I supposed that the documents I had put away were the handwriting specimens of Mr. Hiss."

There were four small sheets of paper, or scratch-pad chits, on which appeared the handwriting of Alger Hiss; sixty-five sheets of onionskin paper, approximately 8½" by 11", typed copies of various State Department documents; four sheets of yellow legal-size paper bearing the handwriting of Harry Dexter White, deceased former assistant secretary of the Treasury; two short strips of developed 35mm film, photographs of State Department documents; three rolls of undeveloped 35mm film cartridges in metal canisters; and a 3" by 5" piece of paper of no significance.

The next day, Monday, Chambers met with his lawyers Richard Cleveland and William Macmillan and informed them he had "found something." Espionage had been involved after all, he confessed, but he had been "shielding" Alger Hiss; he had tried to destroy the Communist conspiracy without harming any more than necessary the individuals involved in the conspiracy. And though he had been protecting Hiss (who had the effrontery to sue!) during the deposition, Marbury had been "baiting me by snide innuendo and sneering skepticism.... I could not avoid knowing that I was being treated, with a blistering condescension, as a kind of human filth." Yet all the while Chambers maintained that he "sat there, covering up for" Hiss.

As Chambers's innate cleverness made him congenitally incapable of leveling with anyone, including his lawyers, he did not reveal to Cleveland and Macmillan the existence of the film. He only turned over to them the typed and handwritten papers — but he asked the attorneys not to show the papers to Marbury just yet, he needed another day to make a final decision. Chambers was scheduled to resume the pre-trial examination the following day but instead sent Esther to testify in his place.

Esther Chambers, like her husband, swore that a close familial relationship was maintained between her family and the Hisses for three or four years in the 1930s. But of the four known Baltimore residences which the Chamberses had occupied between 1934 and 1938, not one of their former neighbors still around could recall ever seeing either Alger or Priscilla Hiss, according to an investigation in preparation for the libel trial against Chambers. And Esther could not furnish the identity of anyone who had possibly seen her with Priscilla or Alger Hiss. When asked if anyone saw the Hisses during the several visits Esther claimed they paid to her various addresses in Baltimore, she responded: "Nobody was there but ourselves when the Hisses were there," or "The Hisses always visited after the maid left for the evening," or "I had no maid at the moment," or "We had a colored woman called Edith. I have not been able to recall what her last name was." At one point Esther became so distraught and confused because of her lies and evasions that she broke down in tears.

While Esther testified, Whittaker Chambers drove back to the farm, where he planned to kill himself. He described his state of mind later in *Witness* as feeling he was separated from the world by the fact that he was really dead, but by some odd torment he still moved and talked. By the time he arrived home he had still not decided whether to shoot himself or inhale cyanide. His gun was upstairs, but he hesitated to use it because of the gruesome scene his wife must encounter, so he walked around the property looking for the cyanide compound that was commonly used on farms. Chambers rationalized that his family would be better off without him. If he went on living he would be nothing to them but a dishonored man, but dead he felt his memory would be cherished.

In a "stupor of distress" Chambers sought guidance in prayer, seeking to lay himself open to God. Was it God's purpose that he live and be a witness of justice by crushing the Communist conspiracy, or kill himself and be a witness of mercy? Either way he was destroying himself, it was only a matter of which form of destruction to choose.

Having turned the written documents over to his lawyers, Chambers had implicated Alger Hiss and Harry Dexter White, who had died in August. If he turned over the film he would implicate others also. By destroying the film — and himself — he could spare these people. He had to finally decide whether to destroy the film and spare those he had so far "shielded," or to expose the conspiracy.

Chambers felt a burden settling upon him, the weight of God's purpose that he must not destroy himself. Therefore, he must not destroy the film. He must remain a living witness, which to him meant a slower means of destruction.

Chambers drove back to Baltimore to pick up Esther. Marbury had given her a rough time. Chambers told his lawyer Richard Cleveland that he had decided to introduce the written documents into the pre-trial examination the next day. He continued to keep the film a secret.

Around two o'clock on Wednesday afternoon, November 17, Chambers, accompanied by his lawyers Cleveland and Macmillan, and Harold Medina, Jr., representing Time-Life, Inc., entered William Marbury's law library to continue Chambers's pre-trial testimony after a twelve-day break. Chambers carried the envelope of documents, minus the film, which he received three days before from Nathan Levine. Alger Hiss was at his Carnegie Endowment office in New York, confident that Marbury could easily handle Chambers's preposterous charges without his attendance. Immediately Macmillan announced that Chambers wished to make a statement in connection with his previous testimony. Then Chambers spoke:

> In response to your request to produce papers from Mr. Hiss, I made a search, and I have certain papers in Mr. Hiss's handwriting and certain other papers. In testifying from the beginning, I have faced two problems.

My first problem was to paralyze and destroy so far as I was able the Communist conspiracy. My second problem was to do no more injury than necessary to the individuals involved in that operation. I was particularly anxious, for reason of friendship, and because Mr. Hiss is one of the most brilliant young men in the country, not to do injury more than necessary to Mr. Hiss.

Therefore, I have carefully avoided testifying to certain activities of Mr. Hiss at any place or any time heretofore. I found when I looked at the papers which I had put by certain documents which I had forgotten I had put by. I thought I had destroyed them. The documents I refer to reveal a kind of activity, the revelation of which is somewhat different from anything I have testified about before.

Marbury asked to see the papers. Macmillan did not want the originals to leave his possession but was willing to give Marbury photostatic copies, and they briefly discussed how the papers should be marked for the record. After the papers were tagged, Marbury resumed the deposition but asked no questions about the papers, nor did Chambers add anything specific concerning them.

Chambers now advanced a decidedly different story, one that previously did not include espionage or Russians. In 1937, Chambers continued, new developments took place in the Washington apparatus. Sometime that summer "J. Peters introduced me to a Russian who identified himself under the pseudonym Peter, I presume for purpose of confusion between his name and J. Peters. I subsequently learned that the Russian Peter was one Colonel [Boris] Bykov." Bykov was extremely interested in the Washington group and questioned Chambers "endlessly," and raised the issue of procuring government documents from them. And so, Chambers maintained, he arranged a meeting between Alger Hiss and Bykov in August or early fall of 1937 in New York; Chambers wasn't sure of the exact location but it was a movie theater "somewhere near the Brooklyn Bridge." The three of them later had supper "at the Port Arthur restaurant in Chinatown."

Bykov raised the question of Hiss supplying documents from the State Department. Hiss agreed to do this, Chambers said, though Bykov refused to speak English and spoke German while Chambers translated. "Following that meeting," Chambers recalled, "Alger Hiss began a fairly consistent flow of such material as we have before us here. The method was for him to bring home documents in his brief case, which Mrs. Hiss usually typed. I am not sure that she typed all of them. Alger Hiss may have typed some of them himself. But it became a function for her to help to solve the problem of Mrs. Hiss's longing for activity, that is Communist activity."

When Hiss was unable to bring out certain State Department documents because they passed through his hands quickly, for example, then he would transmit handwritten notations such as those hidden away in the envelope for ten years, Chambers claimed.

Marbury had no way of knowing that three years earlier, in June 1945, Chambers averred to the FBI that "Peter" was *not* Colonel Boris Bykov — they were two different people. Chambers purposely confused the names Peter and J. Peters because *they* were one and the same person. J. Peters was actually Jozsef Peter, and he was commonly called "Peter" by those who knew him, as Max Bedacht noted in a previous chapter.

"Other people whom he [Chambers] met while in the company of Peter," the 1945 FBI report states, "included an individual who was later identified to him as Boris Bykov by [Walter] Krivitsky. He recalled that during 1936 he met Peter one time in a theatre which he could not recall. Peter was accompanied by a man 5 feet 7 inches tall, red hair, slightly baldy, Jewish, very sloppy appearance, who spoke very little English and poor German, was apparently 36–37 years old in 1937." Peter introduced this man (Bykov, as Chambers later learned) under an alias Chambers could no longer remember. Chambers "sensed" that Bykov was connected with Soviet intelligence.[2]

Typically obfuscatory, Chambers told Marbury that J. Peters introduced him to Bykov (or Peter, later revealed as Bykov), and that subsequently Chambers introduced Hiss to Bykov at a movie theater. But to the FBI three years before, it was Peter who introduced Chambers to Bykov in a movie theater.

Marbury asked again if Chambers had *ever* previously testified that Hiss had committed espionage. He had never told anyone, Chambers replied, including the FBI and the Un-American Activities Committee. Marbury was well-nigh dumbfounded at the sudden revelation of these documents, especially coming almost two months after the suit was filed and two weeks after Chambers was first asked to produce corroboration of his relationship with Hiss. But Marbury thought it would be unwise to proceed with an examination of the typed papers until he had a chance to consult with Hiss. For all Marbury knew, the documents might be fabrications that Hiss could identify as such by scrutinizing the photostatic copies.

The handwritten memoranda which Chambers turned over surely looked like Alger Hiss's handwriting, Marbury believed — and he was "shocked." Barring the possibility of forgery, Marbury wrote forty years later, "it was obvious that the handwritten memoranda really meant the end of the libel suit. I had spent most of my professional life as a litigator and had participated actively in the defense of some fairly important libel cases, and I was fully aware of the devastating effect that these memoranda would be certain to have on Alger's suit." On the other hand, the libel suit would become academic, Marbury recognized, if Chambers were indicted for perjury, for lying to HUAC and a grand jury about knowing nothing about espionage.

That evening Alger Hiss examined copies of Chambers's papers (which became known as the Baltimore Documents) and confirmed to Marbury that it appeared to be his handwriting on the scratch sheets, notes he sometimes jotted to himself when reporting to assistant secretary of state Sayre and later threw away. In the lax security of those years they could have been readily stolen, Hiss said, from his desk or trashcan. Hiss claimed he had never seen the typewritten papers before but acknowledged that their contents were similar to official documents which came across his desk at the State Department, although he had no idea how Chambers acquired them.

Marbury reasoned — correctly, it turned out — that a criminal investigation would now ensue to determine how Chambers came to possess those papers. Were they actually copies of genuine classified documents? Had espionage been involved? Had Alger Hiss given them to Chambers? Marbury knew that only the Department of Justice could marshal the resources for such an inquiry. Moreover, Marbury and his partner, Charles Evans, believed they were legally obliged to immediately tell the Attorney General what had happened. Alger Hiss thoroughly agreed, along with Chambers's own lawyers.

On Friday, November 19, Alexander Campbell, chief of the Justice Department's Criminal Division, arrived in Baltimore to take charge of the investigation. He requested that the libel suit judge, W. Calvin Chesnut, postpone all further actions in the case for two weeks and maintain absolute secrecy while the Justice Department conducted its probe.

After a week passed with no word from Alexander Campbell, William Marbury began to worry. What if the papers turned out to be copies of genuine State Department documents? "In that event," Marbury recalled in his memoir, "it seemed to me that it would be quite likely that Alger and not Chambers would be indicted." He invited the Hisses to lunch on Sunday, November 28, and conveyed his fear that Alger would be indicted. Marbury suggested that the couple make "every effort to locate papers written" on the typewriter they owned in the 1930s, a machine they disposed of around 1938 (the year Chambers's papers were dated) but could no longer remember exactly when or how they got rid of it or even who the manufacturer was. Any typed household letters or papers found, Marbury surmised, could then be compared against Chambers's papers to prove he was lying.

The following Friday, December 3, Marbury wrote to Hiss: "I am troubled by the fact that your inability to explain what became of the typewriter which [Priscilla] had in 1938 might be construed as an attempt to cover up something.... This inference could be rebutted by a voluntary production on your part of papers which were typed by her on that particular machine. I think that she should make every effort to locate some such papers."

But unbeknownst to Marbury, the Justice Department intended to seek an indictment of Chambers only. On November 23, just two working days after Campbell collected Chambers's Baltimore Documents, and presumably after consulting with Attorney General Thomas Clark, Campbell presented J. Edgar Hoover with an exacting directive: "It is desired that an immediate investigation be conducted so that it can be determined whether Chambers has committed perjury. In this connection the photostatic copies of these documents should be obtained together with a copy of the deposition given by Chambers." However, Campbell knew Chambers had indeed committed perjury because of the stark discrepancies between his October grand jury testimony and his libel suit deposition. Campbell also instructed the FBI to question Alger and Priscilla Hiss — but *not* to launch a perjury investigation against Hiss.[3]

At the end of November the House Committee on Un-American Activities "appeared to be going down the drain," in the words of its chief investigator, Robert Stripling. Truman had surprisingly defeated Dewey, HUAC lost its Republican majority, former chairman Thomas was heading to prison, McDowell lost his re-election bid, Rankin and Hébert were forced out because of new committee rules, Mundt won a seat in the Senate, and Stripling was retiring in a month to pursue private business in Texas. What seemed the final insult appeared December 1 on page three of the *Washington Daily News* under the headline "HISS AND CHAMBERS PERJURY PROBE HITS DEAD END."

The report implied that the Justice Department was about to "drop its investigation of the celebrated Alger Hiss-Whittaker Chambers controversy" unless additional evidence was forthcoming. However, the article did not mention Alexander Campbell's probe, nor was there any indication that Chambers had produced evidence in mid–November. The piece read as though the press (the *Daily News* at any rate) was kissing the story goodbye.

But one Nicholas Vazzana, an attorney with Harold Medina's firm representing Chambers on behalf of Time-Life, did not want the case to die, and he looked to HUAC as the last hope to revive it. The morning of December 1 Vazzana dropped in at the committee's offices and asked to speak to Stripling. The committee staffers knew Vazzana from previous visits when he collected copies of files and transcripts from the summer hearings. He told Stripling that new evidence had surfaced in the Hiss-Chambers case, but he was sworn to secrecy and would be held in contempt of court if he talked. Stripling presently introduced Vazzana to Nixon, but Vazzana insisted he couldn't talk to either of them about it. "But I suppose," Vazzana qualified, "I can tell you it has something to do with the Hiss-Chambers libel suit, and it concerns documents." Yet after two hours of friendly questioning by Nixon and Stripling, Vazzana revealed almost everything about the November 17 deposition at Marbury's law office, including the typed documents and notes in Hiss's handwriting surrendered by Chambers, though Vazzana partly honored Campbell's secrecy admonition and would not say what the documents actually revealed.[4]

Nixon was both hurt and angered by the news. He had bet his career on the veracity of Chambers and had even become his friend. Only three weeks before, just after the election, Nixon stopped by the Westminster farmstead, but Chambers had not confided so much as a hint of this. Stripling suggested — and then repeatedly urged — that they immediately drive to Maryland and confront Chambers about Vazzana's revelations. Time was running out. Nixon had booked a cruise to Panama which sailed the next day, the vacation he'd been promising his wife for three years. "I'm so goddamned sick and tired of this case," Stripling recalled Nixon saying. "I don't want to hear any more about it and I'm going to Panama. And the hell with it, and you, and the whole damned business!" Time was short for Stripling also. If Nixon didn't act now, the matter would have to wait until next Congress, by which time Stripling would be gone and HUAC might very well be disbanded by the Democrats. Stripling believed the committee could crack the case wide open by revealing the existence of the Baltimore Documents and perhaps finding more papers at Chambers's home. Stripling's clear thinking finally prevailed over Nixon's tantrums, and they sped out of Washington for Westminster.

Chambers confirmed that he had turned over "documentary" evidence at the pre-trial examination two weeks before, evidence so important that the Justice Department was called in to investigate. Everyone involved was sworn to secrecy, Chambers said, so he couldn't mention what was in the documents. "I will only say that they were a real bombshell." Nixon wanted a second bombshell for HUAC but could pry no more out of Chambers.

On the drive back Stripling recalled that Nixon was again in a surly mood. "I don't think he's got a damned thing," Nixon said. "I'm going right ahead with my plans." But later that evening, while packing for the trip, Nixon called reporter Bert Andrews and told him of the day's events with Vazzana and Chambers. Did Nixon "just ask" for anything Chambers had? Andrews wanted to know. "Or did you slap a subpoena on him?" A subpoena hadn't occurred to him, Nixon replied. Andrews advised Nixon, before he left town on vacation, to tell Stripling to serve a "blanket subpoena on Chambers to produce *anything* and *everything* he still has in his possession."

Nixon also phoned FBI agent Louis Nichols the evening of December 1, according to the agent's records, and apprised Nichols of his cruise to the Canal Zone, and that he would return in two weeks and reopen hearings on the Hiss-Chambers controversy. Nixon was paying the courtesy of advance notice so the bureau wouldn't be caught off guard, and Nixon promised that HUAC would handle the matter so that the FBI would not be criticized.

Before leaving the city the next morning Nixon instructed Stripling to serve Chambers that day with a blanket subpoena which covered evidence he possessed concerning Hiss or anyone else he mentioned during the August hearings. Stripling called, and Chambers agreed to stop by his office on the way to a Loyalty Board hearing, where Chambers was to inform against a Federal official (a veritable second profession now for Chambers) suspected of past Communist associations. Fearing the authorities might ransack the house looking for evidence while he was in Washington, Chambers removed the films from their hiding place in his bedroom and placed them in a hollowed-out pumpkin in his pumpkin patch.

Chambers arrived at Stripling's office about noon, was duly served, and admitted that he had documentary material at his farm. It was decided that Chambers would return after his Loyalty Board testimony, and Stripling would escort him to Westminster. Around seven that evening HUAC investigators William Wheeler and Donald Appell drove Chambers (Stripling was unable to join them) to the Baltimore train station where his car was parked and then followed him home. Chambers led them to the pumpkin patch and gave them all that remained of his life preserver — two strips of developed film wrapped in waxed paper and three canisters of undeveloped film (two sealed with tape, while the lid of the other appeared broken).

Appell kept the films at his home that night and delivered them to Stripling early the next day, December 3. Viewing the developed film strips with an electric enlarging device, the first words which loomed up at Stripling through the glass were "DEPARTMENT OF STATE" and "STRICTLY CONFIDENTIAL." The document was from the office of assistant secretary of state Francis B. Sayre, dated during the period when Alger Hiss was his executive assistant. "That was all I needed," Stripling recalled.[5]

Appell was ordered to take the three undeveloped rolls of film to the Veterans Administration's Identification Division for processing — but not to allow the film to leave his sight even during development. The film in the broken canister had been overexposed and was completely black, Appell testified to the grand jury on December 7, and the frames of the other two rolls were either blank or so foggy he couldn't make out what was on them. Barely legible prints of these films were released by the government in 1975, in compliance with a Freedom of Information Act request. They contained unrestricted Navy Department documents on items such as life rafts, fire extinguishers, and parachutes. Of what value as a "life preserver" these films of easily obtainable and harmless records were to Chambers and why he hid them, undeveloped and certain to deteriorate, no less, remains unknown.

Several public statements issued forth from HUAC on December 3. Karl Mundt declared:

> As the chairman of the subcommittee handling this entire matter, I shall proceed to Washington as soon as possible. I have radioed Congressman Nixon to fly back to Washington, if possible, and am getting in touch with other members of the subcommittee to ascertain the earliest possible date for a public hearing. The evidence before us is so shocking that I do not feel justified in delaying action a day longer than required.... These documents are of such startling and significant importance, and reveal such a vast network of Communist espionage within the State Department, that they far exceed anything yet brought before the Committee in its ten-year history.

Stripling announced that the microfilms — some had Alger Hiss's initials on them — "provided definite proof of one of the most extensive espionage rings in the history of the United States," and "the ones we have developed so far [yield] a stack of letter-sized documents 3 or 4 feet high." (Actually, the pile of prints made from the film — and the fifty-eight frames of the already developed film strips were the only ones readable — was only about an inch high.)

The FBI interrogated Whittaker Chambers the same day, wanting to know why he did not surrender the films two weeks before when he turned over the typed and handwritten papers. Chambers said the films had not been developed and he wasn't sure they were relevant to Hiss. But some of the films, the two strips of fifty eight frames, had long been developed and were quite relevant, though the FBI failed to follow up with that question.

Chambers retold for the agents the basic story he gave Marbury on November 17, but now he added the names of photographers who had worked in the underground with him, David Carpenter and two others, Felix and Keith, whose last names he couldn't remember. He also named Julian Wadleigh, a former employee of the State Department, as one of his sources of official documents. Chambers also recalled, yet again but differently, where he first met Boris Bykov. He was certain it was in front of St. Patrick's Cathedral in Manhattan, whereas three years before Chambers told the FBI he was introduced to Bykov in Brooklyn inside a movie theater.

December 3 was also Nixon's first full day at sea. Late the previous night he received a wire from Bert Andrews indicating that Chambers had produced more evidence, and a few hours later the purser brought Nixon a second wire, this one from Stripling: "Second bombshell obtained by subpoena.... Case clinched. Information amazing. Immediate action appears necessary. Can you possibly get back?" Nixon supposedly radioed Stripling to send a Coast Guard seaplane to fly him back to the mainland.

William Reuben wrote:

[Two days later, Nixon,] with photographers somehow miraculously able to record every phase of the drama, was picked up at sea from a cruise ship by a Navy crash boat and then rushed to a waiting sea plane and flown back to Washington. His first word on the "pumpkin papers" was issued as he sped back to Washington. With no need to even look at the documents, or to ask Chambers a single question for an explanation as to how their existence had never previously been mentioned or even hinted at, Nixon held his first press conference aboard a speeding Navy crash boat. [It was no longer, he told the Associated Press] just one man's word against another's. It will prove to the American people once and for all that where you have a Communist you have an espionage agent.[6]

Nixon and Stripling worked far into the night of December 5, perusing and itemizing not only enlargements of the microfilm but also photostats of the typed and handwritten papers forfeited by Chambers in Baltimore and somehow obtained by HUAC without permission of the Justice Department. Earlier that day the *New York Times* reported that "for the first time, the case seemed to produce hard evidence that there had been an extensive spy ring at work in the American Government, presumably on behalf of Russia.... The dramatic turn of events raised many questions. Among them were these: Where did Mr. Chambers get the new evidence? Why did he not produce it earlier and voluntarily? Would he be prosecuted for espionage? Did the new evidence implicate Mr. Hiss and others?"

The next morning Nixon held a press conference "that drew a record assembly of reporters," according to the *Times.* "Representative Nixon said that the Committee, among its exhibits, had three documents which had been written by hand. He said, too, that a Government handwriting expert had studied them and had declared, conclusively and without qualification, that the penmanship was that of Mr. Hiss."

However, those handwritten notes, along with the typed papers, had been impounded by the Justice Department three weeks earlier. Upon examination they determined no law had been breached and there was no proof, except for the uncorroborated word of Chambers, that any of the papers had been given to Chambers by Hiss. As for the films, they had not yet been examined by experts, or anyone else except HUAC, and Nixon would not allow outsiders to see them. Nor had Nixon yet questioned Chambers, even though he faithfully swallowed whole Chambers's radically revised story. The second phase of HUAC's determination to capture Alger Hiss, this time blatantly accusing him of espionage and treason, was in full swing.

Having absolutely no confidence that the Justice Department would prosecute the case in the manner HUAC wanted (and, most helpfully, lower-level Justice Department employees infuriated by Campbell's execution were informing the House Committee of his every action), which was to vigorously pursue Hiss, Nixon and the committee resolved not to turn over Chambers's films to the FBI or any U.S. Attorney. Nixon wanted to reopen hearings and subpoena Chambers as, once again, their star witness. But the Justice Department beat him to the punch and subpoenaed Chambers to testify before the grand jury, beginning December 6, the day after Nixon returned from sea. As the Justice Department was clamoring for the films, Nixon and Stripling arranged to meet with department officials later that evening in New York.

Before leaving Washington that afternoon, the two men showed the films for the first time to a few journalists and news photographers, one of whom asked Stripling if it had been determined *when* the film was manufactured. No, Stripling blanched, it had not. The Washington representative for Eastman Kodak, Keith Lewis, was summoned to examine the film. (Although DuPont manufactured one of the developed film strips, all the others were by Kodak.) Lewis jotted down the code marks and returned to his office. But the information he was looking for wasn't there, so he phoned headquarters in Rochester. Lewis then immediately called Stripling: "Rochester says they were made in 1947."[7] In Nixon's telling, a "look of complete dismay came over Stripling's face as he took the call. I heard him say, 'You mean this film couldn't have been manufactured before 1945?' Stripling hung up and turned to me. 'Well, we've had it.'" Like a jealous man who has just been told by his best friend that his wife has been cheating on him, Nixon knew instantly that it was true. "This meant that Chambers was, after all," Nixon wrote fourteen years later, "a liar. All the work, the long hours we had put into the investigation had been useless. We had been taken in by a diabolically clever maniac."

Nixon reached Chambers by phone in New York, demanding an answer to Kodak's revelation. In despair, Chambers said only, "I can't understand it. God must be against me." But Nixon was having none of that, and in frustration bordering on rage he ordered Chambers to be at the Commodore Hotel at nine o'clock that night, and slammed the phone down.

Crushed with practically unbearable chagrin and distress, Nixon felt he had no other choice but to call a press conference and get it over with. Five minutes before reporters were due to file in, Keith Lewis called back. "Our Rochester people just telephoned me that they made a mistake," he told Stripling, whose face melted into a smile of sheer joy. "They definitely identify the films as having been manufactured in 1937 — not 1947." Also, the aluminum containers with slip-on lids which housed three of the rolls of film were manufactured only from 1935 to 1941.

Nixon hurriedly called Chambers to apologize but couldn't reach him, so he relayed the good news to his Time, Inc. attorney before catching the train to New York for the meeting with Justice Department officials. The conference, held at the Commodore Hotel, "was marked by considerable table-thumping and raised voices," according to an invited *New York Times* reporter. Justice Department representatives wanted the films and pointed out that HUAC was impeding law enforcement by withholding evidence. Nixon in turn threatened to hold public hearings because HUAC didn't trust the Truman Administration to prosecute the case vigorously (i.e., going after Hiss). A compromise was reached whereby HUAC would furnish Justice with full-size prints of the documents appearing on the films, and Justice permitted HUAC to question Chambers, even though he was bound by their subpoena.

Chambers had been at Harold Medina's law office in Manhattan when Nixon phoned and lambasted him with Kodak's initial dating of the films. Just more bad news for Chambers, who earlier that day was read his constitutional rights by the grand jury — you have the right to refuse to answer any question which may incriminate or degrade you; your answers may be used against you in a criminal prosecution — and Medina likely informed him that the Justice Department was seeking an indictment of him and not Hiss. And topping off the day's reversals, he learned that *Time*'s executives were demanding his resignation. After leaving Medina, Chambers recalled, thinking of God's purpose and that perhaps he had misunderstood it, "I toted my frozen core about the streets of the financial district. I was not going anywhere." He phoned Medina later in the afternoon and was told about Kodak's mistake, but Chambers's mood did not brighten. Instead he felt a "degradation of the soul," and for the second time in three weeks he lapsed into a suicidal funk.

Chambers walked the streets on the west side of the city. At a seed store he bought a canned pesticide containing cyanide, a rodent poison like one he used at his farm. He bought another can at a second supplier and took the wrapped tins to Pennsylvania Station, where he stored them in a lock box. Then he went to the Commodore Hotel and met Nixon's subcommittee.

He reprised for HUAC the new but well-rehearsed version of his former life as an underground Communist courier: Alger Hiss (only one of his sources), for example, would take State Department documents home in his brief case after work and turn them over to Chambers, who had them microfilmed by Communist photographers in Baltimore or Washington and then returned the original documents that same night to Hiss, who restored them to their proper files the next morning. Sometimes Mrs. Hiss would type copies or summaries of official documents at home and pass them to Chambers. They too would be photographed, but Chambers did not return those papers, claiming he destroyed them — except those he kept for his life preserver. All the microfilms were then delivered to New York by Chambers to Boris Bykov, a Soviet intelligence officer, who transmitted them to Russia.

The hearing adjourned after midnight, and the very thought of testifying again in a few hours before the grand jury was further insult to his woes, filling Chambers with lethargy and despair. So without hesitation he retrieved the noxious package from Pennsylvania Station and headed to his mother's house on Long Island for his final sleep.

For all the options Manhattan affords the suicidal person — speeding trains and vehicles, tall buildings and bridges, thousands of secluded spots in which to blow one's brains out — it remains a mystery why Chambers chose to take to his mother's home a gaseous toxin, endangering her life along with his own. "My act was not suicide in the usual sense," Chambers qualified in *Witness*, "for I had no desire to stop living. It was self-execution."

In a parting note, addressed "To All," Chambers justified his decision because he was sparing those he had accused of the ultimate consequences of their actions. He never meant to hurt anyone, only to reveal the conspiracy.

Chambers proceeded with his death ritual, carefully arranging damp towels and a receptacle around his head so the fumes wouldn't diffuse into the outer rooms. He soon fell into a deep sleep. However, he had misread the directions for use on the can, and he awoke abruptly, retching in severe pain. "My first thought," Chambers recalled, "was sheer horror to find that I was still alive; my second, disgust that I had failed."

By the first week of December, just over two weeks after Chambers disclosed the Baltimore Documents, the Justice Department's investigation had not yet determined who originally produced the typed copies of the State Department papers, though the inquiry had revealed that they were, in fact, copies or summaries of official records of the State Department, all dated between January and April 1938. Those copies held no significance whatever to Alger Hiss, and when the FBI asked him on December 4 if Priscilla had ever typed copies of State Department documents, he denied any possibility of it. In a statement to the Bureau, Hiss allowed that "we had a typewriter in our home ... to some time after 1938." He thought the machine was an Underwood but was not at all certain. "Mrs. Hiss," he added, "who was not a typist, used this machine somewhat as an amateur typist, but I never recall having used it. Possible samples of Mrs. Hiss' typing on this machine are in existence, but I have not located any to date, but will endeavor to do so." Hiss believed the typewriter was given or sold to a used typewriter store or dealer subsequent to 1938, "exact date or place unknown. The whereabouts of this typewriter is presently unknown to me."

Priscilla Hiss, interviewed December 7 by FBI agents, also could not recall the make of the machine. Her father, Thomas Fansler, who had been in the insurance business in Philadelphia, gave it to her in 1932 or 1933, and she used it at that time to partially prepare a manuscript for a book later published on fine arts. But she was not a proficient typist and the machine had defects, so she finished the manuscript in longhand. She could not remember how or when they got rid of the typewriter.

J. Howard Haring, a document examiner hired by Hiss's chief lawyer, Edward McLean, after studying the typed Baltimore Documents, identified the typewriter as a Woodstock brand. Sixty four of the sixty five sheets were typed on a Woodstock, pica type, ten characters to the inch. The other sheet was typed on another make. Priscilla Hiss was perhaps in the midst of her interview with the FBI when McLean called Marbury and informed him that among some papers which Priscilla had given him two months before he had found two brief letters which had been typed by her in the mid–1930s — and Haring was certain that Priscilla's typing had been done on a Woodstock, undoubtedly the same Woodstock which produced all the typed Baltimore Documents except one.

This startling news reinforced Marbury's mindset that Alger Hiss would soon be indicted. Not that he believed for a second that his good friend of over twenty years had ever been a Communist or a spy, or that he typed the Baltimore Documents, for Marbury knew Hiss couldn't type a lick, but he felt Hiss was covering up for Priscilla. After McLean's phone call Marbury began distancing himself from Hiss. Perhaps it was a convenient though cynical maneuver to jump ship and escape the political fallout sure to come — and soon, so he foolishly rationalized that Priscilla was involved in an espionage conspiracy with Chambers. What's certain is that Marbury and Priscilla had "never hit it off," according to her and Alger's son Tony. From the day she met William Marbury twenty years before, Priscilla thought he was chauvinistic, stuffy, provincial, and self-absorbed. Marbury found Priscilla too opinionated for a woman in a man's world, even eager to challenge *his* opinions, and a bit radical. Whenever Marbury visited the couple, Priscilla seemed to do most of the talking and acted domineering. One friend of the Hisses said Marbury regarded Priscilla as restless and fanatical, forever taking up new projects only to abandon them for others; and if she was involved in — or "longed for," in Chambers's words — "Communist activity," well that didn't seem too far-fetched either. In short, if Alger was in trouble, Marbury believed Priscilla must be the cause of it.

But it *was* too far-fetched. Marbury's impulsive decision to practically abandon his friend and client was made in the overheated postwar/cold war climate richly composed of political opportunism and guilt by association, a decision different only in degree from Nixon's kneejerk jettisoning of Chambers when the Kodak rep mistakenly told him the film was manufactured in 1947.

Of course, a vital requirement of Chambers's post–November 17 story was that Priscilla Hiss's "longing for Communist activity" manifested itself in feats of typing (the products of which Chambers said he delivered to a photographer and later destroyed, saving the Hisses the bother of disposal) instead of, say, photography, the spy's indispensable discipline and a shorter work process to boot. Although the Baltimore Documents were contrived initially by Chambers to implicate others in his crimes should the need arise, they were prepared by an experienced and accomplished typist, which Priscilla Hiss was not. She may have passed a proficiency test at Columbia in the early 1930s, but she was not a touch typist, did not utilize all her fingers, and constantly looked either at the keyboard or the sheet in the roller. Her top speed in a 1949 typing test was less than fifteen words a minute. She could have printed the Baltimore Documents by hand in block letters faster than she could have typed them.

Throughout 1937, when the Hisses lived on 30th Street, and beginning in January when Chambers was in actuality working at a Federal relief job (using the name Chambers) only a few blocks from Alger Hiss's State Department office across 17th Street from the White House, Chambers claimed he would collect official documents at the Hisses' residence every ten days or so. At first Hiss brought home only original documents, which Chambers would pick up after work and take to Baltimore for photographing, then return the originals to Hiss in Georgetown the same night, often long after midnight and traveling by rail. But in the summer of 1937, Chambers said, Boris Bykov introduced an "innovation." Bykov wanted more documents from Hiss, and he proposed that Hiss should bring home documents every night. The documents were copied using the Hiss family typewriter. When Chambers arrived, Hiss would turn over to him the typed copies made from originals brought home during the week, as well as original documents Hiss had brought home that night. The original documents would be photographed and returned to Hiss. The typed copies would be photographed but not returned to Hiss. Chambers claimed he would destroy them. The typed copies could surely have gone straight to Bykov, but if they were going to be needlessly photographed, why wouldn't Hiss demand their return? Chambers doesn't say. And, of course, the alleged ridiculous typing routine (a typed copy would have no authenticity, no value for a *real* spy) could have been obviated by photographing to begin with. Moreover, the copies Chambers held for his "life preserver" could have been typed (most likely by himself and his wife) from photographed copies or stolen mimeographs of the official documents months or years after their 1938 dates.

Chambers's account of frequent evening and late night visits to Hiss's house was further called into question by the Hisses' 30th Street neighbors Elizabeth and Geoffrey May. The Georgetown residential district where the Hisses and Mays lived in 1936 and 1937 comprised small, recently remodeled old houses set very close together on quiet neighborhood streets. The Mays' two-bedroom house mirrored the Hisses' similar place. Their living rooms and bedrooms faced each other, with little space between the two structures. "And you would hear everything" that went on next door, Elizabeth May remarked years later of the tiny homes with paper-thin walls. But she never heard the sound of typing while the Hisses lived there (though she was often distracted by the typing of a journalist who occupied the house after the Hisses), and she recalled no man who regularly made afternoon or late night visits to the Hiss residence, whose front door was clearly visible from her living room. The Hisses lived there for over a year and soon became friends with the Mays. Elizabeth and Priscilla often saw each other socially and were members of the League of Women Voters together. To Elizabeth, Priscilla was a liberal activist concerned about improving local government but certainly not a political radical. Elizabeth also remembered Timothy Hobson's serious bicycle accident in February 1937, which laid him up for months in the front bedroom of the 30th Street house, an incident known to all of the Hisses' friends. But Whittaker Chambers (whom Hiss maintained he knew as George Crosley and had not seen since some-time in 1936) knew nothing about the accident. Furthermore, Timothy Hobson is certain to this day that he never saw Chambers until he became a public figure in 1948. But they could not possibly have missed seeing each other if Chambers's story of frequent visits to the 30th Street house (his "informal headquarters") had been true.

Not only would a late night visitor to this quiet suburban hamlet alert many of the Hisses' neighbors to his presence, but why would a purported courier for the Soviets risk the possibility of leading counterespionage agents directly to his source? Ladislas Farago, a U.S. Naval Intelligence officer during World War II who later published several popular books on history and espionage, wrote in *War of Wits* (1954) that the courier's job (commenting particularly on Chambers's own delineations in *Witness*), though simple enough, is a "perilous phase of espionage work. First of all, if a ... courier makes numerous visits at regular intervals to the home of the informant, he will invariably attract attention ... where counterespionage is alert. If the [courier] is under surveillance he is certain to lead the counterespionage agent to the informant, thereby destroying this vital source and compromising the whole operation."

"Secondly," Farago added, "documents should not be in transit for too long a time or over great distances. Their security might be easily compromised en route, they could be lost, or something could happen to the person who carries them. If Chambers actually used such a procedure to relay documents from their source to the collector, he not only employed the most primitive and precarious method, but he also violated a very important rule in the Soviet spy book." Soviet instructions for couriers, Farago explained, stipulated that meetings must take place outdoors, on the street, and only once a month. The material received by the courier must be returned the same day or night. And wives of informants must not know that the courier works with and meets their husbands.

If Alger Hiss did not supply Whittaker Chambers with documents from the State Department, including typed and handwritten copies and official records to be photographed, then how would Chambers have obtained them? And most incriminating to Hiss was the fact that a document expert he hired in November 1948 believed that the typed copies of State Department papers surrendered by Chambers in Baltimore on November 17 were produced by the same typewriter on which some found household letters of the Hisses were prepared in the 1930s, though the latest date of any letter ever found was seven months *before* the earliest date of the papers Chambers turned in.

As mentioned above, the Hisses, who asserted the machine was defective and rarely used, could not remember when or how that typewriter had been disposed of, nor could they recall if it was a Woodstock. Their subsequent inquiries, along with investigations by their lawyers, revealed that they had given the typewriter to a former maid's sons, Mike and Pat Catlett, either before or after the Hisses moved locally from 30th Street to Volta Place in late December 1937. The Hisses naturally prayed that the Catlett brothers were positively certain of when they took possession of the Woodstock, and if they got it in 1937 that would prove the Hisses did not have it when the Baltimore Documents were typed in 1938. But on this point the Catletts were not completely in agreement. At first Mike and Pat both remembered loading the typewriter along with other items in a little wagon at the Hisses' 30th Street house just before they moved to Volta Place. But Pat later said he picked up the typewriter at Volta Place in 1938, from an upstairs room by the sun porch. Still later Pat changed his mind again, reverting to his first recollection. And though Alger Hiss himself recalled little if anything about the typewriter or what they ultimately did with it, he said it was common for his family to give items away *prior* to moving, not after, though he admitted in December 1948: "I had a visual memory of the machine being in the Volta Place house" in 1938.

The Woodstock was traced through several more owners subsequent to the Catlett boys, and a book could be written about the search for it by the FBI and Hiss. Investigators working for Hiss eventually tracked it down (or one very similar) in April 1949, and it was presented as a Hiss defense exhibit at both of his perjury trials that year. Though that Woodstock was positively identified at the trials by Priscilla Hiss and the Catletts and others as the machine the Hisses owned in the 1930s, document examiners hired by Hiss after the trials opined that it wasn't, for a variety of reasons. But it's a purely academic point because no expert, whether for the prosecution or defense, claimed in court (or before the trials) that the Woodstock in question had typed either the Baltimore Documents or the personal letters of the Hisses. Only one documents expert, Ramos Feehan of the FBI for the prosecution, testified at Hiss's trials. His conclusion was that the typed Baltimore Documents and the personal letters typed by Priscilla Hiss in the 1930s were typed on the same typewriter, a Woodstock — but *which* Woodstock was never addressed. Feehan's testimony went uncontested by a defense expert, nor was he even cross-examined.

As for how Chambers unlawfully obtained the documents without Hiss providing any of them, security measures at the State Department in 1938, and the types of documents procured, furnish several clues.

Chambers assembled his "life preserver" of documents during and after the four months he worked at a Federal relief job as a report editor, compiling indexes, from October 1937 to the end of January 1938. He worked in Washington, D.C., under the name Chambers, and he lived in Baltimore with his wife and two children, also using his real name. It was a job he was happy to land because he was broke, so he told his old friend Robert Cantwell. Moreover, his position as a Federal employee gave him ready entree to numerous government agencies, even after he was furloughed beginning February 1, 1938, due to lack of work. Building security, access cards, and photo identification badges were still off in the future.

Harrison Salisbury, in 1938 a 29-year-old reporter for the *New York Times* who became one of the paper's chief editors, recalled he "often wandered about unnoticed through the corridors of the old State-War-Navy building where Cordell Hull's State Department was housed.... I recall no guards at the doors, no plastic identification cards, nothing to prevent myself, Chambers or anyone else from poking into just about any office he pleased.... Such a world seems impossible today and no doubt it was fearfully insecure." Also, Chambers's friend and cheerleader Isaac Don Levine swore to HUAC and the grand jury in 1948 and 1949 that Chambers told him he knew his way around *inside* of the State Department in the late 1930s very well.

One of the items of Chambers's life preserver had nothing to do with Alger Hiss. It was four pages of handwritten notes (most likely for a diary) by Harry Dexter White, assistant secretary of the Treasury. The entries were dated January 9 and 10, 1938, and concerned international economic issues. These pages were obviously White's personal records because the notations included questions and reminders to himself to revisit particular issues. Chambers, who claimed White (supposedly one of Chambers's sources) gave him the papers, undoubtedly stole them from White's office, probably the same day he stole the personnel file of Jay Chambers of the Treasury Department, later exploited by Chambers and his wife to establish credit and charge goods to the other Chambers's department store accounts.

The three rolls of undeveloped film Chambers hoarded in 1938 also did not implicate Hiss. These were the overexposed or barely legible photographs of safety paraphernalia such as fire extinguishers — not exactly high value espionage information and as readily available as post office forms. Chambers accused a National Bureau of Standards employee, Ward Pigman, as the source of this pointless material, plus many more documents which Chambers allegedly had passed on to his underground chief, Boris Bykov. However, Ward Pigman emphatically denied it. He was brought before the grand jury four times in December 1948. Pigman swore each time that he had never known Chambers under any name or circumstances, had never even laid eyes on him until a few days before his testimony, and had never given Bureau of Standards documents to anyone not authorized to receive them. Later, and obviously wary of slandering Pigman in public, Chambers did not mention his name in *Witness*, fictionalizing the name of his reputed Bureau of Standards source as Abel Gross instead.

Hiss was the purported source for much of Chambers's life preserver — the handwritten notes, the sixty-four pages typed on a Woodstock, and the fifty-eight frames of developed 35mm film, all of it concerning State Department communications. Notably, Chambers later wrote that his life preserver originally "was not aimed at any individual," and he remarked to the FBI during his long, carefully edited statement in 1949: "It seemed to me that sometime such documentary evidence might prove useful, though I had no definite idea as to how this might work out." In 1938, Chambers's primary targets, should the need arise in his fevered paranoid mind to unveil the life preserver, were most likely Harry Dexter White and Francis B. Sayre, assistant secretary of state charged with economic, tariff, and general trade questions, and for whom Hiss worked as executive assistant. White's memo was part of Chambers's cache, and the material Hiss supposedly contributed could have just as easily incriminated Sayre along with Hiss. Besides, Hiss's official rank and responsibilities were relatively minor in 1938, and secret or highly classified documents remained unavailable to him, though admittedly all of the documents comprising Chambers's life preserver were made public in 1949 — so they were not very important to begin with.

Furthermore, as recounted in an earlier chapter, Chambers told writer Malcolm Cowley in December 1940 that Francis Sayre, who left the State Department in 1939 to become High Commissioner to the Philippines, had been "the head of a Communist apparatus in the State Department." Cowley, astounded by the scurrilous charge and by Chambers's quirky mannerisms during their interview, recapped the encounter in his journal. Yet the year before he met with Cowley, Chambers talked to Adolf Berle soon after the revelation of the Nazi-Soviet Pact and the day after World War II began, specifically to identify government officials who were Communists or fellow travelers; but Chambers made no accusations of, or warnings about, Sayre.

As Sayre's top aide, one of Hiss's daily responsibilities was screening telegrams which poured in, often a thousand a week. Some telegrams were passed on to Sayre to read in their entirety, some were culled, and some Hiss and Sayre briefly discussed, usually during lunch hour meetings. Hiss made talking points notes to himself on scratch paper for these particular telegrams and attached them to the documents. After he and Sayre reviewed it, the note would either be thrown away or left attached to the telegram, which would be gathered with others and sent to the burn room for disposal. Sayre confirmed that Hiss used this note-taking technique, and so did Stanley K. Hornbeck, for whom Hiss subsequently worked in the State Department. Four of these handwritten notes, scribbled from original telegrams dated January and March 1938, found their way to Chambers's life preserver — "handwriting specimens of Mr. Hiss," should Chambers ever need to brandish them.

Of the sixty-four Woodstock-typed pages Chambers had "put by," more than twenty pages were copied from a non-confidential commercial report about business conditions in Manchuria, previously published so that any foreign government, particularly Russia, could have seen the report in a Japanese newspaper. Typed copies of diplomatic telegrams (or cables) accounted for most of the remainder of the typing subterfuge, a hodgepodge of varying importance (some confidential, others available to the press) in which some were copied verbatim, some randomly quoted, and others abbreviated or summarized. The fifty-eight frames of 35mm film contained yet more images of telegrams and three documents that Alger Hiss had initialed, a reckless practice any spy might deem perilous or even deadly. More than forty frames were pages about trade agreement negotiations with Germany. It was demonstrated at Hiss's trials that some of these documents, both typed copies and photographed, never went to Sayre's or Hiss's offices. But all of the documents had been circulated through either the State Department's Far Eastern or Trade Agreements divisions. Julian Wadleigh (to whom we shall return) had worked in Trade Agreements and admitted passing documents to Chambers in 1937 and early 1938.

So much of Chambers's life preserver was composed of copies typewritten, handwritten, or photographed from incoming diplomatic telegrams (about fifty in all), because mimeographs of telegrams were relatively easy to steal from the State Department. They were so easy to walk off with, in fact, that if Alger Hiss had really been Chambers's confederate, it would have been nonsensical for Hiss to have taken telegrams home to make typed copies — or even copies by camera. Extras of information-copy telegrams were plentiful and untraceable, and Hiss could have given them directly to Chambers without fear or threat of detection — be it his own handwriting or typing from the family typewriter, or his telltale initials on a photocopy.

After an incoming telegram to the State Department in 1938 was decoded (if confidential), a stencil was made for the copies. The action copy went to the responsible official, and information copies were sent to interested departments. The single action copy would eventually be returned and filed as a permanent record, but about fifty information mimeographs were run off, and fifteen or more of these would be distributed to various offices, while the remaining thirty-five or so were stored in an unlocked cabinet during business hours. These extra copies were available to officials for the asking — and they were not tracked or accounted for. Also, any one of the dozens of employees who worked in the telegraph room, the decoding room, the revision room, or the typists' room could have pilfered a few of the extra copies without anyone being the wiser. Yet another opportunity for stealing mimeographs presented itself when two or three weeks after issuance they were collected for burning by a messenger who circulated through the building with a frequently unattended pushcart, gathering unwanted information copies to take to the unsecured incinerator room.

Paul Goldsberry, a cryptography (codes and ciphers) specialist of the State Department since 1933, testified before the grand jury on December 10, 1948:

GJ: I wanted to ask this: When you make up a number of copies of incoming telegrams do you keep a record of the number of copies and then later account for all copies? Indicating who it went to, with the box to be checked when it came back?
GOLDSBERRY: I don't believe that there was a record kept of the number of copies. [The record] indicated only to whom an information copy was sent.

GJ: And wasn't that followed up at all to see that it was returned?
GOLDSBERRY: I think not.
GJ: Was there a call-in date as to how long they could hold these information copies out?
GOLDSBERRY: At that time? No.
GJ: Did they come back, as a general practice?
GOLDSBERRY: There is no way of proving that.
GJ: Sitting in my place, you would say it was a very loose arrangement, wouldn't you?
GOLDSBERRY: I'm afraid so.

Richard Nixon and his fellow HUAC members learned to their consternation Wednesday morning, December 8, that assistant attorney general Alexander Campbell was seeking an indictment not of Alger Hiss but of Whittaker Chambers only. The entire House Committee was well aware that Chambers had blatantly lied to the grand jury in October (accepting on faith now that his latest story was indeed true), and he'd lied to HUAC repeatedly for months. But no matter — he was the star witness, the only witness, in any case against Hiss, and his indictment would set Hiss free by default. The problem, in Nixon's view, "was whether or not to expose this Justice Department strategy publicly and risk the political consequences." Nixon took the gamble, hoping public opinion would sway the Justice Department to pursue an indictment of Hiss instead. However, the odds against Nixon's ploy were slim to none at the onset. Hiss's reputation, because of HUAC, was already in tatters — "very seriously damaged," British journalist Alistair Cooke remarked at the time. "It is fair to say that some of this damage had been done by Hiss himself," Cooke argued, "but it was the kind of self-inflicted harm that any witness at bay might do to himself."

The evening of December 8, at a public HUAC hearing well covered by the press, Nixon announced: "We have learned from unimpeachable sources that the Justice Department now plans to indict Chambers for perjury before any of the other people named by Chambers in this conspiracy are indicted." The Truman Administration, he added, was pressuring HUAC to drop its espionage conspiracy investigation and did not want the Committee to hear witnesses who were appearing before the grand jury. "Chambers has confessed," Nixon said with an air of logical finality. "He is in the open. He is no longer a danger to our security.... The Administration is trying to silence this Committee. But we will not entrust to the Justice Department and to the Administration the sole responsibility for protecting the national security in this case."

Chambers, meanwhile, was appearing every day before the grand jury. On December 7 and 8 he was questioned about his alleged former superior in the underground, Colonel Boris Bykov. Though not explicitly stated, Chambers's testimony implied that Bykov was Russian. However, he did not know at the time he worked for Bykov what Bykov's relationship was to the Soviet government or that Bykov was an intelligence agent, or even what his name was; Chambers learned only later (1939), from Walter Krivitsky, Bykov's name and that he was a Soviet military intelligence spy. He delivered film negatives to Bykov and never to anyone else, Chambers said, and always in New York City at widely scattered places, once a week during all of 1937 and a few months after (though earlier he told Marbury he had not met Bykov until mid–1937). Chambers added that he did not know the purpose of the material he was receiving and knew nothing about what Bykov was doing with it — although Bykov supposedly complained about the poor quality of the information Chambers passed on.

Chambers elaborated on Bykov a few weeks later to the FBI, referring to him now as "my last Russian contact," whom he had met in late 1936. Yet Chambers also said that

"Bykov did not in any way indicate to me his true identity, his place of residence or any address or telephone number at which I could locate him in an emergency."

"Bykov had warned me I was not to use an automobile," Chambers told the agents, but "I convinced Bykov that I needed an automobile in order to carry on my apparatus business, and he finally agreed." He asked Bykov to give him five hundred dollars as partial payment for a late-model car. Bykov did not have the money at the time, so Chambers claimed he borrowed the money from Alger Hiss. He then gave the funds to his wife, who "took the money I had borrowed from Alger Hiss, went to the Schmidt Motor Company in Randallstown, Maryland, and purchased a new Ford automobile. Although this automobile was purchased in 1938, it was a 1937 model." In their pursuit to discover corroboration of this purported loan, the FBI checked the Hisses 1937-38 banking records and found that a four-hundred-dollar withdrawal from their savings account was made in mid–November 1937. The Hisses maintained the money was spent on miscellaneous goods for the Volta Place house they moved to in December 1937. But the FBI coached Chambers to change the amount borrowed to four hundred dollars and the date of the automobile purchase from 1938 to November 1937, so it would look as though the Hisses withdrew the funds to give to Chambers, as he asserted, only days before the car purchase. At both of Hiss's trials in 1949 the prosecution entered an exhibit, a photocopy of a single page of a ledger from the Schmidt Motor Company, which indicated that Esther Chambers purchased the Ford on November 23, 1937. This "evidence," which went unchallenged by Hiss's attorneys at trial, was examined closely more than twenty years later by investigative journalist Fred Cook and attorney Ray Werchen, and their findings were published in *The Nation* on May 28, 1973. They concluded that the entry for Esther Chambers "was probably made up and filled in on a blank section of this ledger page at a much later date."

Sometime after Hiss loaned him the five hundred dollars in 1938, Chambers's FBI statement adds (this was, of course, before Chambers changed the date to November 1937 and the amount borrowed to four hundred dollars, the better to match the Hisses' transaction), Boris Bykov gave him an *additional* two thousand dollars—"for my wages and rent for the photographic workshops; for the repayment of the $500.00 loan to Alger Hiss, and as a reserve. This money I kept and I did not repay [the loan to Hiss].... I considered that I was at war with the Communist Party and I confiscated this fund to finance my operations."

And what happened to J. Peters? How was he supplanted by Bykov? And why would Whittaker Chambers, notwithstanding so-called Communist discipline, blindly take orders from a man he didn't really know? Chambers swore that he did not know Bykov's name or where he lived or how to reach him. He assumed Bykov was Russian but did not know he was a Soviet spy, did not know the nature of the stolen documents he delivered to Bykov, did not know what Bykov did with the information.

When Bykov "arrived on the scene," Chambers told the FBI, J. Peters became concerned that Bykov might take over the Washington apparatuses. Peters "felt that he had a vested personal interest in the Washington setup," Chambers said, "and ... he wanted me, if possible, to obstruct Bykov's taking over the Washington apparatuses and that I should not tell Bykov everything. It became apparent, however, that this was impossible and Peters did not press ... further." Chambers could not recall the details of his last meeting with Peters but never saw him after his "break."

The FBI was never able to identify or locate Boris Bykov—but he really did exist, and the information Krivitsky relayed to Chambers about him was basically correct. What little is known of Bykov today has been discovered by historian Svetlana Chervonnaya and compiled on her web site DocumentsTalk.com. Boris Yakovlevich Bukov, not Bykov, was his true name. He was a Russian cadre officer attached to military intelligence whose military rank was equivalent to a Colonel, and he was fluent in German. The consensus of American espionage enthusiasts is that Bykov, who arrived in the U.S. in 1936, vanished soon after Chambers supposedly defected in 1937 or 1938, but he remained an illegal resident of the United States well into 1939, according to Chervonnaya.

Chambers again perjured himself when testifying about Bykov to the grand jury on December 9. "As you know," Chambers lied under oath, "I had been to Washington and talked with Mr. Berle [on September 2, 1939]. I mentioned to him the existence of conspiratorial Communists in government, the names of Colonel Bykov...." But as Berle's notes reveal, or rather do not reveal, Chambers never mentioned Bykov. It was the sort of lie Chambers always told when he was cornered — a desperation move. The grand jury was closing in for the kill. Why had he "held out these documents and failed to disclose their existence" for so many years? Chambers pressed to make it look as though he informed the proper authorities in 1939 yet no action had been taken against the conspirators. But why, the grand jury asked, did he not present the documents to Berle in the first place? "If we had gone further than a conversation," Chambers replied feebly, "those documents would undoubtedly have been disclosed.... Then I heard nothing more for something like two years. In that time the documents had dimmed in my mind ... and my old feeling that I did not want to involve human beings in such a tragic difficulty any more than necessary became paramount again." But how could he take any effective action against a Communist conspiracy without involving those who carried it on? "There are degrees of involvement," Chambers continued beatifically. "And it seemed to me that I could destroy and stop the conspiracy while preserving the human beings involved." "I think there are, in general, two kinds of men," Chambers expanded on his faux reawakened Christian compassion, "one of whom believes that God is a god of justice, and the other believes that God is a god of mercy. I am so constituted that I will always range myself on the side of mercy."

Nevertheless, Chambers produced the documents ultimately, so how did he square that with his "degrees of involvement" otherworldly empathy? Chambers argued that he had all but "forgotten the existence of those documents." And when he went to "get his things" from Nathan Levine only a few weeks before this testimony, he remembered only "handwriting specimens" of Alger Hiss and Harry Dexter White. He was staggered to discover what was in the envelope hidden for a decade. "There then rose the question of what to do," Chambers recalled. But his lawyers told him he had no choice but to disclose the documents, and Chambers rationalized that the libel suit Hiss brought against him "has always seemed to be to me a libel suit of the Communist Party against Whittaker Chambers, a suit very important to the country and one which must not be lost, for that reason.... I would say that I had been forced by the Communist Party to stop shielding the Communists."

The grand jury asked if Chambers believed that the other material, besides the handwriting of Hiss and White, was so unimportant that he had forgotten it was in the envelope?

CHAMBERS: I would put it exactly the other way: that it was so important that I forgot its existence.

GJ: [C]ould there possibly be some additional documents, film, et cetera, that you have completely forgotten.... That are so important that you have forgotten them?

CHAMBERS: I assure you that there is no more.
GJ: Well, you assured us of that once before.

The grand jurors were also disturbed because Chambers had lied while testifying under oath before HUAC the previous summer and then to the grand jury in October. Again, Chambers pleaded he had "shielded" Hiss and others from the "greater damage" of espionage charges.

GJ: Well, did you consider that more important than the fact that you were perjuring yourself before this Grand Jury?
CHAMBERS: I realized that I ran that risk.

In the course of his grand jury testimony the first two weeks of December, Chambers named five former government officials whom he swore provided him in 1937 and early 1938 with documents for transmission to the Soviet Union. Three of the alleged sources: Harry Dexter White (who had forcefully denied Chambers's attacks before he suddenly died in August), Ward Pigman, and Alger Hiss refuted the charges as complete fabrications. White and Pigman avowed they had never laid eyes on Chambers before. The other sources, Franklin Reno, formerly a War Department mathematician at the Aberdeen Proving Grounds, and Julian Wadleigh, who worked in the State Department at the time Alger Hiss was there, admitted having passed restricted and confidential documents to Chambers.

Franklin Reno joined the Communist Party in 1935 when he was a 24-year-old student of astronomy at the University of Virginia. After college he worked for the Works Progress Administration (WPA) in Washington, D.C., as a statistical clerk, a job he held until early 1937. He then left Washington to accept a civilian position as a ballistician at the U.S. Army Proving Grounds in Aberdeen, Maryland.

About a week before commencing duty in June 1937, Reno was introduced to Whittaker Chambers in a basement restaurant in Philadelphia. Reno had gone to Philadelphia specifically to meet Chambers, who, Reno recalled, was using the name Carl Krause. They were introduced by a mutual acquaintance named Bernie, a man who had met Reno through Paddy Whalen of the Communist-run Marine Workers Industrial Union.

At the restaurant meeting Chambers informed Reno that he must cut off all CP contacts, and Reno agreed to provide whatever information he could, though he would only have access to material of the least importance, "restricted." Reno testified to the grand jury on December 14 that he was fully aware of what he had been involved in — "I felt that the defense of the Soviet Union at that time was an important thing."

Reno met Chambers clandestinely perhaps seven or eight times, about once a month, usually in Washington but sometimes in Baltimore or Philadelphia, yet Reno insisted he only passed information to Chambers on maybe three or four occasions: a pair of firing tables consisting of numerical computed data; an openly published textbook on ballistics; an organizational chart of Aberdeen Proving Grounds. Chambers would return the stuff the same night or the next morning, and although no agreement to pay Reno had been arranged, on two or three occasions Chambers reimbursed him for small expenses.

However, Reno's conscience soon began to bother him, or so he told the grand jury, and he was "not fully convinced that I should engage in this work and for that reason I did not openly cooperate to the full extent of my ability and I did hold back on some occasions information which I thought that [Chambers] desired.... I understood what I was doing and I did it anyway. It is true that I steadily acquired more doubts about this matter."

By spring of 1938 Reno had severed all ties to the Communist Party and disavowed their ideology. But Chambers maintained a personal "fix" on Reno, according to Chambers's first biographer, Meyer Zeligs, even though both men had by that time allegedly broken away from Communism. Zeligs's sources characterized Reno as an extremely shy, effeminate, maladjusted, and immature man who drank excessively. Chambers "saw in Reno's emotional struggles and escape into alcoholism," Zeligs wrote, "as well as in his former Communist affiliation, an opportunity" for extortion. Desperate for money, Chambers badgered Reno for fifty dollars, an amount Reno did not have. A colleague of Reno told Zeligs: "We got together and chipped in to raise the fifty dollars for Chambers' blackmail money." To another colleague, Herman Meyer, Reno intimated that "Chambers kept on asking him for something; insisted on getting from him some kind of government document." And if Reno refused, Chambers threatened to inform on him, so Reno gave him an obsolete and useless firing table. By early 1939, Reno heard no more from Chambers. No more until Chambers informed on him a decade later.

Following his appearance before the grand jury in December 1948, Franklin Reno resigned from Aberdeen. He took a job in Wisconsin, but because of his drinking he left after one year. A 1949 FBI report described Reno as appearing in "poor physical, mental, and highly neurotic condition ... [showing] evidence of paranoia." He was indicted for perjury in 1951 because he denied ever belonging to the Communist Party while filling out a loyalty questionnaire at Aberdeen in 1948. He pleaded guilty and served thirty months in prison.

Henry Julian Wadleigh was an economist in the State Department, Division of Trade Agreements, from 1936 to 1943. From 1936 to 1939 he worked under the purview of assistant secretary of state Francis Sayre, Alger Hiss's boss. Born in the U.S. in 1904, the same year as Hiss, Wadleigh traveled abroad extensively as a youth with his parents and was schooled at Oxford and the London School of Economics. In the early 1930s he joined the Socialist Party (but never became a Communist), and by the time he entered the State Department he was increasingly alarmed by the growing power of Nazi Germany, Fascist Italy, and Imperial Japan — and dismayed that the United States government seemed passive about the danger they posed.

Wadleigh remarked at the time to his friend Eleanor Nelson, who was a Communist Party member, that he was willing to collaborate with the Soviets if he could do something useful, such as supplying economic information on Germany and Japan. Now enlisted as an operative for a foreign government, Wadleigh passed in a leather envelope about ten documents a week to his assigned courier, one Harold Wilson. Wilson, Wadleigh did not learn until December 1948, was actually David Carpenter, one of Chambers's purported underground photographers. As documents came across his desk, Wadleigh would select those he thought pertinent or interesting, though he was not privy to anything highly confidential or secret. By prearrangement, Wadleigh and Carpenter would meet at some designated spot for the handoff, and the next morning before work Carpenter returned the papers by a similar procedure. This protocol continued for nearly two years, with some brief gaps, until a few weeks before Wadleigh left for a nine-month official trip to Turkey in March 1938.

Wadleigh first met Whittaker Chambers (who used the name Carl Carlson) in late 1936 or early 1937, introduced by Carpenter at a Baltimore restaurant, and Wadleigh gained the impression Chambers was Carpenter's superior in the operation. They discussed politics and economics, and Chambers plunged into a disquisition on international affairs. "I was enormously impressed with his fund of knowledge of events," Wadleigh recalled. Soon Chambers and Wadleigh were meeting about once a week, usually for lunch or dinner, and a few times Wadleigh gave documents to Chambers instead of Carpenter. "I could scarcely mention a country in the world," Wadleigh said of Chambers's rhetorical arsenal, "but Carl would speak with an intimate knowledge of it ... sometimes discussing it with such a wealth of detailed knowledge that I got the distinct impression that he must have seen it."

Chambers also spoke with inordinate knowledge of people whom he had never known or met — for example, Wadleigh's boss in 1937-38, Charles Darlington. Wadleigh was "amazed" by the abundance of information Chambers had compiled on the assistant chief of the Trade Agreements Division. But snooping into the lives of others who might unwittingly serve his nefarious intrigues was Chambers's ineradicable addiction. "When I asked Chambers," Wadleigh later told an interviewer, "How come you know so much about Charlie Darlington? Chambers answered, 'Well, we naturally like to know about a person who is your roommate so we made inquiries from our friends in the State Department and that is how I got the information.'" Wadleigh added that "Chambers had made it abundantly clear he had other sources [who provided documents] inside of the State Department."

Charles Darlington testified at Hiss's first trial in 1949 that when he was Wadleigh's boss he would occasionally return from lunch to find Wadleigh reading a document off his desk. He had a "well-developed curiosity," Darlington remarked, "in a lot of things that were going on." Darlington also recalled seeing Wadleigh alone in Alger Hiss's office, but he "never gave any particular thought to that."[8]

Wadleigh and Hiss had naturally known each other at the State Department and went to lunch a few times but were not friends outside the office. In 1937 and early 1938 Wadleigh worked what he called a "roving assignment" and was often bored. On his workday wanderings he commonly dropped in on Hiss to chat, regardless of Hiss's workload — usually overwhelming — or to wait in Hiss's office to see Sayre. There's no proof Wadleigh took (or "borrowed" without Hiss's knowledge) any papers from Hiss's office, but he had ample opportunity and hundreds of documents to choose from. Two of the three desks in Hiss's office were always covered with stacks of telegrams, memoranda, reports, and other documents which continually streamed in every hour. However, documents not requiring Hiss's or Sayre's immediate attention might remain on a desk for weeks and could easily have been taken and later replaced.

In his appearance before the grand jury on December 11, 1948, Wadleigh was asked, "Did you ever know that Mr. Hiss was a member of any cell or apparatus?"

> WADLEIGH: No, it never came to my attention. In fact, I would like to say this: that when Alger Hiss' name was mentioned in the newspapers in connection with this I was just as much astonished as any other of Hiss' friends and acquaintances.
> GJ: Do you know whether or not he was a member of the Communist Party?
> WADLEIGH: I have no knowledge of it. And all statements that have appeared in the press, to that effect, have been a source of astonishment to me.
> GJ: Did he evidence any leftist trend that you could detect?
> WADLEIGH: No. My impression of him was that he was a very cautious and rather conservative liberal. "Conservative liberal" may sound funny. By that I mean a person with moderate liberal ideas but with a very conservative temperament.

In early March 1938 Wadleigh went to Turkey to negotiate a trade agreement. He returned to the home office the following December, and a few days later Chambers called to arrange a dinner date. Wadleigh was shocked to learn at their meeting that Chambers had "left the apparatus and the party." He was ordered to return to Moscow, Chambers told Wadleigh, and certain to be executed when he arrived, having been accused of becoming a Trotskyite and converting Wadleigh to Trotskyism. "I realized that my underground work in the State Department was almost certainly ended," Wadleigh recalled, "and I feared that Chambers, embittered as he was, might go to the authorities and tell them of my activities. Knowing that I could no longer trust this man, I feared him…. When we parted, Chambers said: 'Well, now I'm going to become a bourgeois.' Then, patting me on the shoulder, he added: 'That's what you'll have to do, too.'"

Yet Wadleigh was staggered when Chambers phoned his office weeks later, sounding hysterical and desperate, demanding that Wadleigh meet him immediately at Jackson Place, very near the State Department. He imagined "Chambers flanked on either side by an FBI agent, all three of them greeting me with a smile." But Chambers was alone and merely wanted money — ten dollars. Wadleigh gave him a twenty and hurried away, thinking, "I hope I never, never see that man again."

Wadleigh swore to the grand jury on December 11 that Chambers and David Carpenter were the only people he had passed documents to or had contact with in the underground, other than his initial offer of help to Eleanor Nelson. Both Nelson and Carpenter pleaded self-incrimination before the grand jury and refused to testify, and twenty years later Carpenter still refused to talk of those years, even with friendly interviewers.

Another Chambers confederate, Felix, the Baltimore photographer whose last name Chambers had forgotten, was identified by the FBI as Felix Inslerman. He, too, refused to cooperate fully with the grand jury, despite seven appearances and much scolding, lecturing, and cajoling by U.S. attorneys and grand jurors. There were "certain facts," Inslerman said repeatedly, that he did not want to admit to because they were "personal."

Wadleigh recounted for the grand jury a meeting in late 1937 with Chambers and his superior in the underground, ostensibly Boris Bykov. But if Wadleigh's testimony is correct, the man could not have been the real Bykov. The physical descriptions of this man, by Chambers and Wadleigh, are strikingly similar — he was short and stocky, with reddish hair and about forty. The major difference was Wadleigh thought the man had just one arm or was missing part of one arm, and that his name was Sascha. "Chambers characterized this individual as the boss of the outfit," Wadleigh swore. "This individual I recall spoke with an accent, probably Russian. This character talked to me in a rather severe fatherly manner. He told me that the people in Moscow thought that I must be in a position to deliver much more than I had actually delivered."

When Wadleigh returned from Turkey and met with Chambers, who had defected months before, Chambers referred, Wadleigh continued, "to this same person and told me he was a fugitive with whom he spent many a night debating on what the two of them might do and where they might go." That man, Sascha or whatever his name, obviously could not have been the Boris Bykov Chambers was supposedly fleeing after his break.

In its first week of hearings the grand jury was denied by Nixon and HUAC Chambers's pumpkin films for examination, despite the Justice Department's insistence that no one — including the legislative branch of government — could be permitted to withhold evidence vital to a criminal investigation, an action tantamount to "throwing out the courts." So on Saturday, December 11, the Attorney General formally requested that Richard Nixon appear at the U.S. Court House, Foley Square, New York, with said films on Monday, December 13, at ten A.M.

Nixon and staffer Donald Appell arrived punctually, and Nixon briefly displayed for the U.S. attorneys and grand jurors the microfilm. But Nixon declaimed he was there "solely as a messenger for the House. I have the microfilm in my physical custody.... I am here for the purpose of allowing the representatives of your office, Mr. Campbell, to examine it as they like provided it does not leave my custody." He contended that under the rules of the House, the microfilm was evidence entered in a House committee's records and therefore cannot be taken from the committee's custody without permission of the full House.

Alexander Campbell countered that "the investigative agencies of the United States Attorney and the FBI did not permit any person to keep evidence which is vital and essential to the case. We don't permit the sheriffs to keep them, we don't permit anybody to keep them." Yet Nixon reiterated that "the films cannot be left here."

Nixon softened somewhat and allowed that the FBI could examine the microfilm at the House committee's rooms, so long as HUAC retained custody. But this too was unacceptable to Campbell, who remarked that once the FBI began "processing with their secret formulas and methods and rehabilitations which are the greatest in the world," it would be "unthinkable" to return the evidence to HUAC.

The grand jurors immediately voted to sequester the microfilm. Nixon was subpoenaed and brought before a Federal judge, John W. Clancey. Pleading again he was merely a messenger, Nixon promised he would deliver the subpoena to HUAC and the microfilm would be turned over to the FBI. The next day Nixon and HUAC consulted with the Speaker of the House, and all agreed to surrender the evidence to the Justice Department. Thus were Nixon and HUAC checkmated.

In *Six Crises* Nixon contorts this episode into a dramatic constitutional crisis: "Alex Campbell threatened to ask the Judge to cite me for contempt. I, in turn, warned him of the constitutional question that would be raised if a member of Congress, appearing voluntarily before a Grand Jury, were so cited while carrying out a mandate of the Committee which he represented."

Yet a less earnest, more tricky Dick Nixon at the grand jury is unmasked by Donald Appell, who accompanied him that day. In a 1974 interview with Appell, Stephen W. Salant noted: "According to Mr. Appell, between the time that Nixon left the Grand Jury room and the time he entered the Judge's chambers, he gave the films to Mr. Appell," who promptly returned to Washington. "In that way," Salant wrote, "even if compelled by the Judge, Nixon could not have surrendered the films since he no longer had them in his possession. According to the newspapers, Mr. Nixon left Clancey's chambers, thumped his briefcase, and announced to the press that he still retained the films."

The decisive turning point of the Hiss-Chambers Case — the day assistant attorney general Alexander Campbell and his deputies about-faced and sought an indictment of Alger Hiss but not Whittaker Chambers — occurred when FBI document expert Ramos Feehan examined the typed Baltimore Documents and typed letters from the 1930s provided by the Hisses, and determined they were all typed on the same Woodstock machine, a conclusion which Hiss's own hired expert had also arrived at only days before.

Feehan, who had examined thousands of specimens of questioned typewriting, handwriting, inks, stencils, and the like, in over ten years with the Bureau, presented his experienced opinion to the grand jury on December 14, the day before their statutory term ended. Pointing out characteristics of typing which laymen could understand, Feehan demonstrated on a blackboard the defects typical on both sets of documents. Similar typeface irregularities appeared on lowercase letters "g," "e," "o," "i," "d," "a," and "u," and Feehan elaborated on the peculiarities of each flaw. However, Feehan clarified, it was not possible, based on the similar irregularities or similar typographical errors, to determine if the same person typed both sets.

Ramos Feehan appeared briefly only once before the grand jury and spoke fewer than 1,200 words, and many of those words were irrelevant. His expert testimony was subsequently uncontested by other experts or even by defense cross-examination at both of Hiss's trials.

During and before his trials, Hiss and his attorneys and hired document experts simply believed Feehan's testimony was irrefutable. The almost universal assumption was that any particular typewriter was unique, like a fingerprint. Therefore Hiss believed that Chambers, alone or with help, had committed "forgery by typewriter" by actually using Priscilla's old Woodstock. And Hiss may have continued to believe it to his dying day; he certainly never ruled it out. In fact, that scenario (Chambers stealing the Hisses' typewriter and then returning it) is most likely what occurred. Priscilla rarely used the machine—only six or seven of her letters typed on the Woodstock in the 1930s were ever found—and it was always stored in some out-of-the-way spot of the house. It would have been a mere lark for Chambers to steal and return it. He probably took it from their 30th Street house in late 1937, just before the Hisses moved and just before the date of the earliest Baltimore Document, and brought it back to their Volta Place house in 1938 after his dirty work was done. Moreover, Chambers and his underground abettors believed that a typewriter could be traced—that's why *real* tradecraft documents were always reproduced by camera—which is exactly what Chambers wanted in the event he was arrested.

Nevertheless, the *original* typed Baltimore Documents were not available to Hiss until March 1952, two years after his conviction, when his appeals attorney, Chester T. Lane, received permission from the Justice Department to have them examined under FBI guard.

One of the experts Lane consulted, Elizabeth McCarthy, official document examiner for the Boston Police Department and the Massachusetts State Police, concluded, "by all standard tests ordinarily applied by questioned documents examiners, that [all] the documents were typed on the same machine." She based that conclusion not on the identical typeface peculiarities which appeared on the Baltimore Documents and the Hiss letters, "but upon the more convincing fact that I find no substantial consistent deviations in type impression as among the ... documents."

McCarthy closely examined the originals of both sets of papers and stated in her 1952 affidavit:

> No one person typed the Baltimore Documents. There were certainly two typists, whose work varied sharply in evenness of pressure, typing skill, mechanical understanding and control of the machine, style habits, and other similar respects; no one person's work could exhibit such differences. It is quite possible that more than two typists were involved. [Therefore] Priscilla Hiss cannot have typed them all. Furthermore, the characteristics of her typing make it perfectly clear that she was not either of the two principal typists involved. Priscilla Hiss did not in my opinion type any of the Baltimore Documents.

The original Baltimore Documents and the envelope that Chambers alleged they were stored in for ten years were made available to chemist Daniel P. Norman for physical and chemical tests in an attempt to obtain information as to their source and history. He was permitted to cut a section without typing on it from each sheet. Most clippings were about an inch square, but some were larger. He also cut six sections from the envelope, also about an inch square each. The sheets fell into two general size categories: category A sheets were standard letter size 8½" × 11", and category B sheets were 8" × 10½".

"All documents in category A are heavily yellowed," Norman remarked, "and show marks of age over substantial portions of their area to a degree not apparent in any of the documents in category B." The category B paper appeared similar to "government manifold paper" commonly stored in ordinary office cabinets from 1937 to 1952. The category A papers had been "subjected to deteriorating conditions which were not uniform across the area of the sheets." Norman added:

> It is well known that the conditions of storage of paper have a considerable influence on its degree of permanence, variations in heat and humidity being in particular responsible for variations in the rate of aging and yellowing of paper. In view of the fact that most of the papers in both category A and category B are of the same general class (predominantly chemical wood pulp) and show no chemical idiosyncrasies (such as abnormal alum concentrations which would be reflected in abnormal acidity), I conclude that the two categories of documents could not have been stored together under the same atmospheric conditions for most of their existence.

Norman examined the envelope

> for the purpose of determining whether it would nevertheless have been possible that some of the documents might have been stored in it. My examination leads to the conclusion that it would not have been possible. I base this observation on analyses of certain stains appearing on both the front and back of the envelope, and both inside and out, as well as upon observation of the effect made on the envelope by the presence of certain hard physical objects which may have been microfilm containers of one kind or another.

"What I have said," Norman concluded, "indicates that it would have been impossible for all the typed Baltimore Documents to have been stored together over the 10 year period from 1938 to 1948. From this it follows that they cannot have been all stored together during that period in the envelope in which they are alleged to have been stored."

Alger Hiss could have legally side-stepped indictment by refusing to testify. John W. Davis, vice chairman of the Carnegie Endowment, implored Hiss to do just that and take the Fifth. William Marbury felt certain as early as November 18 that Hiss would ultimately be indicted, so the persisting notion that Alger Hiss attempted to brazen out a "reputational defense" to the very end, long after his public reputation had been obliterated, is just another misconception of the enduring myth. In the late 1940s especially, witnesses quite innocent of wrongdoing often asserted their constitutional rights by refusing to testify before congressional committees and grand juries. Hiss mistakenly and naively believed that "our federal judicial system was proof against public prejudice and was free of prosecutorial chicanery," and that "jurors would be insulated from the phobias of the cold war."

Chambers, on the other hand, had no choice but to continue to lie, and the sheer volume of his lies worked to his advantage — no sooner than one lie would be discredited than several others would crop up. "It is no small gift to be an absolute liar," Norman Mailer said. "If you never tell the truth, you are virtually as safe as an honest man who never utters an untruth."

Hiss's principal attorney, Edward McLean, thought both Alger and Priscilla would be indicted, though he had done everything possible to save them. He urged Alexander Campbell to postpone "any action for the new grand jury rather than to rush it through with this one." McLean was hopeful because on December 14, in a conversation with Campbell, they discussed "the question of whether Whittaker Chambers was mentally abnormal and emotionally unstable." McLean recalled that Campbell "said to me in substance that he realized that Mr. Chambers was both unstable and abnormal. I recall that Mr. Campbell said, in substantially the following words, 'I have expected for several days to pick up the paper in the morning and read that Mr. Chambers has jumped out the window.'"[9]

J. Edgar Hoover would have preferred indictments of both Hiss and Chambers, according to Allen Weinstein, "but his superiors at Justice never sought his advice on the question." And if Chambers were indicted, no other possible informants could be expected to come forward with allegations of Communist infiltration or worse. In Campbell's judgment, an indictment of Hiss would only guarantee that a trial be held which was benign and not itself evidence of guilt; but to indict Chambers would nullify the first indictment by invalidating the only witness to the crime.

Hiss had testified before the grand jury almost every day since December 6, and a week later, after word of Feehan's opinion that the personal letters typed by Priscilla in the 1930s were typed on the same Woodstock as Chambers's Baltimore Documents, the nature, tenor, and emphasis of questions asked by Justice Department officials Campbell, Raymond Whearty, and Thomas Donegan became increasingly skeptical and accusatory.

In a memo Hiss wrote of his December 14 appearance, he noted that Donegan stated to the jurors "with great emphasis" that Priscilla's letters and Chambers's typed papers had been produced on the same typewriter, and both Donegan and the jurors pressed him about "the coincidence of the typing." How could Chambers have gained access to the machine? Hiss guessed that Chambers took the machine and kept it for a time "without our being aware of it." He also speculated that Chambers "might have bribed a maid to let him get access to the typewriter." "One of the jurors," Hiss wrote in his memo, "had asked me if I didn't think my theory about how Chambers could have gotten access to our typewriter was fantastic and ... I replied that I thought it was but that I thought Chambers was a fantastic person."

Hiss noted telling the jurors of how he had cooperated with the authorities from the outset:

> I then told the Grand Jury that at noon today, Mr. Campbell had asked to speak to me and had told me that I would be indicted. I said that I wanted the jury to know that I realized the serious nature of the evidence that appeared to militate against me, that naturally I did not know all of the evidence which the jury had had but that I did know that much damaging evidence had been produced by my own direct efforts and had been turned over to the government officials at my direction. I said that I had never failed to answer any questions directed at me, had claimed no privileges and had cooperated as fully as possible in trying to get to the bottom of this matter. I said that I had testified as truthfully as I possibly could and would continue to do so. I said that whatever the evidence, I knew that I had done nothing that was a breach of trust or a dereliction of my duty, that I was proud of my years of government service.... [I told the jurors] Mr. Campbell said in practically these words, "The F.B.I. has cracked the case. You are in it up to your eyes. Your wife's in it. Why don't you go in there and tell the jury the truth?" I said that I had replied that I had continuously told the truth and that I will continue to do so. Mr. Campbell had then said, "You are going to be indicted. I am not fooling...." I said that I had replied that I was not fooling either. Mr. Campbell had then said, "This is your government speaking." That concluded the brief interview but later Mr. Campbell called me back in again and had said, "I want to make it plain, your wife will be included." I had replied that I understood that.

The afternoon of December 15, 1948, the grand jury handed down a two-count perjury indictment against Alger Hiss, but did not indict Priscilla Hiss, based on Hiss's testimony earlier that day, alleging he had perjured himself when denying that "in or about the months of February and March, 1938, [he] furnished, delivered and transmitted to one Jay David Whittaker Chambers, who was not then and there a person authorized to receive the same, copies of numerous secret, confidential and restricted documents, writings, notes and other papers, the originals of which had theretofore been removed and abstracted from the ... Department of State." The second perjury count was rather redundant, charging that Hiss's testimony "was untrue in that the Defendant did in fact see and converse with the said Mr. Chambers in or about the months of February and March 1938."

The grand jury's vote for indictment was only one more than that needed for a majority. One juror said that Hiss's "indictment was a close vote, not a unanimous one. I was never convinced that Hiss was guilty of the crime we indicted him for. Chambers perjured himself many times, but the final decision of the jury was, 'He's our witness, we are not going to indict him.' It was a politically inspired matter."

An interested observer who was in attendance outside the grand jury room each day that Hiss and Chambers testified remarked that Chambers's handlers were careful to see that the two men never met. Hiss always waited with the other witnesses before his appearances, but not so Chambers. He was provided a private room and always entered the building through side entrances. On the day Hiss was indicted, the witness recalled, "I saw a skulking, shambling Chambers. He looked furtive and frightened. He was accompanied by ... an FBI agent. The impression was of a cowed, timid creature being moved from one cage to another by its keeper. He was bent over or stooped, as if this posture might make him less visible."[10]

Appendix

Adolf Berle Notes of Meeting with
Whittaker Chambers, September 2, 1939

The thirteen pages of the Appendix represent notes taken by Adolf Berle, assistant secretary of state for security matters, during his September 2, 1939, meeting with Whittaker Chambers at Berle's residence in Washington, D.C. There is no question by scholars or historians that these notes concern Berle's meeting with Chambers, though the name Whittaker Chambers (or Chambers by any other name) is nowhere written in the notes. The meeting was arranged by Isaac Don Levine, who had known Berle previously. Levine initially did not reveal Chambers's name to Berle in the event the meeting did not come off, but then Chambers agreed to meet Berle (as a substitute for President Roosevelt whom Chambers wanted to talk to). When Levine and Chambers arrived at the Berle residence Chambers was introduced by his real name and even talked to Mrs. Berle about his work at *Time* magazine, according to Levine.

Berle took notes in longhand as Chambers talked. Later a typed copy was prepared by Berle's office. The notes were given to the FBI in 1943. The FBI had known of Chambers since 1941— however, the FBI learned of Chambers's accusations from Berle in 1939 but not his name — and had known of his meeting with Berle since 1942 but did not request his notes until a year later. The FBI prepared a typed copy from the copy given them by Berle. They made some slight changes in text arrangement and punctuation, which make it appear as though Berle was taking notes of a talk with an "underground espionage agent." Chambers, and later many historians, made much out of that forgery, minor though it is. The FBI's copy has been reproduced in many books, including *Witness*. Berle's original notes, long believed lost, were found by the author.

DEPARTMENT OF STATE

FOREIGN ACTIVITY CORRELATION

Personal & Confidential 6/20/43

A - B - Mr. Berle

Chief:

You'll probably want to keep this in your files — you loaned it to me the other day.

Many thanks.

— J —

Adolf A. Berle, Jr. Papers; Subject Files, 1946-1971; File: U.S. Committee on Un-American Activities (Notes-1943), Box 97.

London — Underground Espionage Agent

(1) Dr. Philip Rosenblieett — Formerly of [441st St & B'way, NE]

Dr. Greenberg — M.D. (West 70th ?)

Brother-in-law.

American Liason of British Underground C.

Head in America Mark Moren — (alias Phelipovitc

— allegedly Jugoslav) — :

real name - ?

Rosenblieett — in U.S. —

connected with Dr. Isador Miller — Chemist's Club - 41st St.

Chemist Explosive Arsenal, Picatinny, N.J.

Was "front" behind Mark Moren existed — in

Miller's employ, re —

Knew Pressman — he alias was "Col. Phelps". —

introduced him to Mark Moren, buying arms

for Spanish (Loyalist) Gov't —

Pressman — as counsel helped Moren — made

a flight to Mexico with him; forced down

at Brownsville, Tex in late '36 or early

'37 — probably fall of '36. —

Pressman

Underground organized by the late Harold Ware; Pressman

was in his group — (1932-3 ??) Pressman then

in the A.A.A. —

Nathan Witt — Secretary of the N.L.R.B. — head of the

underground group after Harold Ware —

2

John Abt – followed Witt in test group –
Tax Div'n – Dep't of Justice & head
in CIO (M. Ware's Widow – Jessica Smith
ed. Soviet Russia.
(née Abt) – sister: Marion Bachrach – Secretary
– communist friend Mamie etc.
[Jessica Smith: With Rochers in (1926) –
friend of Louis Fischer.] Smith

Meeting place: John Abt's house – 15th St.
Charles Krivitsky – alias Charles Kramer — (C.I.O)
worked in La Follette Committee –.
Physicist. –

___

Vincent Reno – now at Aberdeen Proving Grounds –
Computer – Math. asst. to Col. Zornig
(Aerial bomb sight Detectors etc)

Formerly
C.P. organized
under alias "June"
Clark?

Philip Reno – in Social Security (??) –
was head of underground Trade Union Group
Political leader etc

Elinor Nelson, treasurer of Fed. Employees' Union –
[Fed. Workers' Union, C.I.O – headed by
Jake Baker]

/3

Reus connected with Baltimore party
organizer - Benjamin (Bundy) Friedman
alias Field - Then California - then Russia
- now organizer for Baltimore & Washington
of Above-Ground party. - Underground connections -

Labor Dep't -
Stanley White - friend of Aubrey Williams - CP -
Red - but not Underground. -

State
Post - editorship, Foreign Service Journal.
Was in Alexandria Unit of CP - in
"Underground Apparatus" -
Duggan - Laurence - [Member CP?? -]

[Wadleigh?]   Wadleigh - Trade Agreement Section -
Lovell -
Communist Study Group
Elinor Nelson - Laurence Duggan - Julian Wadleigh -
West European Div's - - Field - still in -
[Laurence says he is out - work with I L O.
- Then in Committee for Repatriation -
His Leader was Hedda Gompertz -

Field had original contact.
He introduced Duggan to Gumperts (Hede)
Duggan's relationship was casual –
    Still exists? – Where is Hede
    Gumperts? –
        Duggan + Field supposed to have
        been both members of party –

Donald Hiss
  (Philippines Adviser)
  Member of C.P. with Pressman & Witt –
  Labor Dep't – Ross & Thomas Parkin –
  Party wanted him there – to send him
  as Arbitrator in Bredges trial –
  Brought along day twelve –

Alger Hiss
  Ass't to Sayre – C.P. – until 1937 –
  Member of the Underground too – active – ? 1
  Baltimore boys –
  Wife – Priscilla Hiss – Socialist –
  Early days of New Deal

Note – When Loy Henderson interviewed Mrs. Rubens his report
immediately went back to Moscow. Who sent it? – Sent
came from Washington –

4

—

Lauchlin Currie: Was a "Fellow Traveler" —
helped various Communists — never went his
whole way. —

—

<u>S.E.C.</u> —

Philip Reno — used to be
+ are S.E.C.

<u>Treasury</u>

<u>Schloman Adler</u>   (Sol Adler?)
Counsel's Office
<u>Sends</u> weekly reports to C.P. (Gen. Counsel's Office)
Frank Coe —   Now teaches at McGill.
There are two: brothers. One of them
in C.P.'s "Foreign bureau" — Bob Coe

Known from   <u>Peters</u> — formerly in Bela Kun
Gov't — Agricultural Commissariat — called Gändösz (?)
Then to Russia — then here, in Business Office of
Communist Paper " Uj Elöre " — then, after 1929 —
head of C P underground, lived in Hamilton Ap'ts.

5

Woodside, J. I. — under alias "Silers" — +
lectured in Communist Camps —
Freund: "Blake" of "Freiheit". Real name —
Wiener — American: Polish Jew. —
    Peters was responsible for Washington Sector
    — Went to Moscow — where is he now? —
    Wife — a communist courier —
West Coast — Head: "The Old Man" — Volkov is
his real name — daughter a Communist
Courier. He knows the West Coast
underground — Residence: San Francisco
or Oakland —

    Alexander Trachtenberg — Politburo.
      Member of the Exec. Committee
      Head of GPU in U.S.
      Works with Peters —

Plans for two Super Battleships —
secured in 1937 — Who gave —
    Karp, brother in law of Molotov — working
    with Scott Ferris, got them released —
Now: Naval Architect working on it, who??

London - Underground Espionage Agent

1) Dr. <u>Philip Rosenbliett</u> - Formerly of (41st St + B'way, N.E.)

Dr.   Greenberg - MD (West 70^S N.Y.)

Brother-inlaw.

American Liaison of British Underground C.

Head in America Mark Moren - (alias Philipoveter

- allegedly Yougoslav) -

real name - ?

<u>Rosenbliett</u> - in U.S.

connected with Dr. Isador Miller - Chemist's Club-41st St

Chemist   Explosive Arsenal, Picatinny, N.J.

Was "front" behind Mark Moren existed- in

Miller's employ, oc -

Knew Pressman - his alias was "Col Philips" -

Introduced him to Mark Moren, buying arms

for Spanish (Loyalist) gov't. -

Pressman - as counsel - helped Moren - made

a flight to Mexico with him; forced down

at Brownsville, Tex. in late '36 or early

'37 - probably fall of '36 -

<u>Pressman</u>

Underground organized by the <u>late</u> Harold Ware; Pressman

was in his group - (1932-3 ??) Pressman then

in the A.A.A. -

Nathan Witt - Secretary of the NLRB - head of the

underground group after Harold Ware -

2.

John Abt - followed Witt in that group -

Tax Div'n - Dep't of Justice and now

in CIO (M. Ware's Widow - Jessica Smith

ed. Soviet Russia)

hu Abt).   - sister: Marion Bacharach - Secretary

- communist from Minnesota.

(Jessica Smith: With Rauhers in 1926) -

friend of Louis Fisher;)

Meeting place: John Abt's house - 15th St.

Charles Krivitsky - alias Charles Kramer - (C.I.O.)

worked in La Follette Committee -

Physicist -

y.g.

Vincent Reno - now at Aberdeen Proving Grounds -

Formerly
C.P.organizer
under alias "Lance
Clark."

Computer - Math. asst to Col. Zornig

(Aerial bomb sight detectors etc.)

Philip Reno - in Social Security (??) -

was head of Underground Trade Union Group

Political labor Union

Elinor Nelson - treasurer of Fed. Employers' Union -

(Fed. Workers' Union, C.I.O. - headed by

Jake Baker)

3.

    <u>Reno</u> connected with Baltimore party

        organizer - Benjamin (Bundy) Friedman

        alias Field - Then California - then Russia

        - now organizes for Baltimore and Washington

        of Above-Ground party. - Underground connections.

Labor Dep't -

    <u>Stanley White</u> - friend of Aubrey Williams - CP -

        Red - but not underground -

<u>State</u>

    <u>Post</u> - editorship, Foreign Service Journal

        Was in Alexandria Unit of CP - in

        "Underground Apparatus" -

    Duggan - Lawerence - (Member CP ??)

(Wadhigh?)   Wadley - Trade Agreement Section -

    Lavell -   "   "   "

        Communist Study Group

        Elinor Nelson - Lawerence Duggan - Julian Wadhigh -

    West European Div'n -   <u>Field</u> - still in -

        (Levene says he is <u>out</u> - went into I.L.O.

        - then in Committee for Repatriation

    His leader was Hedda Gumpertz -

4.

Field had original contact -

He introduced Duggan to Gumpertz (Hedda)

Duggan's relationship was casual -

    Still exists? - Where is Hedda Gumpertz?

      Duggan and Field supposed to have

      been both members of party -

Donald Hiss

(Philippines Adviser

Member of C.P. with Pressman and Witt -

Labor Dep't - Asst to Francis Perkins -

Party wanted him there - to send him

as arbitrator in Bridges trial -

Brought along by brother -

Alger Hiss

Ass't to Sayre - C.P. - until 1937 -

Member of the underground Com. - Active - ??

    Baltimore boys -

Wife - Priscilla Hiss - Socialist -

    Early days of New Deal

Note - When Leon Henderson interviewed Mrs. Rubens his report
immediately went back to Moscow. Who sent it? - Such
came from Washington -

5.

Laughlin Currie: Was a "Fellow Traveler" -

helped various communists - never went the whole way.

S.E.C. -

Philip Reno - used to be and are S.E.C.

Treasury

Schlomer <u>Adler</u>   (Sol Adler ?)

Counsel's Office

Sends weekly reports to C.P. (Gen. Counsel's Office)

Frank Coe - now teaches at M^CGill

There are two: brother. One of them

in CP's "Forum Bureau" - Bob Coe

Known from   Peters - formerly in Bela Kun

Gov't - Agricultural Commissariat - Called Gandosz (?

Then to Russia - then here, in Business Office of

Communist Paper "Uj Elori" - then, after 1929 -

head of CP Underground, lived in Hamilton Ap'ts

Woodside, L.I. - under alias "Silver" - and

lectured in Communist Camps -

Friend: "Blake" of "Freiheit" Real name -

<u>Wiener</u> - American Polish Jew -

Peters was responsible for Washington Section

- went to Moscow - where is he now? -

Wife - a Comintern Courier -

6.

West Coast - Head: "The Old Man" - Volkov is
        his real name - daughter a Comintern
        Courier. He knows the West Coast
        underground - Residence: San Francisco
        or Oakland -

———

Alexander Trachtenberg - Pihtburo
                Member of the Exec. Committee
                Head of GPU in U.S.
                Works with Peters -
Plans for two Super battleships -
        secured in 1937 - Who gave -
                Karp, brother in law of Molotov -
                working with Scott Ferris, got
                this released -
Now: Naval Architect working on it, why ??

Chapter Notes

Chapter I

1. George F. Kennan, *Russia and the West Under Lenin and Stalin* (Boston: Little, Brown, 1961), p. viii.
2. Theodore H. Draper, *New York Review of Books*, November 20 and December 4, 1997.
3. Lytton Strachey, *Eminent Victorians* (London: Folio Press, 1967), p. 21.
4. Albert Goldman, *Elvis* (New York: McGraw-Hill, 1981), p. 3.
5. Victor Navasky, *Naming Names* (New York: Viking, 1980), p. 4.
6. Whittaker Chambers, *Witness* (New York: Random House, 1964), pp. 741–2.
7. Alger Hiss, *Recollections of a Life* (New York: Seaver Books, Henry Holt, 1988), p. 202.
8. Chambers's testimony before the House Committee on Un-American Activities, August 3, 1948.
9. Hiss's testimony before HUAC, August 5, 1948.
10. G. Edward White, *Alger Hiss's Looking-Glass Wars* (New York: Oxford University Press, 2004), p.52.
11. Chambers, *Witness*, p. 70.
12. Ibid., p. 502.
13. Sam Tanenhaus, *Whittaker Chambers: A Biography* (New York: Random House, 1997), p. 96.

Chapter II

1. Anthony Summers, *Official and Confidential: The Secret Life of J. Edgar Hoover* (New York: Putnam's, 1993), p. 160.
2. Anthony Summers with Robbyn Swan, *The Arrogance of Power* (New York: Penguin, 2000), pp. 41–2.
3. Joseph C. Goulden, *The Best Years, 1945–1950* (New York: Atheneum, 1976), p. 225.
4. Ibid., p. 227.
5. Ibid., p. 235.
6. Ibid., p. 231.
7. Christopher Lasch, *New York Review of Books*, October 10, 1968.
8. Gabriel Kolko, *Main Currents in Modern American History* (New York: Harper & Row, 1976), p. 355.

9. Ibid., p. 279.
10. Gabriel Kolko, *The Politics of War: The World and United States Foreign Policy, 1943–1945* (New York: Random House, 1968), p. 447.
11. Frederick F. Siegel, *Troubled Journey: From Pearl Harbor to Ronald Reagan* (New York: Hill & Wang, 1984), p. 39.
12. Ibid.
13. Allen Weinstein, *Perjury: The Hiss-Chambers Case* (New York: Random House, 1997), p. 316.
14. Summers, *Official and Confidential*, p. 159.
15. Ibid.
16. Ellen Schrecker, *Many Are the Crimes, McCarthyism in America* (New York: Little, Brown, 1998), p. 19.
17. Summers, *Official and Confidential*, p. 160.
18. Summers, *The Arrogance of Power*, p. 65.
19. Goulden, p. 318.
20. Schrecker, p. 214.
21. David Remnick, *The Devil Problem* (New York: Vintage, 1997), p. 125.
22. Meyer Zeligs, *Friendship and Fratricide* (New York: Viking, 1967), p. 10.
23. Weinstein, *Perjury*, p. 15.
24. Hiss, *Recollections of a Life*, p. 203.
25. Summers, *The Arrogance of Power*, p. 67.
26. Richard Nixon, *Six Crises* (New York: Doubleday, 1962), p. 3.
27. Ibid., p. 7.
28. Ibid., p. 9.
29. William A. Reuben, *The Honorable Mr. Nixon* (New York: Action Books, 1958), p. 24.
30. Zeligs, p. 11.

Chapter III

1. Robert Stripling, *The Red Plot Against America* (Drexel Hill, PA: Bell, 1949), p. 117.
2. Chambers's testimony this chapter from the transcript of the August 7, 1948, closed HUAC hearing at Foley Square in New York City.
3. Bert and Peter Andrews, *A Tragedy of History:*

A Journalist's Confidential Role in the Hiss-Chambers Case (Washington, D.C.: Robert B. Luce, 1962), pp. 72–5.

4. John Chabot Smith, *Alger Hiss: The True Story* (New York: Holt, Rinehart and Winston, 1976), p. 158.

Chapter IV

1. HUAC hearing of August 12, 1948.
2. Fred J. Cook, *The Unfinished Story of Alger Hiss* (New York: William Morrow, 1958), pp. 4–5.
3. David Caute, *The Great Fear* (New York: Simon & Schuster, 1978), p. 88.
4. Alistair Cooke, *A Generation on Trial* (New York: Alfred A. Knopf, 1950), p. 8.
5. Schrecker, p. 91.
6. James Aronson, *The Press and the Cold War* (Indianapolis: Bobbs-Merrill, 1970), pp. 31–2.
7. Robert K. Carr, *The House Committee on Un-American Activities, 1945–1950* (Ithaca: Cornell University Press, 1952), p. 19.
8. Gabriel Kolko, *The Age of War: The United States Confronts the World* (Boulder: Lynne Rienner, 2006), p. 4.
9. Frances Stonor Saunders, *The Cultural Cold War* (New York: New Press, 1999), p. 16.
10. D.F. Fleming, *The Cold War And Its Origins, 1917–1960, Volume One, 1917–1950* (New York: Doubleday, 1961), p. 432.
11. Carr, p. 265.
12. Ibid., p. 263.
13. Nixon, p. 14.
14. Stripling, p. 14.
15. Schrecker, p. 152.
16. Carr, p. 266.
17. Goulden, p. 297.
18. Carr, pp. 392–3.
19. Schrecker, pp. 172–4.
20. R. Bruce Craig, *Treasonable Doubt: The Harry Dexter White Spy Case* (Lawrence: University Press of Kansas, 2004), p. 64.
21. Kathryn S. Olmsted, *Red Spy Queen: A Biography of Elizabeth Bentley* (Chapel Hill: University of North Carolina Press, 2002), pp. x–xi.
22. Craig, p. 73.
23. Interview of Mary Price Adamson by Mary Frederickson on April 19, 1976, for the Southern Oral History Program, University of North Carolina at Chapel Hill.
24. Kolko, *The Politics of War*, p. 331.

Chapter V

1. Alger Hiss, *In The Court Of Public Opinion* (New York: Alfred A. Knopf, 1957), p. 15.
2. Zeligs, pp. 278–80.

Chapter VII

1. T.S. Matthews, *Angels Unaware* (New York: Ticknor & Fields, 1985), p. 169.
2. Interview by William A. Reuben in 1969, Reu-ben Papers, Labadie Special Collections, University of Michigan, Ann Arbor, Michigan.
3. Terry Teachout, ed., *Ghosts on the Roof: Selected Journalism of Whittaker Chambers 1931–1959* (Washington, D.C.: Regnery Gateway, 1989), p. xxiv.
4. Louis Kronenberger, *No Whippings, No Gold Watches* (Boston: Little, Brown, 1970), p. 133.
5. Zeligs, p. 309.
6. Matthews, p. 171.
7. Letter, Lael Tucker Wertenbaker to W.A. Reuben, September 17, 1968, Reuben Papers.
8. Tanenhaus, p. 180.
9. Walter Sullivan, "The Crucial 1940's," *Nieman Reports*, Harvard University, Spring 1983.
10. Dorothy Sterling, Letter to the Editor, *New York Times*, February 28, 1984.
11. Thomas Griffith, *Harry and Teddy* (New York: Random House, 1995), p. 138.
12. Teachout, p. xxii.
13. Griffith, p. 118.
14. Ibid., p. 141.
15. Letter, Allen Grover to W.A. Reuben, 1969, Reuben Papers.
16. FBI notes copied from Chambers's personnel file at Time-Life, Reuben Papers.
17. Weinstein, *Perjury*, p. 306.
18. Whittaker Chambers, *Cold Friday* (New York: Random House, 1964), p. 244.
19. Letter, Allen Grover to W.A. Reuben, 1969, Reuben Papers.

Chapter VIII

1. Kenneth Simon interview, 2001, The Alger Hiss Story website, http://homepages.nyu.edu/~th15/.
2. Zeligs, p. 178.
3. Ibid., p. 181.
4. John C. Culver and John Hyde, *American Dreamer, The Life and Times of Henry A. Wallace* (New York: W.W. Norton, 2000), p. 153.
5. Zeligs, pp. 197–8.
6. Letter, Whittaker Chambers to Meyer Schapiro, July 6, 1935, Schapiro Papers, Butler Rare Book and Manuscript Library, Columbia University.
7. Weinstein, *Perjury*, p. 316.
8. Hoover memo, August 18, 1948, Reuben Papers.
9. Amy Knight, *How The Cold War Began: The Gouzenko Affair and the Hunt for Soviet Spies* (Toronto: McClelland & Stewart, 2005), pp. 90–93.
10. Zeligs, p. 340.
11. Knight, p. 75.
12. Dean Acheson, *Present at the Creation: My Years in the State Department* (New York: W.W. Norton, 1969), pp. 250–2.
13. Knight, pp. 90–93.
14. Ibid.
15. Hiss, *Recollections of a Life*, pp. 204–5.
16. Weinstein, *Perjury*, pp. 316–19.
17. Ibid.
18. Ibid., pp. 327–8.
19. Zeligs, p. 341.
20. R. Bruce Craig, article on HUAC Papers, Alger Hiss Web site.
21. Weinstein, *Perjury*, p. 329.
22. Smith, pp. 148–9.

Chapter IX

1. Weinstein, *Perjury*, p. 47.
2. Reuben, *The Honorable Mr. Nixon*, pp. 55–7.

Chapter X

1. Smith, pp. 233–4.
2. Tanenhaus, pp. 283–4.
3. William L. Marbury, *In the Catbird Seat* (Baltimore: Maryland Historical Society, 1988), p. 272.
4. Zeligs, pp. 216–17.

Chapter XI

1. Weinstein, *Perjury*, p. 87.
2. Letter, Sam Krieger to Allen Weinstein, April 11, 1976, Reuben Papers.
3. Letter, Bertram D. Wolfe to W.A. Reuben, May 12, 1969, Reuben Papers.
4. Weinstein, *Perjury*, p. 343.
5. Meyer Schapiro testimony, Grand Jury records, February 9, 1949, p. 6108.
6. Zeligs, pp. 116–25.
7. Whittaker Chambers testimony, Grand Jury records, December 17, 1948, p. 4619.
8. Zeligs, pp. 116–25.
9. Letter, Robert Cantwell to W.A. Reuben, December 14, 1968, Reuben Papers.
10. Zeligs, pp. 116–25.
11. Whittaker Chambers statement to the FBI, January–April 1949, Reuben Papers.
12. Max Bedacht testimony, Grand Jury records, January 5, 1949, p. 5074.
13. Letter, Henry A. Murray to W.A. Reuben, date unknown, Reuben Papers.
14. Phyllis Greenacre, *Emotional Growth* (New York: International Universities Press, 1971), p. 93.

Chapter XII

1. Weinstein, *Perjury*, p. 463.
2. Philip Rahv, "The Sense and Nonsense of Whittaker Chambers," *Partisan Review*, July 1952.
3. Letter, Robert Cantwell to W.A. Reuben, March 13, 1969, Reuben Papers.
4. Zeligs, p. 299.
5. Ibid., pp. 251–2.
6. Ibid., pp. 300–1.
7. Weinstein, *Perjury*, p. 287.
8. Gary Kern, *A Death in Washington, Walter Krivitsky and the Stalin Terror* (New York: Enigma Books, 2003), p. 175.
9. Isaac Don Levine, *Eyewitness to History* (New York: Hawthorn Books, 1973), pp. 189–90.
10. Isaac Don Levine HUAC testimony, December 8, 1948.
11. Ibid.
12. Levine, *Eyewitness to History*, p. 192.
13. J. Edgar Hoover, FBI memo, August 18, 1948, Reuben Papers.
14. Weinstein, *Perjury*, p. 293.

Chapter XIII

1. Nathan Levine testimony, Grand Jury records, December 8, 1948, p. 3615.
2. Zeligs, pp. 292–3.
3. Weinstein, *Perjury*, p. 156.
4. Ibid., pp. 163–4.
5. Stripling, pp. 144–7.
6. Reuben, *The Honorable Mr. Nixon*, pp. 76–86.
7. Ibid.
8. Michael and Morton Levitt, *A Tissue of Lies, Nixon vs. Hiss* (New York: McGraw-Hill, 1979), p. 125.
9. Edward C. McLean, affidavit, October 11, 1950, Reuben Papers.
10. Hiss, *Recollections of a Life*, p. 210.

Bibliography

Acheson, Dean. *Present at the Creation: My Years in the State Department.* New York: W.W. Norton, 1969.

The Alger Hiss Story. Website. http://homepages. nyu.edu/~th15/.

Andrews, Bert, and Peter. *A Tragedy of History: A Journalist's Confidential Role in the Hiss-Chambers Case.* Washington, D.C.: Robert B. Luce, 1962.

Aronson, James. *The Press and the Cold War.* Indianapolis: Bobbs-Merrill, 1970.

Berle, Beatrice Bishop, and Travis Beal Jacobs, eds. *Navigating the Rapids, 1918–1971: From the Papers of Adolf A. Berle.* New York: Harcourt Brace Jovanovich, 1973.

Boyer, Paul. *By the Bomb's Early Light.* New York: Pantheon, 1985.

Buckley, William F., ed. *Odyssey of a Friend: Whittaker Chambers' Letters to William F. Buckley, Jr., 1954–1961.* Privately Printed, 1969.

Carr, Robert K. *The House Committee on Un-American Activities 1945–1950.* Ithaca: Cornell University Press, 1952.

Caute, David. *The Great Fear.* New York: Simon & Schuster, 1978.

Chambers, Whittaker. *Cold Friday.* New York: Random House, 1964.

_____. *Witness.* New York: Random House, 1952.

Chervonnaya, Svetlana. DocumentsTalk.com. Website. http://documentstalk.com/.

Christopher, Nicholas. *Somewhere in the Night.* New York: Free Press, 1997.

Clubb, O. Edmund. *The Witness and I.* New York: Columbia University Press, 1974.

Cook, Fred J. *The Unfinished Story of Alger Hiss.* New York: William Morrow, 1958.

Cooke, Alistair. *A Generation on Trial.* New York: Alfred A. Knopf, 1950.

Craig, R. Bruce. *Treasonable Doubt: The Harry Dexter White Spy Case.* Lawrence: University Press of Kansas, 2004.

Culver, John C., and John Hyde. *American Dreamer: The Life and Times of Henry A. Wallace.* New York: W.W. Norton, 2000.

de Toledano, Ralph, ed. *Notes from the Underground: The Whittaker Chambers–Ralph de Toledano Letters, 1949–1960.* Washington, D.C.: Regnery, 1997.

_____, and Victor Lasky. *Seeds of Treason.* New York: Funk & Wagnalls, 1950.

Fariello, Griffin. *Red Scare.* New York: W.W. Norton, 1995.

Fleming, D.F. *The Cold War and Its Origins, 1917–1960, Volume One, 1917–1950.* New York: Doubleday, 1961.

Goulden, Joseph C. *The Best Years, 1945–1950.* New York: Atheneum, 1976.

Grand jury transcripts, Southern District of New York 1947–1949.

Greenacre, Phyllis. *Emotional Growth.* Volumes 1 & 2. New York: International Universities Press, 1971.

Griffith, Thomas. *Harry and Teddy.* New York: Random House, 1995.

"Hearings Regarding Communist Espionage in the United States Government." *Hearings Before the Committee on Un-American Activities, House of Representatives, Eightieth Congress, Second Session.* Washington D.C.: United States Government Printing Office, 1948.

Hiss, Alger. *In the Court of Public Opinion.* New York: Alfred A. Knopf, 1957.

_____. *Recollections of a Life.* New York: Seaver Books, Henry Holt, 1988.

Hiss, Tony. *Laughing Last.* Boston: Houghton Mifflin, 1977.

Hofstadter, Richard. *The Paranoid Style in American Politics and Other Essays.* Cambridge: Harvard University Press, 1996.

Jowitt, Earl. *The Strange Case of Alger Hiss.* New York: Doubleday, 1953.

Kern, Gary. *A Death in Washington: Walter Krivitsky and the Stalin Terror.* New York: Enigma Books, 2003.

Knight, Amy. *How The Cold War Began: The Gouzenko Affair and the Hunt for Soviet Spies.* Toronto: McClelland & Stewart, 2005.

Kolko, Gabriel. *The Politics of War: The World and United States Foreign Policy, 1943–1945.* New York: Random House, 1968.

Kronenberger, Louis. *No Whippings, No Gold Watches.* Boston: Little, Brown, 1970.

Levine, Isaac Don. *Eyewitness to History.* New York: Hawthorn Books, 1973.

Levitt, Morton, and Michael. *A Tissue of Lies: Nixon vs. Hiss.* New York: McGraw-Hill, 1979.

Marbury, William L. *In the Catbird Seat.* Baltimore: Maryland Historical Society, 1988.

Matthews, T.S. *Angels Unawares.* New York: Ticknor & Fields, 1985.

May, Gary. *Un-American Activities.* New York: Oxford University Press, 1994.

Menand, Louis. *The Metaphysical Club.* New York: Farrar, Straus and Giroux, 2001.

Moore, William Howard. *Two Foolish Men.* Portland, Oregon: Moorop Press, 1987.

Navasky, Victor S. "The Case Not Proved Against Alger Hiss." *The Nation.* April 8, 1978.

_____. *Naming Names.* New York: Viking, 1980.

Nixon, Richard M. *Six Crises.* New York: Doubleday, 1962.

Offner, Arnold A. *Another Such Victory.* Stanford: Stanford University Press, 2002.

Olmsted, Kathryn S. *Red Spy Queen: A Biography of Elizabeth Bentley.* Chapel Hill: University of North Carolina Press, 2002.

Packer, Herbert L. *Ex-Communist Witnesses.* Stanford: Stanford University Press, 1962.

Rahv, Philip. *Essays on Literature and Politics 1932–1972.* Boston: Houghton Mifflin, 1978.

Reuben, William A. *Footnote on an Historic Case: In Re Alger Hiss*, No. 78 Civ. 3433. The Nation Institute, 1983.

_____. *The Honorable Mr. Nixon.* New York: Action Books, 1958.

_____. Papers, Labadie Special Collections, University of Michigan, Ann Arbor, Michigan.

Saunders, Frances Stonor. *The Cultural Cold War.* New York: New Press, 1999.

Schrecker, Ellen. *Many Are the Crimes, McCarthyism In America.* New York: Little, Brown, 1998.

Seth, Ronald. *The Sleeping Truth.* New York: Hart, 1968.

Siegel, Frederick F. *Troubled Journey: From Pearl Harbor to Ronald Reagan.* New York: Hill & Wang, 1984.

Smith, John Chabot. *Alger Hiss: The True Story.* New York: Holt, Rinehart and Winston, 1976.

Stripling, Robert E. *The Red Plot Against America.* Drexel Hill, PA: Bell, 1949.

Summers, Anthony. *Official and Confidential: The Secret Life of J. Edgar Hoover.* New York: Putnam's, 1993.

_____, with Robbyn Swan. *The Arrogance of Power.* New York: Penguin, 2000.

Swan, Patrick , ed. *Alger Hiss, Whittaker Chambers, and the Schism in the American Soul.* Wilmington, DE: Intercollegiate Studies Institute, 2003.

Tanenhaus, Sam. *Whittaker Chambers: A Biography.* New York: Random House, 1997

Teachout, Terry, ed. *Ghosts on the Roof: Selected Journalism of Whittaker Chambers 1931–1959.* Washington, D.C.: Regnery Gateway, 1989.

Tiger, Edith, ed. *In Re Alger Hiss.* Volumes I & II. New York: Hill & Wang, 1979, 1980.

Trilling, Diana. *The Beginning of the Journey.* New York: Harcourt Brace, 1993.

Trilling, Lionel. *The Middle of the Journey.* New York: Scribner's, 1975.

U.S. News & World Report. Interview with Nathaniel Weyl, January 9, 1953.

Wald, Alan M. *The New York Intellectuals: The Rise and Decline of the Anti-Stalinist Left from the 1930s to the 1980s.* Chapel Hill: University of North Carolina Press, 1987.

Weinstein, Allen. *Perjury: The Hiss-Chambers Case.* New York: Random House, 1997.

_____, and Alexander Vassiliev. *The Haunted Wood: Soviet Espionage in America—The Stalin Era.* New York: The Modern Library, 2000.

Weyl, Nathaniel. *Encounters with Communism.* Xlibris Corporation, 2003.

White, G. Edward. *Alger Hiss's Looking-Glass Wars.* New York: Oxford University Press, 2004.

Williams, William Appleman. *The Tragedy of American Diplomacy.* New York: W.W. Norton, 1959, 1962, 1972.

Zeligs, Meyer A. *Friendship and Fratricide.* New York: Viking, 1967.

Index

www.ingramcontent.com/pod-product-compliance
Lightning Source LLC
Chambersburg PA
CBHW080553270326
41929CB00019B/3288